lonely planet

Canary Islands

Miles Roddis
Damien Simonis

D1495672

LONELY PLANET PUBLICATIONS
Melbourne • Oakland • London • Paris

CANARY ISLANDS

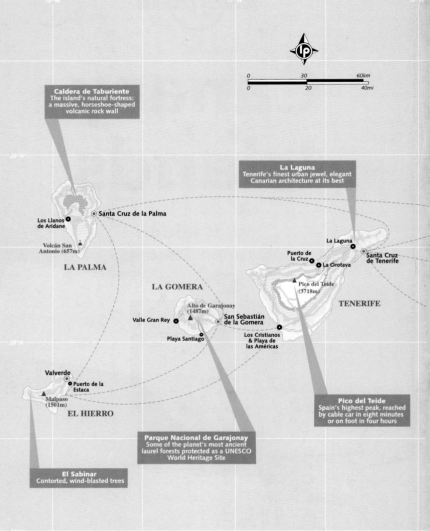

Caldera de Taburiente
The island's natural fortress:
a massive, horseshoe-shaped
volcanic rock wall

La Laguna
Tenerife's finest urban jewel, elegant
Canarian architecture at its best

Los Llanos
de Aridane
• Santa Cruz de la Palma

La Laguna

Volcán San
Antonio (657m)

Puerto de
la Cruz
Santa Cruz
de Tenerife
La Orotava

LA PALMA

Pico del Teide
(3718m)

LA GOMERA

TENERIFE

Alto de Garajonay
(1487m)

Valle Gran Rey
San Sebastián
de la Gomera

Playa Santiago

Los Cristianos
& Playa de
las Américas

Valverde
• Puerto de la
Estaca

Malpaso
(1501m)

EL HIERRO

Pico del Teide
Spain's highest peak, reached
by cable car in eight minutes
or on foot in four hours

Parque Nacional de Garajonay
Some of the planet's most ancient
laurel forests protected as a UNESCO
World Heritage Site

El Sabinar
Contorted, wind-blasted trees

ATLANTIC OCEAN

ATLANTIC OCEAN

15°W   14°W

To Cádiz
(mainland Spain)

Jameos del Agua
César Manrique's 600-seat concert
hall around an underground lake
deep within volcanic caverns

Isla de Alegranza

Montañas del Fuego
A broiling magma chamber 4km
below the surface and ground
temperatures of 100°C

Agujas Grandes (266m) ▲
Isla Graciosa
Monte Corona
(609m)

Timanfaya (510m) ▲   **Arrecife**
LANZAROTE   To Cádiz
(mainland
Spain)

Playa Blanca

Corralejo ●   Isla de Lobos

Playa de Sotavento de Jandía
The most beautiful beaches in the
Canaries -- long stretches of white sand
slipping gently into the Atlantic

La Oliva ●

Betancuria ●   ● **Puerto del
Rosario**
Gran Montaña ▲
(708m)

FUERTEVENTURA

Puerto de ●   ● **Las Palmas de
las Nieves**   **Gran Canaria**

● Morro Jable

▲ Pico de las Nieves
(1949m)

Mogán ●   ● San Bartolomé
de Tirajana

GRAN CANARIA

Maspalomas & Playa
del Inglés

ELEVATION

	2000m
	1500m
	1000m
	500m
	200m
	0

Maspalomas
400 hectares of rolling
sand dunes accessible only
on foot or by camel

To Marrakech

Laayoune

MOROCCO

Canary Islands
2nd edition – May 2001
First published – August 1998

Published by
Lonely Planet Publications Pty Ltd ABN 36 005 607 983
90 Maribyrnong St, Footscray, Victoria 3011, Australia

Lonely Planet Offices
Australia Locked Bag 1, Footscray, Victoria 3011
USA 150 Linden St, Oakland, CA 94607
UK 10a Spring Place, London NW5 3BH
France 1 rue du Dahomey, 75011 Paris

Photographs
All of the images in this guide are available for licensing from
Lonely Planet Images.
email: lpi@lonelyplanet.com.au

Front cover photograph
Eye-catching cacti on Lanzarote (Damien Simonis)

ISBN 1 86450 310 6

Printed by The Bookmaker International Ltd
Printed in China

Although the authors and Lonely Planet try to make the information as accurate as possible, we accept no responsibility for any loss, injury or inconvenience sustained by anyone using this book.

Contents – Text

Contents – Maps

MAP INDEX

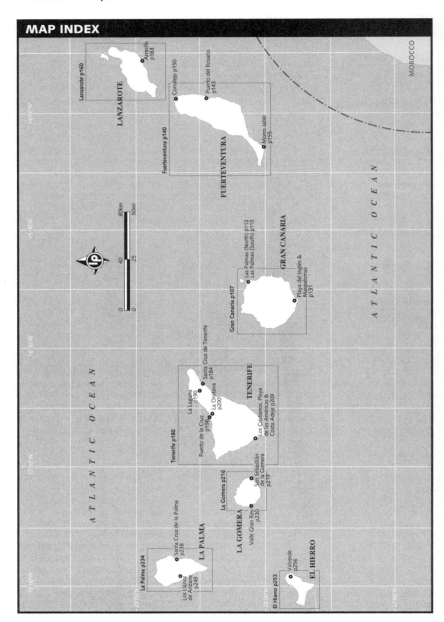

The Authors

Miles Roddis

Always an avid devourer and user of guidebooks, Miles came late to contributing to them. Over 25 years he lived, worked, walked and ran in France, Laos, Iran, Spain, Jordan, Egypt and Sudan. He celebrated a new life by cycling over 18,000km around the rim of the USA.

Now settled in Valencia on Spain's Mediterranean coast, Miles has still to find a cure for his itchy feet. He has contributed to Lonely Planet's *Africa on a Shoestring*, *West Africa*, *Read This First: Africa*, *Lonely Planet Unpacked*, *France*, *Spain*, *Western Europe*, *Europe on a Shoestring*, *Mediterranean Europe*, *Walking in Britain*, *Walking in France* and *Walking in Spain*.

Damien Simonis

With a degree in languages and several years reporting and sub-editing on Australian newspapers (including *The Australian* and *The Age*), Sydney-born Damien left Australia in 1989. He has since lived, worked and travelled extensively throughout Europe, the Middle East and North Africa. Since 1992, Lonely Planet has kept him busy writing for *Jordan & Syria*, *Egypt & the Sudan*, *Morocco*, *North Africa*, *Italy*, *Spain* and *Canary Islands*. More recently he has rattled off titles including *Tuscany*, *Florence*, *Venice*, *Madrid* and *Catalunya & the Costa Brava*, all of which have left him feeling a little dizzy. Damien has also written and snapped photos for other publications in Australia, the UK and North America. When not on the road, he goes to ground in splendid Stoke Newington, deep in the heart of north London.

FROM THE AUTHORS
Miles Roddis

I owe a huge thank you and several tots of the finest Canary Islands rum to Damien Simonis, colleague and author of the first edition of this book. His thorough research and twinkling prose made my own task so much the easier.

As always, thanks to Ingrid for company on the road and back at base. And thanks to Damon for surfing the more arcane Web sites for answers to those knotty questions I always leave until last.

Tourist office staff so often went out of their way to help. Thanks once again to, on Lanzarote, Andrés Rodriguez in Arrecife and Cristina, Alexandra and Lidia, a quite exceptionally cheerful, helpful and well-informed trio in Puerto del Carmen. On Gran Canaria, *gracias* to Clara Sosa, Ayuntamiento de Las Palmas, Juana Rosa Alemán of the Cabildo's Patronato de Turismo, and Nieves Ramirez in Playa del Inglés. On Tenerife, special thanks to

Juan-Carlos Hernández of the Parque Nacional del Teide and to tourist office staff Herbert Dumpfel (La Laguna), Ernesto Estrada (La Orotava) and Vicente Torrents (Puerto de la Cruz).

On La Gomera, thanks to Isabel and Pilar Padilla in San Sebastián, and on El Hierro, thanks to Yaneida Quintero in Valverde. On La Palma, very special thanks to Maite de Paz Martín and colleagues in Santa Cruz de la Palma, and also to Mónica Almeida of the Caldera de Taburiente national park visitor centre.

And in Lonely Planet's London office, an island of cheerfulness in the grey seas of north London, *saludos* to Sara, Imogen and the two Pauls, a particularly friendly crew throughout the book's long journey.

This Book

Damien Simonis wrote the first edition of *Canary Islands*. This edition was revised and updated by Miles Roddis.

From the Publisher

This second edition of *Canary Islands* was edited and proofed in Lonely Planet's London office by Imogen Franks, with assistance from Abigail Hole. Paul Edmunds was responsible for mapping, design and layout. Adam McCrow designed the cover and Jim Miller created the back-cover map. Lonely Planet Images provided the photographs and the illustrations were drawn by Jane Smith. Quentin Frayne and Emma Koch compiled, updated and found the time to make last-minute changes to the Language chapter. Last, but definitely not least, thanks to Miles for all his hard work and endless enthusiasm for these seven islands.

Thanks

Many thanks for the following travellers who used the last edition and wrote to us with helpful hints, useful advice and interesting anecdotes:

Anna Cordon, Audra Howarth, Bela Horvath, Bert Marien, Christopher Drew, Gavin McNaughton, Georgina Gudgeon, Hugh Symons, Ian Hammond, J Vernon, J Winston, Justin Williams, Katharina Sauter, KJ Spriggs, M Fletcher, Maite Segria, Manuel Lopez, Marcel Frenk, Michel de Boer, Nele de Belie, Patrick Buckingham, Sergio Bianco, Stephanie Strand-Muyres, Steve Bailey, Tina Emery

Foreword

ABOUT LONELY PLANET GUIDEBOOKS

The story begins with a classic travel adventure: Tony and Maureen Wheeler's 1972 journey across Europe and Asia to Australia. Useful information about the overland trail did not exist at that time, so Tony and Maureen published the first Lonely Planet guidebook to meet a growing need.

From a kitchen table, then from a tiny office in Melbourne (Australia), Lonely Planet has become the largest independent travel publisher in the world, an international company with offices in Melbourne, Oakland (USA), London (UK) and Paris (France).

Today Lonely Planet guidebooks cover the globe. There is an ever-growing list of books and there's information in a variety of forms and media. Some things haven't changed. The main aim is still to help make it possible for adventurous travellers to get out there – to explore and better understand the world.

At Lonely Planet we believe travellers can make a positive contribution to the countries they visit – if they respect their host communities and spend their money wisely. Since 1986 a percentage of the income from each book has been donated to aid projects and human rights campaigns.

Updates Lonely Planet thoroughly updates each guidebook as often as possible. This usually means there are around two years between editions, although for more unusual or more stable destinations the gap can be longer. Check the imprint page (following the colour map at the beginning of the book) for publication dates.

Between editions up-to-date information is available in two free newsletters – the paper *Planet Talk* and email *Comet* (to subscribe, contact any Lonely Planet office) – and on our Web site at www.lonelyplanet.com. The *Upgrades* section of the Web site covers a number of important and volatile destinations and is regularly updated by Lonely Planet authors. *Scoop* covers news and current affairs relevant to travellers. And, lastly, the *Thorn Tree* bulletin board and *Postcards* section of the site carry unverified, but fascinating, reports from travellers.

Correspondence The process of creating new editions begins with the letters, postcards and emails received from travellers. This correspondence often includes suggestions, criticisms and comments about the current editions. Interesting excerpts are immediately passed on via newsletters and the Web site, and everything goes to our authors to be verified when they're researching on the road. We're keen to get more feedback from organisations or individuals who represent communities visited by travellers.

Lonely Planet gathers information for everyone who's curious about the planet – and especially for those who explore it first-hand. Through guidebooks, phrasebooks, activity guides, maps, literature, newsletters, image library, TV series and Web site we act as an information exchange for a worldwide community of travellers.

Research Authors aim to gather sufficient practical information to enable travellers to make informed choices and to make the mechanics of a journey run smoothly. They also research historical and cultural background to help enrich the travel experience and allow travellers to understand and respond appropriately to cultural and environmental issues.

Authors don't stay in every hotel because that would mean spending a couple of months in each medium-sized city and, no, they don't eat at every restaurant because that would mean stretching belts beyond capacity. They do visit hotels and restaurants to check standards and prices, but feedback based on readers' direct experiences can be very helpful.

Many of our authors work undercover, others aren't so secretive. None of them accept freebies in exchange for positive write-ups. And none of our guidebooks contain any advertising.

Production Authors submit their raw manuscripts and maps to offices in Australia, USA, UK or France. Editors and cartographers – all experienced travellers themselves – then begin the process of assembling the pieces. When the book finally hits the shops, some things are already out of date, we start getting feedback from readers and the process begins again …

WARNING & REQUEST

Things change – prices go up, schedules change, good places go bad and bad places go bankrupt – nothing stays the same. So, if you find things better or worse, recently opened or long since closed, please tell us and help make the next edition even more accurate and useful. We genuinely value all the feedback we receive. A well-travelled team reads and acknowledges every letter, postcard and email and ensures that every morsel of information finds its way to the appropriate authors, editors and cartographers for verification.

Everyone who writes to us will find their name in the next edition of the appropriate guidebook. They will also receive the latest issue of *Planet Talk*, our quarterly printed newsletter, or *Comet*, our monthly email newsletter. Subscriptions to both newsletters are free. The very best contributions will be rewarded with a free guidebook.

Excerpts from your correspondence may appear in new editions of Lonely Planet guidebooks, the Lonely Planet Web site, *Planet Talk* or *Comet*, so please let us know if you *don't* want your letter published or your name acknowledged.

Send all correspondence to the Lonely Planet office closest to you:

Australia: Locked Bag 1, Footscray, Victoria 3011
USA: 150 Linden St, Oakland, CA 94607
UK: 10A Spring Place, London NW5 3BH
France: 1 rue du Dahomey, 75011 Paris

Or email us at: talk2us@lonelyplanet.com.au

For news, views and updates see our Web site: www.lonelyplanet.com

HOW TO USE A LONELY PLANET GUIDEBOOK

The best way to use a Lonely Planet guidebook is any way you choose. At Lonely Planet we believe the most memorable travel experiences are often those that are unexpected, and the finest discoveries are those you make yourself. Guidebooks are not intended to be used as if they provide a detailed set of infallible instructions!

Contents All Lonely Planet guidebooks follow roughly the same format. The Facts about the Destination chapters or sections give background information ranging from history to weather. Facts for the Visitor gives practical information on issues like visas and health. Getting There & Away gives a brief starting point for researching travel to and from the destination. Getting Around gives an overview of the transport options when you arrive.

The peculiar demands of each destination determine how subsequent chapters are broken up, but some things remain constant. We always start with background, then proceed to sights, places to stay, places to eat, entertainment, getting there and away, and getting around information – in that order.

Heading Hierarchy Lonely Planet headings are used in a strict hierarchical structure that can be visualised as a set of Russian dolls. Each heading (and its following text) is encompassed by any preceding heading that is higher on the hierarchical ladder.

Entry Points We do not assume guidebooks will be read from beginning to end, but that people will dip into them. The traditional entry points are the list of contents and the index. In addition, however, some books have a complete list of maps and an index map illustrating map coverage.

There may also be a colour map that shows highlights. These highlights are dealt with in greater detail in the Facts for the Visitor chapter, along with planning questions and suggested itineraries. Each chapter covering a geographical region usually begins with a locator map and another list of highlights. Once you find something of interest in a list of highlights, turn to the index.

Maps Maps play a crucial role in Lonely Planet guidebooks and include a huge amount of information. A legend is printed on the back page. We seek to have complete consistency between maps and text, and to have every important place in the text captured on a map. Map key numbers usually start in the top left corner.

Although inclusion in a guidebook usually implies a recommendation we cannot list every good place. Exclusion does not necessarily imply criticism. In fact there are a number of reasons why we might exclude a place – sometimes it is simply inappropriate to encourage an influx of travellers.

Introduction

'Oh, surely you're not going to the Canary Islands!', travel snobs exclaim in horror. As a sun and fun holiday package destination par excellence, the Canaries are seen by many as the last winter refuge of British lager-louts, German hippies and pensioners from across northern Europe.

To write off the islands in this cavalier and uninformed fashion, however, is to do them, and yourself, a great injustice. The Canary Islands (Islas Canarias), a Spanish archipelago little more than 100km from the coast of Saharan Africa, are in fact a varied and fascinating destination for travellers prepared to look beyond the beaches and bars. You don't have to stray too far from the main holiday resorts to discover an absorbing, multifaceted culture.

Opportunities for many outdoor pursuits abound. On the smaller, less-developed western islands, each scarcely trodden by English-speaking visitors, you can walk through woods of Canary pine or amid sub-tropical rainforest and follow centuries-old trails, linking village with village. On Tenerife, the stark, volcanic grandeur of the Parque Nacional del Teide beckons. Under the ocean, the offshore rocks, caves and sunken wrecks are ideal for diving or a spot of snorkelling. On the surface, the dominant trade winds provide power for windsurfing and sailing, while surfers ride the curling waves off Lanzarote and Fuerteventura.

The island of Gran Canaria alone is often described as a continent in miniature, its countryside an ever-changing pastiche: subtropical and fertile to the north, more arid and reminiscent of the desert in the south. Tenerife is more interesting still. The three small western islands – La Gomera, La Palma and El Hierro – are mountainous, green and dotted with occasional brief strands of black sand. Each presents a startling contrast to the desertscapes and sparkling white beaches of their easternmost counterparts, Lanzarote and Fuerteventura.

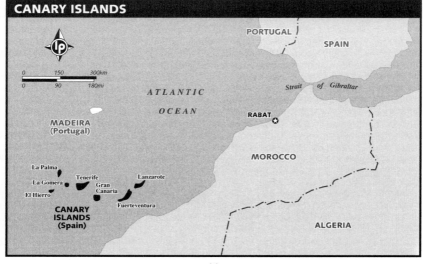

A rich and often bizarre indigenous flora thrives right across this chain of volcanic islands.

As you explore the islands, the back roads and villages bring you in touch with a unique side of Spanish culture, reflecting an unusual mix of influences far removed from the mainland.

Amid the melting pot of Andalucían, Berber, Portuguese, Italian, French and even British migration, the Guanches, the native islanders displaced during the Spanish conquest in the 15th century, also left their mark.

And just as Canarios migrated in search of a better life to Latin America, so in later years South American influences have wafted back across the Atlantic, best sampled in the cuisine and music.

This fascinating mix can be easily (and relatively cheaply) explored – just put aside your preconceptions and go.

Facts about the Islands

HISTORY

The origins of the Canary Islands (Islas Canarias) and their earliest inhabitants are enveloped in thick mists of myth and uncertainty. The islands themselves are estimated to be 30 million years old, relatively young in geological terms.

The existence of the islands was known, or postulated, in ancient times. Plato (428–348 BC), in his dialogues *Timaeus* and *Critias*, spoke of Atlantis, a continent destroyed and sunk deep into the ocean floor in a great cataclysm which left only the peaks of its highest mountains above the water. Whether Plato believed in the lost continent's existence or had more allegorical intentions remains a matter of conjecture. In the centuries since Plato's death, those convinced of the existence of Atlantis have maintained that Macronesia (the Canary Islands, the Azores, Cape Verde and Madeira), constitutes the visible remains of the lost continent.

Legend also has it that one of the 12 labours of Hercules (Heracles to the Greeks) was to go to the end of the world and bring back golden apples guarded by the Hesperides ('daughters of evening'), offspring of Hesperis and Atlas, the latter a mythical Mauritanian king who gave his name to the Atlantic Ocean and the Atlas mountain ranges in Morocco. Hercules supposedly had to go beyond the Pillars of Hercules (the modern Strait of Gibraltar), to reach the paradisiacal home of these maidens. Hercules carried out his task and returned from what many later thought could only have been the Canary Islands – about the only place to fit the ancients' description.

And so the islands gained a reputation, passed down from one classical writer to the next, as a Garden of Eden. Homer identified the islands as Elysium, a place where the righteous spent their afterlife. For all their story-telling, there is no concrete evidence that either the Phoenicians or Greeks ever landed on the Canaries. It is entirely possible, however, that early reconnaissance of the North African Atlantic coast by the Phoenicians and their successors, the Carthaginians, took in at least a peek at the easternmost islands of the archipelago. Some historians believe a Phoenician expedition landed on the islands in the 12th century BC, and that the Carthaginian Hanno turned up there in 470 BC.

The expanding Roman Empire defeated Carthage in the Third Punic War in 146 BC; but the Romans appear not to have been overly keen to investigate the fabled islands, which they knew as the Insulae Fortunatae (Fortunate Isles). A century and a half later, shortly after the birth of Christ, the Romans received vaguely reliable reports on them, penned by Pliny the Elder (AD 23–79) and based upon accounts of an expedition carried out around 40 BC by Juba II, a client king in Roman North Africa. In AD 150, Ptolemy fairly accurately located the islands' position with a little dead reckoning, tracing an imaginary meridian line marking the end of the known world through El Hierro.

The Guanches

That the Canary Islands were inhabited before the birth of Christ is undisputed. But by whom? Carbon-dating of the sparse archaeological finds has pushed back the known date of the earliest settlement to around 200 BC, although earlier occupation is quite conceivable. For a long time, learned observers maintained that the islands were first inhabited by Cro-Magnon man, the Neolithic predecessor of modern *Homo sapiens*. Such conclusions have emerged from the comparison of ancient skulls of indigenous inhabitants with Cro-Magnon remains discovered in the Mediterranean.

Historians tend to wrinkle their noses up at the idea now, although the evidence either way is so flimsy that it cannot be completely ruled out. It throws the doors of speculation wide open, since Cro-Magnon man came onto the scene as long as 40,000 years ago.

A disconcerting clue is provided by European descriptions of locals in the wake of conquest in the 15th century. They found, mainly on Tenerife, tall and powerfully built people, blue eyed and with long fair hair down to their waists. These lanky blond islanders were known as Guanches (from *guan*, 'man', and *che* or *achinch*, meaning 'white mountain' in reference to the snow-capped Teide volcano).

The Tenerife Guanches fascinated the (and ultimately put up the most tenacious resistance to them), but their origin is an open question. If they were not descendants of Cro-Magnon man, where did they come from? Some suggest they were Celtic immigrants from mainland Iberia, possibly even related to the Basques. More fancifully, it is tempting to see a drop of Nordic blood in the Guanches – did Norse raiding parties land here in the 8th or 9th centuries?

Whatever the explanation, the term Guanche came to be used of all the Canary Islands' indigenous people although not all of them fit the description. In the eastern islands in particular, the original inhabitants were almost certainly Berber migrants from nearby Saharan Africa. Place names and the handful of words of the Canary Islands languages (or dialects) that have come down to us bear a striking resemblance to Berber tribal languages. It has also been noted that the occasional case of blue eyes and blondish hair occurs among the Berbers too. This would lend still more credence to the feeling that the islands' original inhabitants were all Berber migrants, and so dispel more imaginative speculation of the kind mentioned above.

When and in what number these people occupied the islands remains a mystery but it appears certain that they came from several tribes. One of them may have been the Canarii tribe, which could explain the islands' present name. Certainly, by the time European swashbucklers started nosing around the islands in the Middle Ages, they were peopled by a variety of tribes often more hostile to one another than to visiting strangers.

Guanche Society For all their differences, the tribes of the Canary Islands had much in common. They all led a primitive existence, their Stone-Age economy reliant on limited farming, herding, hunting and gathering. The main sources of meat were goats (imported from North Africa?) and fish. Barley was grown and, ground and toasted, formed *gofio*, the basic staple which in one form or another is still eaten today.

The women made pottery, often decorated with vegetable dyes. Implements and weapons were fashioned roughly of wood, stone and bone. Goat-skin leather was the basis of most garments, while jewellery and ornaments were largely restricted to earthenware bead-and-shell necklaces.

The majority of islanders lived in caves, mostly artificial. In the eastern islands (now the province of Las Palmas) some built simple low houses, with rough stone walls and wood-beam roofs covered with stones and caked with wet earth. Oddly enough, the Guanches seem to have known nothing of sailing, at best using simple dugouts for coastal fishing or to move occasionally between the islands. Among the Guanches' primitive weapons were the *banot* (lance), rocks and the *tenique*, a stone wrapped up in animal hide and used as a mace.

The Guanches worshipped a god, known as Alcorac in Gran Canaria, Achaman in Tenerife and Abora in La Palma. It appears the god was identified strongly with Magec (the sun). Tenerife islanders commonly held that Hades (hell) was in the Teide volcano, directed by the god of evil, Guayota.

For a people who regarded death and gore with some disdain, they went to enormous trouble to facilitate one's passage from this life to the next. Although not as expert as the Egyptians, the Guanches mummified their dead chiefs and nobles before laying them out in burial caves, usually in barely accessible locations. The embalmers were treated as untouchables, excluded from community life.

The head of a tribe or region was the *mencey*, although on Gran Canaria the chief's title was more commonly *guanarteme*. His rule was almost absolute although justice was administered through a council of nobles *(achimencey)*, sometimes known as a *taoro* or *tagoror*. A little like the ancient Basque parliament that used to sit beneath the Árbol de Gernika (Tree of Guernica), the taoro would usually gather under the ancient branches of a dragon tree *(Dracaena draco)*. Between them, the chief and aristocrats owned all property, flocks and fields, leaving the *achicaxna*, or plebs, to get along as best they could.

Although living in an essentially patriarchal society, women did have some power. On Gran Canaria in particular, succession rights were passed through the mother rather than the father. But when times got tough, they got tougher still for women. Infanticide was practised throughout the islands in periods of famine and it was girls who were sacrificed, never boys.

The island clans were not averse to squabbling and by the time the European conquest of the islands got underway in the 15th century, Tenerife was divided into no less than nine tiny fiefdoms. Gran Canaria had also been a patchwork of minor principalities but by the 15th century these had merged to form two kingdoms, one based around the town of Gáldar, another around Telde. Fuerteventura was another island divided in two and tiny La Palma boasted an astonishing 12 cantons. The other islands were each ruled by one mencey.

First Encounters

Virtually no written record remains of visits to the Fortunate Isles until the 14th century. Rumour has it that Ireland's St Brendan turned up in the 6th century after a remarkable voyage in search of the 'promised land of saints' (immortalised in the 10th-century epic *Navigatio Brendani*). For centuries sailors tried in vain to find 'St Brendan's Island' in the Atlantic.

There is circumstantial evidence that Arabs operating out of Muslim Portugal in the 10th century not only landed in the islands but left behind some settlers.

The first vaguely tenable account of a European landing comes in the late 13th or early 14th century when the Genoese captain Lanzarotto (or Lancelotto) Malocello bumped into the island that would later bear his name: Lanzarote. From then on slavers, dreamers searching for the Río de Oro (the 'River of Gold' route for the legendary African gold trade that many thought spilled into the Atlantic at about the same latitude as the islands), and missionaries bent on spreading the Word all made excursions to the islands.

Of these missions, the most important was the Italian-led and Portuguese-backed expedition of 1341. Three caravels charted a course around all seven islands and took note of even the tiniest islets: the Canary Islands were finally, and more or less accurately, on the map.

The Conquest Begins

On 1 May 1402, Jean de Béthencourt, lord of Granville in Normandy (France) and something of an adventurer, set out from La Rochelle with a small and ill-equipped party bound for the Canary Islands. The avowed aim, as the priests brought along for the ride would testify, was to convert the heathen islanders. Uppermost in de Béthencourt's mind was more likely the hope of glory and a fast buck. With his partner, Gadifer de la Salle, he may have hoped to use the Canaries as a launch pad for exploration of the African coast in search of the Río de Oro. That project never got off the ground, and the buccaneers decided to take over the islands instead. So commenced a lengthy and inglorious chapter of invasion, treachery and bungling. Many Guanches would lose their lives or be sold into slavery in the coming century, the remainder destined to be swallowed up by the invading society.

De Béthencourt's motley crew landed first in Lanzarote, at that stage governed by Mencey Guardafía. There was no resistance and de Béthencourt went on to establish a fort on Fuerteventura.

That was as far as he got. Having run out

of supplies and with too few men for the enterprise, he headed for Spain where he aimed to obtain the backing of the Castilian crown. What had started as a private French enterprise now became a Spanish imperialist adventure.

De Béthencourt returned in 1404 with ships, men and money. Fuerteventura, El Hierro and La Gomera quickly fell under his control. Appointed lord of the four islands by the Spanish king Enrique III, de Béthencourt encouraged the settlement of farmers from his Norman homeland and began to pull in the profits. In 1406 he returned for good to Normandy, leaving his nephew Maciot in charge of his Atlantic possessions.

Squabbles, Bungles & Stagnation

What followed was scarcely one of the world's grandest colonial undertakings. Characterised by continued squabbling and occasional mutiny among the colonists, the European presence did nothing for the increasingly oppressed islanders in the years following de Béthencourt's departure.

Maciot soon revealed how ugly colonial administration could be. The islanders were heavily taxed and many were sold off into slavery; he also recruited them for numerous abortive raids on the remaining three independent islands. Maciot capped it all off by selling to Portugal his rights – inherited from his uncle – to the four islands. This move prompted a tiff with Spain, which was eventually awarded rights to the islands by Pope Eugene V. Low-key rivalry continued for years, with Portugal only recognising Spanish control of the Canaries in 1479 under the Treaty of Alcáçovas. In return, Spain agreed that Portugal could have the Azores, Cape Verde and Madeira.

Maciot died in self-imposed exile in Madeira in 1452. A string of minor Spanish nobility proceeded to run the show, all eager to sell on their rights to the islands almost as soon as they had acquired them.

Numerous commanders undertook the business of attacking the other islands but with extraordinarily little success. While better armed than their Stone-Age adversaries, the Spaniards were repeatedly confounded by their enemies' guerrilla tactics.

Landing a force was rarely a problem but making any headway into the interior was quite another matter. Guillén Peraza died in an attempt to assault La Palma in 1443. In 1464 Peraza's brother-in-law Diego de Herrera, appointed lord of La Gomera, attempted a landing on Gran Canaria and another near present-day Santa Cruz de Tenerife, both ending in failure. By 1466 he had managed to sign a trade treaty with the Canarios, the people of Gran Canaria, and won permission to build a defensive turret in Gando Bay. Intermittent clashes continued over the ensuing years but the Spaniards made no real progress.

The Fall of Gran Canaria

In 1478 a new commander arrived with fresh forces (including for the first time a small cavalry unit) and orders from the Catholic Monarchs of Spain, Fernando and Isabel, to finish the Canaries campaign off once and for all. Juan Rejón landed and dug in at the site of modern Las Palmas. He was immediately attacked by a force of 2000 under Doramas, guanarteme of the island's Telde kingdom. Rejón carried the day but fell victim to internal intrigue by making an enemy of the spiritual head of the conquered territories, Canon Juan Bermúdez, accusing him of incompetence.

The investigator sent from Spain, Pedro de Algaba, sided with Bermúdez and had Rejón transported to the mainland in chains. But, once there, Rejón convinced the Spanish authorities that he'd been unjustly treated and was given carte blanche to return to the Canaries to re-establish his control. One of his first acts was to have Algaba, his erstwhile accuser, arrested and executed. However, this act of vengeance proved his final undoing as Queen Isabel believed the punishment unwarranted and had Rejón replaced by Pedro de Vera.

De Vera continued the campaign and had the good fortune to capture the island's other guanarteme, Tenesor Semidan (known as Don Fernando Guanarteme after his baptism), in an attack on Gáldar by sea.

Tenesor Semidan was sent to Spain, converted to Christianity and returned in 1483 to convince his countrymen to give up the fight. This they did and de Vera subsequently suggested that some might like to sign up for an assault on Tenerife. Duly embarked, de Vera committed the umpteenth act of treachery that had marked the long years of conquest: he packed them off to be sold as slaves in Spain. But the Canarios learnt of this and forced the ships transporting them to put in at Lanzarote.

After the frightful suppression of a revolt in La Gomera in 1488 (see History under San Sebastián in the La Gomera chapter), de Vera was relieved of his post as Captain-General of the conquest.

The Final Campaigns

De Vera's successor was a Galician soldier of fortune, Alonso Fernández de Lugo, who in 1491 received a royal commission to conquer La Palma and Tenerife. He began in La Palma in November and by May of the following year had the island under control. This he achieved partly by negotiation, though the last mencey of La Palma, Tanausú, and his men maintained resistance in the virtually impregnable crater of the Caldera de Taburiente. Only by enticing him out for talks on 3 May and then ambushing him could de Lugo defeat his last adversary on the island. For La Palma, the war was over.

Tenerife provided the toughest resistance to the Spaniards. In May 1493 de Lugo landed in Tenerife, near the site of modern-day Santa Cruz, together with 1000 infantry soldiers and a cavalry of 150, among them Guanches from Gran Canaria and La Gomera.

In the ensuing months the Spaniards fortified their positions and attempted talks with various of the nine menceys, managing to win over those of Güímar and Anaga. Bencomo, mencey of Tahoro and sworn enemy of the invaders, was sure of the support of at least three other menceys, while the remaining three wavered.

In spring of the following year de Lugo sent a column westwards. This proved a disaster. Bencomo was waiting in ambush in the Barranco de Acentejo ravine. The Spanish force was decimated at a place now called La Matanza ('the slaughter') de Acentejo. The survivors beat a hasty retreat and, although foiling a Guanche assault on their positions, de Lugo thought better of the whole operation and left Tenerife.

By the end of the year he was back to engage in the second major battle of the campaign – at La Laguna on 14 November 1494. Here he had greater success but the Guanches were far from defeated and de Lugo fell back to Santa Cruz.

The stalemate was broken by an unexpected ally. At the beginning of the new year a plague known as the *modorra* began to ravage the island. It hardly seemed to affect the Spaniards but soon took a serious toll on the Guanches.

When de Lugo finally moved again from his base at Santa Cruz in December 1495, the mood of the islanders was subdued. On 25 December, 5000 Guanches under Bencomo were routed in the second battle of the Acentejo. The spot, only a few kilometres south of La Matanza, is still called La Victoria ('victory') today. By the following July, when de Lugo marched into the Valle de la Orotava to confront Bencomo's successor Bentor, the diseased and demoralised Guanches were in no state to resist. Bentor surrendered and the conquest was complete. Pockets of resistance took two years to mop up and Bentor, aghast at the loss of his realm, eventually committed suicide.

Four years after the fall of Granada and the reunification of Christian Spain, the Catholic Monarchs could now celebrate one of the country's first imperial exploits – the subjugation in only 94 years of a small Atlantic archipelago defended by Neolithic tribes. Even so, the Spaniards had some difficulty in fully controlling the Guanches. Many refused to settle in the towns established by the colonists, preferring to live their traditional lives out of reach of the authorities. Their agility and cunning in their own land would keep this proud minority a step ahead of the Spaniards for many years to come.

Nevertheless, the Guanches were destined to disappear. Although open hostilities had ceased, the conquistadors continued shipping them as slaves to Spain – a practice that had enticed some of the Europeans here in the first place. Remaining Guanches were converted en masse to Christianity, taking on Christian names and the surnames of their new Spanish godfathers. Some of the slaves, themselves sooner or later brought to conversion, would be freed and permitted to return to the islands. Although the bulk of them were dispossessed of their land, they soon began to assimilate with the colonisers. Within a century their language had all but disappeared: except for a handful of words, all that comes down to us today are the islands' many Guanche place names.

Economic See-Saw & Foreign Challenges

From the early 16th century, Gran Canaria and Tenerife in particular attracted a steady stream of settlers from Spain, Portugal, France, Italy and even Britain. Each island had its own local authority, or *Cabildo*, although increasingly they were overshadowed by the royal court of appeal, established in Las Palmas in 1526. Sugar cane had been introduced from the Portuguese island of Madeira, and soon sugar became the Canaries' main export.

The 'discovery' of the New World by Columbus in 1492, who called in to the archipelago several times en route to the Americas, proved a mixed blessing. It brought much passing transatlantic trade but also led to sugar production being diverted to the Americas where the cane could be grown and processed more cheaply. The local economy was rescued only by the growing export demand for wine, produced mainly in Tenerife; *vino seco* (dry wine), what Shakespeare called Canary Sack, was much appreciated in Britain.

Poorer islands, especially Lanzarote and Fuerteventura, remained backwaters, their impoverished inhabitants making a living from smuggling and piracy off the Moroccan coast – the latter activity part of a

tit-for-tat game played out with the Moroccans for centuries.

Spain's control of the islands did not go completely unchallenged. Moroccan troops occupied Lanzarote in 1569 and again in 1586 but they were dispatched fairly quickly on each occasion. Sir Francis Drake engaged in some gunboat tactics off Las Palmas in 1595 but he too was repelled. A Dutch fleet tried to repeat the effort four years later and managed to reduce the city to rubble. The most spectacular success went to Admiral Robert Blake, one of Oliver Cromwell's three 'generals at sea'. In 1657, a year after war had broken out between England and Spain, Blake annihilated a Spanish treasure fleet (at the cost of only one ship) at Santa Cruz de Tenerife. British harassment culminated in 1797 with Admiral Horatio Nelson's attack on Santa Cruz. Sent there to intercept yet another treasure shipment, he not only failed to storm the town but lost his right arm in the fighting.

Island Rivalries

Within the Canary Islands, a bitter feud developed between Gran Canaria and Tenerife over supremacy of the archipelago. The fortunes of the two rested largely with their economic fate. As demand for Canaries sugar fell and that for wine rose, Tenerife, with land much better suited to the vine, inevitably took the lead. As its exports grew, so too did its ports and overall trade turnover.

When the Canaries were declared a province of Spain in 1821, Santa Cruz de Tenerife was made the capital. Bickering between the two main islands remained heated and Las Palmas de Gran Canaria frequently demanded the province be split in two. The idea was briefly but unsuccessfully put into practice in the 1840s.

Gran Canaria was in any case beginning to redress the economic imbalance. As wine in its turn began to drop off as a major revenue earner, cochineal was introduced as an export commodity. At the same time, Sir Alfred Lewis Jones set up the Grand Canary Coaling Company in Las Palmas and the port was soon every bit as busy as that of Santa Cruz.

Gran Canaria's politicians continued to lobby for division of the region and in 1911 managed to resurrect the old island Cabildos. This restoration of each island's local government sapped Santa Cruz's overall control of the archipelago.

In 1927 Madrid finally decided to split the Canaries into two provinces: Tenerife, La Gomera, La Palma and El Hierro in the west; Fuerteventura, Gran Canaria and Lanzarote in the east.

Flight to the Americas

The cochineal boom was followed by bust in the 1870s as chemical dyes came on to the market. So the Canary Islands turned to other raw export products: bananas and, to a lesser extent, tomatoes and potatoes.

WWI and the British sea blockade of the continent wrecked international trade and the banana began to seem more like a lemon. This time Canarios voted with their feet, choosing to migrate to Latin America. Emigrants shipped out to join their forbears in Cuba, Venezuela, Uruguay, Nicaragua, Mexico and Guatemala.

Civil War & Franco's Spain

The islands' economy picked up slowly after WWI but more shocks were in store. In the 1930s, as the left and the right in mainland Spain became increasingly militant, fears of a coup grew. In March 1936 the government decided to 'transfer' General Franco, a veteran of Spain's wars in Morocco and beloved of the tough Spanish Foreign Legion, to the Canary Islands.

Suspicions that he was involved in a plot to overthrow the government were well founded; when the pro-coup garrisons of Melilla (Spanish North Africa) rose prematurely on 17 July, he was ready. Having seized control of the islands virtually without a struggle (the pro-Republican commander of the Las Palmas garrison died in mysterious circumstances on 14 July), Franco flew to Morocco on 19 July. Although there was virtually no fighting on the islands, the Nationalists wasted no time in rounding up anyone vaguely suspected of harbouring Republican sympathies.

Francoism thus came to the Canary Islands from the outset but the war on the mainland lasted three years. The postwar economic misery of mainland Spain was shared by the islands and again many Canarios opted to emigrate. In the 1950s the situation was so desperate that 16,000 migrated clandestinely, mainly to Venezuela, even though by then that country had closed its doors to further immigration. One-third of those who attempted to flee perished in the ocean crossings.

Tourism & 'Nationalism'

The Canary Islands' latest monoculture has proved the most astounding. When Franco decided to open up the doors of Spain to northern European tourists – sun-starved and on tight budgets – the Canaries benefited as much as the mainland. Millions of holiday-makers now pour into the islands year round.

Not everyone was satisfied with the suntan-lotion-led recovery. Always a fringe phenomenon, Canaries nationalism started to resurface in opposition to Franco. MPAIC (Movimiento para la Autodeterminación e Independencia del Archipiélago Canario), founded in 1963 by Antonio Cubillo to promote secession from Spain, embarked on a terrorist campaign in the late 1970s; Cubillo was expelled, though later allowed to return.

In 1978 a new constitution was passed in Madrid with devolution as one of its central pillars. Thus the Canary Islands became a *comunidad autónoma* (autonomous region) in August 1982 yet they remained divided into two provinces.

The main force in Canary Islands politics since its first regional election victory in 1995 has been the Coalición Canaria (CC). Although not bent on independence from Spain (which would be unlikely), the CC nevertheless puts the interests of the islands before national considerations (see Government & Politics later in this chapter). Its position was consolidated in the June 1999 regional elections – it emerged with 37% of votes cast and 25 seats in a chamber of 58 deputies. In the absence of an absolute majority it's obliged to govern by consensus and to woo the right-wing Partido Popular (PP), which has 14 seats, for support on major issues. Such government by negotiation also puts the brakes upon any extreme policies that the CC might be tempted to introduce. The current president of the inter-islands Cabildo is Román Rodriguez, a member of the Coalición Canaria.

GEOGRAPHY

The Canary Islands are an archipelago of seven islands and six islets. Beginning about 100km west of the Atlantic coast of North Africa, they lie over 1100km southwest of Spain.

The archipelago lies between the 28th and 29th parallels, and the seven main islands have a total area of 7447 sq km.

Their total area may not be great, but packed into them is just about every imaginable kind of landscape, from the long sandy beaches of Fuerteventura and dunes of Gran Canaria to the majestic Atlantic cliffs of Tenerife and mist-enveloped woods of La Gomera, from the almost Saharan desertscape of the easternmost islands to the rock-wall spectacle of the Caldera de Taburiente in La Palma. The highest mountain in all of Spain is the Teide peak (3718m), which dominates the whole island of Tenerife.

None of the islands has rivers and lack of water remains a serious problem. Extracting funds from Madrid for water-conservation projects is always high on the list of priorities of Canarios politicians in the Spanish capital. Instead of rivers, webs of *barrancos* (ravines) cut their way from the mountainous interior of most of the islands to the coast. Water flows along some but others remain dry nearly year round.

Lanzarote and Fuerteventura, the two most easterly islands, would be quite at home if attached to the nearby coast of continental Africa. Volcanic in origin – as is the entire archipelago – their landscapes are otherworldly. Although both are hilly, neither island is blessed with impressive

mountains. The highest point is the Jandía peak (807m) in southern Fuerteventura. Long stretches of beach are Fuerteventura's greatest tourist drawcard. Lanzarote, last rocked by a volcanic eruption in 1824, takes its present appearance from a series of massive blasts in 1730. Eruptions are destructive and scary, but the lava can be good news for farmers, creating fertile ground where before there was nothing. Today Lanzarote produces a wide range of crops including cereals, vegetables and wine grapes, grown mostly on volcanic hillsides. The Montañas del Fuego (Mountains of Fire) in the Parque Nacional de Timanfaya still give off plenty of heat, enough to sizzle a steak. And the island's fine black-sand beaches are an attraction. North of the island are clustered five of the archipelago's six little islets (the other is Isla de Lobos just off the northern tip of Fuerteventura). Of these Isla Graciosa, home to a few hundred people, is the largest.

Gran Canaria is roughly a circular-based volcanic pyramid. Its northern half is surprisingly green and fertile, and still contains more than vestiges of the near-eclipsed banana business. South of the peak of Pozo de las Nieves (1949m) the territory is more arid, reminiscent of Gran Canaria's eastern neighbours. Tourists coming to the southern sandy beaches and dunes have brought more wealth to the island than banana plantations could ever have done. For the variety of its geography, flora and climate, the island is often dubbed a 'continent in miniature'.

Gran Canaria's big brother, at least in terms of size, is Tenerife – every bit as much a 'mini-continent' and last redoubt of the Guanches. Almost two-thirds of the island is taken up by the rugged slopes of the volcanic mountain peak and crater Teide. A further string of mountains, the Anaga range, spreads along the north-eastern panhandle. The only real lowlands are around La Laguna and alongside parts of the coast. The staggering cliffs of the north coast are occasionally lashed by Atlantic rain squalls, arrested by the mountains in such a way that the south-western and south-eastern coasts present a more serene weather picture.

The remaining western islands have much in common with one another. Better supplied with spring and/or rain water, they are green and ringed by rocky, ocean-battered coastlines. La Palma's dominant feature is the yawning funnel known as the Caldera de Taburiente, whose highest peak is the Roque de los Muchachos (2426m). The centre of La Gomera's high *meseta* (plateau) is covered by a UNESCO-listed laurel forest, the Parque Nacional de Garajonay. El Hierro, smallest of the Canary Islands, is mountainous (the highest peak is Malpaso at 1501m) with, again, a coastline that seems designed as a fortress.

GEOLOGY

The Canary Islands, just like similar Atlantic upstarts such as Madeira, the Azores and Cape Verde islands, are little more than the tips of a vast volcanic mountain range that lies below the ocean. Viewed this way, from the Atlantic floor, the highest peak in the Canaries, Tenerife's Teide, is about a 7000m climb!

The volcanoes were thrown up millions of years ago, about the time the Atlas Mountains were formed in North Africa. Behind this event was the movement of great slabs of the Earth's crust known as tectonic plates. As the plate on which Africa rests pulled away from the South American plate and pushed up against Europe, the earth crumpled and folded along what is now a series of mountain ranges, including the Atlas range in Morocco. At the same time, great blocks of rock were thrown up within the Atlantic along much the same latitudes. Up through the cracks in and around these blocks flowed streams of liquid rock while unimaginably powerful forces at work below the crust contributed to the rise of the volcanic islands of the Atlantic.

Nowadays in the Canary Islands you can best get a feel for the rumblings below the surface on Lanzarote, where the Montañas del Fuego still bubble with vigour – although the last eruptions took place way back in 1824. Of the remaining islands, not an eruptive burp has been heard from Fuerteventura, Gran Canaria, La Gomera or El Hierro for centuries; Tenerife's most recent display was a fairly innocuous affair in 1909 and it was La Palma which hosted the most recent spectacle – a fiery outburst in 1971.

Of course, there is still plenty of activity across the floor of the Atlantic Ocean and many peaks lie out of sight below the surface. Occasionally new volcanic islands are puffed up into the light of day but they are generally little more than feeble mounds of loose ash and are quickly washed away.

For centuries the angry Teide mountain loomed menacingly in the imagination of the Guanches and, later, their Spanish overlords. A rumbling god of the underworld was thought to live in its bowels, occasionally giving vent to extreme displeasure by belching up his molten bile from the deepest infernal chambers of the mountain. Teide is indeed an impressive work of nature. Not only is it Spain's highest peak, it is the third-largest volcano in the world, after Hawaii's Mauna Loa and Mauna Kea.

All three are what is known as shield volcanoes – huge and rising in a broad, gently angled cone to a summit which holds a steep-walled, flat-based crater. Teide, like the Hawaiian volcanoes, is formed principally of basalt.

Sometimes such volcanoes, or similar ones known as stratovolcanoes, really blow their tops. Massive explosions cause the whole summit to cave in, emptying the vent, spewing forth the upper levels of the magma chamber and so blasting away an enormous crater. The result is known as a caldera, within which it is not unusual for new cones to emerge, creating volcanoes within volcanoes. There are several impressive calderas on Gran Canaria, most notably Pico de Bandama and Caldera de Tejeda; the latter formed five million years ago. Oddly enough, massive Caldera de Taburiente on La Palma does *not* belong to this group of geological phenomena, although it was long thought to. The generic term 'caldera' (which means 'large cooking pot' in Spanish) was borrowed from the vernacular and first coined in its

Volcanic Origins

Volcanoes spurt in two principal ways. In the **central** variety, magma (molten material from the earth's core) wells up through a single chimney or vent to meet the air at temperatures of 700°C to 1200°C. This forms the characteristic cone shape, such as that of La Gomera. In their **fissured** form, magma is forced through a pipe, or underground crack, within the mountain and erupts from its flank, such as at the Pico Viejo crater on Teide's western side in Tenerife. Often, a mountain may show evidence of both forms. Equally often, as in the case of Teide, today's shape may be the consequence of several eruptions over hundreds of thousands of years, each new deposit overlaying previous layers. A complex form like this is known as a **strato-volcano**.

The way a volcano erupts is largely determined by its gas content. If the material seething beneath the surface has a high gas content, the effect is like shaking a bottle of fizzy drink: once the cap's off, the contents spurt out with force. In the case of volcanoes, what are called **pyroclasts** – cinders, ash and lightweight fragments of pumice – are hurled high into the air and scatter over a wide area.

On the other hand, if the mix is more viscous (like treacle) the magma wells up, overflows a vent, then slows as it slithers down the mountain as lava flow, cooling all the while until its progress is stopped. You'll see several such congealed rivers, composed of clinker (volcanic slag) all spiky and irregular, in the Parque Nacional de Timanfaya on Lanzarote and around the slopes of Teide. Look also for **obsidian**, fragments or layers of smooth, shiny material, like black glass, and **scoria**, high in iron and magnesium and reddish brown in colour since it's – quite literally – rusting.

technical sense by a 19th-century German geologist.

The Las Cañadas depression, running alongside Tenerife's Teide mountain, was similarly formed by the combination of the emptying of a high-level magma chamber and the resultant collapse and lateral movement of the summit.

Although seemingly quieter than Italy's Vesuvius, Etna and Stromboli, all of which still have it in them to cause quite a fright, Teide is by no means finished. Above Etna, in Sicily, there is a constant cloud of steam. Wisps of hot air can sometimes be seen around the peak of Teide too. Where the lava is fairly fluid in such cases, steam pressure can build up to the point of ejecting lava and/or ash in an eruption through the narrow vent. The vent can simply be blown off if there is sufficient pressure.

When volcanoes do erupt, they belch out all sorts of things: ash, cinders, *lapilli* (small, round bombs of lava) and great streams of molten rock. Volcanic eruptions, however, don't just come through one central crater. Often subsidiary craters form around the main cone as lava and other materials force fissures into the mountain and escape that way. See the boxed text 'Volcanic Origins' for more details.

All the Canary Islands are of volcanic rock, dating at least from the Tertiary era – anything up to 65 million years ago (great rock blocks below the surface of Fuerteventura and Lanzarote have been estimated at up to 40 million years old). Basalt is the common denominator throughout the islands. Forming much of their bedrock and also, for example, the mighty walls of Caldera de Taburiente on La Palma, it is also sometimes used in constructing public buildings. Other minerals found include iron, sulphur and copper.

The Canary Islands are far from having exhausted their potential for fireworks. Geologists predict that the islands of La Palma and Tenerife are the most likely candidates for future eruptions.

CLIMATE

The Canary Islands enjoy a particularly benign climate. Indeed, it seems to be endlessly spring, with mean temperatures ranging from 18°C in the winter to about

24°C in summer. Daily highs can easily reach the mid-30s°C in summer. Even on a hot day at the beach, however, it can be pleasantly cool higher up and the snow atop Teide is a clear enough reminder that, in winter at any rate, some warm clothing is essential. This is especially the case if you intend doing any hiking in the mountains.

With the exception of desiccated Lanzarote and Fuerteventura, the north of the islands is sub-tropical while the south is drier, more arid and marginally hotter.

Rainfall is low (rarely more than 250mm annually, except on parts of the windblown northern coasts where it can be as much as 750mm) and what there is tends to fall mainly on the northern side of the more mountainous islands. Rain and cloud are carried in off the Atlantic by *alisios* (trade winds) blowing in mainly from the north-east and prevented from reaching across all the islands by the intervening mountains and hills. Higher alisios from the north-west (mainly dry trade winds that caress the islands) tend to cap the north-easterlies, adding to the pressure which keeps them embracing the hills in a mantle of fog.

The highest rainfall occurs in what passes for winter (from November to February), when it is feasible to be stretched out on a sun-drenched beach in the south of Tenerife or Gran Canaria while to the north it might be grey, cool and even wet. La Palma is the most rain-blessed of the Canaries while the bare and comparatively flat Lanzarote and Fuerteventura receive hardly a drop. This is not so much, as is often assumed, because they lie closest to Saharan Africa but more due to their lack of mountains.

Occasionally, especially in summer, a broiling sirocco (the hot wind off Africa) howls in from the Sahara, bearing swathes of dust and desert sand. Locally known as the *kalima*, it turns the day into twilight, leaving the sun a dull, ineffectual disk in a grey pall. The ocean is agitated and at the end of the day you can feel the grime plastered into your skin. It's a case of, if you won't go to the Sahara, the Sahara comes to you. It's at its worst in the most eastern islands.

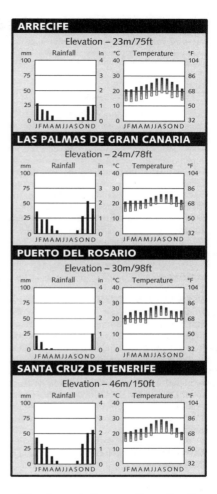

The sirocco is the exception rather than the rule; in fact the islands have long had a reputation as a place for health cures. A Samler Brown, in his *Madeira, Canary Islands & Azores*, first published in 1889, noted on the subject of the islands' invigorating clime:

In the Canaries bronchitis sometimes does well...Rheumatism, neuralgia, Bright's disease, gout, scrofula, venereal and other diseases find the climate most suitable. The first and second stages of consumption show material improvement...If strength permits, excursions should frequently be made to the hills or to the mountains, the change of air, even if only for a few hours, being of great advantage. All hotels will provide luncheon in a basket.

Because all the islands drop away fairly steeply into the ocean, the Gulf Stream moves easily from the north-west through deep channels around and between the islands, although with less force in the eastern islands. Counteracting the warmth of the stream is the chillier Canary Current that embraces the islands as it flows by the African coast towards Senegal, before looping west into the mid-Atlantic. This keeps the average water temperature to a little below what might be expected in these latitudes: 18°C in winter and 22°C in summer. The further west you go, the warmer the water gets.

ECOLOGY & ENVIRONMENT

As in mainland Spain, the 1960s saw the first waves of mass sea-and-sun tourism crash over the tranquil shores of the Canary Islands. The government of the day rubbed its hands in anticipation of filling up the state coffers with easy tourist dollars and local entrepreneurs enthusiastically leapt aboard the gravy train. Few, however, gave a thought to what impact the tourists and the mushrooming coastal resorts might have on the environment.

Tourism, Construction & Pollution

The near-unregulated building and expansion of resorts well into the 1980s has created some monumental eyesores, particularly on the southern side of Tenerife and Gran Canaria. Great scabs of holiday villas, hotels and condominiums have spread across much of the two islands' southern coasts. And the problem is not restricted to the resorts – hasty cement extensions of towns and villages mean that parts of the interior of the islands are being increasingly spoiled by property developers

and speculators. Politics and influence-peddling are often the unsavoury background to a frequent tendency to turn a blind eye to these activities. For most foreign visitors, the ugliness is offset by the chance to party in the sun in winter, when most of Europe lies huddled beneath its thick, cold, grey mantle.

The massive influx of visitors to the islands over recent decades has brought or exacerbated other problems. Littering of beaches, dunes and other areas of natural beauty, both by outsiders and locals, remains a burning issue. Occasionally ecological societies organise massive clean-ups of rubbish along beaches and the like – worthy gestures but equally damning evidence of the extent to which the problem persists.

For the islands' administrators, it's a conundrum. Tourism has come to represent an essential pillar of the Canaries' economy, which quite simply cannot do without it. They argue that profits from the tourist trade are ploughed back into the community. However, this is still fairly haphazard and there have long been calls for more regional planning – and, every year more insistently, for a total moratorium on yet more tourism development.

Some of the damage done over the years, especially to the coastline, is irreversible. The regional government has long been considering an *ecotasa* (eco-tax) to be levied on visitors and channelled into infrastructure and environmental protection, but this has yet to be implemented.

Water

One of the islands' greatest and most persistent problems is water, or rather the lack of it. Limited rainfall and the few natural springs have always restricted agriculture in the islands and water is a commodity still in short supply.

Desalination appears the only solution for the Canaries, which already accounts for 2% of the world's desalinated water production. Pretty much all potable H_2O on Lanzarote and Fuerteventura is desalinated sea water.

In summer, the corollary of the perennial water problem is the forest fire. With almost clockwork regularity, hundreds of hectares of forest are ravaged every summer on all the islands except the already bare Lanzarote and Fuerteventura.

Nature Reserves

Only since the late 1980s have real steps been taken to protect the islands' natural diversity. The 1987 law on the Conservación de Espacios Naturales (preservation of nature areas) earmarked 42% of territory for some form of protection. In 1994, the law passed from being a mere declaration of intent to an enforceable regulatory mechanism. The islands' four national parks, for instance, are largely protected from human interference by rules banning visitors from free camping or straying from defined walking paths (see National Parks & Other Reserves later in this chapter). You can contribute by obeying the rules on where you are permitted to hike and keeping all your trash with you – what you take in you should also take out.

Whales & Dolphins

Several species of whale and dolphin used to find the Canary Islands so friendly that they'd often hang about just 20m off the coast. But then curious visitors started heading out to sea to get a closer look. The more people came, the greater the distance these magnificent mammals put between themselves and the islands. In spite of it all, a colony of pilot whales *(ballenas pilotos)* is based off the south coast of Tenerife. As many as 26 whale and dolphin species (one-third of the world total) have been observed off the Canary Islands. The most common, apart from pilot whales, are bottlenose dolphins *(tursiones)* and sperm whales *(cachalotes)*.

Whale observation is a lucrative, and often aggressive, business with boatloads of tourists jostling for position around schools of these mammals – after all, for many people the Canaries present a unique opportunity to see whales in their natural habitat.

There's now a law which aims to regulate observation of sea mammals. The idea is to limit the number of boats following schools at any one time and to curb unpleasant practices such as using sonar and other devices to attract whales' attention. Four small patrol boats attempt to keep a watchful eye on these activities. There has been much talk of establishing a single marine centre from which all excursions would be organised. It seems extraordinary that, if there is real concern about leaving these animals as undisturbed as possible, such a measure has not already been taken.

There is nothing intrinsically wrong with joining excursions to go whale-watching. Where possible, try to join an outfit that respects the regulations. You could also contact the organisation Whales & Tales in Tenerife (see the next section).

Environmental Organisations

The islands are swarming with environmental action groups, some more active than others. Most are members of the Federación Ecologista Canaria Ben-Magec (Ben-Magec Ecological Foundation of the Canaries; ☎/fax 928 31 10 04), Calle de las Botas 5, Las Palmas. Some of the individual groups you'll find on the islands are listed below. The word 'Apdo' followed by number indicates a post box number only.

Gran Canaria
Asociación Canaria de Amigos de la Naturaleza (ASCAN; ☎ 928 27 36 44) Calle Presidente Alvear 50, 2, Las Palmas

El Hierro
Asociación para la Defensa de la Naturaleza e Identidad del Hierro (ADNIH; ☎ 922 55 82 19) Calle de la Ola 7, La Restinga

Fuerteventura
ASCAN (☎ 928 85 20 71) Calle Juan Tadeo, Puerto del Rosario

La Gomera
Asociación Ecologista y Cultural Guarapo (☎ 922 80 07 10) Apdo 74, 38800 San Sebastián de la Gomera

Lanzarote
Asociación Cultural y Ecologista El Guincho
  (☎ 928 81 54 32, fax 928 81 54 30) Apdo 365,
  35580 Arrecife

La Palma
Asamblea Irichen (☎ 922 44 06 62) Apdo 170,
38700, Santa Cruz de la Palma

Tenerife
**Asociación Tinerfeña de Amigos de la
  Naturaleza** (ATAN; ☎/fax 922 27 93 92) Apdo
  1015, 38080 Santa Cruz de Tenerife
Asociación para la Defensa del Surf (ADES)
  Calle Imeldo Seris 17, Santa Cruz de Tenerife
Whales & Tales (☎ 922 82 05 59) Apdo 7, 38080
  La Laguna. This German-founded group works
  to protect whales and other sealife in the Ca-
  naries, as well as organising whale-observation
  trips and ecologically sensitive excursions on
  the various islands.

FLORA & FAUNA
Flora

A combination of rich volcanic soil and
the varied rainfall and altitude of the more
mountainous islands supports a surprisingly rich diversity of plant life, both indigenous and imported. Despite their small
area the Canary Islands are home to about
2000 species, about half of them unique
to the islands. The only brake on what
might otherwise be a still more florid display in this largely sub-tropical environment is the shortage of water. Budding
botanists will have a field day here.

Up to about 400m, the land is home to
plants that thrive in hot and arid conditions.

Where farmland has been irrigated you'll
find bananas, oranges, coffee, sugar cane,
dates and tobacco. In the towns, bougainvillea, hibiscus, acacia, geraniums, marigolds
and carnations all contribute to the bright
array. Of the more exotic specimens the
strelitzia, with its blue, white and orange
blossoms, stands out. These exotics have all
been introduced to the islands. The dry, un-
cultivated scrublands near the coast, known
as *tabaibales*, host various indigenous
plants such as *cardón* (Eurphorbia).

At elevations of around 700m, the
Canaries' climate is more typical of the
Mediterranean, encouraging crops such as
cereals, potatoes and grapes. Where the
crops give way, stands of eucalyptus and
cork take over. Mimosa, broom, honey-
suckle and laburnums are also common.

Higher still the air is cooler, and common
plants and trees include holly, myrtle and
the laurel. The best place to explore forest
land is in La Gomera's Parque Nacional de
Garajonay, host to one of the world's last
remaining Tertiary era forests and declared
a UNESCO world heritage site. Known as
laurisilva, it is made up of laurels, holly,
linden and giant heather, clad in lichen and
moss and often swathed in swirling mist.

Up to 2000m the most common tree
you're likely to encounter is the Canary
pine *(Pinus canariensis)*, which manages to
set down roots on impossibly steep slopes
that would defeat most other species. It is a
particularly hardy tree whose fire-resistant
timber makes fine construction material.

The Tree with a Long, Shady Past

Among the more curious trees you will see in the Canary Islands is the *drago* (dragon tree; *Dracaena draco*), which can reach 18m in height and live for centuries.

Having survived the last ice age, it looks different – even a touch prehistoric. In shape it resembles a giant posy of flowers, its trunk and branches the stems, which break into bunches of long,
narrow silvery-green leaves higher up. What makes it stranger still is its red sap or resin – known,
of course, as 'dragon's blood' – which was traditionally used in medicine.

The tree played an important role in Canary Island life, for it was beneath the ancient branches
of a drago that the Guanche Council of Nobles would gather to administer justice. The drago is one
of a family of up to 80 species *(Dracaena)* that survived the Ice Age in tropical and sub-tropical zones
of the Old World, and is one of the last representatives of Tertiary-era flora.

Not Just a Pretty Frond

The palm tree is as common in the Canary Islands as it is in North Africa and the Middle East. Apart from the native Canary palm *(Phoenix canariensis)*, the islands boast a fair population of date palms. The latter were largely imported after the Spanish conquest – La Gomera, for instance, had none until Hernán Peraza, the island's ill-fated governor, decided to import some from North Africa. A hybrid between the two has also taken firm root on the islands.

Dates aren't the only product of this graceful tree, which can grow to more than 20m tall. The ribs of its leaves can be used in furniture, while individual leaf strands are handy for basketware. The base of the leaves was traditionally used for fuel, while the fruit stalks and fibre could be used to make rope and other packing material. The devout display palm leaves on their balconies for Palm Sunday, and leaves also feature in the Jewish Feast of Tabernacles.

Dates aren't the only form of sustenance that palms provide. The Gomeros, for example, extract what they call palm honey from the *guarapo* (or sap) of the palm, boiling it into a dark, sticky, sweet liquid.

Spanish missionaries thought palms so versatile that they took samples of the Canarian version to Latin America in the 18th century – yet another example of cross-fertilisation between the Old and New Worlds.

The highest points of Tenerife and La Palma are too harsh for any but the hardiest of Alpine vegetation.

Up in the great volcanic basin of the Parque Nacional del Teide on Tenerife are some outstanding flowers. Apart from the feisty high-altitude Teide violet, one of the floral symbols of the Canaries is the flamboyant *tajinaste rojo*, or Teide viper's bugloss *(Echium wildpretii)*, which can grow over 3m high. Every other spring it sprouts an extraordinary conical spike of striking red blooms like a great red poker. After its brief, spectacular moment of glory, all that remains is a thin, desiccated spear-shaped skeleton, like a well-picked over fish. Leave well alone; each fishbone has thousands of tiny strands, itchy as horsehair.

Although much of the vegetation is common across the islands, there are some marked differences. Fuerteventura, Lanzarote and the south of Gran Canaria distinguish themselves from the rest with their semi-desert flora, where saltbush, Canary palm and other small shrubs dominate. Concentrated in a couple of spots – the cliffs of Famara in Lanzarote and Jandía in Fuerteventura – you will find more abundant flora. This includes the rare *cardón de Jandía* (a cactus-like plant), several species of daisy and all sorts of odd cliff plants unique to these islands.

See Books in the Facts for the Visitor chapter for some suggested reading.

Fauna

The islands are not overly endowed with indigenous animal life. Apart from introduced animals (such as North African hedgehogs, rabbits, mice, and domesticated animals), about the most interesting land-going beasty is a rather large (up to 1m long), ancient and ugly lizard *(lagarto del Salmor)* found only on the island of El Hierro. Its ancestors are thought to have grown as large as 9m but until recently it was deemed extinct. There may be as many as 200 in circulation but you'd be lucky to catch a glimpse of one in the wild. A couple of bat species send up the occasional night patrol – only the *Orejudo canario* is endemic.

Reaching for the sky are more than 200 species of bird, although many of these are not home-grown. Among indigenous birds are the canary (those in the wild are a muck-brown colour, not the sunny yellow colour of their domesticated cousins) and a couple of types of large pigeon, the *rabiche* and the *turqué*. Common throughout the islands are quails, crows, partridges, sparrows, blackbirds, green finches, warblers, blue tits, chaffinches, kestrels and various types of owl.

Several species are seen only in Lanzarote and Fuerteventura. The *hubara* bustard is one, as is the black oyster-catcher.

Nice Dog, Good Dog

If you come across a solid-looking dog with a big head and a stern gaze, you are probably getting to know the Canary dog, known in Spanish as the *Presa Canario*. This beast is right up there with the Pit Bull as a tenacious guard dog, loyal and chummy with its owners but rarely well disposed to outsiders.

The breed is also known as the *verdino* (from a slightly greenish tint in its colouring) and opinion is divided regarding its origins. Probably introduced to the islands in the wake of the Spanish conquest in the 15th century, and subsequently mixed with other breeds, the Canary Dog has been used for centuries to guard farms and cattle. When it comes to stopping human intruders in their tracks, no other dog is so full of fight. It is prized by owners for its fearlessness and loyalty.

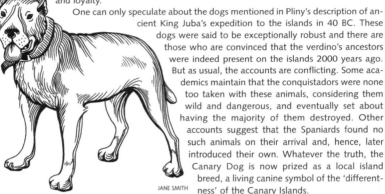

One can only speculate about the dogs mentioned in Pliny's description of ancient King Juba's expedition to the islands in 40 BC. These dogs were said to be exceptionally robust and there are those who are convinced that the verdino's ancestors were indeed present on the islands 2000 years ago. But as usual, the accounts are conflicting. Some academics maintain that the conquistadors were none too taken with these animals, considering them wild and dangerous, and eventually set about having the majority of them destroyed. Other accounts suggest that the Spaniards found no such animals on their arrival and, hence, later introduced their own. Whatever the truth, the Canary Dog is now prized as a local island breed, a living canine symbol of the 'differentness' of the Canary Islands.

JANE SMITH

The odd eagle or vulture can also be seen. Another species to look out for is the hoopoe, whose black-and-white wing patterns, curved beak and striking crest are hard to miss.

Marine Life The waters around the Canary Islands host 350 species of fish, five of them known only here, and about 600 species of algae.

The famous monk seal no longer hangs about Lanzarote and Fuerteventura – the nearest colonies are in Mauritania – but there is talk of attempting to reintroduce it to the archipelago. Out at sea, several species of whale and dolphin can occasionally be spotted and there is no shortage of organised trips for this purpose. See also Whales & Dolphins in the earlier Ecology & Environment section for details.

For those who like to see sub-aquatic species at close quarters, there are dive centres on all the islands – see Activities in the Facts for the Visitor chapter for details.

National Parks & Other Reserves

With 42% of territory falling under one of eight categories of parkland, the Canary Islands are one of the most extensively protected territories in all of Europe – at least in theory.

At the top of the tree are the four *parques nacionales* (national parks), administered at state level from Madrid. The Parque Nacional del Teide has as its centrepiece Spain's highest mountain, the volcanic peak of Teide; the Parque Nacional de Garajonay in La Gomera is a splendid rainforest relic from the Tertiary era; for active volcanic activity, head for the Montañas del Fuego in the Parque Nacional de Timanfaya on Lanzarote; and the enormous eroded-rock cauldron at the heart of La Palma's Parque Nacional de la Caldera de Taburiente encloses another world.

Responsibility for the administration and protection of all other parks and natural areas of interest rests with Spain's regional governments. A 1994 regional law identifies seven other divisions of territory worthy of protection in the Canary Islands. Of these, the *parques naturales* (nature parks) form the second and most extensive tier. They generally have a greater level of human intrusion (in the form of villages, farms, roads and so on) than the parques nacionales.

The remaining six categories are: *parques rurales* (rural parks), *reservas naturales integrales* (integrated nature reserves), *reservas naturales especiales* (special nature reserves), *monumentos naturales* (natural monuments), *paisajes protegidos* (protected countryside) and *sitios de interés científico* (sites of scientific interest).

GOVERNMENT & POLITICS

Well before the Canary Islands were declared a single province of Spain in 1821, competition for primacy between the two main islands, Tenerife and Gran Canaria, was already intense. The selection of Santa Cruz de Tenerife as the provincial capital infuriated politicians and other worthies in Las Palmas de Gran Canaria, and marked the beginning of a long fight to have the province split in two. Tried and shelved in the 1840s, the idea only became reality in 1927. Lanzarote, Fuerteventura and Gran Canaria formed one province, with Las Palmas as the capital, while Tenerife, La Palma, La Gomera and El Hierro were grouped under the leadership of Santa Cruz de Tenerife.

Soon after the 1982 electoral victory of the socialists at national level, the Canary Islands were declared a *comunidad autónoma*, one of 17 autonomous regions across Spain.

The region's flag is a yellow, blue and white tricolour – to which the few militant *independentistas* add seven stars to represent the islands. The provincial division remains intact, as does the bitter rivalry between the two – so much so that the regional government has offices in both provincial capitals, which alternate as lead city of the region every four years.

Article 148 of the national constitution grants considerable power to regional governments, which have authority over areas such as agriculture, transport, tourism, health and local policing. The comunidad raises its own taxes, topped up by contributions from the central state's coffers. In the case of the Canary Islands, a special deal on investment and taxes has to be renegotiated with the European Union every few years. The Canary Islands' government, usually with Madrid's support, argues that their geographical position creates certain disadvantages with respect to the rest of the Union and so requires compensation in the form of its exceptional status. So far, this reasoning has been accepted by Brussels.

To the ordinary Canarios the most important level of government is the *Cabildos* (individual island administrations). Resurrected in 1912, they are directly responsible for each of the islands. The islands are further subdivided into town and district municipalities, or *municipios*. These five tiers of government inevitably lead to a fair degree of bureaucratic overlap.

After Franco's death, the socialist Partido Socialista Obrero Español (PSOE) rose to become the strongest party in the Canary Islands, as in mainland Spain, while the right-wing Partido Popular (PP) tended to run a distant second. There was no shortage of local parties fighting for scraps of the electorate but most struggled through the 1980s. Occasionally, however, one or other tactical local grouping managed to swing enough votes to go into coalition with the major parties.

Since the early 1990s these splintered forces have been able to bury their assorted hatchets (among them the age-old rivalry between Gran Canaria and Tenerife politicians) and form what is today the most powerful political force in the islands, the Coalición Canaria (CC), which has also gone by the name of Coalición Nacionalista.

Its concern is first and foremost to improve the deal the Canaries get from Madrid.

In the latest regional elections, held in June 1999, the CC sustained its position as the single biggest force in the Canaries with 37% of the vote. Both the PP and PSOE lost ground. The former came in on 27% and the PSOE, reeling from a contentious change of leadership, on 19%.

As a result of the March 2000 general elections, which gave a second successive victory to the Partido Popular, the CC has four seats in the national assembly in Madrid. This sounds paltry, but when the CC combines its strength with that of the other major regional parties (the Basque PNV and Catalonian CiU) they can together exert a degree of leverage disproportionate to their individual voting power, extracting concessions and influencing decisions favourable to their autonomous regions.

Key elements of the CC's platform are control of crime and drug abuse, elimination of waiting lists in hospitals, improved finances for education and a host of other socially laudable goals. They press Madrid for cheaper transport between the islands and the mainland; complete local control of ports, airports, public utilities and other enterprises; and the financing of a second runway for La Palma's overstretched airport on Gran Canaria.

However, at local-government level the situation is exactly reversed – the CC governs with support from the PP.

ECONOMY

The fortunes of the Canary Islands have, since the time of their conquest by Spain in the 15th century, always been precarious. An obligatory stop on the old Spanish trade routes to South America, the islands had an economy based on cash crops. Over the centuries sugar, wine grapes, cochineal (used in the production of natural dyes) and bananas were the backbone of the islands' export economy. Predictably, this made the islands and their often struggling inhabitants prey to the vagaries of world markets and boom-bust cycles. Crisis often triggered waves of emigration, mostly to Latin America.

Agriculture and light industry account for about 4.5% and 9% respectively of the islands' gross domestic product. Aside from the big oil refinery at Santa Cruz de Tenerife and some food processing, secondary industry is barely in evidence. By contrast, the services sector (of which a large chunk is tourism-related) represents a whopping 80% of total GDP. With over 8 million tourists (staying on average 10 days) flooding ashore every year, it is easy to identify the islands' latest cash crop. Exporting bananas and tomatoes is a poor earner by comparison.

The islands' exports are fairly limited. Of the total annual income of less than US$1 million from products sold abroad, a little over half comes from fruit and vegetables, with seafood (representing one-sixth) coming in a distant second. A great deal of the islanders' (and tourists') needs are met by imports worth US$6m annually.

The aim of the special tax breaks and regulations is to act as an incentive to business and residents in the islands. There are all sorts of tax discounts for businesses (local or foreign) that want to operate here, while low indirect taxation encourages residents to remain in the islands. Although IVA *(impuesto sobre el valor añadido)*, the Spanish version of VAT, can run to 16% in mainland Spain, the Canary Island equivalent, IGIC *(impuesto general indirecto canario)*, is a flat 5% – compensating for the higher base cost of imported goods and generally resulting in cheaper retail shopping than on the mainland. Petrol, alcohol and tobacco are subject to special low taxes too.

All of this may or may not have a positive effect on the islands' economy. Local statisticians can point to a per capita GDP only a little way behind the Spanish national average. On the other hand, average wages in the islands are lower than on the mainland (the most recent statistics put the average mainland wage at 217,000 ptas per month compared with 182,000 ptas per month in the Canary Islands) and officially 16.5% of the islands' workforce is jobless, higher than the national average of 13%. But keep in mind that the official figures can be deceptive. Unofficially the jobless rate in the islands has been estimated to be as high as 27%, compared with a national rate of about 24%. Also worth remembering is that, by some estimates, the Spanish minimum wage is the lowest in the European Union.

POPULATION & PEOPLE

The total resident population of the Canary Islands at the start of the 20th century was 364,414. It now stands at 1.65 million, growing at the slow rate of 1.15% each year. For every Canary Islander, or Canario, five foreigners visit the islands each year!

The bulk of the population is concentrated in the two main islands – Gran Canaria (716,000) and Tenerife (677,000). Of the remaining islands, the population ranges from 86,000 in La Palma to just 8350 in El Hierro. With an average of 215 people per square kilometre, the Canary Islands are considerably more crowded than mainland Spain, where there are only 77 people per square kilometre.

Only a fraction of all the people who visit the Canaries decide to stay for good. At the last count, 72,000 foreigners called the Canaries home. Of the Europeans, the Germans (10,000) and Brits (7500) were by far out in front. Of the 33,000 from the Americas, many are descendants of Canarios who migrated there generations ago. Venezuelans (24,000), their country the most favoured destination for migrants from these often less-than-fortunate isles, are by far the most numerous.

Although the term Canario has come to designate all the islanders, it once referred more strictly to the people of Gran Canaria alone (now more often as not referred to as Grancanarios or Canariones). The people of Tenerife are Tinerfeños; those of Lanzarote are Lanzaroteños; Fuerteventura, Majoreros (from the Guanche name for much of the island, Maxorata); La Gomera, Gomeros; La Palma, Palmareños; and El Hierro, Herreños.

Most of the locals have the classic Mediterranean looks of the Spaniards (with perhaps a little Berber mixed in) – dark hair, flashing eyes and olive complexion. But talk to some for a while and you might find that they don't think of themselves as all that Spanish.

The *godos* (goths), as the Canarios refer to Spaniards from the peninsula, are not automatically thought of as being part of the family. While mainlanders like to joke about the Canarios being African, there are some in the islands who actually prefer to think of themselves that way (at least insofar as this distinguishes them from the rest of Spain). After all, they are geographically much closer to the African continent than to the Spanish mainland.

EDUCATION

There are more than 150 primary and secondary schools on the islands, catering to a pupil population of a little over 150,000. Education is free and obligatory in the Canary Islands from the age of six to 16. About one third of pupils attend Catholic schools, which are often subsidised by the state. Upon matriculation, students must sit entrance exams for university; there students study for six years or so, taking qualifications such as the *diplomada* after three years and the *licenciado* after another two or three years' study.

There are over 30 universities across Spain but until fairly recently there was only one in the Canary Islands, at La Laguna in Tenerife. Many Canarios find themselves heading for the mainland to pursue their preferred courses. Argument raged for years about whether a second university should be established on Gran Canaria. Long considered by Tinerfeños as an extravagant doubling up of La Laguna, which started as a modest outpost of learning in 1701, the vocation-oriented Universidad de Las Palmas de Gran Canaria was finally set up in 1989. In 1999, there were 48,000 students in higher education.

ARTS
Music
Traditional The symbol of the Canarios' musical heritage is the *timple*, a ukelele-style instrument of obscure origin. Although

many thought it was a variation of the Italian mandolin or the Spanish and Portuguese *guitarillo*, it now appears that Berber slaves, shipped in for farm work by the early Norman invaders under Jean de Béthencourt, might have introduced it to the islands.

It's a small, wooden, five-stringed instrument with a rounded back (it is said the original Berber version was made of a turtle shell) and a sharp tone. There is also a four-string version known as the *contra* or *requinto*, prevalent in Lanzarote.

The timple has travelled widely, as emigrants from the islands took it with them to Latin America, where it was incorporated into their instrumental repertory.

Whenever you see local traditional fiestas, the timple will be there accompanying such dances as the *isa* and *folía*, or if you're lucky the *tajaraste*, about the only dance said to have been passed down from the ancient Guanches.

If you develop a fondness for the timple, look for a CD by Domingo Rodríguez Oramas, who is known as El Colorado.

Los Sabandeños is one of the most widely known folkloric groups in the Canary Islands, and their latest CD, *Gardel*, is a good serving of this light, melodic music.

Verode is a popular group dedicated to traditional Canario music. With six singers, their repertoire includes sentimental island eulogies and melancholy recollections of emigrant life. The CD *Veinte Años* contains a collection of their best work. Watch out too for Taburiente; one of their better CDs is *Nuevo Cauce*. Other groups to bear in mind include Los Gofiones, Mestisay and Añoranza.

Over the centuries there has been no shortage of immigration from Andalucía in the south of Spain, and with it came another musical tradition. Popular Andalucían dances such as the *malagueña* have become part of the local island folk tradition. Flamenco, however, is still pretty much absent.

Contemporary In the mid-1990s a new star burst onto the Spanish music stage and by 1998 looked set to make inroads into the world scene. Rosana Arbelo, born in Lanzarote in 1962, is a fine singer-songwriter whose first CD, *Lunas Rotas*, was a smash hit in Spain and elsewhere in Europe in 1996–7. Her lyrics tend to the melancholy, accompanied by an appealing mix of Cuban, Spanish and African rhythms.

However, the islands' most established *cantautor* (singer-songwriter), and one appreciated across all Spain, is Tenerife's Pedro Guerra. One of his best CDs is titled *Golosinas*.

Las Ratas are a popular rock band whose only CD so far is self-titled.

Literature

Until the arrival of the conquering Spaniards in the 15th century, the Guanches appear not to have known writing. Very much a frontier world even after the conquest, the Canaries were not an immediate source of writers of world renown. Little, if anything, that the islands have produced in the way of literature has made it into English translation.

This is not to say the islanders have been inactive. The Guanches themselves did not write down their verses but some of their oral ballads were transcribed by an Italian historian, Leonardo Torriani. And with the conquistadors came storytellers to chronicle their exploits.

Various historians and poets followed. The first of note beyond the islands was the Tinerfeño José de Viera y Clavijo (1731–1813), an accomplished poet but known above all for his painstaking history of the islands, *Noticias de la Historia General de Canarias*. His contemporary, Tomás de Iriarte (1750–91), born in Puerto de la Cruz, was for years something of a dandy in Madrid court circles. He wrote several plays, but his *Fábulas Literarias*, poetry and tales charged with a mordant wit, constituted his lasting work.

Ricardo Murphy (1814–40) led the way for Romantic poetry in the islands, succumbing at an early age, as did so many ardent poets of the time, to tuberculosis (which he contracted in London).

CRUZ

Architecturally simple yet artistically effective, doors and balconies are the most eye-catching feature of old-style Canarios houses.

From Christopher Columbus and the conquistadors to fishing for food and transporting tourists around the archipelago, boats have been an integral part of Canaries life, past and present.

Nicolás Estévanez (1838–1914), spent much of his life outside the Canary Islands, first as a soldier and politician in Madrid and then in exile for 40 years in France. His poems, in particular one called *Canarias*, marked him as the motor behind the so-called Escuela Regionalista, a school of poets devoting themselves to themes less universal and more identifiable with the archipelago.

Another of the islands' great historians emerged about the same time. Agustín Millares Torres (1826–96) is remembered for his monumental *Historia General de las Islas Canarias.*

Benito Pérez Galdós (1843–1920) grew up in Las Palmas de Gran Canaria, moving to Madrid in 1862. A prolific chronicler of his times, he produced 46 novels and numerous other books and plays. Among his masterpieces is the four-part *Fortunata y Jacinta*, which recounts the lives of two unhappily married women of different social classes. Ángel Guimerá (1849–1924), born in Santa Cruz de Tenerife, moved to the mainland to become one of Barcelona's great lyric poets and a leading figure in Catalan theatre.

Dr Tomás Morales (1885–1921) became in his short life one of the islands' leading exponents of Modernist poetry. A contemporary of his, also of some note, was Alonso Quesada (1886–1925).

The poet Josefina de la Torre (born 1909) first achieved fame in the late 1920s. As the 20th century wore on, the poets of the Vanguardia took the centre stage. Among the Canaries' exponents were Pedro Perdomo Acedo (1897–1977) and Felix Delgado (1904–36).

Isaac de Vega (born 1920) has been one of the 20th century's outstanding novelists in the Canaries. His *Fetasa*, for example, is a disturbing study of alienation and solitude.

Carmen Laforet Díaz's (born 1921) *Nada*, written in the wake of the Civil War, is the partly autobiographical account of a young girl's move from her home in the Canary Islands to study in post-Civil War Barcelona, where she is obliged to live in squalor with her grandmother. She has

followed this up with other novels of lesser impact and, in 1961, *Gran Canaria*, a guide to her home island.

One of the most creative talents to emerge among the post-modern poets of the 1980s was Yolanda Soler Onís (born 1964). *Sobre el Ámbar*, written from 1982 to 1986, is a collection of pieces whose images are sourced largely from an exploration of island poetic traditions.

Other contemporary novelists to look out for are Roberto Cabrera and E Díaz Marrero.

Architecture

Before the Conquest The Guanches lived more often than not in caves; of the rudimentary houses they built nothing remains today.

Gothic & Mudéjar Spaniards, Portuguese, French, Flemish, Italian and even English masters all injected something of their own architectural wealth into the Canaries. It is worth bearing this in mind when contemplating the styles of architecture briefly described below. There is little that can be considered architecturally 'pure' in the handful of outstanding monuments the islands possess.

By the time the conquest of the islands was completed at the end of the 15th century, the Gothic and mudéjar styles already belonged more to the past than the present. The interior of the Catedral de Las Palmas is nevertheless a fine example of what some art historians have denominated Atlantic Gothic. The bell tower of the Basílica de la Virgen del Pino (Teror, Gran Canaria) retains its Portuguese Gothic identity. Don't include the Catedral de Arucas (Gran Canaria) in the equation however – this magnificent edifice, with all the soaring power and complexity of the style, is in fact a neo-Gothic imitation.

The mudéjar style which characterises a swathe of churches and public buildings throughout mainland Spain is barely present in the islands. A hangover from the years of Muslim rule, the use of brick rather than stone, and decorated wooden ceilings set

Spanish Christian monuments apart from anything else in Europe. Only a few scraps of mudéjar influence made it to the islands. Probably the best examples are the fine wooden ceilings (known as *artesonado*) in the Iglesia de la Concepción in La Laguna, Tenerife. Not far behind are those of the Iglesia de Santa Catalina, in Tacoronte, on the same island.

Plateresque & Baroque In mainland Spain, the plateresque (meaning 'silver-smith-like' – so called because it was reminiscent of intricate metalwork) style of decorating monuments marked the arrival of the Renaissance. Its single greatest repository is the Castilian city of Salamanca, whose extraordinary edifices drip with controlled detail, busts and swirling motifs. You can get the merest whiff of such energy at the Catedral de Las Palmas (Gran Canaria) and the Iglesia de la Concepción in La Laguna (Tenerife) – the latter a veritable reference work of styles from gothic through mudéjar to plateresque. The Casa de Colón in Las Palmas also has plateresque features. Baroque, the trademark of the 17th century, left several traces across the archipelago and is best preserved in the parish church of Betancuria (Fuerteventura), built on the ruins of an earlier Gothic church which was destroyed by pirates late in the 16th century.

Modern Times Neo-classical, neo-Gothic and other styles demonstrating a perhaps less creative, more derivative era are represented from the late 18th century onwards in imposing public buildings in the bigger cities. The Catedral de Arucas, already mentioned, is an impressive piece of neo-Gothic – a shame it's not the genuine article.

Modernism, with its use of glass and wrought iron, makes an appearance in such constructions as the Mercado del Puerto in Las Palmas de Gran Canaria, along with private houses in areas such as Las Palmas' Triana district and Las Ramblas in Santa Cruz de Tenerife.

Military Architecture From the earliest days of the conquest until well into the 18th

century, the single most common construction efforts – apart from churches – were castles and forts. This lasted until well into the 18th century. The bulk of these forts were (and are) rough-and-ready affairs, and few have particular artistic merit. Among those to look out for though are the Torre del Conde (San Sebastián de la Gomera), Castillo de la Luz (Las Palmas de Gran Canaria) and the Castillo de San Juan (Santa Cruz de Tenerife).

Popular Architecture Rural houses were and still are simple affairs. The outstanding element is usually the internal courtyard, or *patio*, where a great deal of family life is played out. Another singular element about these houses, usually brilliantly whitewashed, is their wooden upstairs balconies. At their most elaborate, such balconies are intricately carved works of art.

Private houses and mansions in the towns might incorporate various styles with, say, a plateresque entrance, wooden balconies of various types and a striking variety of broad windows. These windows are in some cases true works of art, multi-paned and with varied combinations of wooden shutters, frames and panels. The patio, again, remains a paramount element – usually the most striking and beautiful part of Canario houses. The mix in many cases bears signs of Portuguese and Andalucían influence. If you seek out these urban jewels only once, explore the lanes of La Orotava and La Laguna (Tenerife).

Painting

Guanche Cave Art The Guanches left behind a number of cave paintings, notably in the *cuevas* (caves) of Barranco de Balos, Agaete, Gáldar (all on Gran Canaria), Belmaco and Zarza (La Palma) and Cuevas de El Julán (El Hierro). The paintings appear to date from at least the 13th and 14th centuries, the period immediately preceding the beginning of the Spanish invasion. Some depict human and animal figures, while others (such as in Cueva Pintada de Gáldar) are essentially geometric figures and decorative designs. Circles and ovals seem to have been the preferred symbols and figure among funerary inscriptions on Lanzarote and La Palma.

From the Conquest to the 19th Century It was quite some time after the conquest of the Canary Islands before any painters of note began to appear.

In the 17th century, Gaspar de Quevedo from Tenerife was the first major painter to emerge from the Canary Islands. Quevedo was succeeded in the 18th century by Cristóbal Hernández de Quintana (1659–1725), whose paintings still decorate the Catedral de la Laguna, Tenerife. More important was Juan de Miranda (1723–1805), among whose outstanding works is *La Adoración de los Pastores* (The Adoration of the Shepherds) in the Iglesia de la Concepción in Santa Cruz de Tenerife. His best known acolyte was Luis de la Cruz y Ríos (1776–1853), born in La Orotava and above all a portraitist.

In the 19th century, Valentín Sanz Carta (1849–98) was among the first Canarios to produce landscapes. Others of his ilk included Lorenzo Pastor and Lillier y Thruillé, whose work can be seen in the Museo de Bellas Artes in Santa Cruz de Tenerife.

20th Century The Canary Islands' main exponent of Impressionism was Manuel González Méndez (1843–1909), whose *La Verdad Venciendo el Error* hangs in the Ayuntamiento de Santa Cruz de Tenerife.

Néstor Martín Fernández de la Torre (1887–1938), whose speciality was murals, is best represented by his *Poema del Mar y Poema de la Tierra* (Poem of the Sea and Poem of the Earth). This and other works can be seen in the Museo Nestor, a gallery dedicated mainly to his work, in Las Palmas de Gran Canaria.

The Cuban-Canario José Aguiar García (1895–1976), born of Gomero parents, grew up in Cuba. A prolific painter, he too reached the apogee of his craft in his murals. His works are spread across the islands; the *Friso Isleño* hangs in the casino in Santa Cruz de Tenerife.

All the great currents of European art filtered through to the Canary Islands. Of the so-called Coloristas, names worth mentioning include Francesc Miranda Bonnin (1911–63) and Jesús Arencibia, who did the big mural in the Iglesia de San Antonio de Tamaraceite on Gran Canaria.

The first surrealist exhibition in Spain was held on 11 May 1935 in Santa Cruz de Tenerife. The greatest local exponent of surrealism, Tinerfeño surrealist Óscar Domínguez (1906–57), ended up in Paris in 1927 and was much influenced by Picasso. Cubist Antonio Padrón (1920–68) now has a museum dedicated to his works in his birthplace, Gáldar on Gran Canaria. Others of the period include Felo Monzón (1910–89) and Jorge Oramas (1911–35).

Leading the field of abstract artists is Manuel Millares (1921–72), native of Las Palmas de Gran Canaria. Lanzarote's César Manrique (1919–92) also enjoyed a considerable degree of international recognition.

Canarios currently working hard at the canvas include Cristino de Vera (born 1931), who displays elements of a primitive expressionism in his paintings, and María Castro (born 1930). José Luis Fajardo (born 1941) uses just about any materials that come to hand in his often bizarre works.

Sculpture

The Canaries roll-call of important sculptors is a short one. Two names you may come across are José Luján Pérez (1756–1815) and Fernando Estévez de Salas (1788–1854). The former's most important works are the *Cristo* in Catedral de Las Palmas and the *Cristo de la Columna* (Christ at the Pillar) in the Iglesia de Teror (Gran Canaria). Estévez is at his best in *Jesús Preso* (Christ Captured). *Nuestra Señora de las Angustias*, the masterpiece of Miguel Arroyo (born 1920), stands in the Iglesia del Pilar in Santa Cruz de Tenerife.

More recently, Eduardo Gregorio (1903–74) and Plácido Fleitas (1915–72) were two of the more outstanding modernists. Martín Chirino (born 1925) remains an icon of abstract sculpture, heavily influenced by African and Guanche art. He now divides his time between the Canary Islands and the USA.

SOCIETY & CONDUCT

Politeness is a question of taste and habit, and what it is depends on where you come from. It is always easy to tell a foreigner (especially of the Anglo-Saxon variety) in a bar or shop by the excessive number of '*por favors*' marking each and every request. Your average Canario (and mainland Spaniard) often dispenses with please and thank you and just gets to the point: 'Give me a carton of milk!' How rude, you might think, but then it's not customary for Anglos to routinely greet all and sundry with a cheery *buenos días* (good day) when entering the same establishments. Locals also, as they pass diners on their way out of a restaurant, have an almost distressing habit of smiling and wishing you *que aprovecheis* (bon appetit).

Making friends quickly in these islands is often not difficult. You don't need to be overly outgoing to strike up a chat with people (particularly if you speak passable Spanish), but don't necessarily expect it to go much further than that. Hearty farewells and promises of further meetings are, while not to be dismissed, to be taken with a sizeable grain of salt. Like anywhere else in the world, lasting friendships require spadework.

People socialise in cafes, bars, restaurants and public places. Dinner parties and intimate gatherings in people's homes are the exception rather than the rule.

Canarios are a pretty relaxed lot but, again, relaxation is done in different ways. Like mainland Spaniards and most Latin peoples, the Canarios like to dress well, at least when on show. The more extreme will dress to the nines just to head for the supermarket. No one expects foreigners to emulate this, but the down-at-heel-I-haven't-washed-for-a-week look favoured by some bedraggled tourists is sometimes inappropriate, particularly in restaurants and discos. An eye for what the locals are choosing to wear and a little common sense are handy assets.

Questions of Time

The Canary Islands, in the same time zone as the UK and Ireland, are one hour behind mainland Spain and most of Europe.

By 2 pm most shops, business and government departments are shut and everyone is heading home for a meal with the family or down to their favourite restaurant for a long lunch with colleagues or friends. Lunch can last until 4 pm, and sometimes later. The much mythologised siesta is thus more often than not dedicated to eating, family and friends, although there is time for a quick nap too if you want.

Government offices, banks and the like tend to open in the morning only whereas most shops and businesses re-open around 5 pm and remain so until about 8 pm.

Although in many resorts restaurants and bars cater to foreign habits, locals tend to eat late, rarely arriving at a restaurant before 9 pm. Arrangements to meet in a bar at midnight for the evening's entertainment are the norm.

Canarios are generally family-oriented. So where there's a fiesta or an outdoor cafe on a warm night, you'll see almost as many kids running about as adults – even at 3 am!

RELIGION

One of the primary concerns of the conquistadors from Spain was to convert what they perceived to be the benighted heathen of these far-flung islands to the one true faith. As the protracted and largely inglorious conquest proceeded, the indigenous inhabitants were swiftly converted to Christianity, usually as part of the terms of surrender. When armed resistance ended, the Guanches seem to have protested little at the conversion from their own once-complex faith, about which precious little is known (see the History section earlier in this chapter).

Roman Catholicism quickly took hold in the islands and, as in the rest of Spain, has left a deep-rooted impression. Although the depth of the average Canario's religiosity may be a subject of speculation, the Church still plays an important role in people's lives, at least *pro forma*. Most Canarios are

Don't Mumble, Give a Whistle

The American Indians had smoke signals, the Guanches had the whistle. On the small island of La Gomera, and maybe on other islands too, the original inhabitants developed an ingenious way for transmitting messages across deep ravines and other uncompromising territory. Where the complicated sounds of words could be confused over distance, the Guanches found that whistles were more readily picked up.

What perhaps began as a greeting or danger signal (a little like the Australian bush call 'coo-ee') developed into a veritable language, known today as El Silbo Gomero. Placing different fingers into the mouth in various positions to produce different sounds and cupping their hands so that the sound would travel farther, the Guanches more or less created a limited whistling alphabet. In an age before the telephone, these whistled messages could be heard up to 4km away across deep ravines.

According to more gruesome accounts, the language was developed after the Spanish conquest among those Guanches who had their tongues removed by the authorities for misdemeanours. However, this is probably black propaganda since the shape and position of the tongue are just as important as the fingers in producing each sound.

It appears that Guanches on the other islands may have used the language too. In the wake of the Spanish conquest, a good deal of this 'language' fell into disuse. Only proper names and a few skeletal expressions survived. An Austrian expert on all things Canarian, Dr Dominik Wölfel, compiled all the known words that he could in 1940 and came up with a total of 2909!

Nowadays, there remain a few locals, most of them quite elderly, who are still able to produce some of these whistled words. But this unique language may have been rescued just in time. 'If we take no action, the whistle will die. It used to be the only way that islanders could communicate instantaneously over long distances but the telephone has almost killed it off', says Rogelio Botanz from the island's education department. So whistling has been made a compulsory subject in La Gomera primary schools, taught by those who are still conversant with this unique language, and it can even be pursued at secondary level as an optional subject.

baptised, confirmed, have church weddings and funerals, and attend church for important religious feast days; although fewer than half of the islanders regularly turn up for Sunday Mass. A good number of the colourful and often wild fiestas which take place throughout the year have some religious context or origin.

LANGUAGE

The language of the Canary Islands is Spanish *(español)*, which many Spanish people refer to as *castellano* (Castilian) to distinguish it from other mainland tongues such as Basque and Catalan. See the Language chapter at the back of this book for details and local pronunciation.

Facts for the Visitor

SUGGESTED ITINERARIES

With seven islands to choose from and considerable diversity among them, you can cobble together pretty much any itinerary – from frenetic island-hopping to slothful beach-lazing. The following suggestions assume you want to explore in some depth whichever islands you choose to visit.

Short Trips

With a week or two at your disposal, concentrate your efforts on one or two islands at the most. Tenerife makes a good destination for this length of trip. You could combine excursions to Mount Teide and some walking (say, around the national park, on the Anaga peninsula and down the Masca gorge) with visits to the island's most interesting towns, La Orotava, Santa Cruz de Tenerife and the university town of La Laguna. When satiated with nature and culture, party animals can retire to the south for a few days' sea, sun and drinking. The more active can embark on whale-spotting trips, go diving or deep-sea fishing, or shoot across to the lovely island of La Gomera for a day or more.

Another possibility might be a surf-and-travel tour of the easternmost islands, Lanzarote and Fuerteventura – plenty of ferries operate between the two. There are lots of fine beaches for swimming, surfing and windsurfing, and enough of interest inland, such as the Parque Nacional de Timanfaya, to keep your curiosity well stoked.

Digging Deeper

With a little more time, you can plan wider-ranging trips. The three western islands (La Palma, La Gomera and El Hierro) are the least visited of the archipelago. This is largely due to their lack of long white beaches or hammering nightlife, and makes them a striking alternative to the standard package holiday for which the Canaries are best known.

These three islands are rugged, offering rainforest hiking, exploration of extinct volcanoes or meanderings through verdant countryside and sleepy farming or fishing villages. The seaside is never far away but the beaches are mostly small, black, pebbly and sometimes a little difficult to get to.

Equally, you could visit one or more of these islands as part of your trip to one of the more popular ones in the east – Tenerife is the obvious candidate but there is no reason why you shouldn't spend a week including the great sand dunes of Maspalomas on Gran Canaria and then switch to the relative backwaters of the west.

When planning your trip, do build in time for inter-island travelling – an enjoyable experience in itself if you choose the sea option.

A Grand Tour

To get an impression of all the islands, you need to set aside at least a month, and preferably more like six weeks. Few visitors stay long enough to even consider trying to tackle the lot in one hit. If you do have the time (and the inter-island travel costs are not prohibitive for your budget) there is plenty to keep you occupied, even without considering the myriad sporting activities such as diving, fishing, golf and so on.

On the way, you might include: La Palma's Parque Nacional de la Caldera de Taburiente and the old quarter of its capital, Santa Cruz; walks in the Parque Nacional de Garajonay (La Gomera); a hot volcanic experience in the Parque Nacional de Timanfaya (Lanzarote); excursions in Tenerife's Parque Nacional del Teide and the cabin-lift ascent towards the Teide peak (the highest in all Spain); the towns of La Laguna and La Orotava (Tenerife); Las Palmas de Gran Canaria; some of the smaller villages, such as Masca and Garachico on Tenerife; the great sandy beaches of Maspalomas (Gran Canaria) and Fuerteventura; and perhaps also a walking/driving excursion through the misty heart of El Hierro.

The Best & Worst

Coming up with a Top 12 hit list for the Canary Islands is difficult, but the following made their respective days:

- Riding the cable car up Teide peak (Tenerife)
- Chilling out on the spectacular beaches of the Jandía peninsula (Fuerteventura)
- Feeling the volcanic heat of Lanzarote's Montañas del Fuego
- Exploring the old town centres of La Laguna and La Orotava (Tenerife)
- Hiking in the laurel forest of the Parque Nacional de Garajonay (La Gomera)
- Walking the Ruta de los Volcanes (La Palma)
- Lazing among the rolling dunes of Maspalomas (Gran Canaria)
- Wandering through the old quarter of Santa Cruz de la Palma (La Palma)
- Visiting the spectacular Cueva de los Verdes (Lanzarote)
- Cavorting at the carnaval in Santa Cruz de Tenerife
- Looking at anything designed by César Manrique
- Sipping a freshly squeezed juice – mango, papaya, pineapple – on a cafe terrace

Among the few real turn-offs are:

- Rubbing shoulders with lager louts in Playa de las Américas (Tenerife), or their brothers in Playa del Inglés (Gran Canaria)
- Learning the high price of inter-island air fares
- Visiting damp, charmless Valverde (El Hierro)
- Coping with the touts in the resorts
- Manoeuvring around what feels like the 500th tight bend at the end of a long day's island driving

PLANNING

When to Go

When it comes to sunshine, the Canary Islands are caught in a kind of weather-warp, with an eternal spring-summer climate. They're a year-round destination; you can pretty much take your pick of when to go.

The winter months *are* a tad cooler but still paradise itself compared with mainland Europe, the UK and most of North America. This makes December to March the islands' busiest period, which can mean crowds and higher prices.

Summer is also busy, mainly because that's when mainland Spaniards elect to go (for your average Madrileño, the Canaries can seem refreshingly cool in the height of a scorching mainland summer). Thus July to September is a rival high season; package prices and air fares start coming down by the end of September.

For maximum value on air fares and accommodation, the best periods are from November to mid-December and, better still, April to June (with the notable exception of the intense Easter rush). Spring especially is a great time to be around.

What Kind of Trip?

The vast majority of visitors arrive with a package deal, usually covering flights, transfers and hotels. Such a deal normally means sticking to one of the islands and staying for a week or two.

This, of course, can suit. If you're mainly after some sun and/or intense partying, opting to stay in the one spot is probably ideal.

Independent travellers moving around on a limited budget are very much less common. There's no particular impediment, although accommodation of any kind can be a problem in high season in the big resorts.

Forget about hostels and camping grounds (there is precisely one hostel and camping options are extremely limited), but you can usually find quite affordable rooms in small hotels and apartments.

Those who wish to shun the crowds and enjoy the best the islands have to offer in nature can elect to stay inland, for example in country houses, known as *casas rurales*. There are plenty of walking possibilities and you could easily spend a couple of weeks on hiking excursions, especially in the relatively low-key western islands.

Scuba diving is a popular activity and, with courses available, the Canaries could make a pleasant spot for a diving holiday whether you're a beginner or more experienced. Other aquatic activities, such as surfing, deep-sea fishing, windsurfing and sailing, could easily form the main theme around which to build a holiday.

The Canaries are not terribly hard work. Independent travellers can travel easily by bus and boat across the whole archipelago.

Maps

Regional Maps A good choice, offering all the islands on a single sheet, is Firestone's *Islas Canarias* at 1:150,000, which costs about 750 ptas. Michelin has three excellent sheets, all costing around 875 ptas: *Gran Canaria* (No 220), *Lanzarote & Fuerteventura* (No 221) and *Tenerife, El Hierro, La Gomera & La Palma* (No 222). Scales vary and each includes street plans of the major towns. Worth picking up as well is GeoCenter International's *Canaries* (UK£5), also at 1:150,000. If it's mainly the topography that interests you, you might prefer this as it has superior relief shading.

Spain's Ministerio de Fomento (Ministry of Public Works) produces two maps, each costing 825 ptas and at 1:200,000, one for each province. They look impressively thick – until you realise that most of what is depicted is Atlantic Ocean!

Island Maps Free maps given out by tourist offices are generally adequate for driving around. For walking, the German company Freytag & Berndt does some good ones, including *Teneriffa* (German for Tenerife) at a scale of 1:75,000, *La Palma* (1:50,000) and *La Gomera* (1:35,000). Best of all if you intend to do any hiking are the maps, produced by walkers for walkers, of Discovery Walking Guides. These cover the most promising trekking areas on all islands except Fuerteventura.

Spain's Instituto Geográfico Nacional (IGN) also has a series of detailed island maps, drawn at 1:50,000 but perhaps too cluttered to be attractive to the average hiker. The Servicio Geográfico del Ejército produces still more detailed (but not particularly up-to-date) maps dividing each of the islands into bite-sized pieces at 1:25,000.

City Maps For finding your way around the few major cities and towns, the free maps handed out by tourist offices are usually quite reasonable.

The three Michelin sheets (see Regional Maps earlier in this section) also carry plans of all the major towns.

Where to Buy Maps You can buy the maps you need as you go through the islands. Outside the Canaries, specialist stores such as Stanford's (☎ 020 7836 1321), 12–14 Long Acre, London WC2E 9LP stock a fair range. Check out their excellent Web site at www.stanfords.co.uk.

What to Bring

Bring as little as possible. You can buy pretty much anything you might need in the Canaries.

Luggage If you'll be doing any walking with your luggage, even just from bus stations to hotels, consider something with wheels and a towing strap or handle – or else a backpack. Ones with straps and openings that can be zipped inside a flap are the most secure and least clumsy. A small day-pack is handy.

Clothes & Shoes Although the weather is generally mild year round, pack a light sweater for the evenings and especially if you intend to head inland and explore higher altitudes.

Although rainfall is slight, some light wet-weather gear is advisable, particularly in winter, if you intend to explore the northern sides and mountains of the islands (except arid Fuerteventura and Lanzarote).

See Climate in the Facts about the Islands chapter for the kind of temperatures and rainfall you can expect.

Pack a better set of clothes and shoes (something other than jeans, T-shirts and trainers) for smarter discos and restaurants. Unless all you want to do is hang around beaches and bars, you will need a pair of sturdy shoes along with something light such as sandals.

Useful Items Apart from any special personal needs, consider the following:

- under-the-clothes money belt or shoulder wallet, useful for protecting your money and documents
- towel, soap and a sink plug (often lacking in cheap accommodation)
- small Spanish dictionary and/or phrasebook
- Swiss army knife
- photocopies of your important documents, kept separate from the originals
- minimal unbreakable cooking, eating and drinking gear if you plan to prepare your own food and drinks
- medical kit (see Health later in this chapter)
- padlock or two to secure your luggage to racks
- adapter plug for electrical appliances
- torch (flashlight)
- alarm clock
- sunglasses
- sunhat

Basic drugs are widely available; indeed many items requiring prescriptions in other countries can be obtained easily over the counter in the Canary Islands. If you require specific medication, play safe and bring it with you.

RESPONSIBLE TOURISM

If you've just left a drizzly airport in northern Europe for a sunshine holiday, water conservation won't be uppermost in your mind. But water is very much an issue, particularly in the arid eastern islands where rain rarely falls. On Lanzarote and Fuerteventura, nearly every drop of H_2O is refined from sea water. On Tenerife and Gran Canaria too, where tourist developments continue to expand, an ever-increasing proportion of water consumed never fell from the sky. Fact: incredible as it may seem, a luxury hotel consumes around 600 litres of water per day for every single guest on the register. So do turn off every dripping tap, ask for your towels to be changed less regularly than every day, take a shower rather than a bath and even – hey, you're on holiday – perhaps cut out showers altogether.

An estimated 700,000 visitors each year sign on for whale- and dolphin-watching trips off the coast of the western islands and, in particular, the south coast of Tenerife. Even though the Canaries government talks of limiting numbers to avoid undue stress for these magnificent creatures, there's nothing wrong with joining the throng. One of the more ecologically sensitive operators is Club del Mar in Valle Gran Rey (La Gomera), which also undertakes marine research. See Whales & Dolphins under Ecology & Environment in the Facts about the Islands chapter for more details.

Forest fire is an ever-present hazard; in late 2000, for example, large areas of pine forest in north-western La Palma were devastated by a fire caused by human carelessness when a barbecue wasn't properly extinguished. In drier, more desert-like environments, a shred of paper bowling along in the breeze can be spotted at 100m. So do take particular care not to leave dog ends or litter around.

TOURIST OFFICES
Local Tourist Offices

Each island capital and even many quite small towns have what is generally called an Oficina de Turismo or Oficina de Información Turística. The quality of the information, like opening hours, varies although staff are almost invariably obliging.

Tourist Offices Abroad

Information on the Canary Islands is available from the following branches of the Oficina Española de Turismo abroad:

Canada
(☎ 416-961 3131, e toronto@tourspain.es)
Bloor St West, 34th Floor, Toronto, Ontario
M4W 3E2
France
(☎ 01 45 03 82 50, e paris@tourspain.es) 43
rue Decamps, 75784 Paris, Cedex 16
Germany
Berlin: (☎ 030-882 6036, e berlin@tourspain
.es) Kurfürstendamm 180, D-10707 Berlin
Düsseldorf: (☎ 0211-680 3980, e dusseldorf@
tourspain.es) Grafenberger Allee 100
(Kutscherhaus), 40237 Düsseldorf
Frankfurt/Main: (☎ 069-725033, e frankfurt@
tourspain.es) Myliusstrasse 14, 60325 Frank-
furt/Main
Munich: (☎ 089-538 9075, e munich@
tourspain.es) Schubertstrasse 10, 80336
Munich 15
Netherlands
(☎ 070-346 5900, e lahaya@tourspain.es)
Laan Van Meerdervoort 8a, 2517 The Hague
Portugal
(☎ 01-357 1992 e lisboa@tourspain.es)
Avenida Sidónio Pais 28–3 Dto, 1050 Lisbon
UK
(☎ 020-7486 8077, brochure request 0891
669920 at 50p per minute, e londres@
tourspain.es) 22–23 Manchester Square,
London W1M 5AP
USA
New York: (☎ 212-265 8822, e oetny@
tourspain.es) 666 Fifth Avenue, 35th floor,
New York NY 10103
Los Angeles: (☎ 323-658 7188, e oetla@
tourspain.es) 8383 Wilshire Boulevard, Suite
960, Beverly Hills, Los Angeles, California
90211
Chicago: (☎ 312-642 1992, e oetchi@
tourspain.es) Water Tower Place, Suite 915,
845 North Michigan Ave, Chicago, Illinois
60611
Miami: (☎ 305-358 1992, e oetmiami@
tourspain.es) 1221 Brickell Avenue, Suite
1850, Miami, Florida 33131

VISAS & DOCUMENTS

Although it doesn't look like it geographically, the Canary Islands are part of Spain.
Hence all rules (on passports, visas, residence and so on) that are pertinent to Spain
apply equally here too.

Passport

Citizens of the 15 European Union (EU)
member states and Switzerland can travel to
the Canary Islands just with their national
identity card. Nationals of the UK, which
hasn't got round to issuing ID cards, have to
carry a full passport (UK visitor passports
are not acceptable). All other nationalities
must have a full valid passport.

Check that your passport's expiry date is
at least some months away, or you may not
be granted a visa, should you need one.

By law you are supposed to have your ID
card or passport with you at all times in the
Canaries, in case the police ask to see it. In
practice this is unlikely to cause trouble.
You might want to carry a photocopy of
your documentation instead of the real
thing. You often need to flash one of these
documents for registration when you take a
hotel room.

Visas

Spain is one of 15 countries that has signed
the Schengen Convention, an agreement
whereby all EU member countries (except
the UK and Ireland) plus Iceland and Norway have abolished checks at common
borders for nationals of those countries included in the agreement. Legal residents of
one Schengen country do not require a visa
for another such country. In addition, nationals of a number of other states, including the UK, Canada, Ireland, Japan, New
Zealand and Switzerland, do not require
visas for tourist visits of up to 90 days to
any Schengen country.

Various other nationals not covered by the
Schengen exemption can also spend up to 90
days in Spain without a visa. These include
citizens of Australia, Israel and the USA. If
you are from a country not mentioned in this
section, you should check with a Spanish
consulate whether you need a visa.

The standard tourist visa issued by Spanish consulates is the Schengen visa, valid
for up to 90 days. It's generally good for
travel in all other Schengen countries. However, individual Schengen countries may
impose additional restrictions on certain nationalities. It is therefore worth checking
visa regulations with the consulate of each
Schengen country you plan to visit.

You must apply for the visa in your country of residence. In principle, if you are going to visit more than one Schengen country, you are supposed to apply for the visa at a consulate of your main destination country, or else the first country you intend to visit. It's worth applying early, especially in the busy summer months.

Those needing a visa must apply *in person* at the consulate. Postal applications are not accepted. You can't apply for more than two visas in any 12-month period and you cannot renew them once inside Spain. Options include 30- and 90-day single-entry visas, 90-day multiple-entry visas and various transit visas. Schengen visas are free for spouses and children of EU nationals.

Since passports are often not stamped on entry (unless you arrive by air from outside the Schengen area), the 90-day rule can generally be interpreted flexibly, because no one can prove how long you have been in the country.

Visa Extensions & Residence Nationals of EU countries, Norway and Iceland can virtually (if not technically) enter and leave Spain at will. Schengen visas cannot be extended. Those wanting to stay in Spain longer than 90 days are supposed to apply during their first month for a *tarjeta de residencia* (resident's card). This is a lengthy bureaucratic procedure: consult a Spanish consulate before you go to Spain as you will need to take certain documents with you.

People of other nationalities who want to stay in Spain longer than 90 days are also supposed to get a resident's card, and for them it's a truly nightmarish process, starting with a residence visa issued by a Spanish consulate in your country of residence. Begin the process light years in advance.

Non-EU spouses of EU citizens resident in Spain can apply for residency too. The process is lengthy and those needing to travel in and out of the country in the meantime could ask for an *exención de visa* (visa exemption). In most cases, the spouse is obliged to make the formal application in his/her previous country of residence, which is a real pain.

Travel Insurance

You may never need to call upon your travel insurance, but you'll be glad you've got it if you get into trouble. It should cover you for theft, loss of luggage or tickets, and medical problems, and may also come with coverage for travel cancellation or delays.

Some policies exclude 'dangerous activities', which can include scuba diving, motorcycling and maybe even trekking, while others may impose a surcharge for expensive photo equipment and the like. Check the small print – and also whether the policy covers ambulances or an emergency flight home.

Policies often require you to pay up front for medical expenses and claim from the insurance company afterwards, showing receipts. You might prefer to find a policy under which the insurance company pays the doctor or hospital directly.

The insurance papers, and the international medical-aid numbers that generally accompany them, are valuable documents so treat them as you would air tickets and passports. Keep the details (photocopies or hand-written) in a separate part of your luggage.

Paying for your ticket with a credit card often provides limited travel accident insurance and you may be able to reclaim payment if the operator doesn't deliver.

For documents you need in case of emergency medical treatment if you're a citizen of the EU or Norway, see Health Insurance in the Health section later in this chapter.

Driving Licence

Be sure to pack your driving licence if you intend to hire a car in the Canary Islands. EU licences are recognised here, as throughout Spain. Other foreign licences should be accompanied by an International Driving Permit (in practice your own driving licence will more often than not suffice), available from automobile clubs in your country and valid for 12 months.

Vehicle Papers If you're one of the very rare visitors to bring their own vehicle, you will need its registration papers and an

International Insurance Certificate (or a Green Card). Your third-party insurance company will issue this.

Hostel Card

There's only one Hostelling International hostel on the islands (see Accommodation later). It can issue an HI card on the spot.

Student, Teacher & Youth Cards

An International Student Identity Card (ISIC; 700 ptas), for full-time students, or an International Teacher Identity Card (ITIC; 1000 ptas), for full-time teachers and professors, can get you discounted admission into some museums and sights and may be an asset in getting a cheap flight out of the Canaries. They can also sometimes come in handy for such things as cinemas, theatres and other travel discounts. These cards are issued by student organisations and some travel agents, check out the ISIC Web site (www.isiconline.com) for details.

Anyone aged under 26 can get a GO25 or Euro26 card. Both give similar discounts to the ISIC and are issued by most of the same organisations. The Euro26 is called a Carnet Joven Europeo in Spain. It costs 1000 ptas and you don't have to be Spanish to get one in the country.

Copies

You'd be wise to keep photocopies of all the data pages of your passport and any other identity cards. This will help speed up replacement if they are lost or stolen. If your passport does go astray, notify the police and obtain a statement, then contact your embassy or consulate as soon as possible.

Other worthwhile things to photocopy include airline tickets, travel insurance documents with emergency international medical-aid numbers, credit cards (and international card-loss phone numbers) and driver's licence. Keep these copies, and the serial numbers of any travellers cheques, separate from the originals. Leave extra copies of all this stuff with someone reliable at home.

It's also a good idea to store details of your vital travel documents in Lonely Planet's free on-line Travel Vault in case you lose the photocopies or can't be bothered with them. Your password-protected Travel Vault is accessible on-line anywhere in the world – create it at www.ekno .lonelyplanet.com.

EMBASSIES & CONSULATES
Your Own Embassy

It's important to realise what your own embassy – the embassy of the country of which you are a citizen – can and can't do to help you if you get into trouble. Generally speaking, it won't be much help in emergencies if the trouble you're in is remotely your own fault. Remember that you are bound by the laws of the country you are in. Your embassy will not be sympathetic if you end up in jail after committing a crime locally, even if such actions are legal in your own country.

In genuine emergencies you might get some assistance, but only if other channels have been exhausted. For example, if you need to get home urgently, a free ticket home is exceedingly unlikely – the embassy would expect you to have insurance or to rely upon friends or family. If you have all your money and documents stolen, it might assist with getting a new passport but a loan for onward travel is out of the question.

Some embassies used to keep letters for travellers or have a small reading room with home newspapers, but these days the mail holding service has usually been stopped and even newspapers tend to be out of date.

Spanish Embassies & Consulates

Spanish missions abroad include:

Australia (☎ 02-6273 3555, fax 6273 3918,
 e embespau@mail.mae.es) 15 Arkana St,
 Yarralumla, Canberra 2600, ACT
 Consulate in Brisbane: (☎ 07-3221 8571)
 Consulate in Melbourne: (☎ 03-9347 1966)
 Consulate in Perth: (☎ 09-9322 4522)
 Consulate in Sydney: (☎ 02-9261 2433)
Canada (☎ 613-747 2252, 747 7293,
 e spain@docuweb.ca) 74 Stanley Ave,
 Ottawa, Ontario K1M 1P4

Consulates in Toronto and Montreal.

France (☎ 01 44 43 18 00/53, e ambespfr@mail.mae.es) 22 ave Marceau, 75008 Paris, Cedex 08
Consulates in Marseille, Bayonne, Hendaye, Pau and other regional cities.

Germany (☎ 030-261 60 81, e embesde@mail.mae.es) Lichtensteinallee 1, 10787 Berlin

Ireland (☎ 01-269 1640) 17A Merlyn Park, Balls Bridge, Dublin 4

New Zealand – represented in Australia

Netherlands (☎ 070-364 38 14, e embespnl@mail.mae.es) Lange Voorhout 50, 2514 EG The Hague

Portugal (☎ 01-347 2381, e embesppt@mail.mae.es) Rua do Salitre 1, 1250 Lisbon
Consulates in Porto and Valença do Minho.

UK (☎ 020-7235 5555, e espemblon@espemblon.freeserve.co.uk) 39 Chesham Place, London SW1X 8SB
Consulate in London: (☎ 020-7589 8989) 20 Draycott Place, SW3 2RZ
Consulate in Manchester: (☎ 0161-236 1233)
Consulate in Edinburgh: (☎ 0131-220 1843)

USA (☎ 202-452 0100) 2375 Pennsylvania Ave NW, Washington, DC 20037
Consulate in New York: (☎ 212-355 4080)
Consulate in Boston: (☎ 617-536 2506)
Consulate in Chicago: (☎ 312-782 4588)
Consulate in Houston: (☎ 713-783 6200)
Consulate in Los Angeles: (☎ 213-938 0158)
Consulate in Miami: (☎ 305-446 5511)
Consulate in New Orleans: (☎ 504-525 4951)
Consulate in San Francisco: (☎ 415-922 2995)

Foreign Consulates in Las Palmas de Gran Canaria

The following countries all have their main diplomatic representation in Madrid but also have consular representation in Las Palmas de Gran Canaria:

France (☎ 928 29 23 71) Calle Néstor de la Torre 12

Germany (☎ 928 49 18 80) Calle José Franchy Roca 5

Netherlands (☎ 928 24 23 82) Calle León y Castillo 244

Portugal (☎ 928 23 31 44) Calle Alejandro Hidalgo 3

UK (☎ 928 26 26 58 office hours, ☎ 928 26 25 08 out of hours) Calle Luis Morote 6

USA (☎ 928 22 25 52) Calle de los Martínez de Escobar 3

Foreign Consulates in Santa Cruz de Tenerife

Countries with consular representation in Santa Cruz de Tenerife include:

France (☎ 922 23 27 10) Calle José María 1

Germany (☎ 922 28 48 12) Avenida Francisco La Roche 45

Ireland (☎ 922 24 56 71) Calle del Castillo 8

Netherlands (☎ 922 24 35 75) Calle la Marina 7

Portugal (☎ 922 23 72 50) Calle Velázquez 11

UK (☎ 922 28 66 53 office hours, ☎ 922 28 68 63 out of hours) Plaza General Weyler 8

Foreign Embassies in Mainland Spain

Diplomatic representation for Australia, Canada and New Zealand is in Madrid:

Australia (☎ 91 441 93 00) Plaza del Descubridor Diego Ordás 3–2, Edificio Santa Engrácia 120

Canada (☎ 91 431 45 56) Calle Núñez de Balboa 35

New Zealand (☎ 91 523 02 26) Plaza de la Lealtad 2

CUSTOMS

Although the Canary Islands are part of Spain, for customs purposes they are not considered part of the EU (the same is true, for instance, of the Channel Islands in the UK). For this reason, allowances are much less generous than for goods bought within EU countries. You are allowed to bring in or take out, duty free, a maximum of 2L of still wine, 1L of spirits (or 2L of fortified wine), 60ml of perfume, 50ml of *eau de toilette*, 200 cigarettes and up to UK£145 (or equivalent in other currencies) worth of other goods and gifts.

When returning to an EU country from the Canaries, you must use the green or red customs channels, not the blue EU-only channel.

MONEY

You can get by easily enough with a single credit or debit card that lets you withdraw cash from Automatic Teller Machines (ATMs), but it's also sensible to take some travellers cheques and a second card (if you have it). This combination gives you a fallback if you lose a card or it lets you down.

Currency

Spain's currency until early in 2002 is the peseta (pta). This comes in coins of one, five, 10, 25, 50, 100, 200 and 500 ptas, and notes of 1000, 2000, 5000 and 10,000 ptas. A five-pta coin is often called a *duro*, and it's fairly common for small sums to be quoted in duros: *dos duros* for 10 ptas, *cinco duros* for 25 ptas and so on.

On New Year's Day 2002, the first euro coins and notes will be legal tender. For details of the changeover, see the boxed text '*Adiós* Peseta, *Hola* euro'.

When changing money, old-style or new, try to avoid being stuck with large denomi-

nation notes as they can be difficult to break down.

Exchange Rates

The values of euro-zone currencies against the euro (and therefore against each other) were fixed permanently in 1999. Exchange rates between euro-zone and non-euro-zone currencies fluctuate.

currency	unit		pesetas	euros
Australia	A$1	=	98.29 ptas	€0.59
Canada	C$1	=	118.5 ptas	€0.71
euro	€1	=	166 ptas	–
France	1FF	=	25 ptas	€0.15
Germany	DM1	=	85 ptas	€0.51
Ireland	IR£1	=	212 ptas	€1.28
Japan	¥100	=	153.6 ptas	€0.92
New Zealand	NZ$1	=	79.7 ptas	€0.48
Portugal	100$00	=	83 ptas	€0.50
UK	UK£1	=	261 ptas	€1.57
USA	US$1	=	176.95 ptas	€1.06

Exchanging Money

You can change just about any first-world currency notes at most banks and exchange offices. A minority may be sniffy about travellers cheques or demand an exorbitant commission for accepting them. In this case, just walk on to the next. You'll find exchange facilities at most air and sea ports on the islands.

The Canary Islands have a surfeit of banks, many with ATMs. They're mostly open 8.30 am to 2 pm, Monday to Friday, and 9 am to 1 pm on Saturday. Some don't bother with Saturday opening; very few do between May and September.

In resorts and cities that attract swarms of foreigners you will also find exchange offices – usually indicated by the word *cambio* (exchange). Most of the time they offer longer opening hours and quicker service than banks, but worse exchange rates.

Travellers cheques generally attract a higher rate of exchange than foreign cash but this can be deceiving – often commission is charged on cheques and none on cash. Rates offered *do* vary marginally, particularly from exchange booth to exchange booth, but weigh up the holiday time you're

---

Adiós Peseta, Hola Euro

In early 2002, the euro will become the currency of cash transactions in all of Spain and throughout the EU (except for the three foot-draggers: Denmark, Sweden and the UK). In the lead-up, you'll notice more and more prices and receipts featuring both currencies, preparing people for the change.

Euro coins and notes will appear on 1 January 2002. There will then be a two-month transition period, during which pesetas and euros will circulate side by side and pesetas can be exchanged for euros free of charge at banks. After 28 February 2002, the euro will be Spain's sole currency.

The euro is divided into 100 cents (called *céntimos* in Spain). Coin denominations are one, two, five, 10, 20 and 50 cents, €1 and €2. The notes are €5, €10, €20, €50, €100, €200 and €500.

All euro coins across the EU will be identical on the side showing their value, but there will be 12 different obverses, each representing one of the 12 euro zone countries. All euro notes of each denomination will be identical on both sides. *All* euro coins and notes will be legal tender throughout the euro zone.

---

losing by shopping around for the sake of a few pesetas' gain.

Wherever you change money, ask from the outset about commission, the terms of which differ from place to place, and confirm that exchange rates are as posted. A typical commission is 3% with a minimum deduction of around 500 ptas, but there are places with a minimum of 1000 ptas and sometimes even 2000 ptas. Places that advertise 'no commission' usually make up the difference by offering poorer exchange rates.

Cash Even if you're using a credit card you'll make a lot of your purchases with cash so you need to carry some all the time.

Buying a few pesetas before you come to the Canaries will save a bit of time and hassle on arrival and you often get a better rate on the peseta outside the country. That said, it isn't necessary as changing at the port or airport is straightforward.

You can change leftover pesetas back into your currency, either on returning home or before you leave – you will get a marginally better rate if you change back on Spanish territory. Try not to be stuck with coins as they generally cannot be changed.

Travellers Cheques These are safe and easily cashed at banks and exchange offices (take along your passport) throughout the Canary Islands. Always keep the bank receipt listing the cheque numbers separate from the cheques themselves and log those you have already cashed. This will ease things if they're lost or stolen.

If your travellers cheques are in pesetas (or, from 2002, euros), you should pay no exchange charge when cashing them. Most hard currencies are widely accepted although the New Zealand dollar tends to be greeted with a blank gaze. Buying cheques in a third currency (such as US dollars if you are not coming from the USA) means you pay exchange charges twice: when you buy the cheques and again when cashing them.

Get most of your cheques in fairly large denominations (the equivalent of 10,000 ptas or more) to save on any per-cheque commission charges.

American Express exchange offices charge no commission to change travellers cheques (even other brands). For American Express travellers cheque refunds, call ☎ 900 99 44 26, a Spain-wide number.

Credit/Debit Cards & ATMs Carrying plastic (whether a credit or a debit card) is the simplest way to organise your funds. You don't have large amounts of cash or cheques to lose, you can get money after hours and at weekends, and the exchange rate is usually good if not always the absolute best. By arranging for payments to be made into your card account while you are travelling, you can avoid paying interest.

All major credit/debit cards are widely accepted. They can be used for many purchases (including at petrol stations and larger supermarkets, who sometimes ask to see some form of ID) and in hotels and restaurants (although smaller establishments tend to accept cash only).

Cards can also be used in ATMs *(cajeros automáticos)* displaying the appropriate sign or, if you have no personal identification number (PIN), to obtain cash advances over the counter in many banks. Visa and MasterCard are among the most widely recognised for such transactions.

Check the charges with your bank, but as a rule there is none for purchases on major cards and a 1.5% charge on cash advances and ATM transactions in foreign currencies. Don't expect to find a hole in the wall in every village you visit – always stock up on cash in the main towns.

It's prudent to check with your card's issuer before you leave home on how to report a lost card and what your daily or weekly spending limit is. Perhaps, also whether your PIN will be acceptable (some European ATMs don't recognise PINs of more than four digits). If you think you may go over your credit limit while away, you can make a deposit into your account before you leave to give you access to extra funds.

American Express is fairly widely accepted (although nowhere near as common as Visa or MasterCard). With such a card, you can get cash or travellers cheques from main offices of Viajes Insular (American Express representatives in the Canary Islands) by writing a personal cheque drawn on your home bank account (check this with your bank before leaving home). These offices are in Las Palmas and Playa del Inglés (Gran Canaria), Puerto de la Cruz (Tenerife) and Arrecife (Lanzarote).

If you can, take more than one card and try to keep them separate in case one is lost or stolen. American Express cards tend to be the easiest to replace, you can call ☎ 902 37 56 37 at any time. Other cards may not be replaceable until you get home. Report a lost or stolen card immediately: call ☎ 900 97 44 45 for Visa cards, ☎ 900 97 12 31 for MasterCard/EuroCard and ☎ 91 547 40 00 (a Madrid number) for Diners Club.

International Transfers Frankly, it's scarcely worth the hassle. But if you do run low on funds and ATMs start to spit back your plastic, this is the deal.

You need to organise someone back home to send it to you, through a bank there or – much more rapidly – via a money-transfer service such as Western Union. And you'll have to specify a bank or money-transfer agent in the Canary Islands where you can collect it. If there's money in your bank account at home, you may be able to instruct the bank yourself.

For information on Western Union services, call free on ☎ 900 63 36 33 or visit on-line at www.westernunion.com. You'll find it represented at most island airports and at a few places offering cheap phone calls and the like. To send sums of up to US$400, the sender is charged US$30 to US$40. The money can supposedly be handed over to the recipient within 15 minutes of being sent.

To set up a transfer through a bank, either get advice from the bank at home on a suitable pick-up bank in the Canary Islands, or check with a local bank on how to organise it. You'll need to let the sender have precise details of the Canary Islands bank branch – its name, full address, city and any contact

or code numbers required. A bank-to-bank telegraphic transfer typically costs around US$20 to US$30 and can take as much as a week to clear.

It's also possible to have money sent by American Express.

Electronic Money If you haven't got a debit/credit card, Visa offers another form of electronic cash – a prepaid disposable credit card known as Visa TravelMoney. You buy the card from selected banks or travel agencies (such as Thomas Cook) for amounts from UK£100 to UK£5000 and you are issued with a PIN number. Note that there is a 2% commission and also a £3.50 handling fee. It works for ATM withdrawals wherever the Visa sign is displayed. The first four withdrawals are free. If you haven't used up the money by then, any subsequent withdrawal carries a UK£1.50 fee. Enquire at Thomas Cook or call Visa before you travel.

Security

The Canary Islands are, with the exception of Las Palmas city and the large resorts of southern Tenerife and Gran Canaria, low risk. All the same, it always makes sense to take certain precautions, wherever you're travelling.

Keep only a limited amount of money as cash, and the bulk in more easily replaceable forms such as travellers cheques or plastic. If your accommodation has a safe, use it. If you must leave money and documents in your room, divide the former into stashes and hide them in different places. Lockable luggage is a good deterrent.

On the streets, especially in the big resort areas, keep as little on you as necessary. The safest thing is a shoulder wallet or under-the-clothes money belt or pouch. External money belts tend to attract attention to your belongings and the strap can easily be slashed with a sharp knife.

If you eschew the use of any such device, keep money in your *front pockets* and watch out for people who seem to brush close to you – there is an infinite number of tricks used by teams of delinquents whereby one distracts your attention and the other deftly empties your pockets.

Costs

Daily living expenses in the Canary Islands are lower than those in most countries of Western Europe. They do generally work out a little higher than those of peninsular Spain since just about everything has to be brought from the mainland or from across the Atlantic. Although the islands are not a standard backpacker destination, a prudent traveller might get by on around 6000 ptas per day if sharing a room in the cheapest pensiones and apartments, eating one simple restaurant meal per day, making sandwiches for lunch and travelling slowly by bus and ferry (planes will burn big holes in your pockets).

A breakdown of average costs per person per day at this level might be: 1750 ptas for a bed in a double room (3500 ptas for two); 500 ptas for breakfast (juice, coffee and a *sandwich mixto* – toasted ham and cheese sandwich); 500 ptas to 1000 ptas for lunch (make it yourself); up to 2000 ptas for dinner; and the rest on transport, the occasional sight and a couple of drinks. Luckily, sights for which you have to pay are few on the ground and those that charge are reasonably priced at about 250 ptas. However, one-time splurges such as the cable car up and down the Teide mountain on Tenerife (3000 ptas) can wreak havoc with your daily calculations if you are sailing this close to the wind. Theme and amusement parks are all pricey (1000 ptas to 2000 ptas), and your costs will also rise if you want to go on boat excursions (from 2000 ptas) and the like.

A more comfortable budget if you're one element of a travelling pair would be 9000 ptas to 12,000 ptas per day. With this you could up your daily hotel allowance to at least 3000 ptas each, include a few days' car hire (say an average three days per week of travel time) and consider having a modest sit-down lunch as well as your evening meal.

If money is no object, the sky's the limit. You can easily spend 5000 ptas or more per person on accommodation, and moderate to expensive restaurants can start coming in at 5000 ptas a head. Flying between the islands is expensive (see the Getting Around chapter for details) but time-saving, and with a free-and-easy wallet you can let yourself go in the nightlife hot spots of the main resorts.

Cost-Savers You'll save a little money by avoiding the peak tourist seasons (December to February plus the second half of July and August) when prices tend to sneak upwards and when your choice of cheap accommodation may be limited.

A student or youth card, or a document such as a passport proving you're over 60, brings worthwhile savings on some travel costs and admission fees to some museums and sights. A few museums and sights are also cheaper for EU passport holders.

Single occupancy of rooms costs more per person than doubles, triples and so on. In many of the cheapest pensiones you are charged for a double room even if you're alone. The only way around this is to hook up with another traveller.

In many cafes it is up to 20% cheaper if you stand at the counter rather than sitting at a table.

More information on accommodation, food and travel costs can be found in the Accommodation and Food sections later in this chapter and in the Getting Around chapter.

Tipping & Bargaining

In restaurants, the law requires menu prices to include any service charge, and tipping is a matter of personal choice – most people leave something if they're satisfied: 5% would normally be adequate and 10% is generous. It's common to leave small change at bar and cafe tables.

Porters will generally be happy with 200 ptas, and most won't turn their noses up at 100 ptas. Taxi drivers don't have to be tipped but a little rounding up won't go amiss.

Bargaining is not usual and you risk being regarded as a skinflint. The only exception might be budget accommodation, where you might try negotiating a reduction if you're staying for a few days, and buying electronic and luxury goods.

Taxes & Refunds

The Canary Islands have a special tax regime setting them apart from the rest of Spain. On the mainland, value-added tax (VAT) is known as IVA *(impuesto sobre el valor añadido)* and reaches 16% on retail goods.

In the Canary Islands, however, the equivalent is the IGIC *(impuesto general indirecto canario)*. It is a flat rate 5% on retail goods and services, including hotel accommodation. Since it's so low, there is no tax-refund system for visitors.

POST & COMMUNICATIONS
Post

Stamps & Post Offices Stamps are sold at every post office *(oficina de correos or correos)*, most *estancos* (tobacconist shops: look for the yellow-on-brown 'Tabacos' sign) and some newsagents.

Some towns have more than one post office and most villages have at least one, though its opening hours may be very restricted. The two main provincial post offices in Las Palmas de Gran Canaria and Santa Cruz de Tenerife open 8.30 am to 8.30 pm Monday to Friday, and 9 am to 2 pm on Saturday. Most others open from 8.30 am to 2.30 pm, Monday to Friday, and 9.30 am to 1 pm on Saturday.

Postal Rates A postcard or letter weighing up to 20g costs 35 ptas to send within the islands and to mainland Spain, 70 ptas to other European countries, 115 ptas to North America and 185 ptas to Australia or New Zealand. Three A4 sheets in an air-mail envelope weigh less than 20g. Corresponding prices for letters between 20g and 50g are 45/160/255/325 ptas.

An aerogramme – if you can track one down (only a few post offices stock them) – costs 85 ptas to anywhere in the world.

Certificado (registered mail) costs an extra 175 ptas for international mail. *Urgente*

Street Names

One small, monosyllabic detail that is unlikely to throw you: street names, especially those which commemorate a person (usually long dead), sometimes have an extra 'de' or 'del' in the written form (for example, Calle *de* Juan Tadeo, Gran Viá *de* Católico). It's usually quite arbitrary whether or not they are included on street plaques and you'll rarely hear them if you are asking for directions.

service, which means your letter may arrive two or three days faster, costs around an extra 275 ptas for international mail. You can send the same letter both certificado and urgente if you wish.

Perhaps a day or two quicker than the urgente service is Postal Exprés, sometimes called Express Mail Service (EMS). Available at most post offices, it uses courier companies for international deliveries. Packages weighing between 250g and 500g, for example, cost 3500 ptas to other European countries and 5000 ptas to North America. It's a heck of a lot more expensive than urgente mail but still significantly cheaper than courier services.

Sending Mail It's quite safe to post your mail in the yellow street-postboxes *(buzones)* as well as at post offices. At larger post offices, you may be confronted by the open mouths of several letter boxes. *Península* is for peninsular Spain while all overseas mail is dropped in the one marked *extranjero*.

Delivery times are generally a disgrace: mail to other EU countries routinely takes up to a week – and sometimes just as long to the Spanish mainland; to North America, 10 days; to Australia or New Zealand, as much as two weeks.

Receiving Mail Delivery times are similar to those for outbound mail. Addresses in the Canary Islands have five-digit postcodes, use of which will help your mail arrive a bit quicker.

Poste restante mail can be addressed to you at *lista de correos* anywhere in the Canary Islands that has a post office. In the few towns on the islands with more than one post office, it will fetch up at the main one unless another is specified in the address.

Take your passport when you go to pick up mail. It's a fairly reliable system, although you must be prepared for mail to arrive late. It helps if people writing to you capitalise or underline your surname, and include the postcode. A typical lista de correos address looks like this:

Jane SMITH
Lista de Correos
35080 Las Palmas de Gran Canaria
Islas Canarias
Spain

American Express card or travellers cheque holders can use the free client mail-holding service at those branches of Viajes Insular which represent American Express in Las Palmas and Playa del Inglés on Gran Canaria, Puerto de la Cruz on Tenerife and Arrecife on Lanzarote. Again, take your passport when you go to pick up post.

Telephone

There is no shortage of the distinctive blue pay phones in the Canary Islands. They are easy to use for international and domestic calls. You have the option of using coins or a phonecard *(tarjeta telefónica)* and, in some cases, credit cards. Phonecards are in denominations of 1000 ptas and 2000 ptas and, like postage stamps, are sold at post offices and estancos.

An alternative in some larger towns is a telephone centre, whether belonging to Telefónica, the main Spanish provider, or a small shop, which often doubles up with fax and Internet facilities. These usually have a number of booths where you do your own dialling and then pay someone sitting at a desk when you have finished. These places can be useful if you don't have enough coins or a phonecard, or if pay phones are in short supply. They also usually have a good stock of telephone directories *(guías telefónicas)*.

Coin pay phones (often green) inside bars and cafes normally cost a little more than street pay phones. Phones in hotel rooms can be a good deal more expensive: managements set their own tariffs so it's worth asking about the rates before using one.

Costs Expect a three-minute pay-phone call to cost around 25 ptas within your local area; 65 ptas to other places in the same province; 110 ptas from one of the islands' two provinces to the other (or to mainland Spanish provinces); 230 ptas to other EU countries; 280 ptas to North America; and 820 ptas to Australia. Rates are cheaper between 8 pm and 8 am (6 pm to 8 am for local calls) and all day on Sunday.

A variety of discount cards is available. These can cut costs significantly, especially for international calls – see Phonecards and eKno later in this section.

Domestic Calls Canary Islands telephone numbers, like those throughout Spain, all begin with 9 and consist of nine digits. Phone numbers beginning with 928 are for the province of Las Palmas (Gran Canaria, Fuerteventura and Lanzarote) while those that begin with 922 are for the province of Santa Cruz de Tenerife (Tenerife, La Gomera, La Palma and El Hierro).

To speak to a domestic operator, including for domestic reverse-charge (collect) calls within the Canary Islands and Spain, dial ☎ 1009. A reverse-charge (call collect) communication is called *una llamada por cobro revertido*. For directory enquiries dial ☎ 1003; calls cost about 45 ptas from a private phone – but are free from any phonebox.

The Yellow Pages (Páginas Amarillas) are on-line at www.paginasamarillas.es (Spanish only). For emergency numbers, see the Emergencies section later in this chapter.

International Calls To make an international call, dial the standard international access code (☎ 00) wait for a new dialling tone, then dial the country code, area code and number you want.

For international reverse-charge (collect) calls, dial ☎ 900 99 00 followed by the usual code for the country you're calling (for example, ☎ 33 for France, ☎ 44 for the UK, ☎ 61 for Australia and ☎ 64 for New Zealand). Among the few exceptions are ☎ 15 for Canada and, for the USA, ☎ 11 for AT&T or ☎ 14 for MCI. Country codes are usually posted up in pay phones. You'll get straight through to an operator in the country you're calling. These same numbers (☎ 900 99 00) can be used with direct-dial calling cards.

For international directory enquiries dial ☎ 1025.

Calling the Canary Islands from other Countries The country code, as for Spain as a whole, is ☎ 34.

Phonecards In the larger resorts of southern Tenerife and Gran Canaria you'll find quite a few local and international discount phonecards on sale. Most cards use a 'magic number' and aren't meant to be slotted into the phone. Check carefully the total call costs (including any taxes payable) and exactly where you can use the card; not all are the seductive bargain they'd have you believe.

eKno Lonely Planet's eKno Communication Card is aimed specifically at independent travellers and provides budget international calls, a range of messaging services, free email and travel information, and a safe, secure place to log details of all your important personal documents. Check it out for international calls, where it's usually very competitive; for local calls you're often better off with a local card or jangling pesetas. You can join eKno on-line at www.ekno.lonelyplanet.com or by phone from the Canaries, dialling ☎ 900 98 45 32. Once you're signed up, to use eKno from the islands or mainland dial ☎ 900 98 45 33. It's worth checking out the eKno Web site for joining details and access numbers from other countries – also for updates on budget local access numbers and new features.

Mobile Phones

The Canary Islands use GSM 900/1800, which is compatible with the rest of Europe and Australia but not with the North American GSM 1900 or the totally different system in Japan (though some North Americans have GSM 1900/900 phones that do work here). If you have a GSM phone, check with your service provider about using it on the islands, and beware of calls being routed internationally (very expensive for a 'local' call).

Fax

Most main post offices have a fax service. A single page costs about 350 ptas within the Canary Islands and Spain, 1120 ptas to the EU and 2100 ptas to 2500 ptas elsewhere. You may well find cheaper rates at shops or offices with 'Fax Público' signs.

Email & Internet Access

Travelling with a portable computer is a great way to stay in touch with life back home, but unless you know what you're doing it's fraught with potential problems. If you plan to carry your notebook or palmtop computer with you, remember that the power-supply voltage in the countries you visit may vary from that at home, risking damage to your equipment. The best investment is a universal AC adapter for your appliance, which will enable you to plug it in anywhere without frying the innards. You'll also need a plug adapter for each country you visit – often it's easiest to buy these before you leave home.

Your PC-card modem also may or may not work once you leave your home country – and you won't know for sure until you try. The safest option is to buy a reputable 'global' modem before you leave home, or buy a local PC-card modem if you're spending an extended time in any one country. Phone jacks in the Canaries are the standard American style RJ-11, which should make modem connection easy.

For more information on travelling with a portable computer, see the following Web sites at www.teleadapt.com or www.warrior.com.

Major Internet service providers such as AOL (www.aol.com), CompuServe (www.compuserve.com) and IBM Net (www.ibm.net) have dial-in nodes throughout Europe; check their Web sites for the latest dial-in numbers before you leave home. If you access your Internet email account through a smaller ISP or your office or school network when at home, your best option is either to open an account with a global ISP, such as those mentioned above, or to rely on cybercafes and other public-access points to collect your mail.

If you do intend to rely on cybercafes, you'll need to carry three pieces of information with you to enable you to access your Internet mail account: your incoming (POP or IMAP) mail server name, your account name and your password. Your ISP or network supervisor will be able to give you these. Armed with this information, you should be able to access your Internet mail account from any net-connected machine in the world, provided it runs some kind of email software (remember that Netscape and Internet Explorer both have mail modules). It pays to become familiar with the process for doing this before you leave home.

Another option for collecting mail through cybercafes is to open a free Web-based email account on-line with eKno. You can then access your mail from anywhere in the world from any net-connected machine running a standard Web browser. For more information, visit the eKno Web site at www.ekno.lonelyplanet.com.

The number of Internet cafes and computer shops around the islands is expanding. Web access costs from around 500 ptas per hour.

Telegram

Endearing really: these dinosaurs can still be sent from post offices and remain an expensive but sure way of having important messages delivered the same or next day. It is also possible to send an almost-as-antediluvian telex from post offices, but they too are expensive.

INTERNET RESOURCES

The World Wide Web is a rich resource for travellers. You can research your trip, hunt down bargain fares, book hotels, check on weather conditions or chat with locals and other travellers about the best places to visit (or avoid!).

Start your Web explorations at the Lonely Planet Web site (www.lonelyplanet.com). Here you'll find succinct summaries on travelling to most places on earth, postcards from other travellers and the Thorn Tree bulletin board, where you can ask questions before you go or dispense advice when you get back. You can also find travel news and updates to many of our most popular guidebooks. The subWWWay section links you to the most useful travel resources elsewhere on the Internet. Lonely Planet's Canary Islands' page is at www.lonelyplanet.com/destinations/europe/canary-islands.htm.

A search on key words such as 'Canaria', 'Canarias' or 'Canary Islands' on any of the standard search engines will throw up a plethora of sites. As usual, you have to wade through an awful lot of dross to find anything useful, but some interesting things are swimming around out there. Since many sites are only in their native language, it will be a help if you can read Spanish.

Two sites, each with multiple links to all sorts of others covering just about the whole gamut of Canary Islands-related subjects, are www.candir.com and www.canary-guide.com. The latter has its pages in all major European languages, and offers both general information and island-specific searches. Both have a wealth of links-based information on accommodation, bars, restaurants, property, transport and more.

If you read Spanish and want to get an idea of the issues that move Canarios, you can read their daily news on-line at www.canarias7.es, the Web site of the Canarias 7 newspaper (which covers all the islands).

For a definitive list of Web sites relating to surfing in the Canaries, surfers should visit www.liquidtrips.com/canaries.htm. Topics include Webcams, surf schools, shops and clubs.

Astronomy buffs wanting to know about the latest galaxy-busting developments at the observatories on Tenerife and La Palma can hook into the Web site of the Instituto de Astrofísica de Canarias (IAC) at www.iac.es.

ACANTUR, the leading body for rural tourism in the Canary Islands, has a Web site at www.canary-islands.com. It also gives no-frills information in English, German and Spanish on topics such as general accommodation, national parks and history.

All of the islands have their own Web sites devoted to tourist information (they can all be traced through the Canarian Internet Resources Web site at www.candir.com). Tourist information on the Canaries can also be accessed through the government tourist office at www.spaintour.com/canarias.htm. A German-language service is at www.infocanarias.com.

For general background to the islands, visit www.gobcan.es, the official site of the Cabildo (the local government of the Canary Islands). It gives the latest on the politics of the islands as well as useful facts for the visitor, including an impressive environment page. It's mainly in Spanish with some sections in English.

BOOKS

While there is a wealth of literature in English, Spanish and other languages on Spain, the pickings on the Canary Islands are rather slim. Indeed, outside the islands it is difficult to come by anything much besides...other guidebooks. Except for these, most of the titles listed below will require a good deal of hunting around.

For books in Spanish, one of the best options is Grant & Cutler (☎ 020-7734 2012), 55–57 Great Marlborough St, London W1V 2AY.

Books on Spain (☎ 020-8898 7789, fax 8898 8812, ⓔ keithharris@books-on-spain.com), PO Box 207, Twickenham TW2 5BQ, UK, can send you mail-order catalogues of hundreds of old and new titles on Spain. Check its Web site at www.books-on-spain.com.

In Australia, the Travel Bookshop (☎ 02-9261 8200), 3/175 Liverpool Street, Sydney, is worth a browse. In the USA, try Book Passage (☎ 415-927 0960), 51 Tamal Vista Blvd, Corte Madera, California; and The Complete Traveler Bookstore (☎ 212-685 9007), 199 Madison Ave, New York.

Lonely Planet

Lonely Planet publishes a language-packed yet pocket-sized *Spanish phrasebook* as well as *Spain* (which includes the Balearics), regional guides *Andalucía* and *Catalunya & the Costa Brava*, and city guides *Madrid* and *Barcelona*. It also publishes *World Food Spain* and *Walking in Spain*, which includes a chapter on the Canary Islands.

Travel Photography: A Guide to Taking Better Pictures is written by the internationally renowned travel photographer Richard I'Anson. It's full colour throughout and designed to take on the road.

Travellers' Tales

The Canary Islands, by Florence du Cane, came out in 1911 and is charming mostly because of the paintings by Ella du Cane. Even before the du Canes were wandering around the islands, Olivia Stone had published *Tenerife and its Six Satellites* in London in 1887.

Another early traveller to the islands was Charles Piazzi Smyth, whose colourful impressions were set down in *Tenerife, or the Advantages of a Residence Among the Clouds* in 1852.

History & People

Unless you read Spanish, you won't find a great deal around on the history of the Canary Islands. Even those who can will be underwhelmed by what's on offer. A quirky volume of at times dubious academic worth is *Las Islas Canarias a Través de la Historia*, by Salvador López Herrera, available in English as *The Canary Islands Through History*. Herrera attempts to trace the story of the Guanches and the Spanish conquest of the archipelago.

Felipe Fernández-Armesto, a leading authority on the islands' history, has produced

The Canary Islands After the Conquesta, a fairly specialised work concentrating on 16th-century life in the islands. A classic history, written in 1764, is George Glas' *History of the Canary Islands*.

A fairly straightforward summary of the islands' past is *History of the Canary Islands*, by José M Castellano Gil and Francisco J Macíos Martín. It is published in various languages by the Centro de la Cultura Popular Canaria.

The Guanches – Survivors and their Descendants, by José Luis Concepción, looks at the fate of the islands' first inhabitants. He also wrote a volume on customs, called *Costumbres, Tradiciones Canarias* (published in English and German).

In *La Religión de los Guanches*, Antonio Tejera Gaspar attempts to piece together the puzzle of the islanders' beliefs.

Madeira & the Canary Islands, by A Samler Brown, was first published in 1889 as a precursor to the archetypal traveller's guidebook. Try to get a hold of a later edition of this book, because there is quite a lot of interesting, if highly dated, material in it.

In *Le Canarien*, Alejandro Cioranescu has collected texts by the islands' initial conquerors, Jean de Béthencourt and Gadifer de la Salle.

Art

For a comprehensive review of art and architecture, high and low, in the islands, you might be interested in a series of volumes entitled *El Arte en Canarias*, published by La Biblioteca Canaria.

Flora & Fauna

Budding botanists should check out a series of brochures called *Plants & Flowers of...* (attach the name of whichever island appeals to you). The series is published by Discovery Walking Guides, which also does a series of excellent (you've guessed it!) walking guides to all the islands bar Fuerteventura. Check out its Web site at www.walking.demon.co.uk.

In the Canary Islands themselves you should be able to track down numerous titles devoted to the archipelago's flora. *Flora of the Canary Islands* by David Bramwell is reliable and informative with full-colour photos. *Flowers of the Canary Islands* by Bruno Foggi is also lavishly illustrated but shorter on hard information. *Flowers in the Canary Islands*, by Juan Alberto Rodríguez Pérez, is available in English and German.

A Birdwatchers' Guide to the Canary Islands, by Tony Clarke and David Collins, is the perfect companion for a pair of skyward-pointed binoculars.

Food

Pleasures of the Canary Islands: Wine, Food, Beauty, Mystery, by Ann & Larry Walker, is one of the few introductions to Canaries cuisine in English. Look at it before you go, as you are unlikely to want to lug this hardback around with you.

More portable, but available only in the Canaries, is a paperback volume by various authors called *The Best of Canary Island Cooking*, published by the Centro de la Cultura Popular Canaria. Another possibility is *Typical Canary Cooking* by José Luis Concepción.

If you get hooked on *mojo* (salsa sauce), look out for *Todos los Mojos de Canarias*, by Flora Lilia Barrera Álamo and Dolores Hernández Barrera.

NEWSPAPERS & MAGAZINES

See also Newspapers in the Information section for each island.

Local Press

There is no shortage of local newspapers in the islands. In Tenerife and the western islands, *La Gaceta de Canarias*, *Diario de Avisos* and a relative newcomer, *La Opinión de Tenerife*, are the highest selling dailies.

The most popular dailies on Gran Canaria and the eastern isles are *Canarias 7* and *La Provincia*.

All are useful for their local listings and information – which doesn't always reflect the latest changes – on air and sea timetables and so on. The islands' sporting journal is *Jornada Deportiva*. For the truly parochially inclined, each island gets its own edition of *La Isla*.

Local English-Language Press
The big British and German presence in the islands has led to the growth of a number of foreign-language rags on the two biggest islands. Among the better ones for Tenerife are *Here & Now* and *Tenerife News*. *Island Connections* also has a Gran Canaria edition. *Canarian Weekly* is supposedly circulated in all the islands but you'd be lucky to see it outside the main tourist centres. Most of the other newspapers serve best for wrapping your fish and chips, though all titles, which appear weekly or fortnightly, carry useful listings information and occasionally even job adverts.

Spanish National Press
For a wider view on the world, you can turn to Spain's national press. The main dailies can be identified along roughly political lines, with the old-fashioned *ABC* representing the conservative right and *El País* identified with the Partido Socialista Obrero Español (PSOE; Spain's centre-left socialist party), while *El Mundo*, a paper that prides itself on breaking political scandals, is the liveliest of the big three.

For a good spread of national and international news, *El País* is the pick. One of the best-selling dailies is *Marca*, which is devoted exclusively to sport.

Foreign-Language Press
International publications such as the *International Herald Tribune*, *Time* and *Newsweek*, plus rafts of newspapers from all over Western Europe, reach major cities and tourist areas within a day of publication. Several British newspapers, especially the tabloids, have editions that are published in Madrid.

RADIO
The Spanish national network Radio Nacional de España (RNE) has four stations. RNE 1 has general interest and current affairs programs, RNE 2 plays classical music, RNE 3 (or 'Radio d'Espop') has admirably varied pop and rock music and RNE 5 is a round-the-clock news station. Most listened to of all is the commercial pop-and-rock FM station 40 Principales. Broadcast frequencies vary from place to place.

There is no shortage of local radio stations across the islands, most of them on the FM band – even tiny La Gomera has three stations.

Reception quality varies considerably around the islands and you may find you can pick up only a few stations clearly. Indeed, in the extreme north of La Palma about all you can get is Portuguese broadcasts from Madeira!

In the main resort areas you can also pick up local foreign-language radio. For instance, the English-language music station Power FM broadcasts on 91.2 FM in the Playa de las Américas area in southern Tenerife as does Oasis 101 FM. While on Gran Canaria, you can tune into Radio Maspalomas.

The BBC World Service broadcasts to the Canary Islands mainly on 6195kHz, 12,095kHz and 15,485kHz (short wave). Voice of America (VOA) can be found on various short-wave frequencies, including 1548kHz, 9760kHz and 15,255kHz, depending on the time of day. The BBC and VOA broadcast for much of the day from about 5 am to after 9 pm, but the reception quality fluctuates considerably.

TV
The Canary Islands receive the four main terrestrial channels with national coverage – two from Spain's state-run Televisión Española (TVE1 and La 2) and two independent channels (Antena 3 and Tele 5).

TVAC (Televisión Autonómica de Canarias), usually called TV Canarias or TV Autonómica, is specific to the islands. It produces a few programs of its own, especially local news and sport (with a heavyweight diet of Canarian wrestling), and hooks into regionally produced programs from the mainland, especially Andalucía.

In addition, Tenerife has its own islandwide channel, Teidivision Canal 6. The Gran Canarian equivalent is TeleGC, beaming from Las Palmas.

Many TVs in bars and hotels also pick up Canal Plus, a subscription channel.

News programs are generally decent, if longwinded, and you can occasionally catch an interesting documentary or film. Canal Plus and La 2 offer fairly serious fare. Otherwise the staple diet is soaps (many from Latin America), endless talk shows and naff variety shows.

Many private homes and up-market hotels have satellite TV. Foreign stations usually carried include BBC World (mainly news and travel), BBC Prime (other BBC programs), CNN, Eurosport, the Sky channels and the German SAT 1. Among Spanish satellite channels are Documenta and Canal Clásico, which have some good documentaries and arts programs. Of the new digital networks, Vía Digital is the market favourite so far.

VIDEO SYSTEMS

If you want to record or buy video tapes to play back home, you won't get a picture if the image registration systems are different. TVs in the Canary Islands, and nearly all pre-recorded videos on sale here and in Spain, use the PAL (phase alternation line) system common to most of Western Europe and Australia. France uses the incompatible SECAM system, and North America and Japan use the equally incompatible NTSC system. PAL videos can't be played back on a machine that lacks PAL capability.

PHOTOGRAPHY & VIDEO
Film & Equipment

A roll of 36-exposure 100 ASA Kodak film costs around 700 ptas and you'll spend up to 1800 ptas to get it developed. A roll of 36 slides (diapositivas) costs around 800 ptas and about the same to develop and frame. All the major brands are available, though you may have to visit more than one shop to find your favourite brand of slide film. The quality of processing is as good as anywhere.

Outlets where you can buy films and have your photos processed are numerous. A roll of film is most commonly called a carrete but you will be understood if you ask for 'film'. Shop around a little – all sorts of special offers crop up involving reduced processing costs, free copies or enlargements, and so on.

Technical Tips

Light is the key. As a general rule the midday sun is for mad dogs and not photographers – it is harsh and will lend your snaps a washed-out look. It follows that early and late in the day are the best times to shoot. Use the light's angle and shadows to effect. A basic rule for straightforward shots is to have the light source behind you – but take care not to get your own shadow in shot!

For some handy snapping tips, check out Lonely Planet's full-colour Travel Photography: A Guide to Taking Better Pictures by renowned photographer Richard I'Anson.

Airport Security

Your camera and film will be routinely passed through airport x-ray machines. Make sure that your camera and all your films are in your hand baggage. Although the x-ray machine shouldn't damage film, you can ask for inspection by hand if you're worried. Lead pouches for film are another solution if you're a really serious photo buff.

TIME

Like most of Europe, the Canaries operate on the 24-hour clock, which for those accustomed to 'am' and 'pm' can take some getting used to.

The Canary Islands are on Greenwich mean time (GMT/UTC), plus an hour in summer for daylight-saving time. The islands keep the same time as the UK, Ireland and Portugal, and are always a hour behind mainland Spain and most of Europe. Neighbouring Morocco is on GMT/UTC year round – so in summer it is an hour behind the Canary Islands even though it's further east!

Daylight-saving (summer) time starts on the last Sunday in March, when clocks are put forward one hour. Clocks are put back an hour on the last Sunday in October. When telephoning home you might also need to make allowances for daylight-saving in your own country.

When it's noon in the islands, it's 4 am in San Francisco, 7 am in New York and Toronto, 8 pm in Perth, 10 pm in Sydney, and midnight in Auckland.

ELECTRICITY

The electric current in the Canary Islands is 220V, 50Hz, and plugs have two round pins, like Spain and Continental Europe.

Travellers from the USA need a voltage converter (although many of the more expensive hotels have provision for 110V appliances such as shavers). Make sure you bring plug adapters for your appliances. It is a good idea to buy these *before* leaving home as they are virtually impossible to get in the Canaries. If your appliance's voltage is the same or variable, all you'll need is a European plug to fit onto the one you've brought from home. North American 60 Hz appliances with electric motors (such as some CD and tape players) may perform poorly.

WEIGHTS & MEASURES

The metric system applies in the Canary Islands. See the conversion table at the back of this book. Decimals are indicated with commas and thousands with points.

LAUNDRY

Self-service laundrettes are extremely rare. Small laundries *(lavanderías)* are more common, but not particularly cheap.

Many laundries take in washing by the load. An average price for a load of about 4kg is 800 ptas to 1000 ptas. Your clothes will be returned dried and folded but not ironed. Try not to pay by the garment or you may find yourself doling out as much as 600 ptas to have a pair of trousers done, 450 ptas for a shirt and 550 ptas for a simple skirt!

TOILETS

Public toilets are not common and rarely inviting. The easiest option is to wander into a bar or cafe and use its facilities. The polite thing to do is to have a coffee or something before or after, but you're unlikely to raise too many eyebrows if you don't. This said, some curmudgeonly places in popular tourist areas post notices saying that their toilets are for clients only. Such mean-spirited places are best boycotted – for all needs, including food and drink.

The cautious carry some toilet paper with them when out and about as many toilets lack it. If there's a bin beside the loo, put paper and so on in it – it's probably there because the local sewage system has trouble coping. Here and there you'll still find squat toilets.

HEALTH

The Canary Islands are not exactly a haven for exotic diseases; in fact the climate's positively healthy. The worst many visitors pick up is an extended hangover from too much partying in the resorts. Other potential risks are sunburn, dehydration, insect bites or mild gut problems, usually due to a change in diet.

Predeparture Planning

Immunisations No jabs are normally needed to visit the Canary Islands although it is recommended that everyone keep up-to-date with diptheria, tetanus and polio vaccinations. The story may be different if you're coming from an infected area – yellow fever is the most likely one to be needed. If you've any doubt, check with your travel agent or a Spanish embassy. Depending on your itinerary, your personal risk and the length of your visit, vaccination against hepatitis A, hepatitis B or typhoid may be recommended.

Health Insurance Make sure that you have adequate health insurance. For more information, see Travel Insurance under Visas & Documents earlier in this chapter.

Visitors from other EU countries and Norway are entitled to free emergency medical care (under the Spanish national health system) in the Canary Islands on production of an E111 form, which you must get in your home country before you come.

In Britain, E111s are issued free by post offices; all you need to supply is your name, address, date of birth and National Insurance number. In other EU countries ask your doctor or health service how to get the form.

Even with an E111, you will still have to pay for medicines bought from pharmacies, even if prescribed, and perhaps for a few tests and procedures. Your own national health system may reimburse some of these costs.

An E111 is no good for private medical consultations and treatment in the Canary Islands; this includes virtually all dentists, some of the better clinics and surgeries, and emergency flights home. If you want to avoid paying for these, you'll need adequate medical – as well as theft and loss – insurance on your travel policy.

Most, but not all, US health insurance policies stay in effect, at least for a limited period, if you travel abroad. On the other hand, most other non-European national health plans (including Australia's Medicare) don't, so you must take out special medical as well as theft and loss insurance.

Other Preparations If you wear glasses or contact lenses, pack a spare pair and, if you're ultracautious, your prescription too. If you pop a special medicine take enough with you as it may not be available locally. Take the packet too; if it shows the generic name, and not just the brand, this will make getting replacements easier. It's a good idea to have a legible prescription or letter from your doctor to show that you use the medication legally.

Medical Kit Medicines are easily available in the Canary Islands, and in fact many are cheaper than in countries such as the USA and Australia. Quite a few that would normally require a prescription in other countries can be obtained easily over the counter. In any event, you'd be wise to carry a small, straightforward medical kit, including some or all of the items listed in the boxed text. If you forget, the nearest *farmacia* (pharmacy) should stock them.

Basic Rules

Water Domestic, hotel and restaurant tap water is safe to drink throughout the is-

Medical Kit Check List

Following is a list of items you should consider including in your medical kit – consult your pharmacist for brands available in your country.

- ☐ **Aspirin or paracetamol (acetaminophen in the USA)** – for pain or fever
- ☐ **Antihistamine** – for allergies, eg hay fever; to ease the itch from insect bites or stings; and to prevent motion sickness
- ☐ **Cold and flu tablets, throat lozenges and nasal decongestant**
- ☐ **Multivitamins** – consider for long trips, when dietary vitamin intake may be inadequate
- ☐ **Antibiotics** – consider including these if you're travelling well off the beaten track; see your doctor, as they must be prescribed, and carry the prescription with you
- ☐ **Loperamide or diphenoxylate** – 'blockers' for diarrhoea
- ☐ **Prochlorperazine or metaclopramide** – for nausea and vomiting
- ☐ **Rehydration mixture** – to prevent dehydration, which may occur, for example, during bouts of diarrhoea; particularly important when travelling with children
- ☐ **Insect repellent, sunscreen, lip balm and eye drops**
- ☐ **Calamine lotion, sting relief spray or aloe vera** – to ease irritation from sunburn and insect bites or stings
- ☐ **Antifungal cream or powder** – for fungal skin infections and thrush
- ☐ **Antiseptic (such as povidone-iodine)** – for cuts and grazes
- ☐ **Bandages, Band-Aids (plasters) and other wound dressings**
- ☐ **Water purification tablets or iodine**
- ☐ **Scissors, tweezers and a thermometer** – note that mercury thermometers are prohibited by airlines

lands, though not very palatable. In places with water shortages you might want to check; the lowering of water tables might introduce some undesirable ingredients into the supply. Ask *'¿Es potable el agua?'* if you're in any doubt.

Water from public spouts and fountains is not necessarily reliable unless it has a sign saying *'Agua Potable'*. What's sure is that you shouldn't drink where it says *'Agua No Potable'*. Natural water, unless it's straight from a definitely unpolluted spring, is likewise not always safe to drink unpurified.

Safe bottled water is available everywhere; it generally costs 75 ptas to 85 ptas for a 1.5L bottle in shops and supermarkets.

The surest way of purifying any water you're uncertain about is to boil it vigorously for five minutes. That's usually mightily impracticable if you're out walking so slip a packet of chlorine tablets (Puritabs, Steritabs or other brand names) into your daypack in case your water supply runs out. These will treat the water chemically and kill many pathogens. Iodine, though it tastes fairly vile, is also very effective in purifying water and is available in tablet form (such as Potable Aqua).

Medical Treatment

For serious medical problems and emergencies, the local public-health service provides care to rival that of anywhere in the world. Most of the larger resorts are also well endowed with private clinics, catering in the main to tourists, where English is spoken. Elsewhere, seeing a doctor about more mundane problems can be a frustrating business. If you want to see one quickly or need emergency dental treatment, even quite small towns have a *centro de salud* (health centre) with an *urgencias* (emergencies) section. Failing this, ask for the nearest *ambulatorio* (local clinic) or the urgencias section of the nearest hospital. All are public sector.

The expense of a private clinic or surgery is often worth the saving in time and frustration. A consultation at such a place typically costs somewhere between 3000 ptas and 6000 ptas (not counting medicines). If you have travel insurance you may well be covered for this expense. All dental practices are private anyway.

Take all imaginable documentation (and

photocopies too) – passport, E111, insurance papers – when you deal with medical services. Tourist offices, the police and usually your accommodation, can all tell you where to find doctors, dentists and hospitals, or how to call an ambulance.

Pharmacies can help with many ailments. A system of duty pharmacies *(farmacias de guardia)* operates so that each town or district of a city has at least one open all the time (although often only for filling prescriptions). When a pharmacy closes, it posts the name of the nearest open one(s) on the door. Lists of farmacias de guardia are also often given in local papers.

Environmental Hazards

Heat Exhaustion & Heat Stroke Dehydration and salt deficiency can cause heat exhaustion. Take time to acclimatise to high temperatures, drink litres of liquids and don't overexert yourself in the first few days.

Salt deficiency leads to fatigue, lethargy, headaches, giddiness and muscle cramps. Salt tablets can help – or simply lace your food with extra salt.

Heat stroke, an extreme form of heat exhaustion, is a serious, occasionally fatal, condition. It can occur if the body's heat-regulating mechanism breaks down and the body temperature rises to dangerous levels. Long, continuous periods of exposure to high temperatures, and insufficient fluids can leave you vulnerable to it.

The symptoms are feeling unwell, not sweating very much (or at all) and a high body temperature (39°C to 41°C or 102°F to 106°F). Where sweating has ceased the skin becomes flushed and red. Severe, throbbing headaches and lack of coordination will also occur, and the sufferer may be confused or aggressive. Eventually the victim will become delirious or convulse. Here in the Canaries such an extreme condition is very rare indeed – though you may very well experience some of the symptoms at the end of a good bar crawl!

If it's more than the booze, hospitalisation is essential. In the interim, get the victim out of the sun, remove their clothing, cover them with a wet sheet or towel and then fan continually. Give fluids if they are conscious.

Prickly Heat This is an itchy rash caused by excessive perspiration trapped under the skin. It usually strikes people who have just flown in. Keeping cool, bathing often, drying the skin and using a mild talcum or prickly heat powder, or even resorting to air-conditioning may help.

Sunburn Out on the beach or up in the mountains you can get sunburnt surprisingly quickly, even through cloud. Use a sunscreen, hat, and barrier cream for your nose and lips. Calamine lotion or a commercial after-sun preparation is good for mild sunburn. Protect your eyes with good-quality sunglasses, particularly if you are near water or sand.

Infectious Diseases

Diarrhoea Simple things such as a change of water, food or climate can all cause a mild bout of diarrhoea, but a few rushed toilet trips with no other symptoms are not indicative of a major problem.

Dehydration is the main danger with any diarrhoea, particularly in children or the elderly as it can occur quite quickly. Under all circumstances, fluid replacement (at least equal to the volume being lost) is the most important thing to remember. Weak black tea with a little sugar, soda water, or soft drinks allowed to go flat and diluted 50% with clean water are all good. With severe diarrhoea, a rehydrating solution is preferable in order to replace the minerals and salts lost. Commercially available oral rehydration salts (ORS) are very useful; add them to boiled or bottled water. In an emergency you can make up a solution of six teaspoons of sugar and a half teaspoon of salt to 1L of boiled or bottled water. Urine is the best guide to whether you've been topped up again – if your pee is still little and brightly coloured, you need to drink more. Keep drinking small amounts often, and stick to a bland diet as you recover.

HIV & AIDS A few years ago Spain had the highest AIDS (SIDA in Spanish) rate in Europe, the major reason being intravenous drug use. But the number of new cases (9.3 per 100,000 inhabitants in 1998) is now half what it was in the mid-1990s.

HIV (Human Immunodeficiency Virus) develops into AIDS (Acquired Immune Deficiency Syndrome), which is a fatal disease. HIV is a major problem in many countries. Any exposure to blood, blood products or body fluids may put you at risk. The disease is often transmitted through sexual contact or dirty needles – vaccinations, acupuncture, tattooing and body piercing are potentially as dangerous as intravenous drug use or a dubious sexual partner. There is no cure, as yet, for AIDS.

Sexually Transmitted Diseases Herpes, gonorrhoea and syphilis are among these diseases; sores, blisters or rashes around the genitals and discharges or pain when urinating are common symptoms. In some sexually transmitted diseases (STDs), such as wart virus or chlamydia, symptoms may be less marked or not observed at all, especially in women. Syphilis symptoms eventually disappear completely but the disease continues and can cause severe problems in later years. While abstinence from sexual contact is the only 100% prevention, using condoms is also effective. The different sexually transmitted diseases each require specific antibiotics as treatment. There is no cure for herpes.

Cuts, Bites & Stings

Wash well and treat any cut with an antiseptic. Where possible avoid bandages and Band-Aids (plasters), which can keep wounds wet.

Bee and wasp stings are usually painful rather than dangerous. However people who are allergic to them, may experience severe breathing difficulties and require urgent medical care. In general, calamine lotion or a sting relief spray will ease the irritation while ice packs will reduce the pain and swelling.

Scorpions are mercifully rarer on the

Canary Islands than in mainland Spain. Their sting can be distressingly painful but isn't fatal.

In forested areas, watch out for the hairy, reddish-brown caterpillars of the pine processionary moth. They live in silvery nests up in the pine trees and, come spring, leave the nest to march in long lines (hence the name). Touching the caterpillars' hairs sets off a severely irritating allergic skin reaction.

Check for ticks if you've been walking where sheep and goats graze: they can cause skin infections and other more serious diseases. If you find one clinging to you, smother it in cooking oil or something similar. Once suffocated, it's easy to pick off.

Women's Health
Gynaecological Problems Synthetic underwear, sweating and the use of antibiotics and contraceptive pills can lead to fungal vaginal infections, especially when it's hot. Fungal infections are characterised by a rash, itch and discharge; and can be treated with a vinegar or lemon-juice douche, or with yoghurt. Nystatin, miconazole or clotrimazole pessaries or vaginal cream are the usual treatment. Maintaining good personal hygiene, and wearing loose-fitting clothes and cotton underwear may help prevent these infections.

STDs are a major cause of vaginal problems. Symptoms include a smelly discharge, painful intercourse and sometimes a burning sensation when urinating. Medical attention should be sought and male sexual partners must also be treated. For more details see the section on Sexually Transmitted Diseases earlier. The best thing is to practise safer sex using condoms.

Pregnancy Most miscarriages occur during the first three months of pregnancy. Miscarriage is not uncommon, and can occasionally lead to severe bleeding. The last three months should also be spent within reasonable distance of good medical care. A baby born as early as 24 weeks stands a chance of survival but only in a good modern hospital. Additional care should be taken to prevent illness and particular at-

tention should be paid to diet and nutrition. Avoid alcohol and nicotine, for example.

WOMEN TRAVELLERS
Harassment is much less frequent than the stereotypes of Spain would have you believe and the country has one of the developed world's lowest incidences of reported rape. Any unpleasantness you might encounter is more likely to come from drunken northern European yobs in the big resorts than from the locals.

In towns, you may get the occasional unwelcome stare, catcall or unnecessary comment, to which the best (and most galling) response is indifference. Don't get paranoid about what's being called out; the *piropo* – or harmless, mildly flirty compliment – is deeply ingrained in Spanish society and, if well delivered, even considered gallant.

The advice is really just the common-sense stuff you need to keep in mind anywhere. Think twice about going alone to isolated stretches of beach, lonely country areas or dark city streets at night. Where there are crowds – as there often are very late into the night in towns and cities – you're usually safer. It's inadvisable for a woman to hitchhike alone and not a great idea even for two women together.

Topless bathing and skimpy clothes are generally OK at the coastal resorts, but otherwise a little more modesty is the norm. Not a few local young women feel no compunction about dressing to kill, but equally feel absolutely no obligation to respond to any male interest this arouses.

Recommended reading is the *Handbook for Women Travellers* by M & G Moss.

GAY & LESBIAN TRAVELLERS
Gay and lesbian sex are both legal in Spain and hence in the Canary Islands. The age of consent is 16, the same as for heterosexuals. The Playa del Inglés, on the southern end of Gran Canaria, is where the bulk of Europe's gay crowd heads when holidaying in the Canaries, and the nightlife here bumps and grinds year round. *Guía Gay Visado* is a guide to gay and lesbian bars, discos and

contacts throughout Spain and can be found mostly in gay and lesbian bookshops. Gay magazines in Spanish and on sale at some newsstands include the monthly *Mensual* (600 ptas), which includes listings for gay bars, clubs and so on in the Canary Islands, and the Madrid-based *Entiendes* (500 ptas), which also has a quarterly English edition. Visit Mensual on-line at www.mensual.com (Spanish only).

Before you leave home, check out the *Spartacus Guide for Gay Men* (the Spartacus list also includes the comprehensive *Spartacus National Edition España*, in English and German), published by Bruno Gmünder Verlag, Mail Order, PO Box 11 07 29, D-1000 Berlin 11. Ferrari Publications, Phoenix, AZ, USA, also does travel guides for gay men and *Places for Women*.

There are a few Spanish queer sites on the Internet. Check out http://aleph.pangea .org/org/cgl/guiagaie.html for city and regional listings of bars, clubs, accommodation and the like in the Canary Islands.

For information about gay groups in the islands, you might like to write in advance to the Colectivo de Gays y Lesbianas de Las Palmas, Apartado de Correos 707, 35080 Las Palmas de Gran Canaria.

DISABLED TRAVELLERS

In the UK, Holiday Care (☎ 01293-774535) can send you a fact sheet on hotels and other accommodation in the Canary Islands that cater for the disabled, as well as travel agents who can help organise trips. You might like to pass by their Web site at www.holidaycare.org.uk.

SENIOR TRAVELLERS

Senior citizens get reductions on several inter-island ferries and hydrofoils, and in some museums and sights. The top-end chain of public sector *parador* hotels (see Accommodation later in this chapter) offers attractive discounts for people over 60 and their partners.

TRAVEL WITH CHILDREN

Canarios take quickly to children, who are welcome at all kinds of accommodation and in virtually every cafe, bar and restaurant. Having children with you can often open doors to contact with local people who you otherwise may not have the opportunity to meet.

Many bars and cafes have outside tables, allowing drinking grown-ups to indulge in their favourite tipples while their little ones run around and play – a good sign of a comparatively child-friendly society. Local kids are quite used to staying up late and at fiestas it's commonplace to see even tiny ones toddling the streets at 2 or 3 am. Visiting kids like this idea too but often can't cope with it – or the next day – quite so readily.

Travelling with children usually implies taking a different approach to your holiday. Constant moving around may be fascinating for adults but if you're young you may fail to appreciate the joys of the road. Fortunately, the Canaries are in this sense an ideal location – only those determined to see all seven islands at lightning speed would be tempted to subject themselves, let alone their children, to day after day of tiring movement. As a rule, kids adapt quickly to new environments, but most would never budge if they had a choice. Hanging around the one spot for a few days at a time, or choosing a permanent base from which to make excursions, creates a sense of familiarity (quite nice for adults too!).

The kind of activities that take up most visitors' time in the islands, such as lounging around on beaches, are usually welcomed by kids too. Children will be cheered by the knowledge that the Canaries are not overly laden with museums and other grown-up delights that so often engender desperate, yawn-inducing boredom if you are small.

Much of the stuff put on for tourists appeals to kids. Animal reserves (such as Tenerife's Loro Parque) and all those water and theme parks on the bigger islands provide fun for all the family.

Bring along at least a couple of your kids' favourite toys and/or games to keep them occupied.

There are no particular health precautions you need to take with your children in the

Canary Islands. That said, kids tend to be more affected than adults by unfamiliar heat, changes in diet and sleeping patterns, and just being in a strange place.

Nappies (diapers), creams, lotions, baby foods and so on are all as easily available on the islands as in any other western country, but if there's some particular brand you swear by, it's best to bring it with you. Calpol, for instance, isn't easily found.

Infants generally travel free on ferries and other boats, and those from two to 12 go for half price. Similar reductions apply at most commercial attractions, museums and so on, and on public transport.

Lonely Planet's *Travel with Children*, by Maureen Wheeler, has lots of practical advice on the subject, and first-hand stories from many Lonely Planet authors and others who have done it.

USEFUL ORGANISATIONS

The Instituto Cervantes, with branches in over 30 cities around the world, exists to promote Spanish language and culture in all Spanish-speaking countries. The library at the London branch (☎ 020-7235 0353), 102 Eaton Square, London SW1 W9AN, has a wide range of material on Spain but little specifically on the Canary Islands. It has reference books, literature, books on history and the arts, periodicals, over 1000 videos including feature films, language-teaching material, electronic databases and music CDs. In New York, the institute (☎ 212-689 4232) is at 122 East 42nd St, Suite 807, New York, NY 10168. You can find further addresses on the institute's Web site at www.cervantes.es.

For international student cards and other youth and student services, contact the Dirección General de la Juventud (roughly, department of youth affairs). Their Las Palmas office (☎ 928 30 63 97) is at Calle Profesor Agustín Millares Carló 18. The equivalent office on Tenerife (☎ 922 63 06 90) is at Calle Wenceslao Yanes 6, in La Laguna.

DANGERS & ANNOYANCES

The Canary Islands are not exactly dangerous territory and the vast majority of trav-

ellers to the islands risk little more than sunburn and maybe GBH (grievous bodily hangover).

Petty theft (which isn't so petty if your passport, cash, travellers cheques, credit card and camera all go missing) is something of a problem in Las Palmas de Gran Canaria and the big south coast resorts of Tenerife and Gran Canaria but with a few simple precautions you can minimise the danger.

For some specific hints about looking after your luggage and money, and on safety for women, see the What to Bring (under Planning), Money and Women Travellers sections earlier in this chapter.

Before you leave home, write your name, address and telephone number inside your luggage, and take photocopies of your important documents. See Copies under Visas & Documents earlier in the chapter for suggestions on looking after your important details.

Travel insurance against theft and loss is another good idea; see Travel Insurance under Visas & Documents earlier in this chapter.

Theft & Loss

The risk of theft is highest in the resorts, the main towns and when you first arrive in the islands or a new town and may be off your guard, disoriented or unaware of danger signs. Pickpockets and bag snatchers are the main worry, along with theft from cars. Carry valuables under your clothes if possible – certainly not in a back pocket or in a day pack or anything that could be snatched away easily – and keep your eyes open for people who get unnecessarily close to you. Never leave anything visible in cars – it's an open invitation to break in. If possible, don't even leave anything valuable in the boot (trunk). Hire cars in particular are targeted.

Take care with your belongings on the beach; anything lying on the sand could disappear in a flash when your back is turned. Lone travellers should consider investing in a waterproof neck pouch so that they can keep money, passport and other (light-

TONY WHEELER

Pretty Puerto de Mogán, Gran Canaria, balances a busy fishing port with a bustling tourist trade.

INGRID RODDIS

Traditional basketware is popular on the islands.

DAMIEN SIMONIS

Life in Gran Canaria's fast lane....

So-called Columbus' House was actually a residence for Las Palmas de Gran Canaria's governors.

Standing the test of time, Guanche arts thrive.

Dig those dunes, Maspalomas

Gran Canaria's strange-looking Roque Nublo is often eerily enveloped in cloud.

weight) valuables with them even while swimming.

At night, avoid dingy, empty city alleys and back streets – or anywhere that just doesn't feel 100% safe.

Don't leave anything valuable lying around your room and use a safe if one's available.

If anything valuable is stolen or lost, you must report it to the police and get a copy of the report if you want to make an insurance claim.

If your passport has gone, contact your embassy or consulate for help in issuing a replacement. Such places can give help of various kinds in other emergencies but as a rule cannot advance you money to get home. If your country has no consulate in the islands, you may have to contact your embassy in Madrid.

Annoyances

You would have to be in a bad mood to get all that annoyed in the Canaries but several things can get on your nerves. In the bigger cities and, above all, in the resorts, noise can be a problem. Of course, you can always leave cities and resorts behind in search of more tranquil spots.

While on the subject of resorts, party animals should be aware that some other party animals, when sufficiently tanked, can become quite unpredictable. In most cases, we are talking loud and drunken louts ferried in on charter flights from northern Europe, some of whom can't resist a good fight. It's sad but largely true that the bulk of those who end up in Canary Islands' coolers are foreigners who don't know when enough is enough. The best thing you can probably do is walk away from trouble if you see it brewing and, if warranted, try to contact the police – although locals will probably see to that before you can. See also Legal Matters later.

EMERGENCIES

The best combination to remember is ☎ 112, the pan-European emergency telephone number. Valid in the Canary Islands, it's the one to dial in any major crisis where

you might need urgent medical assistance, the ambulance service, police or fire.

If you're seriously ill or injured, someone should let your embassy or consulate know (see the Embassies & Consulates section earlier in this chapter for telephone numbers).

Alternative emergency numbers that apply on most islands are:

Policía Nacional (National Police)	☎ 091
Policía Local (Local Police)	☎ 092
Guardia Civil	☎ 062
Urgencias Salud (Medical Emergencies)	☎ 061

LEGAL MATTERS

Should you be arrested, you will be allotted the free services of a duty solicitor *(abogado de oficio)*, who may speak only Spanish. You're also entitled to make a phone call. If you use this to contact your embassy or consulate, it will probably be able to do no more than refer you to a lawyer who speaks your language. If you end up in court, the authorities are obliged to provide a translator.

La Policía – Who's Who

Spanish police are, on the whole, more of a help than a threat to a law-abiding traveller. Most are certainly friendly enough to be approached for directions on the street. Unpleasant events, such as random drug searches, do occur but not frequently.

There are three main types of *policía* – the **Policía Nacional**, the **Policía Local** and the **Guardia Civil**. The words policía and guardia refer to the forces, but also stand for each individual member.

Policía Local Often called Policía Municipal and sporting a blue and white uniform, these are under the jurisdiction of city and town councils and deal mainly with minor matters such as parking, traffic and bylaws. There's no real equivalent of 'bobby on the beat' street-patrol police. This said, you'll sometimes see police patrolling the bigger towns and resorts on mountain bikes and where foreign package tourists mass, there's a special category of tourist police who usually speak reasonable English.

Policía Nacional This force covers cities and bigger towns and is the main crime-fighting body because most crime happens on its patch. Those who wear uniforms are in blue. There is also a large contingent in plain clothes, some of whom form special squads dealing with drugs, terrorism and the like. Most of them, though, are to be found in police stations called *comisarías*, shuffling masses of paper concerning things such as the issuing of passports, identity cards for locals and residence cards for foreigners who like Spain enough to opt for long-term entanglement with its bureaucracy.

Guardia Civil The main responsibilities of the green-uniformed members of the Guardia Civil are roads, the countryside, villages, prisons, international borders and some environmental protection. These are the guys who used to wear those alarming winged helmets, phased out in the 1980s but which still resurface on some ceremonial occasions.

The Guardia Civil was set up in the 19th century to quell banditry, but soon came to be regarded as a politically repressive force that clamped down on any challenge to established privilege. Although its image has softened since responsibility for it has been switched from the defence ministry to the interior ministry, it's still a military body in some ways: most officers have attended military academy and members qualify for military decorations.

Contacting the Police Should you need to contact the police, don't agonise over which kind to approach. Any of them will do but you may find that the Policía Local are the most helpful.

Drugs

Cannabis is the only legal drug, and only in amounts for personal use – which means very little.

Public consumption of any drug is, in principle, illegal yet there are some bars where people smoke joints openly. Other bars will ask you to step outside if you light up. The only sure moral of these stories is to be very discreet if you do use cannabis.

Although there's a reasonable degree of tolerance when it comes to people having a smoke in their own home, it would be unwise in hotel rooms or guesthouses and could be risky in even the coolest of public places.

BUSINESS HOURS

Generally, people work from about 9 am to 2 pm and then again from 4.30 or 5 pm for another three hours, Monday to Friday. Shops and travel agencies usually open these hours on Saturday too, although some may skip the evening session. Big supermarkets and department stores often stay open from about 9 am to 9 pm without a break, Monday to Saturday. A lot of government offices don't bother with afternoon opening at all. For bank and post office hours respectively, see Money and Post & Communications earlier in this chapter.

PUBLIC HOLIDAYS & SPECIAL EVENTS
Public Holidays

There are at least 14 official holidays per year in the Canary Islands. When a holiday falls close to a weekend, locals like to make a *puente* (bridge) – meaning they take the intervening day off too. On occasion, when a couple of holidays fall close to the same weekend, the puente becomes an *acueducto* (aqueduct)!

The eight main national holidays, observed throughout the islands and the rest of Spain (though the authorities seem to change their minds about some of these from time to time) are:

1 January Anõ Nuevo (New Year's Day)
March/April Viernes Santo (Good Friday)
1 May Fiesta del Trabajo (Labour Day)
15 August La Asunción de la Virgen (Feast of the Assumption)
12 October Día de la Hispanidad (National Day)
1 November Todos los Santos (All Saints' Day) – gets particular attention on Tenerife
8 December La Inmaculada Concepción (Feast of the Immaculate Conception)
25 December Navidad (Christmas)

In addition, the regional government will set a further five holidays, while local councils allocate another two. Common dates include:

6 January Epifanía (Epiphany) or Día de los Reyes Magos (Three Kings' Day). Children receive presents on this day.

February/March Martes de Carnaval (Carnival Tuesday)

19 March Día de San Juan (St John's Day)

March/April Jueves Santo (Maundy Thursday, the day before Good Friday)

30 May Día de las Islas Canarias (Canary Islands Day)

June Corpus Cristi (the Thursday after the eighth Sunday after Easter Sunday). In Las Palmas de Gran Canaria, La Laguna and La Orotava (Tenerife), locals prepare elaborate floral carpets to celebrate this feast day; the celebration is also big in Mazo and El Paso (La Palma).

25 July Día de Santiago Apóstol (Feast of St James the Apostle, Spain's patron saint). In Santa Cruz de Tenerife the day also marks the commemoration of the defence of the city against Horatio Nelson.

8 September Día del Pino (Pine Tree Day). This is particularly important on Gran Canaria.

6 December Día de la Constitución (Constitution Day)

Fiestas

Like many of their mainland cousins, Canarios love to let it all hang out at the islands' numerous fiestas and local *ferias* (fairs). *Carnaval* is the wildest time, but there are many others in the course of the year – indeed in August alone there are more than 50 across the islands.

The great majority of these fiestas have a religious background (saints' days are common) but all are occasions for having fun. *Romerías* (pilgrimages) are particularly noteworthy. Processions head to/from a town's main church to a chapel or similar location dedicated to the local patron saint or the Virgin Mary, some way away.

Many local festivals are noted in city and town sections of this book and tourist offices can supply more detailed information. A few of the most outstanding include:

2 February Virgen de la Candelaria (festival of the patron of the archipelago). This intense festival derives from the supposed apparition of the Virgin Mary before the Guanches (the event is also celebrated on 15 August); the festival is celebrated in the town of the same name in Tenerife.

February/March Carnaval (carnival). Several weeks of fancy-dress parades and merrymaking across the islands end on the Tuesday 47 days before Easter Sunday. This is at its wildest and most extravagant in Santa Cruz de Tenerife, where the locals put on a display rivalling that of Rio de Janeiro.

21–30 June Bajada de Nuestra Señora de las Nieves. This fiesta is held only once every five years in Santa Cruz de la Palma. The processions, dances and merrymaking constitute the island's premier religious festival.

July Romería de San Benito Abad. This festival is held on the first Sunday of the month in La Laguna (Tenerife).

14 July Día de San Buenaventura. Betancuria (Fuerteventura) celebrates the town's patron saint.

4 August Fiesta de la Rama. This fiesta is held in Agaete (Gran Canaria).

August (dates vary) Romería de San Roque. This festival is held in Garachico (Tenerife).

25 August Día de San Ginés. This is held in Arrecife (Lanzarote).

6–8 September Fiesta de la Virgen del Pino. Held in Teror (Gran Canaria), this is the island's most important religious celebration. Festivities begin two weeks before these final key days.

7–5 September Fiesta del Santísimo Cristo. This fiesta is held in La Laguna (Tenerife).

October Romería de Nuestra Señora de la Luz. Held in Las Palmas de Gran Canaria, this festival is marked by a boat procession.

13 December Día de Santa Lucía. Celebrations occur all over Gran Canaria.

Arts Festivals Las Palmas de Gran Canaria in particular plays host to several important arts festivals including the Festival Internacional de Música (January), the Festival de Opera (February–March), the Festival de Ballet y Danza (May), and the Muestra Internacional de Cine (an international film festival held every two years in October–November).

The Encuentro Teatral Tres Continentes (aka Festival Internacional de Teatro de los Tres Mundos) attracts theatre companies from Europe, Latin America and Africa to Agüimes (Gran Canaria) in September.

ACTIVITIES

Many visitors to the islands are keen to do something more than lounge around on the beaches and hang out in bars. There's certainly no shortage of distractions in the Canaries, where everything from golf to water sports, trekking to diving and sailing to parapente are on offer.

Beaches

OK, so the combination of sun and sand tends to induce inactivity rather than the opposite in many people. All the same, you can't have a section on things to do without highlighting the finest strands on the islands. For rolling dunes, take your umbrella and beachmat to Maspalomas (Gran Canaria) or south-east of Corralejo (Fuerteventura). By contrast, for kilometre after kilometre of flat, natural beach, go to the Jandía peninsula on Fuerteventura. We say 'natural' because quite a few resorts have enhanced their marketability by importing shiploads of sand from the coast of Africa.

Don't necessarily spurn the black volcanic sand beaches of the western islands. From a distance, sun worshippers may seem to be lounging on an extended slag heap. But if you're prepared to be colour-blind, they are (unless they're over-pebbly) as pleasant as and usually less crowded than any yellow one.

Walking

Away from the coast there is plenty of surprising countryside to explore. Tenerife and the three smaller western islands, not strong on beaches anyway, offer some great walking – following attractive trails where, except for one or two well-trodden classics, you may scarcely see another hiker all day. Where else could you plan a one-week walking holiday embracing as many as three national parks?

If you're based on Tenerife, you can tramp the trails through the rugged volcanic scenery of the Parque Nacional del Teide, where park rangers lead daily guided walks, or enjoy the Anaga peninsula, the panhandle in the island's north-east, with its spectacular seascapes.

On La Gomera, a short ferry ride from Tenerife, you can walk within the misty forests, with heather higher than your head, of the Parque Nacional de Garajonay, a UNESCO world heritage site. Alternatively, follow the network of ancient donkey trails, which linked village to village before the advent of the car.

Less-visited La Palma is worth a week's trekking holiday in itself, with a walk around part of the rim of the massive depression of the Caldera de Taburiente (also a national park) a must, and another along the volcanic ridge of the Cumbre Vieja running a close second.

On most islands you can plan your own route, walking wild and free, or join a guided group. Several outfits organise day walks. Prices, which include transport and maybe a picnic, average between 4000 ptas and 5000 ptas per person.

In Playa del Inglés (Gran Canaria), three walking companies offer the opportunity to retreat from the fleshpots into the hinterland: Happy Biking (see Cycling for details), Euroguías (☎ 928 76 41 95) and Rutas Canarias (☎ 928 67 04 66).

On Lanzarote, contact Feetbook Agencia (☎ 928 51 24 41) or Canary Trekking (☎ 609 53 76 84).

Two outfits operate from Valle Gran Rey (La Gomera): Timah (☎/fax 922 80 57 26), long established on the island, and Oko-Tours (☎ 922 80 59 40).

On La Palma, Wanderzentrale (☎/fax 922 40 81 29), a Spanish-German outfit operating from Puerto Naos, organises hikes all over the island, as does Senderos Canarias (☎ 922 43 30 01), based just outside Santa Cruz.

For details of UK-based walking tour operators who offer walking holidays in the western islands, see Organised Tours in the Getting There & Away chapter.

Books & Maps The western isles in particular are well resourced. Lonely Planet's *Walking in Spain* has detailed descriptions of a whole holiday's worth of day hikes around Tenerife and La Gomera. Discovery Walking Guides produces excellent walking maps and descriptions for all the islands (except Fuerterventura) plus their recently published *Walk! La Gomera* in book format. Alternatively, you can pick up the lot in one hit, drawn together on a single CD.

On Tenerife, for hikes at all levels covering the whole island, ask at any tourist office for their free *Footpaths* pack, a box of 22 loose-leaf walks, described in English.

La Palma also has good freebie maps suitable for walking. Ask at the Parque Nacional de la Caldera de Taburiente visitors centre for the standard visitors map to the park and at the tourist office in Santa Cruz de la Palma for three walking maps which together cover the whole island.

Cycling

In many resorts you can rent a mountain bike or tourer. They too are a great way of escaping the crowds and heading for the hills and a less touristy experience.

There's a dearth of explicit maps for mountain biking but a glance at one of the walkers' maps detailed in the previous section will give some good ideas.

Just as hikers can plough their own furrow or join a group, cyclists can pedal alone or join an organised ride, whether on or off the road.

Outfits such as Scott Bike Center (☎ 922 37 60 61) in Puerto de la Cruz (Tenerife), Happy Biking (☎ 928 76 68 32) in Playa del Inglés (Gran Canaria), Tommy's Bikes (☎ 928 59 23 27) in Costa Teguise (Lanzarote), Bike Station Gomera (☎/fax 922 80 50 82) in Valle Gran Rey (La Gomera) and Bike Station (☎/fax 922 40 83 55) in Puerto Naos (La Palma) all offer guided rides. The fee (on average between 4000 ptas and 6000 ptas per day) normally includes hire of cycle and equipment, transport to the start and/or finish of the ride and, in some cases, a picnic lunch.

Surfing

The eastern islands are the best for waves. Here, you're likely to get a reliable combination of satisfying swell and wind that doesn't chop it all up. On Gran Canaria, Playa de las Canteras (the beach for Las Palmas) offers fairly gentle waves. The wilder, less visited and more rugged north coast of Lanzarote has some of Europe's finest surfing breaks and a surf school based at Famara. On Fuerteventura, Corralejo is a popular base for boarders and also has a couple of surf schools. For on-line information, visit www.liquidtrips.com/canaries.

Windsurfing

Wherever you are, you can normally pick up sufficient breeze to make it worth your while to head out with your board and sail. Hiring gear is generally no problem – you'll find outlets at the main resorts.

Gran Canaria is the windiest of the group and thus ideal for those the locals call *windsurfistas*, who choose above all the beach of Bahía de Pozo Izquierdo to practise their sport. It is usually here that world-class competitions are held in summer. Pretty much all the island's beaches are fine for your average windsurfista. Among other spots on this island, all situated between Las Palmas and Maspalomas, are: Playa del Ojo de Garza, Playa del Burrero, Vargas, Arinaga, Mosca Point (near Pozo Izquierdo), Juan Grande, Playa del Aguila, Bahía Feliz, and the Faro (lighthouse) de Maspalomas.

Playa de El Cabezo (near El Médano) on Tenerife, Playa de Sotavento in southern Fuerteventura, and Las Cucharas (near Costa Teguise) on Lanzarote all offer good windsurfing conditions too. For beginners, the quiet bay of Caleta del Fuste (Fuerteventura) is as good a place as any to keep falling into.

In general, the conditions are so good that the PWA (Professional Windsurfers Association) hold three rounds of their World Tour in the islands every year (one each on Gran Canaria, Tenerife and Fuerteventura).

Warning The prevailing trade winds *(alisios)* are particularly strong in April and summer. Various spots, including some of those mentioned above, can also be dangerous for the inexpert. If you are unsure, ask advice from a windsurfing school or shop. It is illegal to head out to sea less than two hours before sunset. That's a hard law to enforce but it's in your own interest to obey it; the idea is that you shouldn't be out there after dark – if something goes wrong, you'll be hard to rescue.

Swimming

Swimming – fun costing absolutely nothing – is something that each island offers in plenty. Many beaches are quite safe and major ones have lifeguards on duty. But a word of warning: the Atlantic can get nasty in winter, with more powerful swells than in summer. This is particularly the case on northern coasts, where swimming can be hazardous away from protected beaches and rockpools. Even strong swimmers should take care. Use common sense. A good rule of thumb is to stay out of the water unless you can see other people cavorting off your chosen beach.

Snorkelling & Diving

The clear waters of the Canaries offer good diving possibilities. Of course, we aren't talking the spectacular reefs of the Red Sea or Australia's Great Barrier Reef, but satisfying ocean diving with the chance to see a variety of rays, grouper, barracuda, turtles, a range of tropical fish and the occasional shark.

There are several marine parks where you can get into this, and many outfits offer wreck-diving and diving safaris. Some of the better diving is around Tenerife and Lanzarote, where the sea life is rich and varied.

One of the best areas for guaranteed offshore diving is the waters around the small resort of Los Gigantes, which boasts three diving schools. Here, the fewest days each year are lost to high winds because the waters are sheltered by giant cliffs.

Around the islets and Famara coast of Lanzarote you can see coral-covered rock walls, octopus colonies, big schools of various fish species and colourful marine flora. The walls and tunnels between Corralejo and Islote de Lobos on Fuerteventura contrast with the shallow terraces off the south coast, teeming with sea life. The marine reserve off La Restinga in El Hierro is also an excellent spot, its underwater life thriving and unthreatened.

The quality of the water means that you can generally rely on around 25m to 30m visibility, especially in summer and autumn.

You'll find about 40 dive centres (centros de buceo) scattered throughout the islands. Most hire out all the necessary gear and some also offer diver-certification courses, such as PADI, CMAS, NAUI and FEDAS courses. You're looking at about 40,000 ptas for a beginners' course. It's better to bring any submarine photographic equipment you are likely to want, as dive centres tend not to have it on hand.

Fishing

Deep-sea fishing is another popular activity for those with a little of Captain Ahab or Ernest Hemingway in them. You can get onto fully equipped fishing trips from the main resorts. A typical price is 7500 ptas for a five-hour trip, including rod hire.

For the elusive big ones, many fisherfolk swear by the waters off Gran Canaria, where more than 30 world fishing records have been set.

Boat Trips

In many resorts, you can sign on for a three-hour or even full-day boat trip, often with a meal (usually of a fairly indifferent standard) and free booze thrown in. Indeed, in the large resorts of southern Gran Canaria and Tenerife, you'll be hounded by touts promoting them. The come-on for many visitors is the opportunity to see whales and dolphins. Take the touts' cajoling with just a pinch of sea salt. At many times of the year, the odds on sightings are indeed very good but they can never be guaranteed. Step aboard prepared simply to enjoy a good sail with the possibility of spotting these magnificent creatures as a welcome bonus. See Whales & Dolphins under Ecology & Environment in the Facts about the Islands chapter for details on how to enjoy a marine-friendly trip.

Considerations for Responsible Diving

The popularity of diving in the waters around all of the Canaries is placing pressure on many sites. Please consider the following tips when diving and help preserve the ecology and beauty of reefs:

- Don't use anchors on the reef. Encourage dive operators and regulatory bodies to establish permanent moorings at popular dive sites.
- Avoid touching living marine organisms. Polyps can be damaged by even the gentlest contact. Never stand on corals, even if they look solid and robust. If you must secure yourself to the reef, only hold fast to exposed rock or dead coral.
- Be conscious of your fins. Even without contact the surge from heavy fin strokes near the reef can damage delicate organisms. When treading water in shallow reef areas, take care not to kick up clouds of sand. Settling sand can easily smother the delicate organisms of the reef.
- Practise and maintain proper buoyancy control. Major damage can be done by divers descending too fast and colliding with the reef. Make sure you are correctly weighted and that your weight belt is positioned so that you stay horizontal. If you haven't dived for a while, have a practice dive in a pool before taking to the reef. Be aware that buoyancy can change over the period of an extended trip: initially you may breathe harder and need more weighting; a few days later you may breathe more easily and need less weight.
- Take great care in underwater caves. Spend as little time within them as possible as your air bubbles may be caught within the roof and leave previously submerged organisms high and dry. Taking turns to inspect the interior of a small cave will lessen the chances of damaging contact.
- Resist the temptation to collect or buy corals or shells. Aside from the ecological damage, taking home marine souvenirs depletes the beauty of a site and spoils the enjoyment for others.
- The same goes for marine archaeological sites (mainly shipwrecks). Respect their integrity; they may even be protected from looting by law.
- Ensure that you take home all your rubbish, and any litter you may find as well. Plastics in particular are a serious threat to marine life. Turtles will mistake plastic for jellyfish and eat it.
- Resist the temptation to feed fish. You may disturb their normal eating habits, encourage aggressive behaviour or feed them food that is detrimental to their health.
- Minimise your disturbance of marine animals. In particular, do not ride on the backs of turtles as this causes them great anxiety.

JANE SMITH

Sailing

Those with looser purse-strings who prefer their own hand on the tiller can charter a yacht or catamaran for day excursions and longer trips. Several of the yacht clubs offer this possibility. Sailing conditions are good year-round and there are ports and facilities on all the islands.

Yellow Submarines

Oh yes, they are all indeed bright yellow! More and more resorts have a submarine offering 'a journey to the bottom of the sea' or suchlike. If you fancy a quick immersion and a peer through a porthole just off the harbour, that's fine. But if you watch from the jetty, you'll see that the – aptly named – conning tower doesn't even get wet. Frankly, you'll see more marine life with a snorkel and mask moseying around the offshore rocks and saving yourself 2000 ptas to 2500 ptas to boot.

Water Parks

Acua Lanza, Aquapark, Aquasur and more: they're all wet and wonderful, offering what can be quite an energetic day out, riding the water slides, tunnels and channels. You'll find such water parks on the outskirts of most major resorts.

Other Water Sports

Most resorts offer other damp diversions, from water-skiing to banana-boat rides. Jet skis abound and you can try parascending (where you dangle beneath a parachute attached to a rocketing speedboat).

Horse Riding

On some islands, there's the opportunity to do a little horse riding at much cheaper prices than on most of the European mainland. Try, for example, Lanzarote a Caballo (☎ 928 83 03 14) near Puerto del Carmen (Lanzarote) or either Tiempo Sur (☎ 922 55 11 68) or La Sanjora (☎/fax 922 55 18 40) in Valverde (El Hierro), both of whom offer a whole gamut of outdoor activities.

Camel Rides

Fancy a more exotic steed? Camels were once used for transport and ploughing on the eastern islands and Tenerife, and you can go for a swaying ride on one. Some of the experiences are a bit cringe-making as they bedeck you as a bedouin and offer some swill purporting to be Arab tea. Others are just a straight, no-messing-about ride. Two of the better ones in the latter category are in Teide national park (Tenerife) and outside the village of Lajares, near Corralejo (Fuerteventura).

Canyon Clambering

On El Hierro, both Tiempo Sur and La Sanjora (see Horse Riding earlier) can set you up with half a day's scrambling down the steep *barrancos*, or ravines, of the interior. They provide transport and all the gear.

Parapente

You don't necessarily have to be experienced to enjoy briefly being a bird. Several parapente outfits offer dual flights with an experienced instructor pulling the reins. One such is Parapente Biplaza (☎ 922 40 81 72, 610 695 570) where the brave hurl themselves off the cliff behind Puerto Naos (La Palma).

Golf

If bashing small white balls with sticks is your thing, you'll find a range of good courses in the Canaries. It was resident British businessmen who established the Real Club de Golf de Las Palmas on Gran Canaria back in 1891. It's still going strong, and the Spanish golf hero Severiano Ballesteros plays here often. There's another club in Maspalomas. On Lanzarote, the only course is at the northern edge of Costa Teguise, while on Tenerife there are three courses. The Real Club de Golf de Tenerife is just south of La Laguna and was established in 1932. The other two clubs are on the south coast near El Médano. Not to be left behind, Fuerteventura inaugurated its first golf course in late 2000, just north of Morro Jable. Most host various national and international tournaments, and plans are afoot to see if yet more courses can't be devised to suck up even more precious water!

LANGUAGE COURSES

A spot of Spanish study in the Canary Islands is a great way not only to learn something but also to meet people – locals as well as other travellers – and get more of an inside angle on life in the islands.

Branches of the Instituto Cervantes (see Useful Organisations earlier in this chapter) can send you lists of places offering Spanish-language courses in the Canary Islands. Some Spanish embassies and consulates also have information on courses.

The Universidad de la Laguna (☎/fax 922 60 33 45) on Tenerife offers a variety of language and culture courses. Write to: Secretaría de los Cursos para Extranjeros, Universidad de la Laguna, Avenida de Trinidad s/n, Edificio Becas 2°, 35015 La Laguna, Tenerife.

The Instituto Cervantes in your country can also supply a list of organisations that arrange study visits to Spain, although few such trips are directed to the Canaries.

Finally, several private language schools are dotted about the islands, especially in Las Palmas de Gran Canaria. Check the local Yellow Pages (Páginas Amarillas) under 'Academias de Idiomas'.

Language courses vary greatly in duration, cost and depth – your choice depends largely on your goals. Those with serious ambitions to learn Spanish will want to consider more intensive classes over an extended period.

It's worth asking whether your course will lead to any formal certificate of competence. The Diploma de Español como Lengua Extranjera (DELE) is a qualification recognised by Spain's Ministry of Education & Science.

Expect to pay around 2000 ptas per hour for individual private lessons.

WORK

Unemployment is as big a problem in the Canary Islands as in southern Spain so there is no great demand for foreign labour. A couple of possibilities exist though, so you might have luck. If you have any contacts in the islands (locals or foreigners) sound them out, as word of mouth counts for a lot.

Nationals of EU countries, Norway and Iceland are allowed to work in Spain without a visa but if they plan to stay more than three months, they are supposed to apply within the first month for a *tarjeta de residencia* (residence card). For information on this laborious process, see Visas & Documents earlier in this chapter. Virtually everyone else is supposed to obtain, from a Spanish consulate in their country of residence, a work permit and, if they plan to stay more than 90 days, a residence visa. These procedures are well-nigh impossible unless you have a job contract lined up before you begin them; in any case you should start the processes a long time before you aim to go to Spain. Quite a few people opt to work discreetly (less politely known as *trabajo negro* – black work) and skip the bureaucracy.

Language Teaching

The greatest employers of foreigners, particularly English speakers, in the Canary Islands are language schools. To get a job, some formal qualification, at least to the level of the RSA First Certificate for the Teaching of English as a Foreign Language (TEFL), makes an enormous difference. The better schools get inundated with requests for employment from English native speakers, ranging from speculative no-hopers to qualified and experienced teachers.

There are schools on all the islands, but only in any great number on Tenerife and Gran Canaria.

You can start your search with the Yellow Pages, looking under 'Academias de Idiomas'. Getting a job in one of them is harder if you're not an EU citizen. Some schools do employ people without work papers, although often at lower than normal rates. Giving private lessons is another avenue, although unlikely to bring you a living wage straight away.

Tourist Resorts

High season work in the islands' main resorts is another possibility, especially if you're prepared to stay a while. Many bars, restaurants and other businesses are run by foreigners, especially in the resort areas such as Maspalomas and Playa de las Américas.

If you have the relevant training and qualifications, you may get lucky and snare work with one of the main dive companies.

Busking

A few travellers earn a crust (and not much more) busking in the resorts.

ACCOMMODATION

The short, sad advice to those who prefer to travel independently and keep their options open is that it's easier and a lot cheaper to buy a Canaries package, including flight and accommodation, before leaving home. If you've started your journey outside Europe, drop into any travel agent in the UK, Germany or Holland and you'll be inundated with brochures.

Yes, this is limiting but it's not as constricting as it at first appears. Many tour operators will offer a two-island holiday – and if they don't, ask the travel agent to get a quote. With the exception of La Palma and El Hierro, to which boats are more limited, there are frequent sailings between the islands (see Boat in the Getting Around chapter).

Unless it's the nightlife you're after, you might want to pick one of the smaller and quieter resorts that only occupies a page or two in the operator's catalogue. And don't think that, once you've arrived, you're trapped for the whole of your stay. On Tenerife and Gran Canaria, buses fan out all over the island and car hire, on whichever island you land up, is less expensive than in mainland Europe.

Seasons & Reservations

Prices at any type of accommodation may vary with the season. Some places have separate price structures for the high season *(temporada alta)*, mid-season *(temporada media)* or low season *(temporada baja)*, all usually displayed on a notice in reception or nearby. Hoteliers are not actually bound by these displayed prices. They are free to charge less, which they quite often do, or more, which happens fairly rarely.

Any time is tourist time in the Canaries. But, contrary to resorts in mainland Spain (and indeed most places in Europe away from the ski slopes) the high season here is in winter, if winter it can be called. Then, unlike their continental competitors, the Canaries can offer sunshine, warmth and an escape from the rigours of the northern European winter.

High season in the Canary Islands runs from about December to April (including the Carnaval period of February/March), and this is when you are likely to find accommodation at its most costly – and elusive. Semana Santa (Easter Week) is another peak time. Summer can also be busy, as this is when mainland Spaniards also turn up in force; July to September marks, for many hotels and apartments, the mid-season. If you can visit during the rest of the year, you'll find less pressure on accommodation with many of those same hotels and apartments offering rates a good 25% below their top prices.

Note that options in individual towns fill up quickly when a local fiesta is on, and those on the smaller islands can be fully taken during important celebrations.

The overwhelming majority of visitors to the Canary Islands come with accommodation booked. This has certain advantages, especially in high season, when going it alone can be difficult.

The biggest problem for budget travellers is that there are often not many cheap-end accommodation options, that is, pensiones, to choose from. Apartments sometimes fill this gap admirably, but not always. Independent travel is quite viable in the Canaries, but there can be moments when you wonder if you'll find a room you can afford. Advance booking really does pay off, even if it's not your usual style and even if it's no more than a phonecall on the morning of the same day.

For obvious reasons, the prices for accommodation in this book are intended as a guide only. Always check the current rate before putting your bags down.

Tax Virtually all accommodation prices are subject to IGIC, the Canary Islands' indirect tax, charged at a rate of 5%. This tax is often included in the quoted price at the cheaper places, but less often at the more expensive ones. In some cases you will only be charged the tax if you ask for a receipt.

Camping

Most islands forbid free camping and have just one token official or private camp site. On most islands, including La Gomera and El Hierro, free camping is totally forbidden. On others, it's allowed at certain primitive camp sites, provided that you arm yourself in advance with a permit. The procedure for getting one varies from island to island; you'll find it described in each island chapter. In most cases, it requires an advance telephone call, perhaps supplemented by an exchange of faxes, and then you have to collect the document in person. Some camp sites (for example, on La Palma) are designed specifically for trekkers and your stay may be limited to a single night.

Note that Camping Gaz is the only common brand of camping gas: other kinds of canisters are near impossible to find.

Youth Hostels

The islands' one youth hostel is on Gran Canaria and has little to recommend it. It's not worth becoming a member if you're just travelling in the Canary Islands.

Pensiones, Hostales, Hotels & Paradores

Officially, all these establishments are either *hoteles* (one to five stars), *hostales* (one to three stars) or *pensiones* (one or two stars).

Compared with mainland Spain, there are precious few of these around. Since the bulk of the islands' visitors arrive with accommodation booked in advance – usually in villas or self-catering apartments – the demand for more standard hotels is low.

The one-star pensión is at the bottom of the ladder and a double room without bathroom will generally start at around 3000 ptas. Often no discount is made for single occupancy. These places are usually adequate, although some are more rundown than others.

The second star usually means there is at least a wash basin in the room and these days most pensiones fall into this category. Hostales are often little different from pensiones. Occasionally pensiones come with different names, for example, *Casa de*

Huéspedes (guest house). In effect they are all the same thing.

Hotels range from simple places, where a single/double room could cost around 4000/6000 ptas, up to wildly luxurious, five-star establishments where your imagination is often the limit on the price you pay. Even the cheapest ones may have a restaurant and most rooms will have a bathroom attached.

The *paradores* (officially *paradores de turismo*), a Spanish state-run chain of high-class hotels with six establishments in the Canary Islands, are in a special category. These can be wonderful places to splurge. They also offer a range of discounts, for example, for senior citizens, under-30s and for staying more than one night. You can find out the current offers via the Web site (www.parador.es) or by contacting their central reservation service, the Central de Reservas (☎ 91 516 66 66, fax 91 516 66 57, @ info@parador.es), Calle Requena 3, 28013 Madrid.

Apartments

Apartments for rent are much more common than hotels. To give a random idea of just how much more common they are, the tourist office on La Gomera has an accommodation list for the island that counts 26 hotels, hostales and pensiones, compared with 169 sets of apartments, ranging from a pair on one floor of someone's house to substantial blocks. Quality can vary greatly, but they can be more comfortable than a simple pensión and also more economical, especially if there are several of you. They certainly give you more living space and, if you want to, allow you to do your own cooking. The two principal categories are studios *(estudios)*, with one bedroom or living room and bedroom in common, and the more frequent *apartamento*, where you get a double bedroom and separate lounge. Both have separate bathroom and a kitchenette.

The downside for the independent traveller is that, particularly in the main resorts of Tenerife, Gran Canaria, Lanzarote and Fuerteventura, many apartment complexes are completely in thrall to the all-powerful tour operators. Obeying the terms of their contract, they can't rent you a room, even if it's empty, since the dog-in-a-manger tour company has snapped up every last one for the season. Even those apartment complexes that do rent to independent travellers may insist upon a minimum stay of three nights to make it worth their while changing the sheets.

In the case of many of the smaller ones, the owner doesn't live in or even near the building so there's no point in just turning up – you need to call. This is particularly the case in the three westernmost islands where small operators predominate. As a rule, the contact phone numbers will be posted at the entrance.

For solo travellers, an apartment usually works out more expensive than a simple room in a pensión.

Apartments are officially categorised as one to three keys. At the bottom of the scale they can cost as little as 3500 ptas or 4000 ptas for a double. At the top you're looking at anything up to 16,000 ptas.

If you arrive somewhere and money is limited, you have no luck finding a pensión and you don't see any of the usual signs for *apartamentos de alquiler* (apartments for rent – this applies above all to the western three islands), keep an eye peeled for the official white-on-red AT sign, which also denotes apartments.

You should get hold of each island's hotel/apartment guide from the main tourist offices as soon as you can after arrival, because of the peculiar difficulties sometimes associated with apartments, and the need in most cases for a phone number. They are often far from complete, the majority giving simply contact details with no indication of price or 'key rating', but at least they give you some information to work with. You can get provincial lists (which do not include the bottom-end, one-star options) at the main offices in Santa Cruz de Tenerife and Las Palmas de Gran Canaria.

Packages The overwhelming majority of people who end up in the apartments are package tourists who book their accommodation with flights at home. The problem here is that you can never really know what you are going to get. Make sure you scan the tour company's brochure carefully before committing yourself. What services does the apartment you have been offered have? Is there a pool? A bar? Children's facilities? Is the beach within walking distance if you've a couple of toddlers in tow?

Casas Rurales
Converted farmsteads or village houses sometimes form the only accommodation option in out-of-the-way places. They are often a highly agreeable option for those seeking to escape the noise and bustle of the resorts by heading into the countryside. It's essential to call ahead as they usually offer limited places and there may be no one in attendance. Many are distant from public transport so check whether a hired car is necessary or desirable. With prices starting at around 6000 ptas for a double and single occupancy rarely attracting a reduction, they don't come all that cheap but they do usually represent excellent value. Each island has its own organisation or you can reserve centrally through Acantur (☎ 922 80 12 48, ⓔ acantur@canary-islands.com), the Asociación Canaria de Turismo Rural. To get an idea of the kind of properties available, visit their Web site at www.canary-islands.com.

Timeshare
It is estimated that as many as three million people around the world buy their slice of holiday pleasure in advance this way. Timeshare involves purchasing a block of time in an apartment or resort that you elect to use regularly for your holidays. Of course, nothing is to stop you lending or renting out your booked time to third parties if, for whatever reason, you decide not to use your annual allocation.

You may well come across timeshare touts if you hang around the main resorts in the Canary Islands. If you like the islands enough to want to return repeatedly for your holidays, timeshare may be worth considering – but you should be careful about how and what you choose. You want to be sure that the place you choose has the amenities you want. You need to have all your rights and obligations in writing, especially where management companies promise to sell your timeshare for you if you decide to buy a new one. Remember that you are not buying property, but time in a property for your future holidays.

The cost variables are many. The type of accommodation (from a cottage through to a luxury resort apartment), its location and the season in which you want the time (high season will cost you more) will all affect the cost.

Find a reputable manager when buying a timeshare. In Europe, your first stop should be your country's member of the European Timeshare Federation. In the UK, the Timeshare Council (☎ 020-7821 8845), 23 Buckingham Gate, London SW1E 6LB, is a founding member of the federation and can advise on timeshare purchases and managers. When you sign a timeshare deal, be sure you are granted a 'cooling off' period. This allows you to back out if you decide it's not such a hot idea. There is an EU-wide directive making such a period compulsory in all timeshare contracts.

FOOD

The cuisine of the Canary Islands reflects a wide range of influences, from Spanish regional to global fast food. Travellers can, if they wish, stick to the resorts and eat English breakfasts, fish and chips and imitation pizzas, all washed down with your favourite northern European lager. But that would be a shame. The Canaries are not a seaside outpost of northern Europe but a fascinating archipelago whose culinary delights are too often overlooked for the easy, known options. If you have an even slightly adventurous approach to your travel, let your taste buds experiment too!

Meal Times

First adjustment – locals eat at times of day when most of us wouldn't dream of it! Breakfast *(desayuno)* is about the only meal of the day which takes place about the same time for everyone – that is, when you get up!

The serious eating starts with lunch *(la comida* or, less commonly, *el almuerzo)*: the famous siesta time, the mid-afternoon, is actually reserved by many locals for this, the main meal of the day. While Canarios tend to eat at home with the family, there is plenty of action in the restaurants too, starting at about 2 pm and continuing until 4 pm.

This late start sets the tone for the evening procedures too. If you turn up for dinner at 6 or 7 pm, you'll be eating alone – if the restaurant is even open. Of course, in the most heavily touristed areas the restaurants *will* be open to cater for the strange habits of foreigners, but you'll be unlikely to see a single Canario dining in them. Dinner *(cena)* is often a lighter meal for your average Canario, although this is not to say that they eschew restaurant outings. In any event, dinner begins, at the earliest, about 9 pm. The bulk of locals wouldn't seriously consider wandering into their favourite eating house until 10 pm. As with lunch, the evening meal can easily last two or three hours – a leisurely and highly social affair.

But don't imagine that you can't eat in the Canaries outside these hours. Snacks are an important part of the Spanish culinary heritage, particularly the bar snacks known as *tapas* (see Snacks later in this section). You can usually pick up a quick bite to eat to tide you over until the main meal times swing around.

Where to Eat

Cafes & Bars Hanging around in bars and cafes, or simply dropping by for a quick caffeine or alcohol injection, is an integral part of life in the Canaries. The distinction between cafes and bars is negligible; coffee and alcohol are almost always available in both. Bars take several different forms, including *cervecerías* (beer bars, a vague equivalent of the pub, although some bars take on the name 'pub' too, as seems to happen right across Western Europe). In *tabernas* (taverns) and *bodegas* (old-style wine bars) you can sometimes get a decent meal too.

Sometimes, you'll get a tapa with your alcoholic drink. Sadly, the days of free tapas are over and more and more often you have to pay. Standing at the bar rather than sitting down can often save you 10% to 20% of the bill, especially where the tables are outside on a picturesque terrace or in a posh attached dining room.

Restaurants These generally open for lunch and dinner (see Meal Times earlier), unless they have a bar attached, in which case they may be open right through the day. Most *restaurantes* close one day per week and advertise this fact with a sign in the window. It is common practice to display a menu *(carta)*, usually with prices, out the front. Any taxes and service charges should also be advertised, but quite often they are not. The scruffier places may not display any prices at all.

Variations on the theme include the *mesón* (traditionally a place for simple home cooking, although this is often no longer the case), *comedor* (literally a dining room, usually attached to a bar or hotel), *venta* (roadside inn) and *marisquería* (seafood specialist).

Staples

Nowadays, a good range of typical Spanish food is widely available in the islands, partly to satisfy the *godos* (Spaniards) who live here, partly to widen the choice on offer for locals and interlopers alike.

The basis of the local cuisine is, however, rather narrow, traditionally restricted to what the islands produced for themselves.

The staple product par excellence is *gofio*, a uniquely Canario product. A roasted mixture of wheat, maize or barley, gofio takes the place of bread in the average Canario's diet. There is no shortage of bread *(pan)* these days, but gofio remains common. It is something of an acquired taste and, mixed in varying proportions, is used as a breakfast food or combined with almonds and figs to make sweets. The Spanish author Antonio Muñoz Molina recalled

in *Ardor Guerrero*, his recollections of conscript days in the Basque city of San Sebastián in northern Spain in the 1980s:

Pepe Rifón had organised a kind of Leninist cell, a clandestine commune to which we all contributed what we could and where everything was shared, whether drugs or food packets sent by our families. The only thing we never managed to share was gofio, that passion of our chums from the Canaries...who at our little food fests, when they had just received some package from their islands, would tear open the packets of gofio and shove fistfuls of the stuff into their mouths with the greed of exiles who, for the first time in years, savour a long lost flavour. 'You mainlanders are the dopes not liking gofio,' they'd say. 'It's God's own food'.

Other basic foods long common across the islands are bananas and tomatoes, but nowadays the markets are filled with a wide range of fruit and vegetables. Beef, pork and lamb are widely available (usually imported) but the traditional goat *(cabra)* and kid *(cabrito)* remain the staple animal protein. Most local cheeses come from goat milk too.

The Canary Islands owe a lot to Columbus; it was from South America that elementary items such as potatoes, tomatoes and corn were introduced. From there also came more exotic delights such as avocados and papayas while from Asia first arrived the sweetest mangoes you've ever tasted. Look out for all three in the valleys and on supermarket shelves.

Canary Islands' Specialities

Away from the standard Spanish fare, and the many bland, tourist-oriented international-style restaurants in the resorts, there is a genuine local cuisine.

The most obvious Canarian contribution to the dinner table is the *mojo*. This sauce has many variants and is used to dip pretty much anything in – from chicken legs to gofio. See the boxed text 'Mojo Rising'.

Papas arrugadas (wrinkly potatoes) are perhaps the next best-known dish, although there is really not much to them. They're

Mojo Rising

Lying at the crossroads of the trade routes between imperial Spain and her vast possessions in Latin America, the Canary Islands were opened up to influences not only from the 'mother country' but also from the developing colonies in Latin America. Explorers and traders brought a wealth of new vegetables, fruit and herbs from the new territories to Spain, dropping samples off in the Canaries along the way. Among them was the humble green pepper (capsicum or *pimiento*) and various kinds of chilli peppers, or *guindillas*.

Just where the original *mojo picón* came from, nobody can tell you. It is a spicy sauce made with red chilli peppers and used as a dip for a huge variety of foods – from *papas arrugadas* (wrinkly potatoes) to chicken wings. There are at least 20 variants on this saucy theme, and good chefs often try to put their own particular spin on it.

Preparing your own mojo is not particularly difficult. For the standard *mojo picón*, try the following recipe:

Ingredients
Half a cup of olive oil
Water
Eight small cloves of garlic, peeled
Quarter cup of wine vinegar
Four small, fresh red chilli peppers
    (more if you can take the heat)
Two ripe tomatoes
Half a teaspoon of cumin
One to two teaspoons of salt
Half a teaspoon of paprika

Method
Pour all the olive oil into a blender and add the paprika, cumin, vinegar, garlic and salt. Boil the chilli peppers in half a cup of water for about 15 minutes, then add to the mixture in the blender. Put the tomatoes on a skewer and lightly roast them over a low flame until the skin is dry. Remove the skin, slice up the tomatoes and put them into the blender. Blend until you are left with a thick, smooth sauce.

You can vary the ingredients quite a lot, for example by adjusting the number of chilli peppers you include. Some people like to add a dash of pepper and even oregano to the mix. If you find what you have made too hot, add more olive oil and vinegar to dilute it.

If you don't like your sauces so hot, you could try the *mojo verde*. This is especially tasty with fish, and is sometimes served up with cheese as a starter. It's a milder version in which you replace the red hot chilli with parsley and *cilantro* (coriander) or green pepper.

Mojo de cilantro is particularly popular on Tenerife owing, it is said, to the one-time presence of a coriander-loving Portuguese community. The trick with this mojo is to finely crush the fresh coriander shortly before the mojo is eaten, because after a while the cilantro oxidises.

Another variant, *mojo colorado*, leans more heavily on the tomatoes and less on the chillies than the *mojo picón* and adds a bit of zing to just about anything.

small new potatoes boiled and salted in their skin and only come to life when dipped in one of the mojos. Potatoes were introduced to the islands from Peru in the 1600s, and connoisseurs identify at least 23 varieties.

euro currency converter €1 = 166 ptas

Of the many soups you'll find, one typically Canarian variant is *potaje de berros*, or watercress soup. Another is *rancho canario*, a kind of broth with thick noodles and the odd chunk of meat and potato – it's very hearty.

Conejo en salmorejo is rabbit in a marinade made of water, vinegar, olive oil, salt and pepper, sweet black pudding and avocado. Although now considered a pillar of local cuisine, the dish's origins lie in distant Aragón.

Sancocho canario is a salted-fish dish with mojo. On La Gomera you might get a chance to tuck into *buche gomero*, basically salted tuna-stomach – it tastes a lot better than it sounds!

Almogrote, a starter from La Gomera, is a goat-cheese spread, flavoured with garlic, chilli pepper and salt.

If you take the time to circulate around the islands, you'll find many variants on standard dishes and quite a few local specialities. Experiment and enjoy!

Breakfast

For those of us unaccustomed to continental practices, breakfast is a flimsy affair, usually involving no more than white coffee and a pastry taken at a bar. If you prefer, you can beef it up a little by ordering some orange juice *(zumo de naranja)* and perhaps a *tostada*, a slice of toast with jam or some such.

Locals would never do it, but you can order eggs in one form or another if you need to, especially in the more touristy areas where Canarios are quite unsurprised by foreign tastes. You can have your *huevos* (eggs) fried *(fritos)*, scrambled *(revueltos* – definitely not normal breakfast fare for locals) or hard-boiled *(cocidos)*. Some people have *churros con chocolate* – a kind of deep-fried finger-shaped doughnut dipped in thick dark chocolate – to start the day.

Snacks

Bar snacks, or tapas, are a well established mainland importation. They range from a tiny saucer with an olive or two and a thin slice of cheese through to quite substantial and delicious mouthfuls of anything from chips to seafood. These are provided at most bars as an accompaniment to your beer or wine. The idea is to stimulate your thirst, and it generally works. There was a time when they came free. Quite often now there is a small charge, and more and more you actually have to ask the barman for the tapa. Generally they are on display – the barman will usually choose whatever he feels like and present you with it, unless you make a specific request.

A larger version of the tapa is the *ración*. You always pay for this and three or four raciones makes a pretty decent meal. But you could even survive a night on beer or wine and tapas, either propping up the one bar or doing the rounds – a popular and highly agreeable pastime. It's much more fun than a sit-down set menu, but if you count your small change at the end of the night you'll almost certainly conclude that it's cost more.

The other standard snack (or *merienda*) is the *bocadillo*, or long bread stick. Typically this will be a rather dry affair with a slice of ham *(jamón)* and/or cheese *(queso)*, or a wedge of *tortilla española* (potato omelette).

All over the islands you'll notice little eateries known as *areperas*. This is where you can order yourself an *arepa*, basically a lightly deep-fried crispy pocket of cornmeal dough with a potatoey flavour and stuffed with chicken, cheese, ham, or whatever you want. It's a Venezuelan import and makes a really filling snack, usually costing 200 ptas to 300 ptas.

Main Meals

The traveller's friend in the Canary Islands, as in mainland Spain, is the *menú del día*, a set meal available at most restaurants for lunch, and occasionally in the evening too. Generally you get a starter or side dish, a main dish, a simple dessert and a drink, all for a modest price – which hovers around the 900 ptas mark at budget establishments and can rise to over 2000 ptas at posh places.

Canarian cuisine is good and reasonably varied without being overly imaginative. Although much of it heavily reflects mainland Spanish tastes, particularly from the south, Latin American influences are also evident. The Muslim heritage in sweets and the use of certain spices such as cumin and saffron are a reminder of the centuries of Arab control of southern Spain (right up until the time of the conquest of the islands).

As a result, you'll see plenty of classic mainland Spanish dishes, including *paella* (saffron rice cooked with chicken and rabbit or with seafood – at its best with good seafood), *tortilla* (omelette), *gazpacho* (a cold, tomato-based soup usually available in summer only), various *sopas* (soups) and *pinchos morunos* (kebabs).

Main meals will generally consist of some form of *carne* (meat), including *ternera* (beef or veal), *cerdo* (pork), *cochinillo* (suckling pig), *cordero* (lamb), *pollo* (chicken), *cabrito* (kid meat) and *conejo* (rabbit), often accompanied by *papas fritas* (chips). Your meat may be done *a la parrilla* (grilled), *asado* (roasted) or come in an *estofado* or *puchero* (stew). Chops *(chuletas)* are popular, and if you are buying your own meat, it's known as *carne picada* when minced (ground).

Otherwise you will have the choice of many kinds of *pescado* (fish) or *mariscos* (seafood).

Your main dish can be preceded by *entremeses*, or starters of various kinds. *Ensaladas* (salads) commonly figure as either starters or side dishes.

Desserts & Sweets

On an ordinary day in a no-nonsense eatery, you may find your dessert options *(postres)* limited to timeless Spanish favourites such as *flan* (crème caramel), *helado* (ice cream) or a piece of fruit.

But the Canarios do have a sweet tooth. And if you are disappointed after your meal, the best thing you can do is head for the local *pastelería* (cake shop) and indulge yourself.

Some of the better known sticky sweets are *bienmesabes* (a kind of thick sticky goo made of almonds and honey – deadly sweet!), *frangollos*, *tirijalas*, *bizcochos lustrados* and *turrón de melaza* (molasses nougat).

La Palma's honey-and-sugar *rapaduras* are a favourite tooth-rotter, and you shouldn't miss the *quesadillas* of/from El Hierro – they've been making this cheesy cinnamon pastry (sometimes also made with aniseed) since the Middle Ages. *Morcillas dulces* (sweet blood sausages), made with grapes, raisins and almonds, are a rather odd concoction; perhaps the closest comparison is the Christmas mince pie consumed with such relish in the UK.

Cheese

Goat cheese is produced across several of the islands, but the best known cheese is probably the *queso de flor*. This is made of a mix of cow's and sheep's milk, which is infused with the aroma of flowers from a type of thistle (the *cardo alcausi*). It is produced exclusively in the Guía area of northern Gran Canaria. Another prize-winning cow-sheep cheese mix is the *pastor*, from around Arucas.

Of the goat cheeses, Fuerteventura's *majorero* – a slightly acidic creamy cheese, is probably the most highly sought after.

The smoked cheese of El Hierro, *queso herreño*, is also much prized – and outside the island costs considerably more than at home.

Vegetarians

The Canary Islands may seem like paradise to some, but they can be more like purgatory for vegetarians, and worse still for vegans. This is meat-eating country, so you will find your choices (unless you cater for yourself) a little limited. Salads are OK, and you will come across various side dishes such as *champiñones* (mushrooms, usually lightly fried in olive oil and garlic). Other possibilities include *berenjenas* (aubergines), *menestra* (a hearty vegetable stew), *espárragos* (asparagus) *lentejas* (lentils) and other vegetables that are sometimes cooked as side dishes. You might be lucky enough to come across a vegetarian restaurant in one of the bigger tourist centres.

DRINKS
Nonalcoholic Drinks

Coffee The Canary Islanders like coffee strong and slightly bitter. Addicts should specify how they want their fix. A *café con leche* is about 50% coffee, 50% hot milk; ask for *grande* or *doble* if you want a large cup (usually a breakfast request), *en vaso* if you want a smaller shot in a glass, or *sombra* if you want lots of milk. A *café solo* is an espresso (short black); *café cortado* (or just *cortado*) is an espresso with a splash of milk (in the islands of Tenerife province it's best to specify *cortado natural* or you'll probably get the default version, *cortado de condensado* – for which, read on....). If you like your coffee piping hot, ask for any of the above to be *caliente*. A café solo or cortado can cost as little as 75 ptas.

There are some local variations on the theme. *Cortado de condensado* is an espresso with condensed milk; *cortado de leche y leche* is the same with a little standard milk thrown in. It sometimes comes in a larger cup and is then called a *barraquito*. You can also have your barraquito *con licor* or *con alcohol*, a shot of liquor usually accompanied by a shred of lemon and sometimes some cinnamon – this is the authentic barraquito, as any Canario will let you know. A good barraquito costs around 200 ptas. Strangely, these options are all but unknown in the province of Las Palmas, while in the western islands they are coming out of your ears. In the easternmost islands you will be asked if you want your milk *condensada* or *líquida*.

For iced coffee, ask for *café con hielo*: you'll get a glass of ice and a hot cup of coffee, to be poured over the ice – which, surprisingly, doesn't all melt straight away!

Tea While coffee is generally preferred, tea is served in most cafes and bars. What you normally get is a cup with a tea bag so you can make it swamp-water strong or weak as gnat's urine. Locals drink it black. If you want milk, ask for it to be separate; otherwise, you'll end up with a cup of milky water with a tea bag floating dismally in it. Most places also offer camomile *(manzanilla)* and mint *(poleo)* infusions, also served in sachets.

Chocolate Spaniards brought chocolate back from the New World and adopted it enthusiastically. At one time it was even a form of currency. The Spanish serve it thick; sometimes it even appears on the dessert section of menus. Generally it's a breakfast drink consumed with *churros*; see Food earlier.

Soft Drinks *Refrescos* (soft drinks) include the usual international brands of soft drinks, local brands such as Kas, and more expensive *granizado* (iced fruit crush).

Clear, cold water from a public fountain or tap is a Spanish favourite – but check that it's *potable*.

The tapwater *(agua del grifo)* won't do you any harm; it just tastes a little unpleasant and makes vile tea. Exceptions are what flows from the cold tap on El Hierro and La Palma, where the water's as sweet as any you've had. Elsewhere, most people go for bottled water from island springs such as Fuente Alta, Fonteide and Pinalito on Tenerife or Firgas, Toscal and Breñalta on Gran Canaria. Water's water and local brands work out cheaper than H_2O imported at cost from the mainland. Bottled water *(agua mineral)* comes in several brands, either fizzy *(con gas)* or still *(sin gas)*. A 1.5L bottle of agua mineral sin gas can cost 75 ptas in a supermarket whereas out and about you may be charged as much as 175 ptas.

A *batido* is a flavoured milk drink or milk shake; the bottled variety is usually oversugared and sickly.

Fruit Juices These are popular with Canarios and you'll find at least one *zumería* (juice bar) in even quite small settlements. Not just boring old *zumo de naranja* (orange juice) but more exotic squeezings such as papaya, mango, pineapple and avocado. At around 300 ptas for a pint pot, they're excellent value. One thing you'll notice in many bars in the bigger centres are the loads of fruit piled up, just waiting to be converted into liquid.

Alcoholic Drinks

Wine Spain is a great wine-drinking and producing country, and plenty of wine is consumed in the Canary Islands. The local wine-making industry is relatively modest, but you can come across the occasional good drop.

Vino comes in white *(blanco)*, red *(tinto)* or rosé *(rosado)*. Prices vary considerably. In general, you get what you pay for and can pick up a really good tipple for under 700 ptas. If it's kick not quality you're after, a bottle of basic plonk (especially if you buy it at a supermarket) need cost no more than 250 ptas. In restaurants, if you are not too particular about brands, you can simply order the house wine *(vino de la casa)*, the cheapest option, which varies from very drinkable to one up on vinegar, depending upon the restaurant.

One of the most common wines across the islands is the *malvasía* (malmsey wine, also produced in Madeira). It is generally sweet *(dulce)*, although you can find the odd dry *(seco)* version. It is particularly common on La Palma.

Tenerife is the principal source of wine, and the red Tacoronte Acentejo was the first Canarian wine to earn the grade of DO *(denominación de orígen)*. This term is one of many employed to regulate and judge wine and grape quality, and is one down from the coveted DOC label *(denominación de orígen calificada)*. Other productive vineyards are in the Icod and Güímar areas of Tenerife. In Lanzarote, the vine has come back into vogue since the early 1980s, and in late 1993 the island's malvasías were awarded a DO. Wine is produced on the other islands too, but the quality is generally not as good.

Beer The most common way to order a beer *(cerveza)* is to ask for a *caña*, which is a small draught beer *(cerveza de barril* or *cerveza de presión)*. A pint-sized version is called a *jarra*. If you just ask for a cerveza you may get bottled beer, usually called a *botellín*, which is more expensive than the draught stuff.

La Dorada, brewed in Santa Cruz de Tenerife, is a very smooth number. Available in cans and on draught, it's as good as – if not superior to – any beer imported from the mainland. Tropical, produced on Gran Canaria and a little lighter, is a worthy runner-up and the preferred tipple of the eastern isles. Volcan beer, made from gofio by the La Dorada company, is a new product. Another recent innovation from a smaller brewery on Tenerife is Rubia. Neither, to our chagrin, were yet in the shops when we completed our research, so feedback (is that *really* the word we're looking for?!) would be welcome.

Even in out of the way places you'll usually have the choice of at least one bottled import from the mainland, such as San Miguel or Heineken.

A *clara* is a shandy, a beer with a dash of lemonade.

Other Alcoholic Drinks Apart from the mainland Spanish imports, which include the grape-based *aguardiente* (similar to schnapps or grappa), brandy *(coñac)* and a whole host of other *licores* (liqueurs), you could try some local fire water.

Although the sugar plantations have all but gone, what remains is put to good use in the production of rum *(ron)*. Ron Aldea of La Palma is considered the best. *Ron miel*, or honey rum, is more liqueur than rum, but interesting enough to taste. Quite a few liqueurs are produced in the islands, including the banana-based *cobana*. Both this and honey rum are produced mainly on Gran Canaria. Another one is *mistela* from La Gomera, a mixture of wine, sugar, rum and sometimes honey – a potent taste!

Sangría, a wine and fruit punch usually laced with spirits, is a recipe imported from the mainland. It's refreshing going down but can leave you with a sore head. *Tinto de verano* is a mix of wine and Casera, a brand of lemonade, or sweet, bubbly water.

The Canaries' Weird World of Sports

Lucha Canaria The Guanches of Tenerife were a particularly robust and warlike crowd, who loved a trial of strength. Any island party was an excuse for indulging in tests of manhood. Apart from jumping over steep ravines and diving into the ocean from dizzying heights, one favourite pastime was wrestling. Rooted in this ancient diversion lies the essence of the modern *lucha canaria*, Canarian wrestling.

You won't find any bull fighting in the Canary Islands, but outdoor sand rings *(terreros)*, very similar to those of a bull ring, still find their use for a little contact sport. Often, however, such rings are in modern buildings known as *luchaderos*. Lucha Canaria is practised throughout the islands. Teams of up to 12 face off for an afternoon of a kind of tag-team wrestling match – something very different from the silly histrionic antics of so-called 'professional wrestling' in TV spectacles such as World Championship Wrestling.

One member of each team faces off his adversary in the ring and, after a formal greeting and other signs of goodwill, they set about trying to dump each other into the dust. The idea is that no part of the body except the soles of the feet may touch the ground, and whoever fails first in this department loses. Each pair fight it out in a best of three competition (each clash is known as a *brega*), and the team with the most winning wrestlers wins the whole show.

There is more skill to this than is perhaps at first apparent. Size and weight are not the determining factors (although these boys tend to be as beefy as rugby front-row forwards), but

JANE SMITH

ENTERTAINMENT
Outside the main cities on Tenerife and Gran Canaria, and the discos and folklore shows put on for tourists in the main resorts, there is generally not an awful lot in the line of entertainment.

Listings
Very few tourist offices, even in the major resorts, produce a 'What's On' brochure, though they will be able to inform you about major upcoming events. On the larger islands, check out the English-language press such as *Here & Now* and *Tenerife News* on Tenerife and Lanzarote's *Gazette*

News and *Island Connections*, which covers the larger islands. In local papers, check under the heading *Cartelera* for entertainment listings.

Bars & Discos
Some holiday-makers come to the Canaries to do little more than party and then sleep off the results on the beach. But the outsiders are not the only ones: late nightlife is in the local blood.

Thursday to Saturday nights are always the wildest, and once you have found the part of town or your resort where all the bars are clustered (as tends to be the case)

The Canaries' Weird World of Sports

rather the skill with which the combatants grapple and manoeuvre their opponents into a position from which they can be toppled. This is not a violent sport, and kicking, punching, pinching and so on are not permitted. Historically, the lucha was staged for fiestas and also often as a means of resolving disputes.

The Canarios, or at least some of them, take this all rather seriously, and there is a major league competition known as the Copa Presidente del Gobierno Canarias. Clashes at this level are often televised.

If you want to find out if any matches are due to be held locally, ask at the nearest tourist office.

Stick Fighting The *juego del palo* (literally, stick game) started off in preconquest days as anything but a game. Two combatants would arm themselves with heavy staves and stones, and attempt to break as many bones in their opponents' bodies as possible. After the arrival of the Spaniards, the 'game' became increasingly marginalised to rural areas and became more a trial of skill than a violent blood sport.

The sport, if it can be called such, is still practised throughout the islands, and there is even a federation devoted to it. The staff is of sturdy wood and about 2m long. The stick goes by various names, *banot* in Tenerife and *lata* in Fuerteventura. You are most likely to see a demonstration of the juego del palo at local fiestas.

A related sport involving poles is the *lucha al garrote*, where opponents wield even longer staves.

Vela Latina Canaria Since the end of the 19th century, the diminutive sail-cum-row boats, which once functioned as ferries between the great ocean-going vessels and the docks of Las Palmas' port, have been sailed in a form of regatta unique to the Canary Islands. For more on this see the boxed text 'Plain Sailing' in the Gran Canaria chapter.

Cockfighting Canarios may not be avid bullfighting fans but cockfighting still has its aficionados. However, the sight of angry feathered roosters armed with spurs attempting to slice each other to shreds is an acquired taste. As with bullfighting, its supporters will beg to differ, taking pride in their birds and assuring you that this is what they are bred to do and that it's what they *like*. You'll need to be in the know to get to see this, and may not want to anyway.

you won't need to move far to keep busy bar-hopping all night. Many locals don't think of going out until about midnight, although there is nothing to stop you making an earlier start.

Bars, which come in all shapes, sizes and themes, are the main attractions until around 2 or 3 am, after which you can move to the discos until 5 or 6 am – or later! Discos can be expensive, and some won't let you in wearing jeans or trainers.

All this is true of the main urban centres and resorts. In farther flung corners of the islands the tempo is very much slower, although you should be able to find the occasional bar open until about 2 am and perhaps even the odd disco or nightclub. La Palma, La Gomera and El Hierro are all fairly quiet.

In even less frenetic mode, one of the great pleasures of Canaries life, day or night, is simply sitting in a roadside *terraza* (open-air cafe terrace) and savouring a long, drawn-out coffee or something stronger.

Live Rock, Pop & Jazz

Live music is alive and kicking in the islands, although the quality at times leaves something to be desired. There are some fun local bands around, and occasionally good mainland and international acts come to town. Look out for music festivals.

Classical Music, Dance & Theatre
For the culturally inclined, the cities and some of the bigger towns are the places to look for classical music, dance and theatre. They often come in the form of festivals. Theatre is almost always in Spanish.

Flamenco
Touristy performances of flamenco can be seen in some of the resorts. However, although some aspects of flamenco migrated to the islands from southern Spain, this is not its natural context; the performance you are likely to see, unless it happens to be by a visiting troupe from Andalucía, will be something of a travesty and low on authenticity.

Cinema
You will be very lucky to find any foreign films that have not been dubbed into Spanish. Cinemas are concentrated in Las Palmas de Gran Canaria and Santa Cruz de Tenerife. Otherwise a few are scattered across secondary towns on the main islands, as well as in Santa Cruz de la Palma. On average, going to the flicks costs 750 ptas, unless you pick the cinema's chosen cheap day, or *día del espectador* (usually Wednesday), when it will cost about 450 ptas.

SPECTATOR SPORT
See the boxed text 'The Canaries' Weird World of Sports' on the previous page for more details.

Football
Across Spain *fútbol* is a national preoccupation and this is as much the case in the Canaries as elsewhere. And just as the Canary Islands are part of yet separate from Spain, so their two major football sides, which yo-yo between the national first and second divisions, almost need a league unto themselves! At the time of writing, UD (Union Deportiva) de Las Palmas from

Gran Canaria was sitting nicely in the middle of the Primera División while Tenerife (arch rivals on the football pitch as in every other field) was struggling in the Segunda División A, the next rung down. To see one of them play at home, get tickets at least a week in advance at the stadium's *taquillas* (box offices). Prices start at 2500 ptas.

Volleyball
This is a popular beachside game across the resorts of the Canary Islands, and it can sometimes get a little more serious. With an ideal climate, the islands often host competitions of world-championship level, which can attract thousands of spectators. Ask the nearest tourist office if any major competitions are due to be held during your stay.

SHOPPING
Shopping for consumer goods in the Canaries has one special attraction: it is virtually tax free (the local indirect tax, the IGIC, is a measly 5% compared with VAT of 16% and more throughout the rest of the EU).

On the larger islands, watches, perfumes, tobacco, alcohol, electronics and so on are the first items that you should investigate, but even things such as jeans can be a good buy. Levis can cost around 7000 ptas in the Canaries, more than in the USA but better than the prices in London stores. Whatever you're after, shop around and try a little bargaining; competition among the mainly Indian traders is keen and there's no such thing as a fixed price. Don't postpone buying goods until you reach the airport on your return journey or you are on the flight back home. You will almost certainly find the same items for less in normal stores in town.

Centros comerciales, or shopping centres, are very much a Canaries phenomenon that you won't find on the Spanish mainland. They're not the giant out-of-town megastores surrounded by bleak car parks that you may be used to visiting at home. Here, they're usually a medium-sized grouping of retail shops, bars and restaurants on two or three floors. There are exceptions of course – such as the truly jumbo

Yumbo Centrum in Playa del Inglés or the Centro Comercial Las Arenas, just outside Las Palmas, both on Gran Canaria.

Prestigious Spanish department stores, such as Corte Inglés and Cortefiel, have got branches in the main centres of the Canary Islands.

If you're on Gran Canaria, it's worth looking round government-sponsored, non-profit making Fedac (Fundación para la Etnografía y el Desarollo de la Artesanía Canaria) for traditional handicrafts. With displays and outlets in Las Palmas and Playa del Inglés, its shops are a good starting point for traditional handicrafts such as pottery, baskets and leatherwork.

You'll find several public-sector *centros de artesanía*, or handicrafts centres, around La Palma, displaying and selling local ware.

Flea Markets
Some of the bigger towns have a weekly flea market, or *rastro*. A lot of the stuff on sale is pure junk, but occasionally you can find some interesting odds and ends.

Village Markets
Much more interesting, if you happen to catch them, are the village markets where local produce and uninspiring international tat sit side by side. Normally held at weekends, they're a joy to browse. Check out, for example, San Bartolomé de Tirajana, Puerto de Mogán and San Mateo on Gran Canaria or the lively weekend market in tiny Mazo on La Palma.

Basketware
Baskets and other similar objects, known as *cestería* (basketwork), fashioned of palm leaves, reeds, wicker and even banana leaves are popular (though not particularly sturdy) items.

On La Gomera, in particular, this is something of an art form. You'll also find such products on La Palma. The Lanzaroteños concentrate more on the straw version.

Ceramics
Before the arrival of the Europeans, the Guanches were at their most artistically

expressive in their pottery *(alfarería)*. Sadly, most of the contemporary pottery thrown on the island is little more than anachronistic reproductions of these fairly lumpy, leaden designs; there's little sign of the innovative flare that you'll find on the Spanish mainland. If you fancy a Guanche reproduction on your mantelpiece, call by the village of Chipude on La Gomera or the folk museum in the unassuming hamlet of Arguayo on Tenerife.

Embroidery, Lace & Silk
A very few women in certain parts of the islands, such as El Hierro, still make their own thread-and-weave bedspreads, rugs and bags on primitive wooden looms. Embroidered table cloths and napkins also make convenient and tasteful souvenirs. Embroidery is one of the most widely available quality handicrafts in the Canary Islands, and only in La Gomera is there little or nothing to speak of.

Ingenio (Gran Canaria) is famous for its embroidery, and Vilaflor (Tenerife) is known for its high-quality lace. For silk, keep your eyes peeled on the island of La Palma.

Musical Instruments
If you have a hankering for a timple (the islands' most popular folk instrument, akin to a ukelele) – even in reduced size for display only, Telde (Gran Canaria) – where timples are made – is the place to look.

Liquor, Cigars & Honey
The rum of La Palma is a very fine drop indeed, as are some – but not all – of the strange concoctions made with it. Honey rum which is special to the islands is one of them, along with *mistela* on La Gomera, and nonalcoholic liqueurs made with bananas. All are hard to find outside the islands and can make original gifts. See Drinks earlier in the chapter for more details.

Cigar smokers should stock up on the cigars made in La Palma which, say the cognoscenti, rival the more expensive and more renowned Cuban versions.

Honey, some of it made not by bees but with palm sap, is another product you are likely to come across in the western islands and Gran Canaria.

Woodwork

The Canary Islands' pine, chestnut, mulberry and beech trees are all sources of timber for the carving of various household implements ranging from ladles, spoons and bowls to a kind of giant tweezers used for picking prickly pears.

The local version of castanets, known as *chácaras*, make a nice souvenir item.

Getting There & Away

With an agreeable climate year round, the Canary Islands are an especially popular holiday destination with Europeans, particularly those coming from the wintry northern reaches. As a result, there are plenty of air links between many European cities and the islands. By contrast, there's precisely one sea link – the weekly boat from Cádiz on the Spanish mainland.

Despite its proximity, Morocco is a lousy launching pad for flights to the Canaries and direct flights to the rest of Africa are close to nonexistent.

AIR
Airports & Airlines

All seven islands have airports – OK, so La Gomera's only receives three flights daily but it's still an airport for all that! Tenerife, Gran Canaria and Lanzarote absorb nearly all the direct international flights and those from mainland Spain, while the others are principally for inter-island hops.

There are two main airports on Tenerife. Tenerife Norte (Los Rodeos) handles just about all inter-island flights and most of those to the Spanish mainland. The remainder of the scheduled flights and virtually all charter flights to the island are channelled to the more modern Tenerife Sur (Reina Sofia). Gran Canaria's airport, Aeropuerto de Grande, is 16km south of Las Palmas. Lanzarote's Guasimeta airport lies a convenient 6km south-west of the 'capital', Arrecife.

The bulk of international flights serving the islands directly are charters. Remember that for charter flights you are obliged to ring in and check within 72 hours of departure.

From Spain, Air Europa, Iberia and Spanair all fly to the Canary Islands. They connect the islands with international destinations, usually via Madrid or Barcelona.

Buying Tickets

World aviation has never been so competitive, making air travel better value than

ever. But you have to research the options carefully to make sure you get the best deal. The Internet is an increasingly useful resource for checking air fares.

Full-time students and those aged under 26 (under 30 in some countries) have access to better deals than other travellers. You have to show a document proving your date of birth or a valid International Student Identity Card (ISIC) when buying your ticket and boarding the plane.

Generally, there is nothing to be gained by buying a ticket direct from the airline. Discounted tickets are released to selected travel agents and specialist discount agencies, and these are usually the cheapest deals going.

One exception to this rule is the expanding number of 'no-frills' carriers, which normally only sell tickets direct to travellers (usually over the Internet). Unlike the

Air Travel Glossary

Alliances Many of the world's leading airlines are now intimately involved with each other, sharing everything from reservations systems and check-in to aircraft and frequent flyer schemes. Opponents say that alliances restrict competition. Whatever the arguments, there is no doubt that big alliances are the way of the future.

Cancelling or Changing Tickets If you have to cancel or change a ticket, you need to contact the original travel agent who sold you the ticket. Airlines only issue refunds to the purchaser of a ticket – usually the travel agent who bought the ticket on your behalf. There are often heavy penalties involved; insurance can sometimes be taken out against these penalties.

Courier Fares Businesses often need to send urgent documents or freight securely and quickly. Courier companies hire people to accompany the package through customs and, in return, offer a discount ticket which is sometimes a bargain. However, you may have to surrender all your baggage allowance and take only carry-on luggage.

Fares Airlines traditionally offer 1st class (coded F), business class (coded J) and economy class (coded Y) tickets. These days there are so many promotional and discounted fares available that few passengers pay full fare.

Lost Tickets If you lose your airline ticket an airline will usually treat it like a travellers cheque and, after enquiries, issue you with another one. Legally, however, an airline is entitled to treat it like cash and if you lose it then it's gone forever. Take good care of your tickets.

Onward Tickets An entry requirement for many countries is that you have a ticket out of the country. If you're unsure of your next move, the easiest solution is to buy the cheapest onward ticket to a neighbouring country or a ticket from a reliable airline which can later be refunded if you do not use it.

Open-Jaw Tickets These are return tickets where you fly out to one place but return from another. If available, this can save you backtracking to your arrival point.

Overbooking Since every flight has some passengers who fail to show up, airlines often book more passengers than they have seats. Usually excess passengers make up for the no-shows, but occasionally somebody gets 'bumped' onto the next available flight. Guess who it is most likely to be? The passengers who check in late. If you do get 'bumped' you are normally offered some form of compensation.

Reconfirmation Some airlines require you to reconfirm your flight at least 72 hours prior to departure. Check your travel documents to see if this is the case.

Restrictions Discounted tickets often have various restrictions on them – such as needing to be paid for in advance and incurring a penalty if they are altered or cancelled. Others are restrictions on the minimum and maximum period you must be away.

Round-the-World Tickets RTW tickets give you a limited period (usually a year) in which to circumnavigate the globe. You can go anywhere the carrying airlines go, as long as you don't backtrack. The number of stopovers or total number of separate flights is decided before you set off and they usually cost a bit more than a basic return flight.

Ticketless Travel Airlines are gradually waking up to the realisation that paper tickets are unnecessary encumbrances. On simple one-way or return trips, reservations details can be held on computer, and the passenger merely shows ID to claim his or her seat.

Transferred Tickets Airline tickets cannot be transferred from one person to another. Travellers sometimes try to sell the return half of their ticket, but officials can ask you to prove that you are the person named on the ticket. On an international flight tickets are always compared with passports.

'full-service' airlines, no-frills carriers often make one-way tickets available at around half the return fare, so it is easy to put together an open-jaw ticket (see the Air Travel Glossary for details).

The other exception is booking on the Internet. Many airlines offer some excellent fares to Web surfers. They may sell seats by auction or simply cut prices to reflect the reduced cost of electronic selling.

Many travel agencies around the world have Web sites and there is also an increasing number of on-line agents such as www.travelocity.co.uk and www.deckchair.com that operate only on the Internet. On-line ticket sales work well if you are doing a simple one-way or return trip on specified dates and the Internet is a useful tool for comparing fares and routes. However, on-line superfast fare generators are no substitute for a travel agent who knows all about special deals, has strategies for avoiding layovers and can offer advice on everything from which airline has the best vegetarian food to the best travel insurance on offer.

You may find the cheapest flights are advertised by obscure agencies. Most such firms are honest and solvent, but there are some rogue fly-by-night outfits around. Paying by credit card generally offers protection, as most card issuers provide refunds if you can prove you didn't get what you paid for. Similar protection can be obtained by buying a ticket from a bonded agent, such as one covered by the Air Travel Organiser's Licence (ATOL) scheme in the UK – for more details, see ATOL's Web site at www.atol.org.uk. Agents who only accept cash should hand over the tickets straight away and not tell you to 'come back tomorrow'. After you've made a booking or paid your deposit, call the airline and confirm that the booking was made. It's generally not advisable to send money (even cheques) through the post unless the agent is very well established – some travellers have reported being ripped off by fly-by-night mail-order ticket agents.

Many travellers change their routes halfway through their trips, so think carefully before you buy a ticket which is not easily refunded.

Travellers with Specific Needs

If they're warned early enough, airlines can often make special arrangements for travellers, such as wheelchair assistance at airports or vegetarian meals on the flight.

Children under two years travel for 10% of the standard fare (or free on some airlines) as long as they don't occupy a seat. They don't get a baggage allowance. 'Skycots', baby food and nappies (diapers) should be provided by the airline if requested in advance. Children aged between two and 12 can usually occupy a seat for half to two-thirds of the full fare, and do get a baggage allowance.

Guide dogs for the blind usually have to travel in a specially pressurised baggage compartment with other animals, though smaller guide dogs may be admitted to the cabin. All guide dogs will be subject to the same quarantine procedures (which may include a period in isolation) as any other animal when entering or returning to countries currently free of rabies, such as Britain or Australia.

Deaf travellers can ask for airport and inflight announcements to be written down for them.

The disability-friendly Web site, www.everybody.co.uk, has an airline directory that provides information on the facilities offered by various airlines.

Departure Taxes

There are departure taxes when leaving the Canary islands by air (fluctuating around 1000 ptas for European flights) but these are included in the price of the ticket at purchase. This said, some discount travel agents will quote the net price (exclusive of tax) to you so make a point of asking when you book.

The UK & Ireland

Discount air travel is big business in London. Travel agencies advertise in the travel pages of the weekend broadsheet newspapers, in *Time Out*, the *Evening Standard* and in the free magazine *TNT*.

For students or travellers aged under 26, popular travel agencies in the UK include:

STA Travel (Europe ☎ 020-7361 6161, Longhaul ☎ 7361 6262), which has an office at 86 Old Brompton Rd, London SW7, and branches across the country.
Web site: www.statravel.co.uk

Usit Campus (☎ 0870 240 1010), which has an office at 52 Grosvenor Gardens, London SW1, and branches throughout the UK.
Web site: www.usitcampus.co.uk

Usit Now (Europe & North America ☎ 01-602 1600, Rest of the world ☎ 602 1700) which has an office at 19–21 Aston Quay, O'Connell Bridge, Dublin, and other offices throughout Ireland.
Web site: www.usitnow.ie

These agencies sell tickets to all but cater especially to young people and students. Another good travel agency, which offers flights to the Canaries for all age groups, is Flightbookers (☎ 020-7757 2000), 177–178 Tottenham Court Rd, London W1, with a Web site at www.ebookers.com.

Spanish Travel Services (STS; ☎ 020-7387 5337), 138 Eversholt St, London NW1 1BL, uses scheduled airlines and charter flights. It has charter flights starting at UK£130 return to Gran Canaria and the other main islands.

Another good source of cheap flights to the Canaries is the Charter Flight Centre (☎ 020-7565 6755), 15 Gillingham St, London SW1 V1HN. It also offers packages. You can check out their special deals online at www.charterflights.co.uk.

The two flag airlines linking the UK and Spain are British Airways (☎ 020-7434 4700, 24-hour line ☎ 0345 222111), 156 Regent St, London W1R 5TA, and the Spanish airline Iberia (☎ 020-7830 0011 in London, ☎ 0990 341341 rest of UK), Venture House, 27–29 Glasshouse St, London W1R 6JU. Visit their Web sites, www .british-airways.com and www.iberia.com, for more information.

Iberia flights all go via Madrid, and the standard return fare from London to Gran Canaria, valid for six months, was UK£283 at the time of writing. Of the two, BA is more likely to have special deals lower than the standard scheduled fares. At the time of writing, high-season return fares with BA were £250 (low-season £185). The discount travel agents can get you across for much less, usually on charter flights.

Air Europa (☎ 0870 240 1501) has one flight per weekday from London (Gatwick) to both Gran Canaria and Tenerife via Madrid. Monarch (☎ 0870 040 5040), principally a charter company, also offers a scheduled flight to Tenerife. Charter airlines linking the UK and the Canary Islands include Air 2000, Airtours, Britannia and JMC, a relative newcomer to the skies which has the only direct flight to La Palma from the UK (leaving on Fridays, November to March).

Go (☎ 0845 605 4321), one of the no-frills airlines, flies to Tenerife four times per week. At the time of writing, one-way fares were available from UK£120 – check their Web site (www.go-fly.com) for special deals.

In the low season, fares to the Canaries can fall as low as UK£99 return. If your quotes are still way above this rock bottom, you might try calling the Air Travel Advisory Bureau (☎ 020-7636 5000). You tell the bureau your destination and it provides a list of relevant discount travel agents that it has on its books.

The cheapest time to fly is midweek on a night flight. Always check the arrival and departure times on these flights, as inconvenience is usually part of the price you pay for a low fare. You should not be surprised, in peak times at any rate, to find your flight delayed. Remember too that, once booked, you cannot alter your charter flight details. If you miss a charter flight, you have lost your money.

If you're looking to go in winter but wish to avoid the high-season crush and price rises, you'll need to fly out in late November or early December and return before Christmas.

You needn't necessarily fly from London; many good deals are just as easily available from other major centres in the UK.

If you're travelling from Ireland, several

charter flights leave every weekend for the Canary Islands. Check them out, then perhaps compare what is available with prices from London – getting across to London first may save you a few quid.

In the Canaries Check around the budget travel agents. In the main resorts and cities especially, if you can be flexible on times and dates, you can often dig up some extraordinary last-minute bargains.

V.Travel 2000 (also called Flight Line) can set you up with a flight to just about any UK airport at budget rates. For current offers, phone its airport kiosks, Tenerife Sur (☎ 922 75 95 31) or Lanzarote (☎ 928 84 63 36), or its downtown office in Playa del Inglés on Gran Canaria (☎ 902 44 33 88), which also covers flights from Fuerteventura.

Packages & Fly-Drive The vast majority of visitors to the islands come on a package deal. This generally consists of flights, transfers and accommodation. This can work out well and is usually quite substantially cheaper than going it alone, but it does limit you. See also the Organised Tours section towards the end of this chapter.

It could work out marginally cheaper to book a hire car before arriving in the islands, so you might want to investigate a fly-drive package. Most reputable travel agents and tour operators can organise this. But think about how long you will actually want a car first. Those staying on one island may find they can dispense with one after a few days while those island-hopping will find it expensive to haul a hire car from island to island, if the hire company permits this – you'd be better off hiring a car on each island as you go.

Spain

You might think of Spain as the obvious place to get a flight to the Canary Islands, since in effect it represents an internal flight. However, such are the inconsistencies of air travel that it's often just as cheap or even cheaper to fly in from northern Europe (more than twice the distance away).

Aside from charters, Air Europa, Spanair and Iberia operate regular scheduled flights between Tenerife, Gran Canaria and Lanzarote and both Madrid and Barcelona, from where each has connections to a wide range of mainland provincial cities.

Both Air Europa and Iberia have a few direct flights per week to Sevilla, Valencia and Malaga.

An average return flight with Iberia, valid for up to one month, from Madrid to either Tenerife or Gran Canaria costs around 45,000 ptas (about 55,000 ptas from Barcelona) but much depends on the season.

The Rest of Europe

As a result of the popularity of the Canary Islands with sun-starved northern Europeans, there are plenty of enticing charter options from a number of cities across Europe.

France The student travel agency OTU Voyages (☎ 01 40 29 12 12) has a central Paris office at 39 ave Georges Bernanos and many others around the country. Visit its Web site at www.otu.fr.

USIT-Voyages (☎ 01 42 44 14 00) does reasonable student and cut-price travel. It has four offices in Paris, including one at 85 blvd St-Michel, and other branches in the provinces, and a Web site at www.usit .connect.fr. STA Travel's Paris agent is Voyages Wasteels (☎ 01 43 25 58 35) at 11 rue Dupuytren. Visit its Web site at www.voyages.wasteels.fr.

Germany Munich is a haven of discount travel agents and more mainstream budget-travel outlets. Council Travel (☎ 089-39 50 22), Adalbertstrasse 32, near the university, is one of the best. STA Travel (☎ 089-39 90 96), Königstrasse 49, is also good.

In Berlin, Kilroy Travel-ARTU Reisen (☎ 030-310 00 40), at Hardenbergstrasse 9, near Berlin Zoo (with five branches around the city) is a good travel agent, as is STA Travel (☎ 030-311 09 50) at Goethestrasse 73. In Frankfurt, you could try the STA Travel office (☎ 069-70 30 35) at

Bockenheimer Landstrasse 133 or in Bornheim (☎ 069-43 01 91), Bergerstrasse 118. For information on other branches, check its Web site at www.statravel.de. Connections (☎ 069-70 50 60) at Adalbertstrasse 8, in Bockenheim, is another consolidator.

Lufthansa's subsidiary airline, Condor, has frequent flights from many towns in Germany to Tenerife Sur, Las Palmas de Gran Canaria, Santa Cruz de la Palma, Arrecife (Lanzarote) and Puerto del Rosario (Fuerteventura).

Other airlines with frequent direct flights between Germany and various of the Canary Islands include Hapag-Lloyd Flug, Air-Berlin, Germania, Aero Lloyd and LTU.

The Netherlands Amsterdam is a popular departure point. The student travel agency NBBS Reiswinkels, Rokin 38 (☎ 020-624 09 89), offers reliable and reasonably low fares. Compare with the pickings in the discount travel agents along Rokin before deciding. NBBS has several branches throughout the city, as well as in Brussels (Belgium). Check out its Web site at www.nbbs.nl.

Transavia Airlines and Martinair have several direct flights between Amsterdam and Tenerife Sur every Monday and Friday.

Italy A reliable place to look for cheap flights is CTS (Centro Turistico Studentesco). It has branches all over the country. In Rome (☎ 06-46791), it's at Via Genova 16.

Portugal Portugalia Airlines flies between Lisbon and Tenerife Sur twice a week and both Air Europa and Spanair each have a weekly connection. A monthly excursion return fare is 36,000 ptas.

Morocco
Although barely 100km away, the shores of Morocco are expensive to reach. If you're really intent on going there, it will probably work out cheaper to backtrack on a flight to Malaga, on the Spanish mainland, and then take a ferry across the straits from Algeciras to Tangier or Ceuta.

A monthly excursion return to Agadir from Las Palmas de Gran Canaria with Spanair, who fly the route daily, costs 72,200 ptas. A similar ticket to Casablanca will set you back 96,200 ptas.

If you are thinking about making a brief excursion into Morocco while in the Canaries, a package, starting from around 50,000 ptas for a week with half board, offers much better value.

The Rest of Africa
At the time of writing, the only option was an Iberia service from Las Palmas de Gran Canaria to Dakar (Senegal). This flies three times per week and a return ticket, valid for up to a month – and cheaper than the single fare – costs 72,170 ptas.

The USA
There are no direct scheduled flights from the USA to the Canary Islands. The options are to take a package trip with a charter airline (see Organised Tours later in this chapter for details) or to fly to mainland Spain or another European destination and take a connecting flight on to the islands. It is also worth considering getting a cheap flight to Europe and then finding a package deal or charter flight to the Canaries from there.

If your European trip is not going to be confined to the islands, consult your travel agent about how best to incorporate them into your vacation.

The *New York Times*, *LA Times*, *Chicago Tribune* and *San Francisco Examiner* produce weekly travel sections in which you'll find any number of travel agents' ads. Two reliable discount travel agents are Council Travel (☎ 800 2COUNCIL) and STA Travel (☎ 800 781 4040), both of which have offices in major cities nationwide, and Web sites at www.counciltravel.com and www.sta-travel.com.

Iberia (☎ 800 772 4642) flies non-stop between Madrid and New York. Return fares can range from US$500 to over US$12,000, depending on the season and your place of departure (the West Coast is inevitably more expensive). You may get a better deal with another airline if you are prepared to fly via other European cities, so

Emigration

The Canarios have long looked across the Atlantic to farther shores and a high proportion of Cubans and continental Americans can claim a Canarian gene or two.

Following in the wake of Columbus, Canarios were among the earliest colonisers. In the early days, the most popular destinations were Cuba, La Hispañola (today's Dominican Republic and Haiti) and Puerto Rico in the Caribbean. On the mainland, pioneers settled around Buenos Aires in Argentina, Montevideo in Uruguay, and Caracas in Venezuela. Further north, Canarios were well represented in Florida, Louisiana, Yucatán and Nueva España (Texas) – it was a group of Canaries emigrants who, on 9 March 1731, founded San Fernando, today's San Antonio, Texas.

Those who packed their bags and left everything didn't always leave voluntarily. The Spanish imperial government, its officers thin on the ground, maintained only a superficial control over its vast American colonies. Under increasing threat from French and British incursions, it was keen to beef up the Spanish presence by importing its own kind – and the Canarios were the nearest to hand. So it organised the forcible transfer of families, primarily to Cuba, Florida, Texas and Mexico, where they were given rudimentary supplies and sent out to establish new settlements.

There were two later surges in emigration, both spurred as much by poverty on the islands and the need to escape as by hope of a new life and new deal over the waters. In the Canaries, the 1880s are called the decade of *la crisis de la cochinilla*, when synthetic dyes swamped the international market and killed off the local cochineal cottage industries. Later, the hard times that the Canary Islands shared with mainland Spain following the Spanish civil war and WWII were even harder on the archipelago and lasted right through until the 1960s.

But life was often just as tough at first on the other side of the ocean. In the Franco era, many left without passport or papers and arrived illegally in the new land. Here, they would be interned in camps and then set to work, cutting cane in the sugar plantations in order to earn their keep – arduous labour from which they escaped to better-paid work at the first opportunity.

Venezuela is often called the 'eighth island' of the Canaries. So strong are business, family and cultural links that many Canaries newspapers carry a whole page each day of news from Caracas and Televisión Autonómica, the islands' TV channel, has a similar daily news program.

Nowadays the Canary Islands, for so long a region of net emigration, admit more people than they export – workers for the hotel, restaurant and construction industries, and migrants from northern Europe seeking a place in the near-perpetual sun.

And, as the wheel turns full circle, the eastern islands in particular are a staging post for a new generation of economic migrants – from Morocco and West Africa come folk who risk their lives crossing illegally from the African mainland in fragile rowing boats. The motives are just the same: fleeing poverty in the hope of creating a new life on a new continent.

---

shop around. Spain's Air Europa (☎ 902-410 501) occasionally has good deals between Madrid and New York.

The very cheapest way of getting from the USA to Europe is by stand-by or courier flights. Stand-by fares are often sold at 60% of the normal price for one-way tickets. Airhitch (☎ 212-864 2000, 800 326 2009), 2641 Broadway, New York, NY 10025, specialises in this sort of thing. You will need to give a general idea of where and when you need to go, and a few days before your departure you will be presented with a choice of two or three flights.

Airhitch has several other offices in the USA, including Los Angeles (☎ 310-726 5000). In Europe they operate a central office in France (☎ 01 47 00 16 30) at 5 rue de Crussol, 75001, Paris. Seasonal offices (which means they may be shut from November to April) operate in Berlin, Amsterdam, Prague and Rome. Contact its Madrid representative on ☎ 91 366 79 27 or try the Web site at www.airhitch.org. A one-way fare from the USA to Europe costs from US$160 (east coast) to US$240 (west coast) plus taxes.

Another travel agent specialising in budget air fares is Discount Tickets in New York (☎ 212-391 2313).

Courier flights are where you accompany a parcel to its destination. Courier prices can be 10–40% below scheduled fares and tend to drop if you are prepared to fly at short notice. You'd be very lucky to get anything directly to the islands, but a New York–Madrid or New York–London return on a courier run can cost under US$300 in the low season (more expensive from the west coast). Always check conditions and details with the company.

For more information, contact either Now Voyager (☎ 212-431 1616), Suite 307, 74 Varrick St, New York, NY 10013 or the Denver-based Air Courier Association (☎ 303-278 8810), who both specialise in courier flights. You may be able to organise such flights directly with the courier companies themselves – try the Yellow Pages.

Canada

Iberia has no direct flights from Canada to Spain, let alone its offshore islands. To reach them, you'll need to travel via the USA or a European hub. As with the USA, the thing to do is work out the best possible route/fare combination; again a direct flight to London combined with an onward charter or package can often work out the cheapest and simplest method for reaching the Canaries.

Canada's main student travel organisation is Travel CUTS (known as Voyages Campus in Quebec). Represented in most major cities, its two main offices are in Toronto (☎ 416-977 0441), 74 Gerrard St East, and Montreal (☎ 514-398 0647), Université McG, McGill, 3480 rue Mc-Tavish. Check out fares and routes on-line at www.travelcuts.com.

For courier flights originating in Canada, contact FB on Board Courier Services (☎ 514-631 2077 in Toronto). Airhitch (see the USA section) has stand-by fares to and from Toronto, Montreal and Vancouver.

South America

There's precisely one scheduled direct flight per week between the Canaries and South America – Iberia's Monday run between Caracas (Venezuela) and Tenerife. In low season, a single ticket costs 91,000 ptas and a return, valid for up to two months, costs 120,000 ptas. For all other transatlantic destinations, you will need to go via Barcelona or Madrid.

Australia

There are no direct flights from Australia to the Canaries, so you'll have to book connecting flights via Madrid, Barcelona or another European capital.

STA Travel (☎ 1300 360 960) and Flight Centre (☎ 1300 362 665) are major dealers in cheap airfares. Check out their Web sites at www.statravel.com.au and www.flight centre.com.au respectively. Heavily discounted fares can often be found at your local travel agent too.

The Saturday travel sections of the Melbourne *Age* and the *Sydney Morning Herald* have many advertisements offering cheap fares to Europe, but don't be surprised if the very cheapest happen to be 'sold out' when you contact the agents – they are usually low-season fares on obscure airlines with conditions attached.

Low-season return fares to Madrid or Barcelona are from around A$1499 on airlines such as Olympic Airways, Thai International and Lauda Air. High-season fares can climb to A$2000. You then have to tack on the cost of the return flights between Europe and the Canaries.

New Zealand

From New Zealand, flights to Europe are via the USA and Asia. You can also fly from Auckland to pick up a connecting flight in either Melbourne or Sydney. Expect to pay around NZ$2400 for a return to Barcelona or Madrid in the low season and NZ$2700 in the high season.

As with Australia, STA Travel and Flight

The windmills around Antigua, Fuerteventura – rusting or restored, you can't miss 'em.

Life's a beach and then you die: sand sculptures on Playa Corralejo, Fuerteventura

Playa de Barlovento de Jandía is wilder and less crowded than Fuerteventura's eastern beaches.

Surf breaks over a volanic reef to create the 'Bubbles' of Fuerteventura's north coast.

Centres International are popular travel agents in New Zealand. Flight Centre (☎ 09-309 6171) has a large central office in Auckland at National Bank Towers (corner Queen and Darby Sts) and many branches throughout the country. STA Travel (☎ 09-309 0458) has its main office at 10 High St, Auckland, and has other offices in Auckland as well as in Hamilton, Christchurch, Palmerston North, Wellington and Dunedin.

Asia
Although most Asian countries are now offering fairly competitive deals, Bangkok, Hong Kong and Singapore are still the best places to shop around for discount tickets. Return fares from Bangkok and Singapore to Madrid start from around US$780. From Hong Kong expect to pay around US$1020.

STA Travel has branches in Hong Kong, Singapore, Bangkok and Kuala Lumpur.

SEA
Just about everyone flies to the Canaries. The only other alternative (apart from a very long swim!) is to take the Trasmediterránea ferry, which carries vital supplies and up to 135 cars to the islands. It sets out from Cádiz, on Spain's Mediterranean coast, every Tuesday at 7 pm. After a long and often bumpy voyage, it puts in to Las Palmas de Gran Canaria at 9 am on Thursday. It then proceeds to Santa Cruz de Tenerife, arriving at 2 pm and hanging around before sailing on to Santa Cruz de La Palma, which it reaches around 8 am on Friday.

The boat back to the Spanish mainland leaves Santa Cruz de La Palma on Friday at 2 pm and arrives in Santa Cruz de Tenerife at 8.30 pm. It leaves there at 9 am on Friday and calls by Arrecife (Lanzarote), from where it sets sail at 10.30 pm, returning to Cádiz at 11 am on Monday.

Unless you especially like rough ocean voyages for their own sake or have a car that you simply must get to the islands, you're much, much better off just hopping on a plane.

Fares per person range from 30,500 ptas to 63,000 ptas depending on the type of

cabin and – we should hope so at such prices – include all meals. A car up to 2m long costs 25,370 ptas one way and a motorcycle costs 10,300 ptas. You generally need to book at least a month in advance if you want to get a car aboard.

Representatives for Trasmediterránea in the UK are Southern Ferries (☎ 020-7491 4968), 1st Floor, 179 Piccadilly, London W1V 9DB.

ORGANISED TOURS
Plenty of operators provide travel services to the Canary Islands from anywhere in Europe and North America. The Spanish tourist office in your country (see Tourist Offices in the Facts for the Visitor chapter) can provide extensive lists of companies offering all kinds of holidays, although the emphasis is very much on flight and accommodation packages. Ask in particular for the Holidays of Special Interest list, which categorises companies thematically (for example, coach tours, birdwatching, golf and fishing).

It is worth shopping around and comparing what's on offer. Remember that while packages do take a lot of the hassle out of travelling, they also remove much of the adventure and liberty of movement. Once you've paid for your apartment for two weeks, you're stuck with it. If you have a couple of weeks at your disposal, perhaps think of a two-island holiday. Even if such an option doesn't feature in a company's brochure, many can line this up if you ask. If you plan to travel the islands more extensively, independent travel is really the way to go, the only proviso being that in high season, especially on the smaller islands, it is possible to be left out on a limb with nowhere to stay.

Package Tours All of the major tour companies in the UK have holidays in Tenerife and Gran Canaria on their books. Most too will offer Lanzarote and maybe Fuerteventura. Scarcely any feature the smallest three islands.

Key to the Canaries (☎ 0161-834 1187) at 16 Lloyd St, Manchester M2 5WA, more focussed than the giants, specialises in all-inclusive packages to the Canary Islands.

In the USA, you could have a look at Spanish Heritage Tours (☎ 800 456 5050) 116–47 Queens Blvd, Forest Hills, NY 11375. From New York you would be looking at from US$900 per person for a week, including flights, transfers, accommodation and breakfast. You can visit their Web site at www.shtours.com.

Walking Tours Specialising in the western islands is recommended small-scale, small-group Wilderness Walks (☎ 01227-779199). It organises walking holidays on La Gomera and Tenerife, and is one of the very rare operators to offer trekking on El Hierro and La Palma.

Several UK-based activity holiday and walking-tour operators also offer the Canary Islands as a destination. Explore Worldwide (☎ 01252-319448, fax 343170, ⓔ info@explore.co.uk) has trekking tours to La Gomera, El Hierro and Tenerife. Sherpa Expeditions (☎ 020-8577 2717, fax 8572 9788, ⓔ sherpa.sales@dial.pipex .com) offers La Gomera, which is also on offer from Headwater (☎ 01606-813333, fax 813334, ⓔ info@headwater.com). Exodus (☎ 020-8675 5550, fax 8673 0779, ⓔ sales@exodustravels.co.uk) has a full week of hiking on Tenerife, radiating out from the small village of Vilaflor. The daddy of them all, Ramblers Holidays (☎ 01707-331133, fax 333276, ⓔ ramhols @dial.pipex.com), an offshoot of the Ramblers Association, offers walking holidays to both Tenerife and La Gomera.

Cruises & Freighters If travelling is more important to you than arriving, and money

is no object, you could take a leisurely cruise out to the Canary Islands.

Fred Olsen Cruise Lines (☎ 01473-292222, fax 01473-292345) at White House Rd, Ipswich, Suffolk IP1 5LL, offers a range of cruises into the Atlantic. For example, fares for a 13-night cruise from Southampton, calling in at the main islands, plus Gibraltar and Madeira, start from as little as UK£675 per person.

An alternative is Festival Cruises (☎ 020-7734 0005) at 5th Floor, Victory House, 99–101 Regent St, London W1B 4EZ, offering 12-day cruises starting at UK£760 per person in four-berth cabins. Cruises start in Genova (Italy – return flights from Gatwick included) and cruise along the Spanish coast, out to the islands and back along the Moroccan coast.

With both companies, enquire about extra charges for on-shore activities and discounts for early booking.

The Cruise People Ltd can organise you on to still more expensive cruise ships doing the Canaries, as well as anything from an expedition ship to the Antarctic to a West Indies banana boat. Check out its Web site at www.cruisepeople.co.uk.

Its London office (☎ 020-7723 2450), 88 York St, London W1 1QT, can get you passage on a German container ship departing Hamburg on two- and three-week trips to the Canaries. You can opt for a one-way trip. You'll be looking at roughly UK£1500 for the full three weeks. Again, make sure you know exactly what is included in the price.

The Cruise People Ltd also have a Canadian office (☎ 416-444 2410) at 1252 Lawrence Ave, East, Suite 202, Don Mills, Ontario, Canada M3A 1C3.

Getting Around

AIR

Flying isn't a cheap way to get around but, for longer inter-island journeys, it can work out substantially quicker than taking a ferry. Binter, a subsidiary of Spain's national airline Iberia and now in the throes of being privatised, connects all seven islands with fairly regular flights. Note, however, that you can only fly between La Palma and El Hierro by passing through Tenerife Norte airport and you'd have to pass through Gran Canaria if flying between Fuerteventura and Lanzarote (not that there's much point since ferry connections are so good). With ferries between Tenerife and La Gomera so frequent and rapid, there's also little incentive to take one of the three flights per day that land at the latter's spanking new white elephant of an airport.

In business since 1988, Binter operates 11 ATR-72 prop aircraft. See the table 'Domestic Flights' for a rundown of available flights and fares. Frequency and fares are the same in reverse and there's no reduction for getting round-trip tickets. If you take a return flight between Fuerteventura and Lanzarote via Tenerife Norte or between El Hierro and La Palma via Gran Canaria, there's a discount.

For more information, contact Binter on ☎ 902 40 05 00 or visit their Web site at www.bintercanarias.es (Spanish only).

The *Cabildo* (regional government) is trying to foment competition on inter-island routes. Small companies come and go but there's nothing constant so far. At the time of writing, Air Atlantic covers some routes but their flights are advertised as Binter's – and Iberia sells the tickets. All rather incestuous! Also, especially for the shorter hops, many people still elect to take the less environmentally damaging and cheaper sea option.

Two other airlines serving the Spanish mainland have a few flights connecting the bigger islands. They are Air Europa (Tenerife, Gran Canaria, Lanzarote) and Spanair (Tenerife, Gran Canaria, Lanzarote and Fuerteventura).

BUS

A bus in the Canary Islands is called a *guagua*, pronounced 'wa-wa'. If you've bounced around Latin America, you'll be familiar with the term. Still, if you ask about *autobuses*, you'll be understood.

Every island has its own inter-urban

Domestic Flights

departure point	destination	frequency	flight time	one-way fare
Tenerife Norte	Gran Canaria	Up to 12 daily	30 minutes	6360 ptas
Tenerife Sur	Gran Canaria	2 daily	30 minutes	6360 ptas
Tenerife Norte	Lanzarote	4 daily	50 minutes	11,310 ptas
Tenerife Norte	Fuerteventura	2 daily	45 minutes	10,460 ptas
Tenerife Norte	La Palma	up to 8 daily	30 minutes	6860 ptas
Tenerife Norte	El Hierro	2–3 daily	40 minutes	7160 ptas
Tenerife Norte	La Gomera	2 daily	30 minutes	8060 ptas
Gran Canaria	La Palma	2–3 daily	50 minutes	10,410 ptas
Gran Canaria	Lanzarote	8 daily	45 minutes	8860 ptas
Gran Canaria	Fuerteventura	8 daily	40 minutes	7760 ptas
Gran Canaria	La Gomera	1 daily	40 minutes	11,310 ptas
Gran Canaria	El Hierro	2 weekly	45 minutes	11,160 ptas

Bus Routes

island	departure point	destination	fare
Gran Canaria	Las Palmas de Gran Canaria	Mogán	805 ptas
Fuerteventura	Puerto del Rosario	Morro Jable	1045 ptas
Lanzarote	Arrecife	Playa Blanca	415 ptas
Tenerife	Santa Cruz de Tenerife	Playa de las Américas	950 ptas
La Gomera	San Sebastián de la Gomera	Valle de Gran Rey	675 ptas
La Palma	Santa Cruz de la Palma	Los Llanos de Aridane	570 ptas
El Hierro	Valverde	La Restinga	300 ptas

service. One way or another, they can get you to most main locations but in many cases there are few runs each day. This is especially so on the smaller islands where the population is low and most people are obliged to have their own wheels.

The bigger islands of Tenerife and Gran Canaria each have an impressive public transport system that covers the whole island. Frequency, however, varies enormously: from a regular service between major towns to a couple of runs per day for transporting workers and school kids into and out of the capital.

Check the timetable carefully before travelling at the weekend. Even on major runs on the bigger islands, a frequent weekday service can trickle off to just a few departures on Saturday and one, or none, on Sunday.

In the larger towns and cities, buses leave from a bus station *(estación de guaguas)*. In villages and small towns, they usually terminate on a particular street or plaza.

You buy your ticket on the bus.On some of the islands you can buy a Bonobus card (called a Tarjeta Insular on Gran Canaria), which usually costs 2000 ptas. They're sold at bus stations and shops such as newsagents. Insert the card into the machine on the bus, tell the driver where you are going and he will deduct the fare from the card. You get about 30% off standard fares with one, so they are a good investment if you intend to use the buses a lot.

Fares, especially if you invest in a Bonobus card, are reasonable. See the table 'Bus Routes' for sample standard one-way

fares. These indicate the most you are likely to pay for any one ticket on each island. Other destinations within each island are calculated pro rata according to distance.

CAR & MOTORCYCLE

Unless you're intending to settle on the islands, there's no advantage whatsoever in bringing your own vehicle. Transport costs on the one ferry per week from Cádiz in mainland Spain are savage and car-hire rates on the islands are significantly cheaper than in most countries of the European Union.

Road Rules

The minimum driving age is 18. If fitted, rear seatbelts must be worn. Fines for failure to comply range from 50,000 ptas to 100,000 ptas – though, as for those spectacular fines for dog owners whose pets foul the pavement (sidewalk), we've never met anyone who's been charged.

In principle, motorcyclists should use headlights at all times though few locals do. Crash helmets are obligatory when riding any motorised bikes. The minimum age for riding bikes and scooters up to 50cc is 16 (no licence is required). For anything more powerful, you'll need to produce your driving licence.

In built-up areas the speed limit is generally 40km/h, rising to a maximum of 100km/h on major roads and 120km/h on *autovías* (motorways).

The blood-alcohol limit is 0.08% and random breath-testing is carried out. The fine can be up to 100,000 ptas if you are caught driving under the influence of alcohol.

Fines for other traffic offences range between 50,000 ptas and 100,000 ptas. Non-resident foreigners are fined on the spot – the cold comfort being that immediate settlement brings a 20% reduction.

Road Maps

If you are planning to drive on only one island, the map that tourist offices hand out is quite adequate. If you're likely to be island hopping, you might want to invest in Fire stone's *Islas Canarias* map, which includes all seven islands at a scale of 1:150,000. Michelin too is reliable. Its sheet No 220 covers Gran Canaria (1:150,000), No 221 takes in Lanzarote at the same scale and Fuerteventura at 1:175,000. For the western isles, sheet No 222 embraces Tenerife at 1:150,000 and El Hierro, La Gomera and La Palma, all at 1:125,000. See also the Books and Maps section in the Facts for the Visitor chapter and under each island.

Road Assistance

In practice, you'll almost certainly be driving a hired car. Check before you set out that the phone number of the rental company features on the copy of the rental agreement that you should be given (you're required by law to carry this with you). Some agents also offer a 24-hour mobile phone contact.

City Driving & Parking

Driving, even in the biggest cities of Las Palmas de Gran Canaria and Santa Cruz de Tenerife, doesn't present particular difficulties although the traffic can be a little intense.

Parking, however, can be more problematic. Most city centres and several smaller towns operate restricted meter parking. Otherwise, there are several paying car parks in the two capitals.

If you double park or leave your vehicle in a designated no-parking zone, you risk being towed – recovering the vehicle costs 6000 ptas. If you get a ticket on your windscreen, don't hit the sunroof; in most towns

you can annul it (unless you're more than an hour into the red) by running to the nearest machine and paying in a mere 100 ptas.

Don't leave anything in the car unless you have to. If so, lock it in the boot (trunk). Theft from cars, and hire cars in particular, is always a threat.

Petrol

Gasolina is much cheaper in the Canary Islands than elsewhere on Spanish territory since it's free of normal consumer taxes.

You'll not find regular, leaded petrol anywhere nowadays, but lead-free *(sin plomo)* is available pretty much everywhere. Prices vary slightly between service stations and fluctuate according to oil tariffs, OPEC arm twisting and tax policy, so the following prices can only serve as a guide. Super, when we were last on the islands, cost 112 ptas per litre and the increasingly popular diesel *(gasoil or gasóleo)* was 87 ptas per litre. Lead-free (95 octane) cost 102 ptas and 98 octane super, sometimes known as *Súper Star*, came in at 106 ptas. You can pay with major credit cards at most service stations.

Rental

To break free from your resort, it's well worth hiring a car for a few days and exploring the island. If you're contemplating this, remember to pack your driving licence, which is required for any vehicle over 50cc. You need to be at least 21 years old and have held a driver's licence for a minimum of two years. It's easier, and with some companies obligatory, to pay with a credit card – although they do then have a hold over you if something goes wrong. Out on the road, always drive with your licence, passport and rental agreement on board.

All the big international car rental companies are represented in the Canary Islands and there are plenty of local operators. If you intend to stay on one island for any length of time, it might be worth booking a car in advance, for example in a fly/drive deal

No matter what you rent, make sure you understand what is included in the price (unlimited kilometres, tax, insurance, collision damage waiver and so on) and what your liabilities are, and that you examine the rental agreement carefully – difficult if it is in Spanish only!

Multinational companies operating in all or most of the islands include Hertz (☎ 901 10 07 77), Avis (☎ 902 13 55 31) and Europcar/BC Betacar (☎ 922 37 28 56). The largest local operators are Euro Dollar/Atesa (☎ 902 100 101) and Cicar (☎ 928 59 70 19).

There are plenty of local companies, which often work out quite significantly cheaper than the international big boys. Indeed, you may prefer to put your money their way. Prices vary a little from island to island but, in general, if you manage in the region of 4000/10,000/20,000 ptas per day/three days/week for a small saloon car, you've done well. A day's fun in a Suzuki 4WD will cost around 7000 ptas. Wherever you rent, the longer you hire the car for, the lower the daily rate.

It's well worth shopping around and picking up a few brochures. Especially in the big resorts, some operators quote rates that are seductively and misleadingly low. That's because insurance, which can more than double the cost, hasn't been included. And there are other incidentals, some optional, such as collision damage waiver, extra passenger cover and 5% IGIC tax.

You can't generally take a hire car from one island to another without the firm's explicit permission. Some companies, such as Hertz, offer a special rate that allows you to island-hop. Most flexible of all is local company, Orlando Rent a Car (central reservations ☎ 928 76 55 02). Represented on all seven islands, it allows you to drop off a car on any of them on payment of a piddling 1000 ptas supplement. Another exception for most companies is the Fuerteventura–Lanzarote sea crossing – most have no problem with you taking your car from one to the other, and in some cases you can hire on one and drop the car off on the other.

Renting motorbikes and mopeds can be expensive. A sample rate is 6500 ptas per day for a Honda Enduro X250. You have to leave a refundable deposit of at least 20,000 ptas (or a credit card). An 80cc scooter will cost around 3000 ptas per day.

Purchase
Only residents in Spain can buy a car there, and only those who can prove residence in the Canary Islands may avail themselves of the local tax breaks to buy a car cheaply.

Taxi
You *could* tour around an island by taxi but it's a very expensive way to go. A few taxi drivers operating between towns are sharkish and reluctant to set the meter. It's wise to confirm the fare (in most cases there are set tariffs) before taking (or being taken for) a ride.

BICYCLE
You can rent mountain bikes, city bikes and beach tourers in various resorts and in the more tourist-orientated areas of the islands. Expect to pay 1000 ptas per day for the simplest machine.

If you plan to bring your own bike, check with the airline about any hidden costs and whether it will have to be disassembled and packed for the journey.

Fill all your water bottles – and then add one more; it can be hot on the open road and, more often than not, you won't find anything between villages.

HITCHING
Hitching is never entirely safe in any country in the world, and we don't recommend it. Travellers who decide to hitch should understand that they are taking a small but potentially serious risk. People who do choose to hitch will be safer if they travel in pairs and let someone know where they are planning to go.

Hitching is illegal on the islands' few *autovías* (motorways) and can be difficult on major highways. You really need to choose a spot where cars can safely stop before the highway slipways, or use minor roads.

You're wasting your time trying to hitch from city centres. Take local transport to town exits and carry a sign with your destination in Spanish.

In all, hitching is a bit hit-and-miss in the islands. With so many tourists getting around in hire vehicles it can often seem a breeze. At other times the lack of traffic on back roads can be frustrating, and locals are not always so keen on giving strangers a lift.

BOAT

The islands are connected by ferries, 'fast ferries', and jetfoils. There are three companies: Naviera Armas, Fred Olsen and Trasmediterránea. See the tables 'Inter-Island Ferries' and 'Inter-Island Jetfoils' for a summary of routes. For more detailed information, refer to the Getting There & Away sections under each island's port(s).

Do bear in mind that (especially since Trasmediterránea's monopoly on inter-island travel was broken) times, prices – even routes – are constantly changing. Trasmediterránea, buffeted by the competition and still adjusting, is a particular culprit. This isn't so important on major routes where there's plenty of choice but can mean a big delay if you're planning to travel a route which has only a couple of boats per day – or even week.

At the time of writing, Naviera Armas had no service to La Gomera or El Hierro.

To check routes, fares and sailing times, phone the company or visit their Web site:

Naviera Armas

Web site: www.naviera-armas.com
Fuerteventura (☎ 928 86 70 80) Corralejo; (☎ 928 54 21 13) Morro Jable
Gran Canaria (☎ 928 26 77 00) Las Palmas
Lanzarote (☎ 928 51 79 12) Playa Blanca
La Palma (☎ 922 41 74 82) Santa Cruz de la Palma
Tenerife (☎ 922 53 40 52) Santa Cruz de Tenerife

Fred Olsen

Web site: www.fredolsen.es
El Hierro (☎ 922 55 14 24) Puerto de la Estaca
Fuerteventura (☎ 928 53 50 90) Corralejo; (☎ 928 53 21 27) Puerto del Rosario
Gran Canaria (☎ 928 55 40 05) Agaete/Puerto de las Nieves; (☎ 928 49 50 46) Las Palmas
La Gomera (☎ 922 87 10 07) San Sebastián
Lanzarote (☎ 928 51 72 66) Playa Blanca; (☎ 928 80 50 10) Arrecife
La Palma (☎ 922 41 74 95) Santa Cruz de la Palma
Tenerife (☎ 922 62 82 00, 922 29 00 11) Santa Cruz de Tenerife; (☎ 922 79 05 56) Los Cristianos

Trasmediterránea

Web site: www.trasmediterranea.es
☎ 902 45 46 45 (all routes)

Ferry

There are roll-on roll-off car ferries between major ports around the islands. Naviera Armas, for example, has one fast ferry daily between Santa Cruz de Tenerife

Inter-Island Ferries

route	duration	one-way fare
Las Palmas de Gran Canaria–Santa Cruz de Tenerife	4 hours	3005 ptas
Las Palmas de Gran Canaria–Puerto del Rosario (Fuerteventura)	8 hours	3900 ptas
Las Palmas de Gran Canaria–Arrecife (Lanzarote)	10 hours	3900 ptas
Las Palmas de Gran Canaria–Morro Jable (Fuerteventura)	3 hours	5000 ptas
Las Palmas de Gran Canaria–Santa Cruz de la Palma	8 hours	5120 ptas
Los Cristianos (Tenerife)–Santa Cruz de la Palma	5 hours	3100 ptas
Los Cristianos (Tenerife)–Puerto de la Estaca (El Hierro)	5½ hours	2540 ptas
San Sebastián de la Gomera–Puerto de la Estaca (El Hierro)	3 hours	2615 ptas
Los Cristianos (Tenerife)–San Sebastián de la Gomera	45 minutes	2420 ptas
Playa Blanca (Lanzarote)–Corralejo (Fuerteventura)	45 minutes	1700–1850 ptas

euro currency converter €1 = 166 ptas

and Las Palmas de Gran Canaria. This runs on from Las Palmas to Morro Jable (Fuerteventura). Fred Olsen operates six fast ferries per day from Santa Cruz de Tenerife to Agaete/Puerto de las Nieves on Gran Canaria and offers a free bus connection on to Las Palmas.

From Las Palmas, the three companies between them run around 12 ferries per week to both Arrecife (Lanzarote) and Puerto del Rosario (Fuerteventura). There *are* boats between the island capitals of Puerto del Rosario and Arrecife but it's much swifter to take one of the regular Naviera Armas or Fred Olsen ferries between Corralejo in the north of Fuerteventura and Playa Blanca in Lanzarote's south.

From Los Cristianos (Tenerife), Fred Olsen runs a fast ferry five times daily and Trasmediterránea has two sailings daily to San Sebastián de la Gomera.

Trasmediterránea and Fred Olsen have daily ferries from Los Cristianos to El Hierro and Fred Olsen runs a daily boat to Santa Cruz de la Palma via La Gomera.

Jetfoil

High-speed Trasmediterránea jetfoils make the crossing between Las Palmas de Gran Canaria and Santa Cruz de Tenerife in 80 minutes. There are three to five departures daily, depending on the day and season. A Trasmediterránea jetfoil also links Las Palmas with Morro Jable (Fuerteventura). There is generally one departure per day except Sunday, although in low season (such as November), services can drop as low as two per week.

Fares & Travel Times

See the tables 'Inter-Island Ferries' (on the previous page) and 'Inter-Island Jetfoils' for sample fares and travel times for the main sailings between the islands. As a rule, fares between rival companies don't vary substantially. Do remember that sea schedules are particularly subject to change, so you should check out the latest information on the spot.

Infants travel free and children aged two to 12 years pay half price. EU nationals over 60 years old should always ask about 20% reductions. Holders of the Carnet Joven (Euro26) get 35% off.

Bicycles go for free with Trasmediterránea but not with their competitors, whose charges vary according to the route.

LOCAL TRANSPORT

With the possible exception of long, thin Las Palmas de Gran Canaria, in the handful of cities throughout the islands large enough to need a public-transport system, the average visitor won't need to use it that much anyway. Accommodation, restaurants, bars and attractions are in most cases concentrated in a small area.

Bus

Bus companies operate fairly extensive services in the two main capitals, allowing you to get from the centre to bus stations and airports cheaply and with little fuss.

Taxi

Taxis in the cities use meters. The flagfall is 160 ptas in Tenerife and 175 ptas in Gran Canaria. After that you pay 60 ptas per

Inter-Island Jetfoils			
departure point	destination	duration	one-way off-peak/ tourist/premier-class fare
Las Palmas de Gran Canaria	Santa Cruz de Tenerife	1 hour 20 minutes	3840/6265/7890 ptas
Las Palmas de Gran Canaria	Morro Jable	1½ hours	3840/6265/7890 ptas

kilometre. Surcharges of 55 ptas (60 ptas in Tenerife) apply to travel between 10 pm and 6 am, travel on Sunday and holidays, fares to airports, fares to the docks in Las Palmas de Gran Canaria and Santa Cruz de Tenerife, and for each piece of luggage carried (Tenerife only). By European standards, city taxis in the Canaries are cheap.

On the roof of taxis is a green light and the numbers 1, 2 and 3. When the green light is on, the cab is available. The numbers refer to the kind of fare. No 1 is what you should expect, as this is the standard city zone. Fare types 2 and 3 apply to trips that take the cabs out of their city zone (Las Palmas to the airport falls into this category). In these cases, the passenger doesn't pay a flagfall or any surcharge. And don't worry, you can stop a cab saying No 1 even if you want to go as far as a No 2 or even 3!

ORGANISED TOURS

You'll stumble into a forest of tour possibilities in the main tourist resorts. They range from bog standard tours of whichever island you happen to be on to whale-spotting and deep-sea fishing excursions. Various options are mentioned in each island chapter.

Gran Canaria

The Canariones, as the islanders tend to refer to themselves, like to think of Gran Canaria as a 'continent in miniature'. And although the startling range of terrain, from the fertile north to the arid interior and desert south, largely justifies the claim, it has to be said that this is no more the case than, say, on Tenerife.

The island, covering 1560 sq km, is the third largest of the group but, with 716,000 residents, it accounts for almost half the archipelago's population.

In many respects this is perhaps the least attractive of the Canary Islands. But it all depends on your tastes. If you're after a ball-breaking beachside nightlife with the one-week charter-flight crowd, then the Playa del Inglés scene is marginally preferable to Tenerife's equivalent, Playa de las Américas – if only because of the pretty dunes of Maspalomas.

Otherwise, the capital Las Palmas is a busy, happening city and worth a visit for its historic old quarter, nightlife and the golden sands of Playa de las Canteras. Surfers can pick up some waves here and off Maspalomas, and windsurfers are in heaven on the south-eastern coast.

The interior is a world away from both the capital and the southern resorts, and worth exploring. It is nevertheless a somewhat arid affair and frankly less captivating than the volcanic splendours of Tenerife or the mountainous western islands.

History

Gran Canaria was known to its original inhabitants as Tamarán, which scholars have linked with the Arabic name for date palms *(tamar)*. This sounds feasible but could not go back much beyond the 7th century, when the Muslim Arabs invaded Morocco.

The Romans – who, as far as is known, never landed here – first called the island Canaria. Just why is discussed in the boxed text 'Dogs & Purple Prose' later in this chapter. How Canaria came to be thought of

Highlights

- Strolling through the cobbled streets of the historical Vegueta quarter of Las Palmas
- Enjoying a seafood lunch on the waterfront in Puerto de las Nieves
- Wandering over the expansive sand dunes of Maspalomas
- Exploring the resort and fishing port of Puerto de Mogán
- Cruising the bars of Las Palmas, followed by a lazy day on Playa de las Canteras
- Driving the scenic coastal route from Agaete to Aldea de San Nicolás

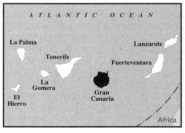

as Gran (big) is also open to question. Some say it was because the Spaniards thought the locals put up a big fight while resisting conquest, and others that the island was thought to be the biggest in the archipelago.

Conquest began in earnest with the landing of a Spanish force led by Juan Rejón. Despite carrying the day and beating off a furious counterattack by Doramas, the *guanarteme* (chief) of the island's Telde kingdom, Rejón was supplanted by Pedro de Vera, who pressed home the campaign in the following five years.

The turning point was the conversion of the Guanche chief Tenesor Semidan to Christianity. In April 1483 he convinced his countrymen to submit.

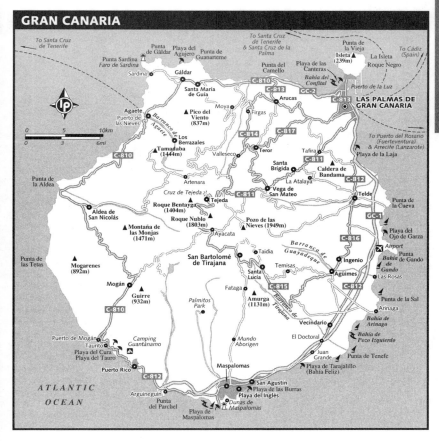

GRAN CANARIA

The island was soon colonised by a rag-tag assortment of adventurers and landless hopefuls from as far away as Galicia, Andalucía, Portugal, Italy, France, the Low Countries and even Britain and Ireland.

Initially, the island boomed on the back of sugar exports and trans-Atlantic trade between Spain and the Americas. But, as the demand for Canary Islands sugar fell and the fortunes of wine grew, the island declined before its main rival and superior wine-grower, Tenerife. It was not until the late 19th century that Gran Canaria recovered its position. To this day the two islands remain rivals and, between them, are home to most of the islands' permanent populace.

Information

Books & Maps One of the best of a number of competing maps of the island is *Gran Canaria*, published by Distrimapas Telstar (500 ptas). It comes with accurate city maps of Las Palmas, Maspalomas, Playa del Inglés and various other towns.

For walking maps, call by Grafcan, Calle Malaga 23, in Las Palmas. Discovery Walking Guides produces two titles for walkers: *Gran Canaria Mountains* and *Gran*

Dogs & Purple Prose

To the ancient Greeks, the fabled islands beyond the Pillars of Hercules (today's Straits of Gibraltar) were known as the Hesperides or Atlantes, after the daughters of Atlas who Hercules supposedly visited. Long thought to be abundant in every possible kind of fruit, the islands were also often referred to as the Garden of Hesperides. Some writers have also identified Elysium, the field of perfect peace where the ancient Greeks believed the good and great spent the afterlife, with the Canaries.

The Romans, who apparently never set foot on the islands, knew them as the Insulae Fortunatae (Fortunate Isles). The Spaniards, when they set about conquering them in the 15th century, also began by calling them the Islas Afortunadas.

Juba II, the North African king who told Pliny the Elder about the islands, referred to them as the Insulae Purpuriae (Purple Isles) because of the purple dyes extracted from the orchil lichen on Fuerteventura and Lanzarote. Juba's report can't have been all fiction as he at least got the number of islands right – seven. The Romans gave them the following names: Canaria (Gran Canaria), Nivaria (Tenerife), Capraria (Lanzarote), Planaria (Fuerteventura), Junonia Mayor (La Palma), Junonia Minor (La Gomera) and Pluvialia (El Hierro).

JANE SMITH

Which came first, the Canary or the islands?

The Guanches had their own names for the islands, some of them preserved to this day: Achinech (Tenerife), Tamarán (Gran Canaria), Tyterorgatra (Lanzarote), Maxorata (Fuerteventura), Benahoare (La Palma), Gomera (La Gomera) and Hero (El Hierro).

Why Canaria? One improbable tale talks of an adventuresome Latin couple, Cranus and Crana, who went off in search of a challenge, bumped into what is now Gran Canaria and liked it so much they stayed. They dubbed the island Cranaria, which was later simplified to Canaria.

Another theory suggests the name was inspired by the trilling canary birds, thought by some to be native to the islands. However, most ornithologists claim the bird took the name from the islands rather than the other way around.

Others reckon the name came from the Latin word for dog *(canus)* because members of Juba's expedition came across what they considered unusually large dogs. On the other hand, there was a minority school of thought which held that the natives of the island were dog-eaters!

And maybe none of these fanciful solutions to the riddle is near the mark. Yet another theory claims that the people of Canaria, who possibly arrived several hundred years before Christ, were in fact Berbers of the Canarii tribe living in Morocco. The tribal name was simply applied to the island and later accepted by Pliny. Canaria became 'great' *(gran)*, according to some chronicles, after its people put up a tough fight against the Spanish conquistadors. Equally unclear is at precisely what point the islands came to be known collectively as Las Islas Canarias, although probably this came with the completion of the Spanish conquest of the islands at the end of the 15th century.

Canaria South while Sunflower's *Landscapes of Gran Canaria* by Noel Rochford gives more ideas for walks, car tours and picnic sites.

Newspapers The most widely read local newspapers on Gran Canaria and the two most eastern islands are *Canarias 7* and *La Provincia*.

Of the several English-language weeklies, *Island Connections* – for sale at newsagents but available free from most tourist offices – is the most widely distributed.

Activities
Many visitors come to simply relax and escape the workaday world but if you're looking for something more active, there is ample potential. The Bahía de Pozo Izquierdo, on the south-eastern coast, has demanding, world-class surfing while Maspalomas and Playa de las Canteras (Las Palmas) have more gentle waves. There are several diving and deep-sea fishing outfits in the southern resorts while, on land, you can bike or trek independently or join a guided group.

Accommodation
Away from Las Palmas and the southern coastal resorts, accommodation is remarkably thin on the ground. As a rule you should not have too much trouble in the capital but the resorts can be full to overflowing in high season.

For something a thousand metaphorical miles from the package tour resorts, consider renting a *casa rural* (house in the country). They don't come cheap (count on anything from 10,000 ptas to 15,000 ptas per night for a place that will sleep up to four) but they usually represent good value for what you pay. Contact Gran Canaria Rural (☎ 928 46 25 47, fax 928 46 08 89, ℮ info@grancanariarural.com), AECAN (☎ 922 24 08 16, fax 922 24 40 03), who have an all-islands remit, or RETUR (☎ 928 66 16 68, fax 928 66 15 60).

Getting There & Away
Air Gran Canaria's Aeropuerto de Gando is, along with the two airports on Tenerife, the main hub in the islands. There are connections to all other islands as well as regular flights to mainland Spain, and a raft of international scheduled and charter flights.

Binter connects the island with Tenerife (6360 ptas) over 10 times daily (all but one to Tenerife Norte airport). It has three flights daily to La Palma (10,410 ptas), two per week to El Hierro (11,160 ptas, Friday and Sunday) and regular connections to Lanzarote (8860 ptas) and Fuerteventura (7760 ptas). Air Europa has one daily scheduled flight to Tenerife Norte.

Iberia has six flights daily to Madrid while Spanair has three and Air Europa has one (daily except Saturday). To Barcelona, Iberia flies daily and Spanair flies daily except Sunday.

The Aeropuerto de Gando (☎ 928 57 91 30) is 16km south of Las Palmas. At the airport you'll find a tourist information office on the ground floor (it doesn't have much information though, and only opens at peak arrival times), car-rental outlets, a post office and money-changing facilities (including a Western Union representative).

Boat Ferries and jetfoils link Gran Canaria with Tenerife, Lanzarote and Fuerteventura, using Las Palmas and Agaete ports. See the Getting There & Away sections under each port for more details and Sea in the Getting There & Away chapter for details of the ferry to/from Cádiz (mainland Spain).

Getting Around
Blue Global buses provide the island with a first-class network of routes, although the number of runs per day to many rural areas is pretty thin. In Las Palmas, yellow municipal buses provide a similarly efficient service that deserves to be the envy of many a larger city.

If you're travelling around the island, it's probably worthwhile investing in a Tarjeta Insular, an island-wide discount card, for 2000 ptas. Instead of buying individual tickets on the bus for each trip, you stick your card in the machine, tell the driver your destination and he endorses your card – when compared to the standard fare for a

GRAN CANARIA

journey, it represents at least a 30% saving on each trip. Cards are on sale at bus stations and from many newsagents and *estancos* (tobacconists).

The general number for enquiries is ☎ 902 38 11 10.

Las Palmas de Gran Canaria

postcode 35080 • pop 556,000

Las Palmas is the big smoke, the only place in the Canary Islands with that unmistakable big-city feel. OK, it oozes the kind of sunny languor you'd associate with the Mediterranean or North Africa, but the snarled traffic, bustling shopping districts and thriving port all give off the energy of *the* city, Spain's seventh largest.

The historic centre, if small, is rich in interest, and the restaurant- and bar-lined Playa de las Canteras could keep the average hedonist busy for days. The flavour is Spanish, with a heavy international overlay. Unlike in the southern resorts, however, the foreign crowd in Las Palmas is an eclectic mix of tourists, container-ship crews, and the flotsam and jetsam that tends to drift around port cities.

For visitors in search of nothing more than peace and quiet, or an uncomplicated beach-bar scene with English breakfasts thrown in, Las Palmas may seem like too much of a headache. But if you've come to the Canaries to experience Spain, and like a little city bustle plus a museum or two, the place rewards at least a couple of days' attention.

HISTORY

Although Jean de Béthencourt's partner in mischief, Gadifer de la Salle, sailed past here in 1403, it wasn't until 1478 that Europeans made a determined landing in the area. That year Juan Rejón and his troops set up camp just south of La Isleta, naming it Real de las Palmas. As the conquest of the island proceeded, the original military camp began to take on a more permanent look, and so the *barrio* (district) of San Antonio

Abad, later known as Vegueta, began to expand.

By the time Christopher Columbus sailed by on his way to the Americas in 1492, the busy little hub of the old town had already been traced out. Everybody likes to claim a hero for their very own and the Gran Canarian version of history has it that Columbus briefly put in here for repairs before pushing on to La Gomera.

Las Palmas grew quickly as a commercial centre, and in recognition of its importance the seat of the bishopric of the Canary Islands was transferred here from Lanzarote halfway through the 16th century.

The city, along with the rest of the archipelago, benefited greatly from the Spanish conquest of Latin America and the subsequent transatlantic trade. But you have to take the good with the bad, and the islands were a favourite target for pirates and buccaneers of all nations. In 1595 Sir Francis Drake raided Las Palmas with particular gusto. Four years later a still more determined band of Dutch adventurers reduced much of the town to ruins.

In 1821, Santa Cruz de Tenerife was declared capital of the single new Spanish province of Las Islas Canarias. This left the great and good of Las Palmas disgruntled but redress was some time in coming.

The fortunes of the port city fluctuated with those of the islands as a whole as boom followed bust in a chain of cash-crop cycles. However, Las Palmas began to go its own way towards the end of the 19th century, due in no small measure to the growing British presence in the city.

The trading families of the Millers and the Swanstons were already well established by the time Sir Alfred Lewis Jones set up the Grand Canary Coaling Company in Las Palmas. The city flourished as a crucial refuelling stop for transatlantic shipping. It was the British who introduced the first water mains, electricity company and telephone exchange to the city in the early years of the 20th century. However, it all came apart before the outbreak of WWII, as coal-fired ships gradually made way for more modern vessels.

Still, the city's prosperity had become such that Madrid could no longer resist calls for the islands to be divided into two provinces. Las Palmas thus became capital of Gran Canaria, Fuerteventura and Lanzarote in 1927.

It was from Las Palmas that Franco launched the coup in July 1936 that sparked the Spanish Civil War.

Since the 1960s, when the tourism boom was first felt in the islands, Las Palmas has grown from a middling port city of 70,000 souls to a bustling metropolis of over half a million. And while it shares evenly the status of regional capital with Santa Cruz de Tenerife, there is no doubt about which of the two is the main centre.

ORIENTATION

Las Palmas stretches from the old historical centre in the south, centred on the Vegueta and Triana districts, up a series of long boulevards towards bustling Santa Catalina and, the port, Puerto de la Luz – a good 3km. From there it continues up to what was once an islet off the island, still called La Isleta.

Most of what will be of interest to sightseers is concentrated in Vegueta. The bulk of the hotels are around Santa Catalina, close to the 3km-long golden sands of Playa de las Canteras, the bars, shops and port. You'll find plenty of authentic bars and restaurants in Vegueta and Triana.

The heavier, more international action is around Santa Catalina, which is also where the majority of the discos and nightclubs are.

Map N refers to the Las Palmas (North) map, Map S to the Las Palmas (South) map.

Maps

You'll find a free map sponsored by the Corte Inglés department store all over the place. The street-plan map (green cover) handed out by tourist offices is clearer to navigate by. For bus travel, pick up the local public-transport map, called *Guaguas Muncipales* (yellow cover). All three are available from tourist offices.

INFORMATION
Tourist Offices

Few towns can boast so many tourist information points. Most, alas, are fairly inept at answering queries that can't be resolved by simply handing over a brochure.

The *Cabildo* (regional government) tourist office (Map N; ☎ 928 26 46 23), in Parque de Santa Catalina, has an island-wide remit. It opens 9 am to 2 pm, Monday to Friday.

There's a municipal tourist office (Map S) in the town hall on Plaza de Santa Ana. It too observes jobsworths' hours – 10 am to 3 pm, Monday to Friday – as does the office (Map N) just inside the entrance to the Pueblo Canario complex, which functions 9 am to 2.30 pm, Monday to Friday.

The information kiosk in the southwestern corner of Parque San Telmo (Map S) opens 3.30 to 8 pm, Monday to Friday, and 10 am to 3 pm on Saturday. The tourist office (Map S) at the bus station is red-hot on island-wide transport info and also provides a general service. It opens 6.30 am to 8.30 pm on weekdays and 7.30 am to 1 pm at weekends.

There's also a wooden information kiosk (Map N) at the northern end of Playa de las Canteras, open 10 am to 7.30 pm on weekdays and 10 am to 1 pm on Saturday.

Finally, if – as is quite possible – you *still* haven't got the information you're looking for, try the information booth (Map N) on Avenida de Mesa y López by the Corte Inglés department store.

Foreign Consulates

For a list of foreign consulates in Las Palmas, see Embassies & Consulates in the Facts for the Visitor chapter. All the foreign consulates can be found on Map N.

Money

Viajes Insular (Map N; ☎ 928 22 79 50), at Calle Luis Morote 9, represents American Express. Western Union, for emergency money transfers, has an office at the airport. It is also represented by Office Services (Map N), Calle los Martínez de Escobar 5.

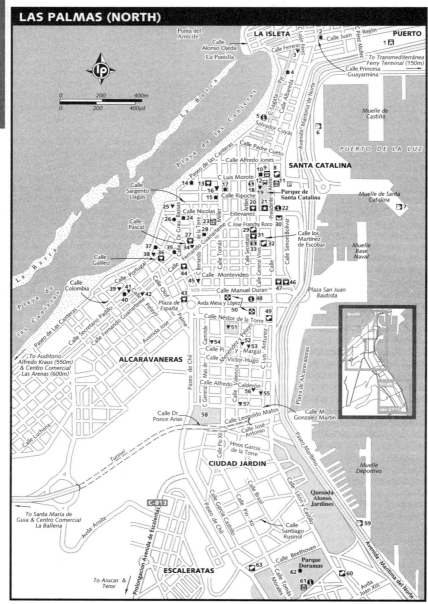

LAS PALMAS (NORTH)

LAS PALMAS (NORTH)

PLACES TO STAY
2   Pensión Princesa
4   Apartamentos Sol Canteras
10   Pensión Plaza
14   Apartamentos Playa Dorada
15   Apartamentos Catalina Park
17   Hostal Residencia Majorica;
     Hersoji Launderette
24   Apartamentos Marmoral
35   Hotel Olympia
37   Apartamentos La Goleta
40   Hotel Tamadaba
62   Hotel Santa Catalina; Casino
     de las Palmas

PLACES TO EAT
3   Mesón Condado
16   Casa Pablo
19   Restaurante Porto Vigo
25   Pans't & Bueno't
34   Restaurante Balalaika
38   Pat's Place
39   Rincón de la Pampa
41   Pasta Real
42   Fuji
45   Restaurante Tehran
51   Covered Market
52   Centro Vasco Aterpe Alai
53   Anthuriun
54   Mesón La Cuadra

55   Casa Rafael
56   Restaurante El Coto
57   Restaurante Hermanos
     Rogelio

CONSULATES
8   UK Consulate
29   German Consulate
32   US Consulate
49   French Consulate
60   Netherlands Consulate
63   Portuguese Consulate

BARS & DISCOS
13   Palacio Latino
20   Área
27   Gas
31   Sheehan's
36   Donde López
43   Persepolis; El Cinco; Geiser
     (Terrazas)
44   Pequeña Habana
46   Pick Up
47   Mogambo

OTHER
1   Castillo de la Luz
5   Tourist Information Booth
6   Naviera Armas Ferry
     Terminal

7   Estación Marítima;
     Trasmediterránea Jetfoils to
     Santa Cruz de Tenerife &
     Morro Jable
9   Telephone Office
11   Museo Elder de la Ciencia y
     la Tecnología
12   Fred Olsen Bus for
     Agaete
18   Viajes Insular (American
     Express)
21   Police Station
22   Tourist Office (Cabildo)
23   Zona Internet
26   Gran Canaria School of
     Languages
28   Buceo Canarias
30   Post Office
33   Office Services (Western
     Union & Telephone Office)
48   Tourist Information
     Booth
50   Corte Inglés Department
     Store
58   Estadio Insular
59   Bahia Cat (Boat Trips)
61   Pueblo Canario;
     Museo Néstor;
     Tourist Office Pérez
     Galdós

Post & Communications

The main post office (Map S) is at Avenida Primero de Mayo 62. Another big post office (Map N) is south-east of Parque de Santa Catalina.

Supplementing street phones, several phone offices are dotted about Santa Catalina. One office (Map N) is at Calle Luis Morote 12, another at Office Services (see Money earlier in this section).

Email & Internet Access

You can send email from Zona Internet (Map N), Calle Joaquin Costa 32, just southwest of Parque de Santa Catalina. It opens 9.30 am to midnight daily (from 6 pm on Sunday) and charges 475 ptas per hour (150 ptas for 15 minutes). Down in Triana, log on at Cyberspacio, Calle Peregrina 7. It opens 11 am to 2 pm and 5 to 11 pm, Monday to Saturday, and 5.30 to 11 pm on Sunday. On-line time costs 400 ptas per hour.

Gay & Lesbian Information

For information about gay groups on the islands, write in advance to the Colectivo de Gays y Lesbianas de Las Palmas, Apartado de Correos 707, 35080 Las Palmas, a group of volunteers.

Bookshops

For titles in Spanish, probably the best bookstore in town is the Casa del Lector (Map S), Paseo de Tomás Morales 46. For all you ever wanted to know about the Canary Islands, and more, try the Librería del Cabildo Insular de Gran Canaria (Map S), Calle del Travieso 15. Nearly all titles are in Spanish but they have a few shelves of English titles.

Grafcan (off Map S), Calle Malaga 23, is the best place on the island for maps.

Laundry

Las Palmas has plenty of dry cleaners and *lavanderías*, traditional laundries where you leave your washing and collect it later the same day. Hersoji (Map N), Calle Ripoche 22, beside Hostal Residencia Majorica, is conveniently central.

Emergency

There's a police station (Map N) on Parque Santa Catalina, just west of the Cabildo tourist office.

Dangers & Annoyances

Las Palmas is not only the largest city in the islands but palpably the dodgiest. There's a lot of drug abuse and, as a major port, Las Palmas attracts its share of shady characters.

All this means is that you should take the standard city streetwise precautions. Carry as little money and as few valuables on you as possible. Leave *nothing* of value (preferably nothing at all) in cars, especially the hired variety.

At night, avoid dark, quiet streets and parks. Parque San Telmo (Map S) and Parque de Santa Catalina (Map N) are safe enough in daylight, although even then, down-and-outs wander among the courting couples and playing children. At night, Parque de Santa Catalina becomes an informal camp site for the latest illegal immigrant arrivals from Africa – if the poor devils can get any sleep at all among the gibbering weirdos.

If hookers with attitude hanging around in doorways are your scene, head for Calle Molinos de Viento, a block west of Calle León y Castillo. Otherwise, it is perhaps best to avoid this louche zone.

VEGUETA & TRIANA

Unless indicated otherwise, the places listed appear on the Las Palmas (South) map. Map N refers to the Las Palmas (North) map.

Casa/Museo de Colón

This museum is a beautiful example of Canarian architecture, built around two patios overlooked by fine wooden balconies. The exterior itself is something of a work of art, with some showy plateresque elements mixing in original fashion with the brown-stained balconies so typical of the islands.

Although it's called Columbus' House (it's possible he passed by here to present his credentials to the governor in 1492), most of what you see was the residence of Las Palmas' early governors.

The museum's four sections present Columbus' voyages, the Canaries as a staging post for transatlantic shipping, pre-Columbian America and the city of Las Palmas. Upstairs is an art gallery whose most interesting canvases are from the Hispanic-Flemish school.

It opens 9 am to 7 pm Monday to Friday, and 9 am to 3 pm at weekends. Admission is free.

Catedral de Santa Ana & Museo Diocesano

The city's main place of worship was begun in the early 15th century, soon after the Spanish conquest, but took what must be a record 350 years to complete. The neoclassical facade contrasts with the interior, which is a fine example of what some art historians have denominated Atlantic Gothic that betrays the earlier beginnings of construction. The Gothic retable above the high altar comes from Catalunya (mainland Spain) and the exquisite lamp hanging before the altar was made in Genova (Italy). It also holds a number of paintings by Juan de Miranda, the islands' most respected 18th-century artist.

Entry to the cathedral is via the **Museo Diocesano** at Calle Espíritu Santo 20. The museum is set on two levels around the Patio de los Naranjos (Orange Tree Courtyard), once home to the Inquisition. It contains a fairly standard collection of religious art and memorabilia, including centuries-old manuscripts, a good deal of wooden sculptures and other ornaments.

The museum and cathedral open 9 am to 1.30 pm and 4 to 6.30 pm, Monday to Friday. Admission costs 300 ptas.

Iglesia de San Antonio Abad

Just behind the Casa/Museo de Colón (heading towards the waterfront), this little

GRAN CANARIA

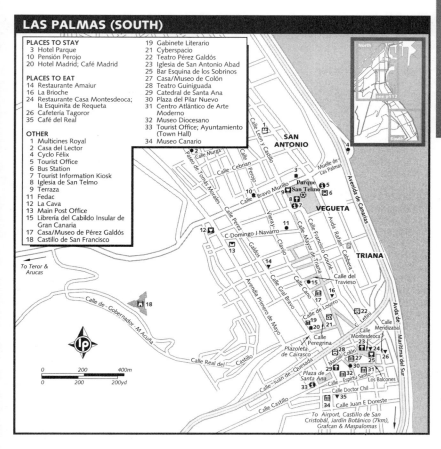

LAS PALMAS (SOUTH)

PLACES TO STAY
3 Hotel Parque
10 Pensión Perojo
20 Hotel Madrid; Café Madrid

PLACES TO EAT
14 Restaurante Amaiur
16 La Brioche
24 Restaurante Casa Montesdeoca;
    la Esquinita de Requeta
26 Cafetería Tagoror
35 Café del Real

OTHER
1 Multicines Royal
2 Casa del Lector
4 Cyclo Félix
5 Tourist Office
6 Bus Station
7 Tourist Information Kiosk
8 Iglesia de San Telmo
9 Terraza
11 Fedac
12 La Cava
13 Main Post Office
15 Librería del Cabildo Insular de
    Gran Canaria
17 Casa/Museo de Pérez Galdós
18 Castillo de San Francisco

19 Gabinete Literario
21 Cyberspacio
22 Teatro Pérez Galdós
23 Iglesia de San Antonio Abad
25 Bar Esquina de los Sobrinos
27 Casa/Museo de Colón
28 Teatro Guiniguada
29 Catedral de Santa Ana
30 Plaza del Pilar Nuevo
31 Centro Atlántico de Arte
    Moderno
32 Museo Diocesano
33 Tourist Office; Ayuntamiento
    (Town Hall)
34 Museo Canario

church of modest Romanesque-Canarian design is where, according to tradition, Columbus prayed for divine help before sailing for the Americas.

Museo Canario

The island's main museum chronicles Gran Canaria's pre-conquest history. It claims to be home to the biggest collection of Cro-Magnon skulls in the world – no mean boast! Some heads come attached to other body parts in the form of mummies. There's also a fair collection of pottery and other Guanche implements. The material comes

from across the island, and a mock-up of the Cueva Pintada of Gáldar (see Gáldar later in this chapter) has been set up to compensate for the fact that the real thing is, until mid-2002, closed to visitors.

The museum, at Calle Doctor Chil 25, opens 10 am to 8 pm, Monday to Friday, and 10 am to 2 pm on Saturday and Sunday. Admission costs 500 ptas.

Centro Atlántico de Arte Moderno

The city's main museum of modern art (☎ 928 31 18 24), at Calle Los Balcones 11, hosts temporary exhibitions. It opens 10 am to 9 pm, Tuesday to Saturday, and 10 am to 2 pm on Sunday. Admission is free.

Gabinete Literario
This sumptuous one-time theatre, with its gracious interior patio, has been declared a national monument. It's an old-world display of faded elegance, illumined by chandeliers and lined with bookcases crammed with learned-looking volumes. The place now functions as a kind of well-to-do club, but lesser mortals can eat outside on Plazoleta de Cairasco.

Calle Mayor de Triana
Traditionally, Calle Mayor de Triana, now a pedestrianised mall, was the main shopping street in Las Palmas. As you browse the shop windows, keep your head up and eyes peeled to enjoy the little architectural gems, among them some nice examples of modernism, that line this busy thoroughfare.

Casa/Museo de Pérez Galdós
In 1843 the Canary Islands' greatest writer, Benito Pérez Galdós, was born in this house in the heart of old Las Palmas. He lived the first 19 years of his life here before moving on to Madrid and literary greatness.

The house, at Calle Cano 6, contains a reconstruction of the author's study, various personal effects and other objects related to his life. It opens 9 am to 9 pm (to 8 pm from July to September) on weekdays, 10 am to 6 pm on Saturday and 10 am to 2 pm on Sunday. Admission is free.

Parque San Telmo
The Iglesia de San Telmo, on the southwestern side of the park, was one of the first religious buildings in the nascent town. Beside it is a tourist information kiosk and in the north-western corner, an attractively restored modernist kiosk which these days functions as a cafe. Its *terraza* (open air cafe) is a pleasant shady spot for a drink. The square can be a bit dodgy after dark (see Dangers & Annoyances earlier).

CIUDAD JARDÍN
The Parque Doramas is the nucleus of this area of the city, laid out by the British towards the end of the 19th century, when British businessmen dominated the economic life of Las Palmas. That said, this leafy, upper-class suburb is a decidedly eclectic mix of architectural styles, ranging from British colonial to Andalucían. The following all appear on Map N.

Pueblo Canario
Designed by the artist Néstor Martín Fernández de la Torre and built by his brother Miguel, the Pueblo Canario borders the gardens of the Parque Doramas. With a restaurant, terraces, shops and kiddies' play area, it is designed as a pleasant bit of escapism in a clearly Canarian architectural style. The small central plaza, surrounded by buildings reflecting that traditional style, makes for an agreeable drinks stop.

Museo Néstor
An art gallery originally dedicated purely to the works of Néstor, who died in 1938, the Museo Néstor was later expanded to accommodate a broader collection of works – displayed in the Gallery of Contemporary Canarian Art (rooms 11 to 13). It also houses period furniture and other memorabilia. The gallery opens 10 am to 1 pm and 4 to 8 pm, Tuesday to Friday, and 11 am to 2 pm on Sunday. Admission costs 150 ptas (students free).

Casino
If you remembered to bring along your black-tie evening wear and want to have a flutter in style, head for the **Casino de Las Palmas**. It's within the city's prestige Hotel Santa Catalina (see Places to Stay later), built in 1904 in the heart of the Parque Doramas. The casino opens nightly at 8 pm and closes between 4 and 5 am.

SANTA CATALINA
Unless indicated otherwise, places listed appear on the Las Palmas (North) map. Map S refers to the Las Palmas (South) map.

Plain Sailing

In the 1880s, when Puerto de la Luz (Las Palmas) was developing as a port, merchant and passenger ships had to moor some way from the docks. So a local variety of shuttle boat, equipped with oars and sails up to 13m high, was developed to service offshore vessels. From poop to prow these boats measured no more than 7m, and they were soon doing a brisk trade ferrying people and goods from ship to shore.

Like any business, these little *botes* knew both busy and slack times. During the latter their captains and crews organised regattas in the port area. An idea born to ease the boredom of empty days sitting on the docks slowly transformed itself into a regular competition, and the tradition has been maintained.

Eighteen of these curious craft remain today and they regularly gather for an afternoon's racing on Saturday (usually from 5 pm) and Sunday (around noon) from April to October. Crewed by eight to 12 people, each boat represents a *barrio*, or quarter, of Las Palmas.

Apart from the odd appearance of the participating vessels, the race itself is a little peculiar in that competitors race only *en bolina* (against the wind) but in such a way as to get maximum power from it. The fact that the prevailing wind is pretty much the same in the competition months off the east coast of Gran Canaria makes it the ideal spot for such races. The botes start at Playa de la Laja, a few kilometres south of the southern suburbs of Las Palmas, and finish at Playa de Alcaravaneras.

Playa de las Canteras

The 3km stretch of narrow, golden sandy beach is the main attraction. It has made the Santa Catalina district the city's main tourist drawcard. There's an attractive *paseo marítimo* (promenade) – the Paseo de las Canteras – which, once major construction works are completed in its central section, will allow walkers, cyclists, joggers and roller bladers to cover the entire length, free from traffic. The whole area fairly hums with the activity of bars, restaurants, nightclubs and shops.

This is by far the nicest beach, so there is little need to use small **Playa de las Alcaravaneras**, in the port, or **Playa de la Laja**, south of the city in a pretty grim, barren and partly industrial setting.

Museo Elder de la Ciencia y la Tecnología

This 21st-century museum of science and technology (☎ 928 011 828), Parque de Santa Catalina s/n, full of things that whirr, clank and hum, occupies a revamped docks warehouse to the east of Parque de Santa Catalina. It opens 11 am to 10 pm daily except Monday and admission costs 500 ptas (those aged under 18, 350 ptas).

Castillo de la Luz

Built in the 16th century (as were most other such fortresses around the Canary Islands) to ward off pirate attacks, the castle has traditionally been used for occasional art exhibitions. It was closed at the time of writing, when its environs were being extensively landscaped.

Other forts around town include the dilapidated hulk of the Castillo de San Francisco (Map S), high up above Vegueta, and Castillo de San Cristóbal to the south of the city.

JARDÍN BOTÁNICO CANARIO VIERA Y CLAVIJO

About 9km south-west of the city, just before the village of Tafira Alta, this vast botanical garden (☎ 928 35 36 04) – Spain's largest, encompassing 27 hectares – hosts a broad range of Macronesian flora from all seven Canary Islands, including many species on the verge of extinction. It opens 9 am to 6 pm daily and admission is free. Wear trainers or stout shoes as some of the stony paths are uneven.

Bus Nos 301, 302 and 303 all pass by the garden's upper entrance. By car, take the C-811 road from Las Palmas.

ACTIVITIES

Surfing

Playa de las Canteras is not the world's greatest surf break but you can catch some good waves, and plenty of locals are out there at the weekend. It is one of the better beaches on the island. Unfortunately, there's nowhere to hire gear so pack your own board.

Diving

Buceo Canarias (Map N; ☎ 928 26 27 86), Calle Bernardo de la Torre 56–58, organises courses at all levels and both rents and sells diving gear. It opens Tuesday to Saturday.

Boat Trips

Bahia Cat (Map N) does twice-daily one-hour boat-trips around the port (1500 ptas per person) from the Muelle Deportivo.

Walking

Las Palmas has two great paseos marítimos, seaside promenades that hug the coast. For the shorter one, see Playa de las Canteras earlier in this section. The other extends from the northern limit of Playa de Alcaravaneras for nearly 5km, the downside being that it's sandwiched between the shore and a six-lane highway for too much of its length.

For something a little more strenuous ring Rutas Canarias, a local walking group, on ☎/fax 928 25 40 09. Using public transport, they set out on hikes every weekend (1975 ptas, including transport).

Cycling

Not serious cycling, this, but you can trundle up and down the prom on a machine from the stall of Cyclo Felix (Map S) on the paseo marítimo just east of Parque San Telmo. Open 4 to 8 pm, Tuesday to Friday, and noon to 8 pm at weekends, it rents tandems, trikes, bikes and even four-wheelers which can take up to six people.

LANGUAGE COURSES

There are a dozen or so language schools in Las Palmas, some of which offer Spanish classes – check the Yellow Pages.

The Gran Canaria School of Languages (Map N; ☎ 928 26 79 71, fax 928 27 89 80), at Calle Doctor Grau Bassas 27, for example, offers intensive courses for 16,600 ptas per week – and you can enrol for as short a period as one week.

SPECIAL EVENTS

Fiestas

Although overshadowed by its more famous version in Santa Cruz de Tenerife, Carnaval is nevertheless a big event in Las Palmas. Three to four weeks of madness and fancy dress mark the first rupture with winter in February (the dates move depending on when Lent falls) – not that winter out here is any great trial! The bulk of the action takes place around Parque de Santa Catalina.

In late June the Fiesta de San Juan, patron saint of the city, coincides with midsummer's day. Cultural events are staged across the city while big fireworks displays and concerts take place on Playa de las Canteras.

Corpus Christi, another feast with moveable dates that takes place around June, is marked in particular by the laying out of extraordinary floral 'carpets' in some of the central streets of the old city.

Among the oldest religious festivals in Las Palmas is the *romería*, or pilgrimage/procession in honour of the Virgen de la Luz, held in October. Most of the action takes place around Playa de las Canteras and in La Isleta. The battle with Sir Francis Drake is commemorated at the same time.

Festivals

Las Palmas hosts a range of international festivals including the Festival Internacional de Música (January), Festival de Opera (February–March), Festival de Ballet y Danza (May) and the Muestra Internacional de Cine (an international film festival held every two years (October–November).

PLACES TO STAY – BUDGET

The bulk of the accommodation of all classes is around Santa Catalina beach and the port.

Vegueta & Triana (Map S)

The pick of the crop, in a ramshackle sort of way, has to be friendly *Hotel Madrid* (☎ *928 36 06 64, fax 928 38 21 76, Plazoleta Cairasco 4)*, right by the Gabinete Literario. Simple singles/doubles cost 3500/4500 ptas while those with bathroom cost 4500/5500 ptas. Ask for a room overlooking the square.

A scrupulously clean and acceptable alternative is *Pensión Perojo (☎ 928 37 13 87, Calle Perojo 1)*, which has basic rooms for 2500/3500 ptas (3000/4000 ptas if you're only spending one night).

Santa Catalina (Map N)

Many of the clientele at *Pensión Plaza* (☎ *928 26 52 12, Calle Luis Morote 16)* might have tumbled off the latest container ship. Still, it's OK and there's usually a room going. Basic singles/doubles cost 2400/3400 ptas, while those with bathroom cost 2800/3800 ptas.

Hostal Residencia Majorica (☎ 928 26 28 78, Calle Ripoche 22) is even more multi-ethnic but not so cheerful with it. It's right in the heart of Santa Catalina but perhaps a little too much so for some – it can be pretty noisy. Spartan singles cost 1500 ptas, doubles between 3000 ptas and 3500 ptas.

Pensión Princesa (☎ 928 46 77 04, Calle Princesa Guayarmina 2) offers bleak rooms with bathroom for 2200/3200 ptas.

A couple of steps up, *Hotel Tamadaba* (☎ *928 22 07 92, Calle Pelayo 10)* has rooms with bathroom for 5000 ptas.

Apartamentos La Goleta (☎ 928 38 09 78, Paseo de las Canteras 58) is nothing flash but it's right on the beach and is very good value. Apartments for two cost 3500 ptas, while those sleeping up to four cost 5000 ptas.

PLACES TO STAY – MID-RANGE
Vegueta & Triana (Map S)

There really isn't a lot in this area. To stay near the old centre and enjoy a little luxury, about your only option is recommended *Hotel Parque (☎ 928 36 80 00, fax 928 36 88 56, Muelle de Las Palmas 2)*, where singles/doubles cost 7400/14,700 ptas, including breakfast – and what a breakfast, with a great view over town from the 6th-floor restaurant. All rooms have aircon and the hotel has its own garage (800 ptas per night).

Santa Catalina & the Port (Map N)

Moving up the line a tad from the cheapies, *Hotel Olympia (☎ 928 26 17 20, fax 928 26 26 17, Calle Doctor Grau Bassas)* offers plain singles/doubles with bathroom for 5500/6500 ptas. At this level, you may prefer to consider an apartment.

Apartamentos Marmoral (☎ 928 27 12 08, Calle Doctor Grau Bassas 38) has functional ones at 5800/6000/6400 ptas for single/double/triple occupancy.

Better are *Apartamentos Catalina Park* (☎ *928 26 41 20, Calle Tomás Miller 67)* where apartments for two/three cost 6000/7000 ptas.

Apartamentos Sol Canteras (☎ 928 26 65 58, fax 928 26 65 58, Calle Sagasta 76) is another step up in quality. Interior apartments, which can take up to four, cost 6000 ptas. Those for up to three with ocean views go for 7000 ptas; that 1000 ptas extra is a worthwhile investment.

Also right on the beach are *Apartamentos Playa Dorada (☎ 928 26 51 00, fax 928 26 51 04, Calle Luis Morote 69)* where apartments with balcony cost 9000/11,500/13,000 ptas for two/three/four people. Like several places, they're around 25% cheaper in May and June.

PLACES TO STAY – TOP END

Hotel Santa Catalina (Map N; ☎ 928 24 30 40, fax 928 24 27 64), at the heart of Parque Doramas, is *the* address in Las Palmas. It exudes the class of another era and, if the 15,840/24,750 ptas price tag doesn't sufficiently dent your life savings, you can always throw away more at the hotel's casino.

PLACES TO EAT
Vegueta & Triana (Map S)

A good little place for breakfast is *La Brioche*, on the corner of Calle Mayor de Triana and Calle Losero. A ham-and-cheese croissant, orange juice and coffee will cost about 700 ptas.

Café Madrid, beneath the hotel of the same name (see Places to Stay), is great for breakfast or an aperitif, whether you're sitting inside or on the terraza. *Café del Real (Calle Doctor Chil 21)* is an elegant place for a cup of coffee or even a *bocadillo* (French-bread sandwich).

For something simple, *Cafetería Tagoror (Calle Mendizabal)* is unbeatable value. It does a huge range of tapas and has a good choice of *platos combinados* (mixed dishes) for 600 ptas. From 6 pm, it also serves *arepas* (an envelope of maize – corn – with a savoury filling) for 250 ptas.

Restaurante Casa Montesdeoca (Calle Montesdeoca 10) is set in an exquisitely maintained 16th-century Canarian colonial style house. The patio (internal courtyard) is cool and relaxing. Mains cost between 1700 ptas and 2300 ptas. The fish is deliciously fresh and they specialise in *bacalao* (cod), prepared in 12 different ways.

Another good up-market establishment is popular *Restaurante Amaiur (Calle Pérez Galdós 2)*, which offers mainly Basque cuisine. Mains cost between 1700 ptas and 2500 ptas.

Santa Catalina & the Port (Map N)

For quick food, *Pans't & Bueno't (Paseo de las Cantera 38)* is OK for bocadillos and pizza.

Mesón La Cuadra (Calle General Mas de Gaminde 32) has an excellent set menu for 1600 ptas.

A promising little Lebanese joint is *Restaurante El Coto (Calle Alfredo Calderón 21)*. Not far away, *Casa Rafael (Calle Luis Antunez 25)* represents a return to more traditional local cooking and is popular with Canarios. Mains cost between 1800 ptas and 2200 ptas.

For good Basque cooking you can't beat the *Centro Vasco Aterpe Alai (Calle Menéndez y Pelayo 10)*. This prized cuisine very rarely comes cheap, so you'll be looking at up to 3000 ptas per head.

Another expensive place with a fine reputation is *Anthuriun (Calle Pi y Margall 10)*, where mains come in at about 2000 ptas.

More modest is *Restaurante Hermanos Rogelio (Calle Valencia 4)*, where you can dine on hearty mainstream Spanish and Canarian food for about 2000 ptas per person.

Those with a hankering for the British Isles can gather at *Pat's Place (Calle Galileo 3)*. It opens evenings only, Monday to Saturday, and from 12.30 pm on Sunday.

Pasta Real (Calle del Secretario Padilla 28) is not so much an Italian eatery as a haven for vegetarians. It caters for carnivores too, and the food is tasty and inventive with mains starting at 1250 ptas.

Serious meat eaters should head round the corner. If it's a fat, sizzling steak you're after, settle into the friendly, Argentinian *Rincón de la Pampa (☎ 928 22 26 00, Calle Colombia 6)*.

Mesón Condado (Calle Ferreras 22) serves up a mix of Galician food (concentrating on shellfish) from the north-west of Spain, Canarian and more mainstream Spanish dishes. Count on spending the best part of 2000 ptas.

Casa Pablo (Calle Tomás Miller 73) has Spanish mains for about 1000 ptas. It's a popular little spot, oozing atmosphere.

If you fancy a special night out, up-market *Restaurante Porto Vigo (☎ 928 27 65 18, Calle General Vives 90)*, whose main entrance is in Parque de Santa Catalina, serves up very good cuisine from Galicia. It specialises in octopus and other seafood, washed down with a crisp Gallego Ribeiro white wine. Main dishes cost between 2400 ptas and 3000 ptas.

As befits a big port, you can eat exotically if you look around. For Japanese food at less than the usual Japanese restaurant prices, visit the unassuming *Fuji (Calle Fernando Guanarteme 56)*. Tempura and other mains start at 900 ptas.

For Middle Eastern food with a difference, *Restaurante Tehran*, at the angle of Calle Bernardo de la Torre and Calle Rafael Almeda, specialises in Iranian cuisine. There's even caviar on the menu, starting – that's *starting*! – at 5100 ptas. Your more normal main dishes cost between 1100 ptas and 1500 ptas.

From the other side of the Caspian Sea – and also offering caviar – is **Restaurante Balalaika** *(Fernando Guanarteme 25)* with a Russian menu and mains costing around 1500 ptas.

Self-Catering

If you're cooking for yourself, shun the big supermarkets and take your custom to the *covered market* (Map N) between Calles Barcelona and Nestor de la Torre. Open mornings only, daily except Sunday, it's relatively small for such a large city yet full of atmosphere.

ENTERTAINMENT
Bars, Pubs & Terrazas

There is no shortage of watering holes in Las Palmas, especially in Santa Catalina and around Playa de las Canteras.

Three popular terrazas are **Persepolis**, **El Cinco** and **Geiser** on Plaza de España (Map N), good for a daytime drink or as places to kick off the evening's fun.

If you're in need of a Guinness or just feel like being in a spot of almost Irish territory, **Sheehan's** *(Map N; Calle los Martínez de Escobar 8)* is the place for you.

The Vegueta area also gets busy at this time, although for some tastes it's a little too rowdy to be fun.

Bar Esquina de los Sobrinos *(Map S; Calle Montesdeoca 3)* is a great old place with huge hams dangling from the ceiling.

By contrast, **La Esquinita de Requeta** *(Map S)*, just around the corner on Calle Mendizabal, is a smart designer bar. Both open evenings only until late.

La Cava *(Map S; Avenida del Primero de Mayo 57)* is easy to miss and has a rather conspiratorial air about it. It stays open until about 3 am.

The bars around the Muelle Deportivo (Map N) offer a more sedate and posey scene (this is yachtie territory after all).

Late-Night Bars & Discos

The late-night bars and discos are mostly in the Santa Catalina-beach-Puerto de la Luz

area. Don't expect to pay less than 500 ptas per glass, whatever's in it.

Gas *(Map N; Calle Pascal 1)* is a late-night hangout, although it starts up at the uncommonly early hour of 10.30 pm.

Pequeña Habana *(Map N; Calle Fernando Guanarteme 45)* is a cool salsa-bar open until 3.30 am. Drinks cost an equally cool 800 ptas – no wonder the locals need the dancing to loosen up!

Donde López *(Map N; Calle Galileo 9)* doesn't get going until after midnight. It's a slightly louche little place but has a great atmosphere if it doesn't get too crowded.

Palacio Latino *(Map N; Calle Luis Morote 51)*, as the name implies, throbs to a South American beat. It attracts a varied crowd, some of it definitely off the boats.

Mogambo *(Map N; Calle Montevideo 5)* and **Pick Up**, next door at No 3, are both good dance places that don't bother opening before midnight. The former attracts a younger, marginally wilder set, while the music in the latter is fairly mainstream stuff.

Área *(Map N; Calle Secretario Artiles 48)* is a disco that plays mainly Spanish pop music and opens Thursday to Saturday only.

Live Music

You can enjoy free performances of Canarian folk music in the Pueblo Canario every Sunday morning from about 11.30 am.

The Auditorio Alfredo Kraus is used for quite a few big-name concerts. Otherwise, in summer lots of events are staged on Playa de las Canteras. Tickets are usually available at the Corte Inglés department store.

Classical Music & Opera

The spectacular **Auditorio Alfredo Kraus** (☎ 928 49 17 70) designed by the Catalan architect Óscar Tusquets, is what one French expert described as 'a boat of air, sea and light'. Constructed partly of volcanic rock and with a huge window affording the spectators (up to 1700) broad ocean views, it is the dominant feature of the southern end of Playa de las Canteras.

Concerts are also sometimes performed in the Teatro Pérez Galdós.

Cinema

There are three *multicines* complexes in Las Palmas. The chances of getting to see undubbed versions of foreign movies are slight. *Multicines Royal (Map S; Calle León y Castillo 85)* is central.

Theatre

Teatro Pérez Galdós (Map S; ☎ 928 36 15 09, Calle Lentini 1) has some theatrical performances and more frequent music recitals.

The other mainstream theatre, *Teatro Guiniguada (Map S; ☎ 928 38 09 86, Calle Mesa de León)*, gets the lion's share of the better quality productions, be they classics or more modern pieces.

SPECTATOR SPORTS
Football

Union Deportiva (UD) de Las Palmas, to give the club its full name, celebrated the millennium and its 50th anniversary by being promoted to the first division. What gave added piquancy was that the team's ascent coincided with relegation to Division Two for Tenerife – arch rivals on the football pitch and in every other field. To see UD in action, join the throng heading for the Estadio Insular (Map N) on Calle Pio XII.

SHOPPING

Before buying handicrafts and other souvenirs, make first for the Fedac (Fundación para la Etnografía y el Desarollo de la Artesanía Canaria; Map S) shop at Calle Domingo J Navarro 7 – a government-sponsored non-profit-making store where prices and quality are a good standard by which to measure those of products sold elsewhere. You'll find traditional handicrafts such as pottery, baskets, and leatherwork.

The traditional shopper's street has for centuries been Calle Mayor de Triana (Map S). The street is nowadays more interesting for its jumble of modernist architecture than its stores.

Las Palmas' self-promoted chic shoppers' hangout is Avenida de Mesa y López

(Map N). Here you'll find a gigantic Corte Inglés and a host of other shops and boutiques. Nearby, Indians have moved in to many of the shops around Parque de Santa Catalina to sell cheap electronic goods (or sell electronic goods cheaply, depending on how you view these things).

Dedicated shoppers may want to take a look around the Centro Comercial Las Arenas, out by the Auditorio Alfredo Kraus at the southern end of Playa de las Canteras. It's got everything from fashion stores to a cinema complex. One better still is the 120,000 sq metre Centro Comercial La Ballena (Carretera del Norte 113), built in the shape of a whale!

GETTING THERE & AWAY
Air

See Getting There & Away at the beginning of the chapter for details.

Bus

The bus station (Map S; ☎ 928 36 83 35 or ☎ 902 38 11 10 for timetable enquiries) is at the northern end of the Vegueta district, beside Parque San Telmo. You should be able to pick up a copy of Global's island-wide schedules from any tourist office.

Bus Nos 30 and 50 (non-stop) go to Maspalomas (650 ptas), No 1 to Puerto de Mogán (805 ptas), Nos 12 and 80 to Telde (165 ptas) and Nos 101, 102, 103 and 105 to Guía and Gáldar (325 ptas). There are frequent services to all these destinations.

A night owls' bus, No 5, links the capital and Maspalomas. It leaves on the hour from Las Palmas and on the half hour from Maspalomas, beginning at 8/9.30 pm and continuing until 3/4.30 am.

If you plan to travel much outside town, a Tarjeta Insular (see Getting Around at the beginning of this chapter) may well save you money.

Car & Motorcycle

There are car rental firms at the airport, jetfoil terminal and scattered across the Santa Catalina district of the city. Three possibilities are Autos Canaria (☎ 928 27 08 61),

Calle Tenerife 6; Agencia Guanche (☎ 928 36 88 77), Calle Bravo Murillo 13; and Avis (☎ 928 26 55 37).

Boat

For details of the weekly ferry to/from Cádiz (mainland Spain), see Sea in the Getting There & Away chapter.

The quickest way to Santa Cruz de Tenerife is by Trasmediterránea (☎ 902 45 46 45) jetfoil (one hour 20 minutes). They leave five times daily (three times on Sunday) and the standard fare is 6265 ptas (3840 ptas off-peak – which is most of the time). Naviera Armas (☎ 928 26 77 00) also has one fast ferry daily except Sunday on this route (5000 ptas). Both companies run one service daily on to Morro Jable in Fuerteventura (fare as for Tenerife). The jetfoil takes 1½ hours and the Naviera Armas boat exactly double.

For a bus/ferry combination to Santa Cruz de Tenerife with Fred Olsen, see Getting There & Away under Agaete & Puerto de las Nieves later in this chapter. If you enjoy the sea trip for its own sake, you might want to take Trasmediterránea's weekly standard ferry, which sets sail on Thursday (3005 ptas, four hours).

Three Trasmediterránea ferries per week serve Puerto del Rosario on Fuerteventura (3900 ptas, eight hours) and Arrecife on Lanzarote (3900 ptas, 10 hours). It also has one sailing per week to Santa Cruz de la Palma (5120 ptas, eight hours).

Naviera Armas has two weekly ferries to Puerto del Rosario (3605 ptas) and three to Arrecife (3705 ptas).

Fred Olsen (☎ 928 55 40 05 in Agaete/ Puerto de las Neives, ☎ 928 49 50 46 in Las Palmas) has a daily service to Puerto del Rosario (3080 ptas), continuing to Arrecife (a further 1850 ptas).

GETTING AROUND
To/From the Airport

Bus No 60 runs between the airport and Las Palmas bus station every hour around the clock and twice hourly between 7 am and 7 pm. The journey takes about 25 minutes, traffic permitting, and costs (245 ptas). A taxi between the airport and central Las Palmas is likely to cost you about 3000 ptas.

Bus

Yellow buses serve the metropolitan area. Pick up a route map from the tourist office at the bus station or from one of the other information offices around town.

The Tarjeta Insular (see Getting There & Away at the beginning of this chapter for details) also works on urban routes. Just stick it in the machine and it will deduct 90 ptas. A standard single ticket, bought on the bus, costs 130 ptas.

Yellow buses No 1, 12, 13 and 15 all run from Triana northwards as far as the port and the northern end of Playa de las Canteras, calling by the bus station and Parque de Santa Catalina.

For 1000 ptas, you can buy a ticket giving you unlimited hop-on-hop off travel for one day on the Bus Turística (Tourist Bus). It departs from Parque de Santa Catalina irregularly 12 times daily, making it almost impossible to plan a day around Las Palmas and rely on it for getting around. This said, if you just jump on and stay aboard for the round trip, it's an excellent way of getting an initial overview of the town.

Car & Motorcycle

Driving and parking in Las Palmas are a pain. It's not really any worse than many mainland Spanish cities, but rush-hour traffic jams are frustrating, as is the sometimes misleading one-way street system. Most of the centre operates meter parking. Otherwise there are several private car parks, where you pay up to 200 ptas an hour.

Taxi

If you need a taxi, call ☎ 928 46 00 00, 928 46 56 66 or ☎ 928 46 22 12. You can flag them down or pick them up at one of the 34 taxi stands across the city.

Bicycle

Biciguagua ('beeseewawa') is a great scheme, operated by Global, the island bus company, which ought to be emulated across Europe. For 1000 ptas per day, you can rent a bike from the bus station tourist office, open 8 am to 8 pm. Take along your passport or ID and be prepared to leave 5000 ptas as a refundable deposit.

Around the Island

With your own transport, you can get a reasonable look at the entire island in two to three days. Buses connect most towns and villages, but you will use up more time this way. Cyclists not averse to some tough inclines will enjoy the lightly trafficked roads of the interior.

CENTRAL CIRCUIT

Starting from Las Palmas you can enjoy a one-day circuit, heading first south and then cutting inland to take in the mountainous Tejeda region before swinging northeastwards back towards the capital.

Telde

postcode 35200 • pop 99,500

Telde is the island's second city. It was founded *before* the Spanish conquest, by monks from Mallorca seeking to set up a bishopric in the Fortunate Isles, and is known for its production of string instruments, above all the timple – a kind of ukelele – the islands' musical emblem.

The 12km trip south from Las Palmas passes through an arid, semi-industrialised landscape. But it's worth taking the trouble to visit Telde's San Juan and San Francisco areas, the nucleus of the old town. Here, the houses positively gleam with whitewash as the town preens itself and tries hard to live down its industrial image.

The tourist office (☎ 928 68 13 36), at Calle León y Castillo 2, just off Plaza de San Juan, opens 8 am to 3 pm weekdays.

Among the well-aged noble houses of the San Juan area, the 15th-century **Basílica de San Juan** stands out. As you enter, your eye is drawn to the elaborate 16th-century altarpiece, all gilt and gold, and with a Crucifixion at its heart. On the large silver cross the Christ figure, made of a corn-based plaster by Tarasco Indians in Mexico, dates from the earliest days of cultural contact between the two continents.

The **Museo León y Castillo** at Calle León y Castillo 43–45 is devoted to the family of the same name and in particular a late 19th-century politician – you'll want to be a serious Spanish history buff to get much out of this.

More interesting for most is the short walk to the **Iglesia de San Francisco**. From the Plaza de San Juan, take cobbled Calle Inés Chanida westwards as it runs alongside an old aqueduct with orange and banana groves below. In the church, note the three polychrome stone altars on the northernmost of the twin naves and the fine artesonado ceilings.

On Plaza de San Juan is *La Alameda*, a pleasant cafe with an interior patio by day and a lively pub at night.

Bus Nos 12 and 80 run to/from Las Palmas every 20 minutes.

Ingenio & Agüimes

A short bus ride south of Telde brings you to the towns of Ingenio and Agüimes, separated from one another by the Barranco de Guayadeque (see the next section) and in themselves of little interest. Of the two, Agüimes boasts a marginally more attractive town centre, the centrepiece of which is shady Plaza del Rosario, bounded on one side by the **Iglesia de San Sebastián**, considered one of the best examples of Canarian neo-classicism.

What does make Agüimes special is the Encuentro Teatral Tres Continentes, an annual gathering of theatre companies from Europe, South America and Africa. During this September festival, an otherwise fairly dull place becomes a temporary hotbed of international creativity. For advance information, you could try ringing Agüimes' Concejalía de Cultura (☎ 928 78 41 00).

Plenty of buses connect the two towns with Telde and Las Palmas. From Agüimes, bus No 22 heads south-east to the coast and **Arinaga**, a popular local spot for swimming even though there's no beach.

Barranco de Guayadeque

The real reason for being hereabouts lies *between* Ingenio and Agüimes. The Barranco de Guayadeque (Guayadeque Ravine) rises up into central Gran Canaria in a majestic sweep of crumpled ridges, its close-cropped vegetation softening the otherwise arid terrain with a little green. Most curiously, about halfway along the 9km road leading into the barranco from Agüimes (there is another road from Ingenio) you'll find an odd relic of bygone ages – a troglodyte hamlet. Some of the handful of inhabitants here live in cleverly decked-out caves.

Another 4km and the road peters out in an impassable (for vehicles) track and a couple of restaurants. *Restaurante Tagoror* is recommended and modestly priced.

Temisas

If you have a vehicle, you can take a back road from Agüimes to Santa Lucía (or Santa Lucía de Tirajana to give its full name). The C-815 highway, which all the buses and coaches take, also heads this way.

If you decide to opt for the narrow, little-frequented and only just two-lane back road, as it weaves its way around the mountains notice the terracing up each side valley and incised into many of the flanks. All the terraces were worked until quite recently. Then came mass tourism and with it plenty of less-gruelling, better-paid work.

The setting for sleepy Temisas, with its backdrop of impenetrable cliffs, is impressive. And the village itself has preserved a good deal of its older stone houses.

Bus No 34 connects Temisas with San Bartolomé de Tirajana and El Doctoral (in the south-east) every two hours.

Santa Lucía

Despite its pretty position in the upper reaches of a palm-studded valley, the place is something of a tourist-fuelled travesty. Someone has seen fit to build a very cheap-looking Disney castle and shoved inside, any which way, several hundred Guanche artefacts and a jumble of more modern tools and implements. Admission costs 300 ptas,

but you need a healthy sense of the silly to savour this 'Castillo de la Fortaleza'. Just behind it is the *Restaurante Hao*, a well-advertised and patronised tour-bus eating stopover.

At the western exit of the village are the less strident and more modest *Restaurante Casa Antonio* and *Restaurante Mirador Santa Lucía*.

San Bartolomé de Tirajana
postcode 35290 • pop 3573
• elevation 850m

San Bartolomé has no notable sights but the views out over the Tirajana valley are pleasing and you could choose a worse spot to get stuck for the night. *Hostal Santana* (☎ 928 12 71 32), on the main drag, has simple singles/doubles for 2000/3200 ptas. Along the same street are several eateries and bars. If you're planning a visit, make it on Sunday morning, when there's a lively farmers market known as Mercatunte.

Fataga

A 7km detour south from San Bartolomé (or a 30-minute drive north from Playa del Inglés) brings you to the charming hamlet of Fataga, sitting squat on a small knoll, humbled by the tall cliffs that overhang it to the west. Its narrow, car-free cobbled lanes are a joy to roam. Several houses have already been tastefully renovated; get there soon before it becomes over-gentrified.

Bar Restaurante La Albericoque (☎ 928 79 86 56, Calle Nestor Álamo 4–6), on the main road, has a couple of rooms at 4000 ptas. *El Molino del Agua* (☎ 928 17 20 89, fax 928 17 22 44) 1.5km north of the village, is something of a package-tour circus during the day with camel rides and a good quality feed-the-five-thousand restaurant. But, set amid a mature palm grove, it's a very pleasant, tranquil place – once the coaches have rolled off into the distance. Singles/doubles are good value at 5000/7500 ptas. If the camels (1000 ptas per ride) fail to turn you on, you can always hire a bike for the day for the same price.

Bus No 18 (from Maspalomas to San Bartolomé) calls by four times daily.

Tejeda & Around

postcode 35360 • pop 880
• elevation 1050m

Tejeda is 33km north of San Bartolomé along a road that twists its way through splendidly rugged scenery of looming cliffs and deep gorges. It is a quiet, unprepossessing hill village whose main attraction is its marvellous setting. A good place for lunch is the ***Restaurante Tejeda*** (☎ 928 66 60 55), near the southern exit from town. If you are tempted to stay overnight in this pretty spot, rooms with bathroom cost 4000 ptas.

Cruz de Tejeda The greenish-stone cross – from which this spot, north of Tejeda, takes its name – marks the centre of Gran Canaria and its old *caminos reales* (king's highways), along which it is still possible to cross the entire island.

From the lookouts here you can contemplate the island's greatest natural wonders:

JANE SMITH

Cruz de Tejeda marks the centre of Gran Canaria.

to the west the Roque Bentayga (and in clear weather the great cone of Teide on Tenerife), to the south Pozo de las Nieves (the island's highest point) and the odd-looking **Roque Nublo** (1803m), which as often as not truly is enveloped in a wad of cloud, and dropping away to the north-east the plains of San Mateo.

You can also buy souvenirs and ride donkeys if you feel the urge.

Cheery ***Hotel El Refugio*** (☎ 928 66 65 13, fax 928 66 65 20) is a rural hostelry that makes a great base for a few days' walking. It has singles/doubles for 8500/10,000 ptas in high season (6800/8500 ptas in low season) and a good restaurant. The one-time *parador* is being all but rebuilt and won't be back in action for ages.

Bus No 305 from Las Palmas (via Santa Brígida and Vega de San Mateo) passes by five times daily on its way to Tejeda. From the south of the island you're better off by bike or car; there's precisely one bus per week from Playa del Inglés (No 18), leaving at 8 am on Sunday and returning at 12.30 pm.

Roque Bentayga About 10km south-west of Tejeda village rises up the Roque Bentayga (1404m), it's signposted – you need your own transport. Around the Roque itself, and farther afield, there are various reminders of the Guanche presence here – from rock inscriptions to granaries and a sacred ritual site. There's also a Centro de Interpretación, which seems to be permanently shut.

Pozo de las Nieves Those with their own wheels can drive the 15km east to this, the highest peak on the island at 1949m. Follow the signs for Los Pechos and keep an eye on the military communications post which sits atop the rise. The views are breathtaking on a clear day. Directly west is the distinctive Roque Nublo.

San Mateo

Descending from the barren, chilly heights of Tejeda, you'll notice the scene around you quickly transforming itself as you approach San Mateo – or Vega de San Mateo, to give the town its full title. The plain *(vega)* of San Mateo is a sea of green. As with most of the northern strip of the island (but especially the north-east), the area is busily cultivated and receives enough rain to keep local farmers well occupied. You'll notice too that the area is much more densely populated – most of the island's population lives in the north. There's not an awful lot to San Mateo but it makes a pleasant stop.

If you happen to be around in September, try to make it for the romería and celebrations of the patron saint, St Matthew, on 21 September.

Statistically, you've a greater chance of catching the large weekend market. Held every Saturday and Sunday just south of the bus station, it pulls in regulars from all over the island.

Bus No 303 comes up from Las Palmas every 30 minutes.

Santa Brígida

About 9km farther east on the road to Las Palmas, the next town of any note is Santa Brígida, whose centre repays a wander. The narrow streets are tree-lined and attractive, and from the parish church you have nice views inland over fields and palm groves to the central mountains.

Back on the road to Las Palmas, after 4km there is a turn-off south for the **Caldera de Bandama**, one of the biggest extinct volcanic craters on the island, which offers superb views. Close by is **La Atalaya**, the largest pottery-producing village on the island.

Bus No 311 from Las Palmas to the village of Bandama passes through La Atalaya and takes you close to the crater – get off at the end of the line.

THE NORTH

As on most of the islands, the rain-blessed fertile north of Gran Canaria presents a radically different picture from its rugged, monochrome interior and south. Rolling hills, intensively tilled fields and terraces, and myriad villages and hamlets make up a busy and interesting picture as you wind along twisting roads, negotiating ravines and an ever-changing terrain. Only as you reach the west does the green give way to a more austere, although no less captivating, landscape – the west coast is the most dramatic on the island.

Teror
postcode 35330 • pop 6067
• elevation 543m

In spite of its name, Teror, 22km south-west of Las Palmas, does anything but inspire fear. The central Plaza de Nuestra Señora del Pino and Calle Real, leading from it and lined with fine old houses, have survived the modern age more or less intact.

Among them is **Casa de los Patronos de la Virgen**, which nowadays serves as a museum. Smelling pleasantly musty, it's full of all sorts of intriguing odds and ends, mostly from the Las Palmas families who owned it and used it as their second home in the hills. The ancestors of Simón Bolívar's wife, the Venezuelan María Teresa Rodríguez del Toro, lived here at one point. It opens 11 am to 6.30 pm, Monday to Thursday and Saturday, and 10.30 am to 2 pm on Sunday. Admission costs 300 ptas.

Dominating the square is the **Basílica de la Virgen del Pino**, a neo-classical 18th-century edifice. Inside, the most compelling detail is the 15th-century carving of the enthroned Virgen de la Nieve, illuminated in her place of honour at the heart of a particularly ornate gilded altarpiece.

The Virgen is the patron of the island and Teror, hence, is the religious capital. The Fiesta de la Virgen del Pino, held in the first week of September, is not only a big event in Teror – it's the most important religious feast day on the island's calendar.

Cheerful, excellent-value *Mesón Los Parranderos (Calle de la Diputación 6)* belongs to Pepe el Feo (Ugly Pete), 40 years in the trade. He does mains for between 700 ptas and 900 ptas and a filling set menu for 1375 ptas. The restaurant is just off the central square.

Bus No 216 connects with Las Palmas and No 215 with Arucas. Both run hourly.

Arucas

postcode 35400 • pop 29,400

The extraordinary grey, neo-Gothic **Iglesia de San Juan**, begun in 1917 and completed over 60 years later, stands sullen watch over the bright white houses of Arucas in a striking display of disproportion. Inside, a fine 16th-century Italian Crucifixion, hanging above the altar, and the wooden *Cristo Yacente* (*Reclining Christ*), behind in the ambulatory, are the most noteworthy artworks. It opens 9.30 am to 12.30 pm and 4.30 to 7.15 pm daily.

From the church, walk down Calle Gourié and turn right into Plaza de la Constitución, whose most interesting building is its restrained modernist *ayuntamiento* (town hall). Opposite are the somewhat ragged municipal gardens and, within them, the tourist office (☎ 928 62 31 36) open 8 am to 7 pm on weekdays and 9 am to 2 pm on Saturday.

Calle de la Heredad flanks the gardens on the southern side. It's dominated by the neo-classical **Heredad de Aguas de Arucas y Firgas** building, completed in 1908.

More to the taste of many visitors is the **Destilerías Arehucas** (Arehucas rum distillery). Free guided visits, culminating in a little tipple, take place between 10 am and 2 pm on weekdays.

If you have wheels – it's a fairly hard grind, mind you, if you only have two – take the well-signed route to **La Montaña de Arucas**, 2.5km north of the town. From here there's a splendid panorama of Las Palmas to the north-east, the northern coast of the island, fruit orchards, banana groves – and hectare upon hectare of plastic greenhouses.

The *restaurant* here – which controls access to the finest views westwards – is among the best in town. The set menu is a little pricey at 1650 ptas, but you can be pretty sure of the quality.

About 1.5km west of town is the *Hacienda de Buen Suceso* (☎ 928 62 29 45), a fine rural hotel, and the equally splendid **Jardín de las Hespérides** botanical garden, open 9 am to noon and 2 to 6 pm on weekdays and 9 am to noon on Saturday. Owned by the Marquésa de Arucas, they may not be to every democrat's taste but both are very beautiful. Rooms at the Hacienda cost 20,000 ptas, including breakfast, and admission to the gardens costs 600 ptas.

Bus Nos 205 and 206 provide a regular service to/from Las Palmas while No 215 runs hourly to Teror.

Moya

postcode 35562 • pop 895
• elevation 490m

The spectacular 13km drive between Arucas and Moya follows a corniche, incised into the flank of the mountain, which gives spectacular views of the northern coast. Moya hasn't a lot to hold you except for the **Casa/Museo Tomás Morales**, opposite the 16th-century church on the main road through town. Once home to the Canarian poet, who died in 1922 when he was only 37, it also promotes temporary art exhibitions. It opens 8 am to 8 pm on weekdays and 10 am to 2 pm and 5 to 8 pm on Saturday. Admission is free.

Heading westwards along Calle Alejandro Hidalgo, you can get a hearty set meal for a bargain 850 ptas at *Mesón Casa Plácido* at No 6.

Bus Nos 116 and 117 between them run 15 times daily to/from Las Palmas.

Santa María de Guía

postcode 35450 • pop 8740
• elevation 180m

Just off the main C-810 highway 25km west of Las Palmas, Santa María de Guía (or just Guía) was for a while home to the French composer Camille Saint-Saëns (1835–1921), who occasionally tickled the ivories in the town's 17th-century neo-classical church.

In the 18th century the town and surrounding area were devastated by a plague of locusts. To rid themselves of this blight, town and country people got together to implore the Virgin Mary for help. This has remained a tradition and on the third Sunday of September the townsfolk celebrate La Rama de las Marías, in which they dance their way to the doors of the church to make

Tiles add a splash of colour to plain white walls.

Testing the water at Playa del Papagayo

Lanzarote's best beach, Puerto del Carmen, stretches 6km long and four rows of sun-shades deep.

Clean living: a typical whitewashed church

Go cactus crazy in Lanzarote's Cactus Garden.

Castillo de San Gabriel, Arrecife, Lanzarote

Coming into port at Playa Blanca, Lanzarote

offerings of fruits of the earth to Mary. The town is also known for its *queso de flor* (flower cheese).

Bus Nos 101, 102, 103 and 105 all pass through on their way from Las Palmas.

Gáldar
postcode 35460 • pop 15,450
• elevation 124m

Gáldar's tourist office (☎ 928 89 58 55), in the Edificio Heredad de Agua building, opens 8 am to 2.30 pm, Monday to Friday.

Possibly the most important archaeological find in the islands is the **Cueva Pintada** (Painted Cave), near the Agaete exit of town. Its walls bear deteriorating designs in red, black and white that were left behind by the Guanches. The area around it, which has yielded some remains of a Guanche settlement, has been declared an archaeological park and a museum is due to open at the cave in mid-2002. It's closed to visitors until that time but you can see a replica at the Museo Canario in Las Palmas. Contact the tourist office for more details.

A couple of kilometres out of town at Playa del Agujero is the **Necrópolis de Gáldar**. Mummies, objects used in Guanche funeral rites and domestic items have been discovered among these tombs. The area has, however, been fenced off and seems likely to stay that way.

Bus Nos 103 and 105 head east for Las Palmas (325 ptas). Southbound, No 103 links Gáldar with Agaete and Puerto de las Nieves (465 ptas).

Agaete & Puerto de las Nieves
postcode 35480 • pop 4375

There's little to attract visitors to the town of Agaete, just 10km south of Gáldar. By contrast, nearby Puerto de las Nieves – until the 19th century the island's principal port and nowadays the terminal for the ferry to Santa Cruz de Tenerife – isn't a bad place at all. It's nothing to go overboard about and the beach is small, black and pebbly but its buildings are low, the Atlantic thunders in and there's a cluster of pleasant fish restaurants by the port. It was there before

tourism, and now co-exists with but is not over-dominated by it.

Just in from the beach is the striking **Iglesia de Nuestra Señora de la Concepción**. Built in 1874, it is quite unique in the islands for its pronounced Mediterranean style. For a moment it feels like you've landed in Greece! Inside are two parts of a 16th-century Flemish triptych. The middle panel is preserved in nearby **Ermita de las Nieves**, a small chapel.

Around Agaete the coast begins to take on a sterner countenance than farther north. From the jetty you can see the **Dedo de Dios** (God's Finger), thrusting up from the sea beneath the cliffs to the east of the port. This basalt monolith has weathered the elements for 100,000 years.

If you have children – or should it just take your fancy – a small herd of jaded-looking camels and donkeys would probably quite welcome your taking them for a ride.

Special Events If you manage to be in Agaete around 4 August you'll witness the Fiesta de la Rama, whose origins lie in an obscure Guanche rain dance. Nowadays locals, accompanied by marching bands, parade into town brandishing tree branches and then get down to the serious business of having a good time.

Places to Stay & Eat In Agaete, the unmarked *Pensión Tecla* (☎ 928 89 81 66, Calle Saulo Torón 2) has a couple of rooms without bathroom at 4000 ptas. Fifty metres south of the church, go up the steps on your left.

In Puerto de las Nieves you can stay at *Apartamentos El Angosto* (☎ 928 55 41 92, Paseo del Obispo Pildaín 11), near the cemetery, where apartments cost 6000 ptas. At the brand new four-star *Hotel de las Nieves* (☎ 928 88 62 56, fax 928 88 62 67, e hpnieves@intercom.es), singles/doubles start at 10,350/15,350 ptas, which includes breakfast.

Fronting the port, you have a choice of seafood restaurants. Cheap and cheerful *La Granja*, right by the dock entrance, does a *menú* for 950 ptas. Smarter *Restaurante el Cápita* also has a menú at 900 ptas but you'll do better picking a la carte. Fresh fish dishes cost around 1400 ptas.

Getting There & Away Bus Nos 102 and 103 link the town and port with Las Palmas at least hourly. Bus No 101 heads south for Aldea de San Nicolás three times daily.

Fred Olsen (☎ 928 55 40 05) operates six fast ferries per day to Santa Cruz de Tenerife from Puerto de las Nieves. The standard fare is 3700 ptas. There is a free bus connection to Las Palmas (Parque de Santa Catalina). Going the other way, the bus leaves Las Palmas 1½ hours before the ferry is due to depart.

Los Berrazales

An 8km diversion up the tight Barranco de Aguete (follow the signs for El Valle) leads you to Los Berrazales (325m), whose mineral waters have curative qualities. At the end of the road is the two-star *Hotel Princesa Guayarmina* (☎ *928 89 80 09; fax 928 89 85 25)*, a healthy place which grows its own vegetables, has a pool and lays on all kinds of water treatment. It also makes a good base for a few days' walking in the surrounding hills. Singles/doubles cost a very reasonable 4860/7500 ptas.

Bus No 102, which runs between Las Palmas and Puerto de las Nieves, pushes on to Los Berrazales seven times daily.

Aldea de San Nicolás

Usually known as San Nicolás de Tolentino, this town is the kind of place where you might well arrive in the evening and then stop and recharge your batteries before heading on round the island.

The treat here is travelling, not arriving. The road between Agaete and San Nicolás takes you on a magnificent cliff-side journey. If you head south-west in the late afternoon, the setting sun delights the eyes with a soft light display, marking out each successive ridge in an ever-darker shadowy mantle. There are numerous lookouts along the way to take in the rugged views.

The approach from Mogán and the south

(see Around Playa del Inglés & Maspalomas later in this chapter), though lacking the seascapes, is almost as awesome.

The rather scruffy town has little to excite the senses. However, *Hotel Los Cascajos* (☎ *928 89 11 65, Calle de los Cascajos 9)* offers decent singles/doubles with bathroom for 4000/6000 ptas, including breakfast. The owner also has *Pensión Segundo* (☎ *928 89 09 09)*, nearby on the main square, and the bar/restaurant beneath it. Simple rooms cost 3000/4000 ptas without breakfast.

Bus No 38 runs four times daily to Playa del Inglés via Puerto de Mogán and on to Las Palmas twice daily. No 101 goes to Las Palmas via Puerto de las Nieves and Santa María de Guía three times daily.

Artenara

A back road climbs eastwards up the valley from Aldea de San Nicolás to the hilltop village of Artenara, from where you are only a short distance from Tejeda. The sparsely populated countryside of bare ridges and rugged hills is dotted with troglodyte caves, some still inhabited.

Bus No 220 runs three times daily from Las Palmas via Teror. No buses connect the village with Aldea de San Nicolás.

PLAYA DEL INGLÉS & MASPALOMAS
postcode 35100 • pop c.40,000

This is the international party end of the island. It appeals to many, but it won't appeal to all. A good chunk of the coast has basically been converted into a giant holiday home, with drinks. You come here for sun (especially if escaping the European winter) and nocturnal fun. Of course, there is nothing to stop you exploring the rest of the island – and we'd recommend hiring a bike or car and breaking free for a day or two to do just that.

But don't come to Maspalomas and Playa del Inglés (not an Englishman at all, but a French fellow who was one of the first foreigners to live in the area early in the 20th century) for the history and impressive monuments – there aren't any. And don't come expecting to savour Spain. Playa del Inglés in particular is a foreign-tourist destination, where mainland Spanish visitors are very much in a minority.

The heart of the resort is Playa del Inglés, and the heart of the heart is the Yumbo Centrum, a big four-level shopping jungle. You could spend your entire holiday in here. By day it's like an Arab bazaar, bursting with all sorts of goods from rags to radios while innumerable restaurants compete for your attention with 'international' food. Here you will also find banks, doctors, telephone and fax offices, a laundrette and supermar-

kets. The main tourist office is just outside the centre, on the same block.

As day gives way to night the scene transforms itself so that by the wee small hours the leather handbags and wallets in the stores have been replaced by leather gear in steamy gay bars. The vaguely wholesome bustly family atmosphere evaporates as the discos, straight and gay, swing until dawn, barrels and bottles are drained by the dozen in pubs and bars, and the drag shows, saunas and sex shops all do a roaring trade.

Beyond Yumbo is the rest, which in many respects is not unlike Yumbo. This is, of

PLAYA DEL INGLÉS & MASPALOMAS

PLACES TO STAY
4 Bungalows Sonnenland Club II & III
9 Pensión San Fernando
13 Hotel Continental; Happy Biking
14 Hotel Lucana
16 Apartamentos Liberty
18 Apartamentos Duna Flor
29 Apartamentos Oasis

PLACES TO EAT
1 Restaurante Grill Marguarita
2 Mesón Motino
3 Casa Vieja
8 Restaurante Viuda de Franco
10 Alprende del Amo (Casa Antonio)
19 Restaurante La Toja
20 Restaurante Riás Bajas
25 Restaurante La Liguria
27 Restaurante El Tenderete

OTHER
5 Ayuntamiento (Town Hall)
6 Local Police
7 Post Office
11 Viajes Insular (American Express)
12 National Police
15 Diving Center Sun-Sub (Hotel Buenaventura)
17 Tourist Office
21 Laundrette; Papelería Grafos
22 Cabildo Tourist Office; Fedac
23 24-Hour Clinic
24 Blue Explorers Dive Center (Apartamentos Igazú)
26 CiberBeach
28 Tourist Office
30 Faro de Maspalomas

course, an artificial settlement and you feel it immediately – the neatly traced boulevards and roundabouts betraying all the spontaneity in town design of a Five-Year Plan. It's all hotels, apartments, restaurants and bars, and then some.

In Maspalomas especially the street names are revealing – Avenida del Touroperador Saga Tours, Avenida del Touroperador Alpitours, Neckerman, Tui, Thomson and so on and so on. No plain old streets *(calles)* either – all avenues, no matter how small.

To the south are the beaches and the only natural item of genuine interest – the deeply impressive dunes of Maspalomas. Maspalomas itself is the quieter, you might say more exclusive, western perimeter of the resort. East of Playa del Inglés the resort continues but thins out in the areas known as Veril and San Agustín.

There are bus stops all over the resorts, a couple of them right by Yumbo.

Information
Tourist Offices The Cabildo tourist office (☎ 928 77 15 50) is on the corner of Avenida de España and Avenida de los Estados Unidos, just outside the Yumbo Centrum. It opens 9 am to 9 pm on weekdays (9 am to 2 pm and 3 to 8 pm, July to September) and 9 am to 1 pm on Saturday.

There are two municipal tourist offices; one (☎ 928 76 84 09) beside the beach at Playa del Inglés and the other (☎ 928 76 95 85) stuck out by a roundabout that few visitors pass on Avenida del Touroperador Neckermann. Both open 9 am to 9 pm on weekdays and 9 am to 2 pm on Saturday.

Money American Express is represented by Viajes Insular (☎ 928 76 05 00), at Avenida de Moya 14.

Laundry There is a coin-operated, self-service laundrette in Lot 411 on the 4th floor of the Yumbo Centrum. Machines whirl 8 am to 8 pm weekdays and 8 am to 1 pm on Saturday.

Email & Internet Access The best place to log on is CiberBeach, Apartamentos

Taidia, Avenida Tirajana 11, a serious centre with a pleasant, helpful young manager. It opens 9 am to 2 pm and 5 to 10 pm daily.

If you want to check your emails while your smalls spin, log on at one of the trio of computers at Papelería Grafos, next door to the laundrette in the Yumbo Centrum.

Medical Services The resort is swarming with clinics, their business no doubt enhanced by the aftermath of drunken brawls and ecstasy casualties.

There's a 24-hour clinic (☎ 928 76 12 92) opposite the tourist office on the corner of Avenida de España and Avenida de los Estados Unidos.

Emergency The local police are near the town hall beside the Barranco de Maspalomas. The national police office is beside the C-812 highway.

Theme Parks
There's a multitude of theme parks in the south of the island. You'll soon know about them because brochures, and the touts who promote them, are everywhere.

Palmitos Park (☎ 928 14 02 76), a few kilometres north of the resort area, is a sub-tropical oasis crammed with exotic flora and 1500 species of birds, along with a butterfly house, an aquarium and 15 performing parrots. It opens 9.30 am to 6 pm daily. Buses run there regularly from various stops in Playa del Inglés.

Mundo Aborigen (☎ 928 17 22 95) on the road north to Fataga, is where 100 or so model Guanches stand in various ancient poses designed to give you an idea of what life was like here before the conquistadors turned up to build theme parks about how the Guanches once lived. It opens 9 am to 6 pm daily.

Aqua Sur (bus No 45) and **Ocean Park** (bus Nos 30, 32 and 45) are basically pools with slides and rides.

Want to see a showdown (maybe even a hoe-down?). Then it's off to **Sioux City** (bus No 29), where good guys and bad guys shoot 'em up, round 'em up and generally get (mildly) wild for your entertainment. It closes on Monday.

After the west, a trip to the Orient? Try **La Baranda** (☎ 928 79 86 80), open 10 am to 5 pm, on the road to Fataga. According to the brochure you can come and enjoy the oasis of palms and 'relax listening to the singing of the birds and the murmur of the camels'. Murmur?!

The list goes on, but you probably get the general idea by now. Admission generally ranges from 1000 ptas up, so keep your wallets full!

Swimming

For many, the only energy left after partying at night will be just enough to get down to the beach and collapse for the day. Beaches from east to west are Playa de las Burras, Playa del Inglés and Playa de Maspalomas. Basically they all link up to form the one beach.

The best part about Maspalomas is the dunes, which fold back from the beach. Their inland heart has been declared a nature reserve with restricted access.

There is a nudist area about where the dunes begin if you are approaching from Playa del Inglés. Although mixed, it's a popular gay cruising area.

Diving

Two reliable operators are Diving Center Sun-Sub (☎ 928 77 81 65), based in the Hotel Buenaventura, Plaza de Ansite, and Blue Explorers Dive Center (☎ 928 77 45 39), who operate from Apartamentos Iguazú, Avenida Tirajana 24.

Surfing & Windsurfing

Although surfing is possible here (the best waves tend to break off the western end of Maspalomas by the lighthouse, or *faro*), this is not mind-blowing surfing territory. Windsurfers hang around in the same spot, but are better off heading east beyond the resorts to Bahía Feliz, Juan Grande and, best of all, Pozo Izquierdo, which is for experienced windsurfers. Club Mistral (☎/fax 928 15 71 58) in Playa de Tarajillo, Bahía Feliz, rents equipment and offers courses.

Other Watery Activities

Everything from deep-sea fishing to yacht trips or an excursion in an old schooner or glass-bottomed catamaran can be organised here through travel agents and many of the hotels and apartments. You often get a better price through them than you would by going direct to the operator.

Thalassotherapy

To save you looking it up – as we had to – it's a health treatment based on warmed-up sea water, designed to remove stress and other more physical aches. Whether or not it works, it's quite a sensual experience in its own right. The Centro de Talasoterapía (☎ 928 76 56 89), Europe's largest, occupies a huge complex attached to Hotel Gloria Palace, Calle Las Margaritas s/n. This kind of seawater doesn't come cheap, however. A day's dunking and use of the various appliances costs between 8500 ptas and 14,500 ptas, risking inducing the very stress the centre claims to alleviate.

Cycling

Happy Biking (☎ 928 76 68 32) – now there's a nice name! – rent out a range of cycles from 900 ptas per day. They're based within the Hotel Continental, Avenida de Italia 2. Take your passport along. They also organise cycle tours, mostly quite gentle, which start at 3900 ptas, including bike hire, transport to and from the ride and a picnic.

The Cabildo tourist office has a brochure in Spanish describing four recommended day routes radiating from Maspalomas.

Walking

There's really no excuse for not pulling on those trainers and getting away from the coastal hordes!

The friendly folk at Happy Biking organise day walks (4900 ptas) every Monday and Wednesday to the island's high spots (both literally and figuratively). 'For hikers who want to let dangle their soul between heaven and earth', says their brochure in charming so-near English. Go on, let it dangle; you'll feel all the better for it!

Euroguías (☎ 928 76 41 95), based at Lot

58 on the first floor of the Centro Comercial San Agustín, also organises day walks (4700 ptas). Both will pick you up from your accommodation or a nearby point.

Rutas Canarias sets out by bus for a full-day walk (3500 ptas) from the Cabildo tourist office beside the Yumbo Centrum at 10 am on Monday, Wednesday and Friday. Just turn up or ring ☎ 928 67 04 66 for information.

For all, transport to/from the walk is included within the fee.

To enjoy an exhilarating 5km and more for free, simply follow the promenade which, sometimes at shore level, sometimes above it, extends eastwards from Playa del Inglés.

Places to Stay

There are over 500 hotels, apartment blocks and bungalows in Playa del Inglés and Maspalomas; in peak periods many are full to bursting. It's much safer and certainly cheaper to book a package outside Spain; the rate some hotels and apartments quote to independent visitors can be as much as 100% over what a tour operator offers. Travel agents in Britain, Ireland, Germany and the Netherlands brim with deals and special last-minute offers.

If you're going it alone, it's almost impossible to assess where you should head. You get, in reasonable measure, what you pay for. In moderate to high season you are unlikely to find an apartment (cheaper than a hotel) for less than 5500 ptas for two people.

All we can do is give some indicative places and prices. With no taxi fare in the urban area above 600 ptas – and taxis rolling through the night – consider taking a place away from the beach, even away from Playa del Inglés itself.

If you haven't reserved in advance, pick up an accommodation list and town map from one of the tourist offices and let your fingers do the walking. Many apartments don't have anyone in permanent attendance so it's often useless to simply turn up with hope in your heart.

The following places are fine in their category – but remember the other 500....

Pensións There's precisely one pensión in town and if you can get in, it's excellent value. A basic room at *Pensión San Fernando* (☎ *928 76 39 06, Calle La Palma 16)*, just south of San Fernando's Centro Comercial, costs 2500 ptas.

Apartments In Playa del Inglés, *Apartamentos Liberty* (☎ *928 76 74 54, fax 928 72 00 32, Avenida Tirajana 32)*, fairly near the beach, has not-very-special apartments for 10,000 ptas.

Close to the seafront in Maspalomas, *Apartamentos Oasis* (☎ *928 14 19 52, Avenida Oasis 14)* lets run-of-the-mill apartments, overshadowed by multistorey luxury blocks, for 11,000 ptas (9000 ptas in summer).

Moving north, *Apartamentos Duna Flor* (☎ *928 76 76 75)*, with its huge central swimming pool, is like a mini-village. Its 282 pleasantly appointed bungalows come in at a reasonable 8000 ptas.

Retreating even farther, *Bungalows Sonnenland Club II & III* (☎ *928 14 24 62, fax 928 14 09 53, Calle Millares Carló s/n)*, with pool and restaurant in the bleak suburb of Sonnenland, offer spacious apartments for 5500 ptas (6000 ptas in high season) and they run a free shuttle bus to Maspalomas.

Hotels There's no such thing as a budget hotel hereabouts. Singles/doubles at pleasant *Hotel Lucana* (☎ *928 77 40 40, fax 928 77 41 41)*, one block back from the shore, cost 12,000/15,000 ptas. A better deal in this mid-range category is *Hotel Continental* (☎ *928 76 00 33, fax 928 77 14 84, Avenida de Italia 2)*, which offers half-board for 8500/13,500 ptas.

The premier top-end establishments are out by the dunes in Maspalomas. Perhaps the finest is *Hotel Maspalomas Oasis* (☎ *928 14 14 48, fax 928 14 11 92)*, at the end of Avenida del Oasis, where doubles begin at 15,200 ptas per person, including breakfast.

Places to Eat

The place is predictably swarming with eateries. The bulk of them serve up a pretty bland array of 'international' dishes designed to keep any stomach filled without upsetting any palates.

Restaurante Viuda de Franco, on the roundabout where the C-812 highway intersects with Avenida de Tirajana, has been serving up tapas and solid meals since WWII. Nowadays – and despite the fact that the menu's available in seven different languages – the food still makes no concession to non-Canary palates and is not too pricey.

Casa Vieja is just north of the GC-1 motorway, along the road to Fataga. OK, so it's a little out of the way but the effort to get here is well repaid. The 'old house' is indeed a charmingly bucolic affair. Plants – real, not the ubiquitous plastic – festoon the low-roof, canaries trill and a particularly hearty meal (such portions!) costs around 2000 ptas.

A pair of family restaurants in the outer working-class suburb of El Tablero could be a couple of light years away from the tourist joints to the south. At **Restaurante Grill Marguarita** (Avenida de las Américas 58), closed Sunday, the decor's naff and the TV drones but there's no better value in town than their three-course *menú* at 850 ptas. Or perhaps there just is, though it's a very close call; along the street at No 40, **Mesón Motino** does a midday special, equally filling, costing 800 ptas. Both are good on local fare.

Alprende del Amo (Calle del Alcalde Marcial Franco 3), also called Casa Antonio, is a good place for grills costing from 1200 ptas to 1500 ptas.

Restaurante Rías Bajas, just off the Yumbo Centrum at the corner of Avenida Tirajana and Avenida de los Estados Unidos, is primarily a solid fish and seafood place. Expect to pay a good 3500 ptas for a full meal with wine.

For quality Canarian food, albeit at premium prices, you can't beat **Restaurante El Tenderete** (☎ 928 76 14 60, Avenida Tirajana s/n), its walls scarcely visible for the framed certificates and awards it has picked up. Recommended, especially for the fresh fish – pick your piece from the fridge – but

make sure your credit-card account is topped up first.

Restaurante La Toja (Edificio Barbados II, Avenida de Tirajana) is a quality establishment blending the best of cuisines from France and Galicia. You shell out for it though – don't be surprised to see 5000 ptas or more slip effortlessly out of the pocket for a three-course meal with wine. It closes Sunday lunchtime.

Of the myriad Italian joints, **Restaurante La Liguria** (Avenida Tirajana 24) is not bad. Most pasta and pizza dishes cost between 900 ptas and 1200 ptas.

Entertainment

Naming particular bars and discos is as pointless as listing hotels. You could stagger around Yumbo Centrum – as many do – for weeks and not have sampled all its bars and discos. Quite a few are gay venues but there are plenty of straight places too.

If you ever break out beyond Yumbo Centrum, all the big shopping centres (centros comerciales) have at least some bars and discos in them. And beyond them, there are still more bars and discos.

It's a Gay Old Life

Gran Canaria is gay Europe's winter escape playground. Or, rather, the Playa del Inglés on the southern side of the island is. A seemingly endless string of bars, discos and clubs are crammed into the Yumbo Centrum, right smack in the heart of the Playa del Inglés. It is predominantly a gay men's scene, although of course this doesn't stop small numbers of lesbians and straights from wading in.

Little happens before 10 pm. From then until about 3 am the bars on the fourth level of the Yumbo Centrum bear the brunt of the fun, after which the clubs and discos on the second level take over.

At dawn, people stagger out for some rest. Some make for the beach at Maspalomas across the dunes, which are themselves a busy gay-cruising area.

Shopping

About the only interruption to the hectares of apartments, hotels, restaurants and bars comes in the form of the afore-mentioned shopping centres. In them you can buy anything from children's wear to electronics. There's a lot of junk in there, so take care. If you're after local handicrafts, an initial visit to the small Fedac store, co-located with the Cabildo tourist office, repays a visit. Fedac is a government-sponsored non-profit-making store, whose prices and quality are a good standard by which to measure those of products sold elsewhere. It opens 10 am to 2 pm and 4 to 7 pm on weekdays.

Getting There & Around

Bus Bus No 66 runs to/from Gando airport (430 ptas) hourly until 9 pm.

Buses also link regularly with other points along the coast, westwards as far as Puerto de Mogán and eastwards to Las Palmas. For Las Palmas (650 ptas, about 50 minutes), take No 5 (night bus), 30 or 50 (non-stop). Pick up a pair of Global bus-route maps from a tourist office. One shows routes and bus stops throughout Maspalomas and Playa del Inglés while the other gives details of routes throughout the island. Global also runs buses to many of the theme parks listed earlier. The fare for a standard run within town is 130 ptas. If you plan to travel out of town, a Tarjeta Insular (see Getting Around at the beginning of this chapter) is a good investment.

Car & Motorcycle If you really *must* take your car down to the beach, there's a large paying car park beside Playa del Inglés.

Taxi Taxis and taxi stands abound and are reliable. To call a cab, ring ☎ 928 76 67 67. From Playa del Inglés, no destination within the urban area costs more than 600 ptas. To Gando airport, budget for about 3500 ptas from Playa del Inglés and 4200 ptas from Maspalomas.

Bicycle For information on bike rental, see Cycling earlier.

AROUND PLAYA DEL INGLÉS & MASPALOMAS
Puerto Rico & Arguineguín

If Maspalomas has redeeming features in the shape of its great dunes and nightlife, little good can be said of the chain of its resort cousins farther west along the coast.

The port area of **Arguineguín** still remains true to itself as a small, active fishing settlement but it's a charmless town with no beach to speak of. Two things, however, might draw you here. Dive Center Arguineguín (☎ 928 73 61 96), Calle Graciliano Alfonso 14, overlooking the beach, is run by a friendly Dutch couple and explores reefs up and down the coast. And good seafood can be had at modest prices in the down-to-earth *restaurant* of the Cofradía de Pescadores, the fishing cooperative within the port. It even does *gofio* (a roasted mixture of wheat, maize or barley), which you rarely find in big city restaurants or the resorts.

The original fishing town of **Puerto Rico** must be in there somewhere, but it's been submerged below serried ranks of apartment blocks scaling the barren cliffs and hills of what must once have been a spectacular if harsh coastline. Not even the beach is noteworthy (nor are those farther west still, such as Playa del Cura, Playa del Tauro and the resort of Taurito).

There's no point singling out specific apartments, hotels and the like. As in Maspalomas, you're much better off booking ahead from outside the islands.

Camping Guantanamo (☎ *928 56 02 07*), one of the few official camp sites on the island, is beside the C-812 highway, just east of Playa del Cura. But it's a dusty, scruffy place where you'd only want to overnight as a last resort.

Restaurant Oliver puts an imaginative French spin on international cuisine. You'll be lucky to get any change from 2500 ptas but the food is good and makes a nice change from both Spanish and British fare!

Buses connect both places with Maspalomas and Playa del Inglés (275 ptas) regularly and with Puerto de Mogán and Las Palmas (790 ptas) less frequently.

Lineas Salmon and Blue Bird have eight

and seven services, respectively, each day to/from Puerto de Mogán and the former runs every two hours eastwards to Arguineguín. Prices for all are 700 ptas single, 1200 ptas return.

Puerto de Mogán
After Taurito, a couple of kilometres of rugged and pretty much unspoiled coastline recall what this whole southern stretch of the island must have been like 40 years ago before mass tourism came to the Canaries.

Finally you round a bend; below you is a smallish crescent of sandy beach and next to it a busy little yacht harbour and fishing port. Puerto de Mogán, although now largely given over to the tourist trade, is light years from its garish counterparts to the east.

The waterfront is a purpose-built holiday zone, but tastefully done with low two- and three-storey apartments, covered in bougainvillea and other exotic flora, the whole exuding an air of quiet charm despite the artificiality of the place. Here, there really is a fishing port and small town clustered behind the tourist facade. It's a fairly admirable balance – but how long can the balancing act last?

The charm is agreeably disturbed on Friday morning by the weekly market.

Activities Atlantik Diving (☎ 689 35 20 49, e atdiving@clubdemar.com), based at Hotel Club de Mar, offers courses at all levels. A yellow submarine submerges seven times daily – and its owners run a free bus as far as Playa del Inglés to pick up punters. Above the waterline, you can take a half-day deep-sea fishing trip (6500 ptas per fisher and 4500 ptas for spectators).

Places to Stay The apartments along the waterfront are generally let by local people. Start by asking around the shops below them – even if they don't let themselves, they can point you in the right direction. Prices vary from about 7000 ptas up to 15,000 ptas according to the kind of apartment, views and season. In the town itself you can also hunt down apartments for around 5000 ptas.

There are three pensión possibilities. ***Pensión Salvador*** (☎ 928 56 53 74, *Calle de la Corriente 13*) has small but clean rooms in a ramshackle house for 2500 ptas. Among the last houses on the left, about 750m inland as you head north, are ***Pensión Lucrecia*** (☎ 928 56 56 43, *Calle Lomo Quiebre 16*) and ***Pensión Eva*** (☎ 928 56 52 35), next-door-but-one at – bizarrely – No 35. All three charge 2500 ptas for simple rooms.

For greater comfort, try **Hotel Club de Mar** (☎ 928 56 50 66, fax 928 56 54 38), right by the harbour. Its rooms and apartments range from 7000 ptas to 15,500 ptas for doubles, depending on season and views.

Places to Eat The yacht harbour is lined with cafes and restaurants with pleasant terrazas offering fresh fish. You'll not find it fresher than at *Restaurante Cofradía*, the no-frills fishing cooperative eatery in the south-western corner of the quay.

Inland, *Restaurante Calipso (Pasaje de los Pescadores)* is another no-nonsense local fish place. Just over the small footbridge, the name is masked by its blue-and-white awning,

Getting There & Away There is no shortage of buses heading east to Puerto Rico and Playa del Inglés (440 ptas). You also have regular departures for Las Palmas (925 ptas).

Between them, Lineas Salmon and Blue Bird run 15 ferry boats daily to/from Puerto Rico.

North of Puerto de Mogán
Just as Puerto de Mogán is a relief from the south coast's relentless armies of apartments, bungalows and 'true British pubs', so the C-810 road north from the port is another leap away from the crowds.

As it ascends gradually up a wide valley towards **Mogán**, you pass orchards of subtropical trees such as papaya, mango and avocado. Mogán's a pleasant place with a handful of restaurants and bars, but nothing in particular to see or do. From here, you can retrace your steps or join the North and

Central Circuits (see those sections earlier in this chapter).

To press on, you have two choices: the C-810 winds off to the north-west through spectacularly austere landscapes to Aldea de San Nicolás (26km). Alternatively, take a minor turning 2.5km north of Mogán to head north-east up the barranco to **Ayacata**. About 5km of this road, which climbs tortuously up the barren and lonely ravine, is dirt track.

From Ayacata you can hang a left and head for Tejeda and the highest points of the island.

Fuerteventura

If you were to close your eyes and fly in from Laayoune, little more than 100km east in Moroccan-occupied Western Sahara, you could be forgiven for thinking you hadn't gone anywhere. Lapped (and sometimes lashed) by the Atlantic, the dunes, shrub-studded plains, and arid, knife-edge mountain ridges of Fuerteventura present a parched picture. Its villages and towns, with their bundles of whitewashed, flat-roofed houses, largely modern and unimaginatively fashioned of poured concrete, would be right at home cast across the semi-desert wastes of North Africa.

Fuerteventura's 1660 sq km make it the second-largest island in the archipelago but, with only 49,000 inhabitants (known as Majoreros or Maxoreros, from the Guanche name for the northern kingdom of the island – Maxorata), it is one of the least populous. It is also rather flat – the highest peak, known variously as the Orejas del Asno and the Pico de la Zarza, in the southern Jandía hills, reaches 807m.

The empty interior, where for centuries tough herdsmen have scratched out a living with their flocks of equally hardy goats, holds a certain fascination although for most visitors the coast is the main attraction. And the miles of white sandy beaches are not only a sun-seeker's delight. Serious surfers and windsurfers will find near-ideal conditions year round.

The ocean is not just for frolicking in – it is the islanders' life blood. Rainfall here is negligible, so virtually all the water consumed on the island is desalinated Atlantic. Diving and big-game fishing are also hooks to hang your holiday on. Blue and white marlin, various kinds of tuna, wahoo and skipjack all ply the waters off the island.

Tourism is here to stay, but Fuerteventura is still a long way from the resort horrors of southern Gran Canaria and Tenerife. Perhaps it's just a question of time but for the moment the oficial line seems to be to keep development under control.

Highlights

- Relaxing on the endless strands of the Jandía peninsula's Playa de Sotavento
- Strolling and sunning yourself among the rolling dunes of Corralejo
- Surfing and windsurfing around Corralejo and El Cotillo
- Having a lazy lunch on Isla de Lobos

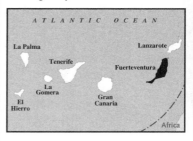

The two main resorts are at opposite ends of the island. At the northern tip (and the point of entry if you're coming in by boat from Lanzarote) is Corralejo – loud, brash and beloved of British budget tour operators. Deep down south is Morro Jable, where a knowledge of German is almost as useful as Spanish. It's an altogether more sophisticated place – and ideal if you have a passion for surfing or sand.

History

The island was known (at least in theory) to the Romans as Planaria, but the Guanches called it (or most of it at any rate) Maxorata. What the Europeans came to dub Fuerteventura ('strong winds') was in fact divided into two tribal kingdoms: Jandía, which took up the southern peninsula as far north as La Pared, and Maxorata, which occupied the rest of the island.

Fuerteventura was the second island to fall to the initial wave of conquerors under

FUERTEVENTURA

Jean de Béthencourt in January 1405. He had already established a fort there in 1402, but had been obliged to seek aid for his ambitions from the Castilian crown in Spain before proceeding. Although the islanders resisted the Spaniards, they could not hold out for long.

De Béthencourt set up a permanent base in the mountainous zone of what came to be known as Betancuria. He had a chapel built and the village that grew up around it, Santa María de Betancuria, became the island's capital. The choice of location was determined not by aesthetics but by hard reason-

ing. The area provided one of the island's few water supplies and the terrain gave a measure of natural defence against attacks from Guanches and, later, pirate raids.

New settlements spread slowly across the island but not until the 17th century did the Europeans occupy El Cotillo, once the seat of the Guanche Maxorata kingdom. At this time the Arias and Saavedra families took control of the *señorío*, the island government deputising for the Spanish crown. By the following century, however, officers of the island militia had established themselves as a rival power base in La Oliva.

Los Coroneles (the Colonels) gradually took virtual control of the island's affairs, enriching themselves at the expense of both the *señores* and the hard-pressed peasantry.

The militia was disbanded in 1834 and in 1912 the island, along with others in the archipelago, was granted a degree of self-administration with the installation of the Cabildo.

Information

Landscapes of Fuerteventura by Noel Rochford, published by Sunflower Books, gives some useful suggestions for drives and walks around the island of varying duration. See Maps in the Facts for the Visitor chapter for details on the maps available.

Activities

The sea offers most of the action. From Caleta de Fuste, Morro Jable and Corralejo, you can both dive and windsurf (Morro Jable regularly hosts a leg of the Windsurf World Cup). The waters off Corralejo are good for deep-sea fishing and the curling waves nearby draw in surfers.

Accommodation

Finding a place to stay in the coastal resorts can be problematic. In the case of many apartments you can't even book ahead as they deal exclusively with tour operators and their clientele.

If things look grim, head for Puerto del Rosario where you should encounter few problems getting a room. With a roof over your head you can work out your next strategy (hiring a vehicle of some sort will simplify life greatly).

There are no camp sites on the island. To camp in one of the very few areas where it is permitted (including the Isla de Lobos), you need a special permit.

Getting There & Away

Air The airport (☎ 928 86 06 00) is 6km south of Puerto del Rosario. Binter has at least six flights daily to Gran Canaria (7760 ptas, 35 minutes) and two daily to Tenerife Norte (10,460 ptas, 50 minutes).

Otherwise, charter flights, generally op-

erating only two or three days per week, connect the island with mainland Spanish cities and several European centres (including London, Manchester, Amsterdam, Munich and Frankfurt). For a charter seat to the UK, contact V.Travel 2000 (see Getting There & Away at the beginning of the Lanzarote chapter).

At the airport there's a tourist information office (☎ 928 85 12 50) in the arrivals area, open 9 am to at least 5 pm daily.

Boat At least six ferries weekly link Puerto del Rosario and Las Palmas de Gran Canaria while faster jetfoils speed between Morro Jable and Las Palmas.

There *are* boats between Puerto del Rosario and Arrecife on Lanzarote but you're better off taking one of the regular ferries that make the one-hour crossing between Corralejo in the north and Playa Blanca in Lanzarote's south.

Getting Around

Given the scant public transport cover on most routes, having your own wheels will greatly enhance your capacity to get around the island.

To/From the Airport You can get buses or taxis to Puerto del Rosario (see Puerto del Rosario later in this chapter) and, from there, buses to other parts of the island. Taxis from the airport to Corralejo cost around 4400 ptas, to El Cotillo 5000 ptas and to the Jandía beaches around 9700 ptas.

Bus Tiadhe (☎ 928 85 21 66) provides a limited service, with 13 lines operating around the island. The most frequent runs link Puerto del Rosario with Corralejo (No 6) in the north and with Caleta de Fuste via the airport (No 3) to the south. Bus No 5 from Morro Jable to Costa Calma is also fairly regular.

On other routes, do check times carefully before setting out. A number have only one service daily, primarily to transport schoolchildren and workers into Puerto del Rosario and bring them back at the end of the day. They tend to leave the village about

FUERTEVENTURA

6.30 am and return from Puerto del Rosario shortly after 4 pm – little help if you're planning a day in the country.

If you intend to use the buses a lot or even for one return trip between Morro Jable and Corralejo, changing at Puerto del Rosario, it is worth investing in a Tarjeta Dinero, a discount card that costs 2000 ptas. Instead of buying individual tickets on the bus for each trip, you tell the driver your destination and he endorses your card – it represents about a 30% saving on each trip.

Taxi You can belt around in taxis, but it soon becomes an expensive habit. The trip from Puerto del Rosario to Corralejo costs about 3900 ptas and to Morro Jable, you'd pay 9200 ptas or so.

The Centre

The central chunk of Fuerteventura offers some of the most varied countryside a desert island can manage. The mountains of the Parque Natural de Betancuria are sliced in their southern reaches by a palm-studded ravine starting at Vega del Río de Palmas. The west and east coasts are largely rocky cliffs interspersed with small black-sand beaches and fishing hamlets. By contrast, the central, copper-coloured plains around Antigua are dotted by old windmills in various states of repair and dating back a couple of centuries.

PUERTO DEL ROSARIO
postcode 35600 • pop 20,100
Puerto del Rosario, the island capital – and only place of consequence which exists for reasons other than tourism – is home to almost half the island's population. It's a relatively modern little port town that only really took off in the 19th century. If you fly to the island or use the buses, you may well find yourself passing through. It's a scruffy sort of place, spreading like a thick clump of white clotted cream over the dusty earth. Mediocre, higgledy-piggledy concrete housing developments seep slowly into the surrounding dry country.

When Spain pulled out of the Sahara in 1975, it sent about 5000 Legión Extranjera (Foreign Legion) troops to Fuerteventura to keep a watch on North Africa. Their huge barracks in Puerto del Rosario – a cross between a prison and a Beau Geste fort – are still in use, although remaining troops now number under 1000.

History
Puerto del Rosario, for long little more than an insignificant cluster of houses, became the island's capital in 1860, due to its growing importance as a harbour.

Until 1956 it was known as Puerto de las Cabras, named after the goats for which it had long been a watering hole (before becoming the main departure point for their export in the form of chops). In an early rebranding exercise, it was renamed Puerto del Rosario (Port of the Rosary) – altogether more dignified, you must agree, and befitting a capital! All the same, it remains unexciting.

Orientation
The centre of town backs away from the port, and anything you might need is within fairly easy strolling distance.

Information
Tourist Offices The main tourist office (☎ 928 53 08 44, fax 928 85 16 95), Avenida de la Constitución 5, is a fairly desultory, dingy place. It opens strictly civil servants' hours: 8 am to 2 pm, Monday to Friday. If you fly in, you're much better off consulting the friendly folk at the airport office (see Getting There & Away at the beginning of the chapter for details). Alternatively, call by the green tourist kiosk near the port. It opens 9.30 am to 1.30 pm and 4.30 to 7 pm on weekdays and 9.30 am to 1.30 pm on Saturday morning.

Post & Communications The central post office is at Calle Primero de Mayo 58.

Medical Services & Emergency The island's Hospital General (☎ 928 53 17 99) is on the highway towards the airport. There's

PUERTO DEL ROSARIO

PLACES TO STAY
2 Pensión Ruben Tinguaro
3 Pensión Macario
10 Hotel Valerón
11 Hotel Palace Puerto Rosario
22 Hostal Tamasite

PLACES TO EAT
1 Mesón Las Brasas
12 Restaurante Casino El Porvenir
20 Cafetería Tinguaro V
21 Pizzeria El Patio
23 Taberna Getaria

OTHER
4 Centro de Salud
5 Police Station
6 Intercity Bus Stop
7 Cruz Roja
8 Tourist Office
9 Trasmediterránea Office
13 Iglesia de Nuestra Señora del Rosario
14 Casa Museo de Unamuno
15 Pub Evening
16 Oficina del Medio Ambiente (Environment Office)
17 Taxi Rank
18 Cabildo Insular
19 Post Office
24 Paco's Bar
25 Tourist Information Kiosk
26 Taxi Rank
27 Naviera Armas Ticket Office
28 Estación Marítima
29 Hospital General

FUERTEVENTURA

a Centro de Salud (health clinic) on Calle Primero de Mayo.

The main police station (☎ 928 85 09 09) is on Avenida Juan de Béthencourt.

Things to See

About the only place worth a visit is **Casa Museo de Unamuno**, Calle Rosario 11. The philosopher Miguel de Unamuno, exiled for his opposition to the dictatorship of Primo de Rivera, briefly stayed in this house, then the Hotel Fuerteventura, in 1924. He later escaped to France before returning to his position at Salamanca University when the Republicans came to power in 1931. Part of the house has been turned into a period piece, with furnishings and other odds and ends from Unamuno's day, including his desk. It opens 9 am to 1 pm and 5 to 7 pm on weekdays and 9 am to 1 pm on Saturday. Admission is free.

During his exile, Unamuno used to seek solace on the **Playa Blanca**, about a 45-minute walk south of the town centre.

Special Events

The town puts on its party clothes on the first Sunday of October to celebrate the

The Big Cheese

Be sure to sample a hunk of the local goat cheese while you're in the Canaries.

Goats milk is curdled by stirring in rennet, an enzyme that was traditionally taken from the stomach of a kid. The liquid whey is squeezed from the resultant soggy blob. Then, the still damp (and usually circular) cheese is left to mature between two wooden disks; look for the characteristic multiple 'V' shaped imprint on the top and bottom.

Three islands in particular produce this white, usually flaky, musty scented delicacy and each has its own distinctive flavour.

So renowned is *Majorero*, the cheese from Fuerteventura, that, just like a fine wine, it bears a *denominación de origen* label, certifying that it's indeed from the island and the genuine article. It's the first Canary Island cheese to receive this accolade – and the first goat's cheese in the whole of Spain to bear the label.

At the heart of the process is the Majorero goat, a high-yielding hybrid of indigenous goats and those that were originally imported from the Spanish mainland, which can give as much as 750L of milk in one year. Whole cheeses weigh between one and six kilos but shop assistants will happily cut you a slice as thick or as thin as you like. You can buy it young and soft with a powdery white rind, which becomes yellow with ageing. Cheeses that are to be stored for some time are often given a coating of oil, corn meal or paprika to preserve them.

The cheeses of La Palma, whether young and fresh or more mature, are usually smoked. Nowadays they're mostly produced in large dairies but the smoking reflects an earlier practice where families would leave a cheese to hang and cure above the fireplace.

Milk from all over the island of El Hierro is brought to the cooperative outside the village of Isora and transformed into a cheese which is particularly prized.

None are easy to obtain outside the Canaries so, if you're a cheese lover, stock up before you leave – and perhaps add an extra slab for friends back home.

Fiesta de la Virgen del Rosario, the capital's patron.

Places to Stay

There are few good reasons for staying but if you have a hard time getting a room elsewhere on the island, you're more likely to find something here.

Hostal Tamasite (☎ 928 85 02 80, Calle León y Castillo 9) is a well situated pensión with charmless but clean singles/doubles for 4000/5000 ptas. Rooms have a bath, phone and TV. It's one of the better choices in town but not if you are a light sleeper as the noise from the bar in the same building can be intrusive at weekends.

At *Pensión Macario* (☎ 928 85 11 97, Calle Juan de Austria 24), rooms with bathroom cost 5000 ptas (3000 ptas without). They're spick and span, but the area is forlorn and the welcome is lukewarm, even grumpy.

Altogether more inviting is *Hotel Valerón* (☎ 928 85 06 18, Calle Candelaria del Castillo 10), which has singles/doubles with full facilities – including mini-bar – for 3500/5000 ptas.

Pensión Ruben Tinguaro (☎ 928 85 10 88, Calle Juan XXIII 48) offers singles/doubles/triples/quads with bathroom for 3000/4500/5500/6500 ptas.

Recently privatised *Hotel Fuerteventura* (☎ 928 85 11 50, fax 928 85 11 58, Calle Playa Blanca 45), previously a parador hotel, overlooks Playa Blanca, 3km south of the town centre. Unfortunately, it's also right under the flight path for the nearby airport. Rooms cost 9200/11,500 ptas.

Rooms at the recently renovated *Hotel Palace Puerto Rosario* (☎ 928 85 94 64, fax 928 85 22 60), beside the port, are more pleasant than its gaunt exterior would suggest. Singles/doubles come in at 9000/13,800 ptas.

Places to Eat

Beside Hostal Tamasite is the small and friendly *Taberna Getaria (☎ 928 85 94 11)*, which does a midday *menú* (set lunch) for 1200 ptas. This apart, don't expect a printed menu; it all depends what's on offer in the market that day. Expect to pay about 2500 ptas for three courses. It opens Monday to Saturday.

Nearby, with rather more airs yet comparable prices, is *Restaurante Casino El Porvenir (Calle de la Cruz)*.

For pizza, or a reasonable approximation thereof, you could do worse than *Pizzeria El Patio (Plazoleta de Lazaro Rugama Nieves 3)*.

If you're staying at Pensión Ruben Tinguaro, *Mesón Las Brasas (Calle Juan XXIII 68)* is a handy place, serving a fair range of fish and meat dishes for between 1000 ptas and 1600 ptas.

For *churros* (doughnuts) and chocolate, stop by *Cafetería Tinguaro V (Plaza de España 7)*.

Though no longer a parador, the *restaurant* of Hotel Fuerteventura (see Places to Stay earlier) maintains that chain's high culinary standards. Try their *milhojas de puerro y gambas*, an island of puff pastry lapped by a rich creamy sauce of leek and shrimp, or the local speciality, *cabrito en adobo Majorero* (marinated kid). They also do a good value menú at 2000 ptas.

Entertainment

First-floor *Paco's Bar (Calle Doctor Mena 8)* is a popular late-night hangout.

If you are looking for a drink even later in the evening, at weekends at any rate, head for *Pub Evening* (Calle Profesor Juan Tadeo Cabrera 17).

Getting There & Away

Air See Getting There & Away at the beginning of this chapter for details.

Bus Tiadhe buses leave from the main bus stop on the corner of Avenida León y Castillo and Avenida de la Constitución. The following services operate from Puerto del Rosario:

No 1 Morro Jable via Tuineje (1055 ptas, two hours, nine daily)
No 2 Vega del Río Palma via Betancuria (400 ptas, 50 minutes, twice daily)
No 3 Caleta de Fuste via the airport (150 ptas, 20 minutes, frequent)
No 6 Corralejo (360 ptas, 40 minutes, frequent)
No 7 El Cotillo via La Oliva (450 ptas, 45 minutes, three daily except Sunday)
No 10 Morro Jable via the airport (1045 ptas, 1½ hours, three daily except Sunday)

Boat Trasmediterránea ferries leave from the Estación Marítima at 1 pm on Tuesday, Thursday and Saturday, and at 3 pm on Sunday, for Las Palmas de Gran Canaria (3895 ptas, seven hours). It has an office (☎ 928 85 08 77) at Calle León y Castillo 58.

Naviera Armas runs to Las Palmas on Wednesday and Friday (3605 ptas, six hours). Its office is in the grey and white striped building just east of the port entrance. You can also buy tickets at any travel agency.

Getting Around

To/From the Airport Take bus No 3 (see Bus under Getting There & Away earlier). It stops at the airport about 10 minutes before reaching Caleta de Fuste. The trip between town and airport takes 10 to 15 minutes and costs 130 ptas. A taxi will rack up about 700 ptas.

Bus One municipal bus does the rounds of the town every hour, but you are unlikely to need it.

Taxi If you need a cab, call ☎ 928 85 00 59 or ☎ 928 85 02 16.

BETANCURIA

Jean de Béthencourt thought this the ideal spot to set up house in 1405, so he had living quarters and a chapel built. To this nascent settlement he gave his own name, which with time was corrupted to Betancuria (or the Villa de Santa María de Betancuria in the unexpurgated version). In the course of the century Franciscan friars moved in and expanded the town, which remained the island's capital until 1834. The island's proximity to the North African coast made it easy prey for Moroccan and European pirates who, on numerous occasions, managed to defy Betancuria's natural mountain defences and sack it. Tucked prettily into the protective folds of the basalt hills, the town is now home to fewer than 600 people.

Things to See

If you approach from the north, your gaze will be drawn down to the left, where ruins of the island's first **monastery**, built by the Franciscans, stand proud.

The centre of the settlement is watched over by the 17th-century **Iglesia de Santa María**. Pirates had destroyed its Gothic predecessor in 1593. A short walk away is the **Museo de Arte Sacro**. This contains a mixed bag of religious art, including paintings, gold and silverware. Admission to both is covered by one 200 ptas ticket; the custodian races back and forth to open the church and museum alternately every half hour from 11 am to 4 pm, daily except Sunday.

Of modest interest also is the **Casa Museo de Betancuria**. Housing a modest collection of Guanche artefacts plus objects from the time of the early colonisers, it opens 11 am to 5 pm, Tuesday to Saturday, and 11 am to 2 pm on Sunday. Admission costs 100 ptas.

If you have 800 ptas to burn, you can enter the Restaurante Casa de Santa María's **theme show**, in which pottery and weaving workshops have been set up; the price includes a bit of wine and cheese tasting.

Special Events

On 14 July, townspeople celebrate the Día de San Buenaventura, patron saint of the town, a fiesta dating from 1456.

Places to Eat

Restaurante Casa de Santa María, part of the tourist complex opposite the main portal of the church and open lunchtime only, wins hands down on atmosphere. Mains cost between 1500 ptas and 2900 ptas and they do a menú at 2000 ptas.

Food at the inconspicuous *Restaurante Valtarajal* at the southern exit of town is less enticing but will do half the damage to your purse.

Getting There & Away

Bus No 2 passes through here twice daily on its way between Puerto del Rosario (400 ptas) and Vega del Río de Palmas, a short distance south.

AROUND BETANCURIA

A couple of kilometres north of Betancuria, the **Mirador Morro Veloso** offers mesmerising views across the island's weird, disconsolate moonscape. If the barrier is closed, the view is almost as spectacular at the col over which the FV-30 highway climbs before it twists its way north through the barely perceptible settlements of Valle de Santa Inés and Los Llanos de la Concepción.

In **Casillas del Ángel** the petite Iglesia de Santa Ana contains an 18th-century wooden carving of St Anne.

For a hearty meal of goat meat, try the appropriately named *El Cabrito* at the western end of the town.

Heading south for Pájara, you soon hit **Vega del Río Palma**. As you proceed, the reason for the name becomes clear – the road follows the course of a near-dry watercourse, still sufficiently wet enough below the surface to keep a stand of palms alive.

ANTIGUA

This is one of the bigger inland villages but there is not much to do except make a quick visit to the 18th-century church.

Scarcely 1km north of the pueblo is the **Molino de Antigua**, a fully restored windmill. Admission is free to the windmill and its trim grounds, planted with cactuses. and indigenous species. It opens 9.30 am to 5.30 pm daily except Monday and Saturday.

Piccolo Mondo, a pizzeria and sandwich place across the road from the church, is handy for a snack or you could try the *restaurant* next door to the Molino for a classier lunch.

Bus No 1 passes through here en route between Puerto del Rosario and Morro Jable.

AROUND ANTIGUA
La Ampuyenta
If it's open, the 17th-century **Ermita de San Pedro de Alcántara** merits a quick stop. The *ermita* (chapel) is surrounded by a stout, protective wall built by French from the Normandy area. Within, the walls of the nave are decorated with large, engagingly naive paintings, contrasting with the more sophisticated works embellishing the wooden altarpieces.

Tiscamanita
Visit this tiny hamlet, 9km south of Antigua, to see a working restored mill (and find out what a hard grind it all was). With its infectiously enthusiastic guide, the Windmill Interpretation Centre opens 9.30 am to 5.30 pm daily except Monday and Saturday. Admission costs 300 ptas – including a free fistful of *gofio* (a roasted mixture of wheat, maize or barley). Ask for the English version of the explanatory leaflet.

PÁJARA
What makes the 17th-century **Iglesia de Nuestra Señora de Regla** unique in the islands are the pair of *retables* behind the altar, simpler and more subdued than the Baroque excesses of mainland Spain (stick 100 ptas in the machine on the right after you enter the church to light them up). They are an example of influences flowing back from Latin America – in this case, Mexico. Lift your gaze to the fine wooden ceiling. Outside, the decoration above the main portal is said to be of Aztec inspiration.

Right next to the church you can eat well at the ***Centro Cultural***. Across the road, ***Restaurante La Fonda*** has a more pleasant ambience, although the food and prices are much of a muchness.

Two to three buses daily (No 13) run between Pájara and Gran Tarajal, then on to La Lajita. The trip to Gran Tarajal takes about 30 minutes. The bus calls in at the beach villages between Gran Tarajal and La Lajita.

AROUND PÁJARA
The drive directly north towards Betancuria is one of the most spectacular on the island and the journey south towards the Jandía peninsula via La Pared is almost as attractive. Fuerteventura ranks as relatively flat when compared to Lanzarote and the other islands to the west, but you would never think so as you wend your way through this lonely and spectacularly harsh terrain.

Ajuy & Puerto de la Peña
If you have your own wheels, a 9km side trip from Pájara takes you north-west to Ajuy and contiguous Puerto de la Peña. A dishevelled fishing settlement, its black-sand beach makes a change from its illustrious golden neighbours to the south in the Jandía peninsula. The strand is fronted by a couple of simple eateries serving up the day's catch.

CALETA DE FUSTE
Of the main resorts on the island, this is the most convenient for the airport but the least attractive.

The none-too-clued-up tourist office (☎ 928 16 32 86) is in the Centro Comercial Castillo. It opens 9 am to 3 pm (to 2 pm, July to September) on weekdays.

The squat, little, round tower (hyperbolically known as El Castillo) has been turned into an appendage of the ***Barceló Club El Castillo*** bungalow complex. The beach, while perfectly pleasant, is a poor relation compared with what's on offer at Corralejo and Jandía.

Activities
Diving Deep Blue (☎ 606 27 54 68, ✉ info@deep-blue-diving.com) is conveniently sited beside the port. A single dive costs 3900 ptas and a pack of ten costs 35,000 ptas. Add 1500 ptas per dive for equipment hire. They do beginners courses

for PADI certification and a wide range of specialist courses.

Windsurfing Between port and beach, Fanatic Fun Center (☎ 928 53 59 99, e ucop@jet.es) offers beginners courses costing 15,300/23,800 ptas for six/12 hours, including equipment. The hire of gear alone costs 4000/6000/23,800 ptas per half-day/day/week.

Sailing & Subbing From the port, Catamaran Excursions (☎ 928 16 35 14) sail daily at noon, returning at 4 pm. The price of 6900 ptas (children 3500 ptas) includes lunch on board, the use of snorkelling equipment and also a visit to their small Oceanarium.

Nautilus, a small yellow submarine, sets out on the hour daily for a 45-minute dive. Tickets cost 2500 ptas (children under 12 free).

Cycling Bike-Nort rents bicycles for 1200/3100/6000 ptas per day/three days/week. Sign on at the reception desk of Barceló Club El Castillo. See the following section for details.

Places to Stay & Eat
As in other resorts, most places fill with package guests and some deal only with tour operators.

Bungalows Castillo Beach (☎ 928 16 30 01, fax 928 16 32 03) is among the less expensive options, not least because it's up the hill 750m west of the FV-1 (about a 15-minute walk from the beach). It has bungalows for two at 6500 ptas.

Hotel El Mahay (☎ 928 16 33 53, fax 928 16 33 51, e mhr@idecnet.com), 150m south-west of the tourist office, has very limited capacity once the tour operator has taken its slice. Singles/doubles are good value at 6300/8900 ptas, including breakfast. Its mid-priced *restaurant* offers a good range of Spanish and international cuisine.

Top of the range is *Barceló Club El Castillo (☎ 928 16 31 00, fax 928 16 30 42, e elcastillo@barcelo.com)*, right beside

the beach and port. At this veritable mini-village, a bungalow accommodating up to three is between 9000 ptas and 12,000 ptas.

SOUTH-EAST BEACHES
Giniginamar & Tarajalejo
These two quiet fishing hamlets go about their business largely undisturbed by tourists – though Tarajalejo, with a couple of hotels and apartment blocks at its southern limit, is under siege. Their brief, grey beaches make a dull show compared with their brilliant white cousins further south – but at least they're not crowded.

Just west of the FV-2 highway outside Tarajalejo, El Brasero has a tiny aquarium where admission costs 500 ptas (children 250 ptas). It also offers horse riding for 2000/5000 ptas per hour/3 hours.

Bus No 1 between Puerto del Rosario and Morro Jable stops at Tarajalejo, but not in Giniginamar.

La Lajita
This unremarkable little fishing village presents yet another black-sand and pebble beach. At its southern exit is one of those theme-park arrangements which have so utterly overrun Fuerteventura's big sister island, Gran Canaria.

At Zoo Camel Safari (☎ 928 16 11 35) you can wander around the little zoo, populated by monkeys, exotic birds and other unfortunates, and/or join a 30 minute camel trek, which costs 1200 per person (children 700 ptas). The zoo opens 9 am to 7 pm, admission costs 1000 ptas (children 500 ptas). Bus No 1 stops at the highway exit to town, from where it's a short walk south to the complex.

The North

ROAD TO LA OLIVA
The FV-10 highway shoots westwards away from Puerto del Rosario into the barren interior of the island. Before crossing the ridgeback that forms the island's spine, it passes through the sleepy hamlets of **Tetir** and **La Matilla**. The demure chapel in the

latter is a good example of the simple, bucolic buildings of the Canaries – functional, relatively unadorned and aesthetically pleasing.

About 7km south of La Matilla along the FV-207 and 1km beyond the village of Tefía is the **Ecomuseo la Alcogida** – a restored agricultural hamlet complete with furnished houses, outbuildings and domestic animals. There's an optional audio commentary in English (500 ptas) and a self-guiding pack (400 ptas) in Spanish (an English version is currently being prepared). This open-air museum opens 9.30 am to 5.30 pm daily except Monday and Saturday. Admission costs 700 ptas.

Follow the road out of Tefía and swing right (west) on the FV-211 for **Casa de los Molinos**. On the way you can't miss the old mill, sitting squat in the grounds of what is now a handicrafts school. Casa de los Molinos itself is little more than a few simple houses overlooking a small black pebble beach. You can eat seafood at ***Restaurante Los Molinos*** while gazing over Atlantic breakers.

Tindaya is a sprawling centre where much of the island's goat cheese *(queso majorero)* is produced. See the boxed text 'The Big Cheese' earlier in this chapter for more details of this renowned cheese.

Just to its north, the Basque sculptor, Eduardo Chillida, has caused considerable controversy with his plan, officially supported, to bore a huge hole into Montaña de Tindaya. The 50-cubic-metre space is designed to make its visitors 'feel small in their physical dimension, and brotherhood with all other people'. Opponents perceive all sorts of less lofty interests behind the project. Yet despite anonymous threatening phone calls and letters, plus a major related financial scandal involving the disappearance of nearly 2,000 million ptas, Chillida remains undeterred – and, let's face it, there are plenty more undisturbed volcanice mountains to be explored on Fuerteventura.

The No 7 bus from Puerto del Rosario to El Cotillo passes through all but Tefía and Casa de los Molinos three times daily. Bus No 2 between Puerto del Rosario and Vega del Río de Palmas passes by Tefía twice daily. There are no buses to Casa de los Molinos.

LA OLIVA
pop 2300

One-time capital of the island, in fact if not in name, La Oliva still bears a trace or two of grander days. The weighty bell tower of the 18th-century **Iglesia de Nuestra Señora de la Candelaria** is the town's focal point. To the south, the 18th-century **Casa de los Coroneles**, more foreign legion fortress than simple *casa* (house), stands in decrepit isolation, overrun by goats, its promised restoration still unfulfilled.

From the early 1700s, the officers who once presided here virtually controlled the affairs of the island. Amassing power and wealth, they so exploited the peasant class that in 1834 Madrid, faced with repeated bloody mutinies on the island, disbanded the militia. Problem was, the now ex-colonels still held onto their appropriated wealth.

About 250m north of the church is the **Casa de la Cilla**, a small museum, which is devoted to grain and its production. Closed for renovations at the time of writing, like other official museums, it normally opens 9.30 am to 5.30 pm, daily except Monday and Saturday.

Bus No 7 between Puerto del Rosario and El Cotillo passes through three times daily.

CORRALEJO
postcode 35660 • pop 4000

Tourism is what makes this place tick. For the moment, it has been kept to manageable levels – the town has its tacky side but the bulk of the holiday apartments remain low rise and the town centre still retains the faintest resonance of what was once a simple fishing village.

What make Corralejo are the blinding white sand dunes to the south of town, sweeping back in gentle sugar-loaf rolls from the crystal blue ocean. Protected as a nature park, no one can build on or near them.

FUERTEVENTURA

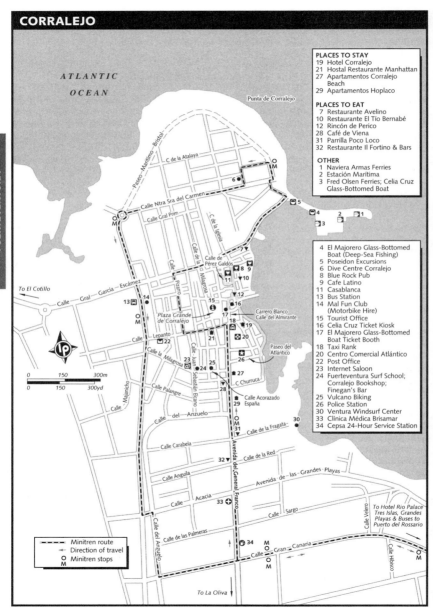

CORRALEJO

PLACES TO STAY
19 Hotel Corralejo
21 Hostal Restaurante Manhattan
27 Apartamentos Corralejo Beach
29 Apartamentos Hoplaco

PLACES TO EAT
7   Restaurante Avelino
10 Restaurante El Tío Bernabé
12 Rincón de Perico
28 Café de Viena
31 Parrilla Poco Loco
32 Restaurante Il Fortino & Bars

OTHER
1   Naviera Armas Ferries
2   Estación Marítima
3   Fred Olsen Ferries; Celia Cruz Glass-Bottomed Boat
4   El Majorero Glass-Bottomed Boat (Deep-Sea Fishing)
5   Poseidon Excursions
6   Dive Centre Corralejo
8   Blue Rock Pub
9   Cafe Latino
11 Casablanca
13 Bus Station
14 Mal Fun Club (Motorbike Hire)
15 Tourist Office
16 Celia Cruz Ticket Kiosk
17 El Majorero Glass-Bottomed Boat Ticket Booth
18 Taxi Rank
20 Centro Comercial Atlántico
22 Post Office
23 Internet Saloon
24 Fuerteventura Surf School; Corralejo Bookshop; Finegan's Bar
25 Vulcano Biking
26 Police Station
30 Ventura Windsurf Center
33 Clínica Médica Brisamar
34 Cepsa 24-Hour Service Station

ATLANTIC OCEAN

Punta de Corralejo

To El Cotillo

Plaza Grande de Corralejo

Carrero Blanco Calle del Almirante

Paseo del Atlántico

Calle Acorazado España

To Hotel Rio Palace Tres Islas, Grandes Playas & Buses to Puerto del Rossario

To La Oliva

Minitren route
Direction of travel
Minitren stops

0   150   300m
0   150   300yd

Information

Tourist Offices The tourist office (☎ 928 86 62 35), Plaza Grande de Corralejo, opens 9 am to 2 pm and 4 to 7 pm, Monday to Friday, and 9 am to noon on Saturday.

Post & Communications The main post office is on Calle Lepanto.

Internet Saloon (aka Crumuri Service) on Calle Juan Sebastián Elcano is wired 9 am to 1 pm and 8 to 10.30 pm on weekdays and 10 am to 2 pm on Saturday.

Bookshops The best place on the island for books in English is Corralejo Bookshop, bang opposite Internet Saloon. It stocks mainly novels, both new and second hand.

Medical Services Clínica Médica Brisamar (☎ 928 53 64 02) on Avenida General Franco is one among several private clinics set up primarily for tourists.

Emergency There's a police station on Paseo del Atlántico.

Things to See & Do

Parque Natural de Corralejo The beach dunes of this protected nature park stretch along the east coast for about 10km from Corralejo.

It can get breezy here, and your predecessors have already applied their ingenuity to the problem – the little fortresses of loose stones, most commonly erected atop shrub-covered sandy knolls, are designed to protect sun-worshippers from the wind.

Diving Dive Centre Corralejo (☎ 928 53 59 06, fax 928 86 62 43) on Calle Nuestra Señora del Pino, just back from the waterfront, organises two-dive day trips for experienced divers from Monday to Saturday. They also rent equipment and offer courses.

Windsurfing Conditions along much of the coast and in the strait between Corralejo and Lanzarote, the Estrecho de la Bocaina, are ideal for windsurfing.

The Ventura Windsurf Center (☎ 928 86 62 95) is one of several in the area which cater for beginners – or you can just hire the gear. It is on the beach at the end of Calle de la Fragata.

Surfing Corralejo is a popular base for surfers. If you need equipment, lessons or advice on where to get the best breaks, you could try Fuerteventura Surf School (☎ 928 86 74 42) at Calle Acorazado España 14. Out at Grandes Playas, try Flag Beach Windsurf Center (☎ 928 86 63 89).

Boat Trips Three-hour mini-cruises aboard El Majorero allow a couple of hours on the Isla de Lobos. They leave at 10 am and noon. Tickets cost 1700 ptas. Alternatively, simply use the boat to get across to the islet for 1300 ptas return. The last boat back leaves at 5 pm. On Wednesday, they do a day cruise to and around the islet; lunch is included in the price (4500 ptas). Get tickets from the booth at Calle Almirante Carrero Blanco or at the port.

The Poseidon and the catamaran Celia Cruz do similar return trips to Isla de Lobos. The latter also offers one-hour mini-cruises (1500 ptas, daily except Sunday).

Fishing At the port, you can sign up for deep-sea fishing trips with Barvik (☎ 928 17 51 55), Pez Velero (☎ 928 86 61 73) or Siña María. All will cook your catch.

Places to Stay

It can be a real hassle finding somewhere to stay. Without wheels it can be worse as a lot of the apartments are strung out along the beach south of the town. Still more of a pain, many deal only with tour operators. So, if you don't come with a package, be prepared to move on to, say, Puerto del Rosario until you can organise something in one of the resorts.

Hotel Corralejo (☎ 928 53 52 46, Calle Colón 12) is right in the heart of town and offers spacious singles/doubles/triples with bathroom for 4180/5250/6270 ptas. Most rooms overlook the little town beach. Otherwise, try *Hostal Restaurante Manhattan (☎ 928 86 66 43, Calle Gravina 19),* open Monday to Saturday only, which has

FUERTEVENTURA

basic singles/doubles with bathroom for 3500/6000 ptas. Both are often full.

An apartment, with greater space, may work out cheaper. Within its shady compound, ***Apartamentos Hoplaco*** *(☎/fax 928 86 60 40, Avenida General Franco 7)* has two/three-person apartments from 4700/6700 ptas.

More upmarket, ***Corralejo Beach*** *(☎ 928 88 63 15, fax 928 86 63 17, Avenida General Franco s/n)* has apartments for two/four costing from 7000/10000 ptas (8000/12000 ptas from July to September). It's handy for accessing the town centre but far enough away not to be disturbed by the whoops of the partying.

Hotel Rio Palace Tres Islas *(☎ 928 53 57 00, fax 928 53 58 58, Avenida de las Grandes Playas)* is a luxury seaside fortress on the edge of the dunes. Singles and doubles with view of the dunes cost 11,930 ptas per person, while doubles with ocean views come in at 15,700 ptas per person. Prices include half board.

Places to Eat

If you want to try gofio, followed by a plate of *cabrito* (goat meat – an island speciality for reasons which have probably become apparent by now) head for ***El Rincón de Perico***, where Calle Iglesia runs into Plaza Chica. These local delicacies and a beer will set you back 1800 ptas.

Also on Calle Iglesia, ***El Tío Bernabé*** carries a wider range of Canaries cuisine. Count on spending about 2500 ptas for a three-course meal, excluding drinks.

Parrilla Poco Loco *(Avenida General Franco 16)* is great for grills – a healthy T-bone costs 2000 ptas.

Il Fortino, in the gaudy yellow shopping centre on the corner of Avenida General Franco and Calle Anguila, serves quality Italian food at reasonable prices – but can you entirely trust a place where the menu is over 140 items long?

For a civilised cup of coffee or breakfast, ***Café de Viena*** *(Calle Juan de Austria 27)* hits the spot.

Away from the tourist mainstream and still very Spanish (the Guardia Civil drink there) is ***Restaurante Avelino*** *(☎ 928 53 51 95)* at the corner of Calle García Escámez and Calle Ballena.

Entertainment

Finding a drink in Corralejo doesn't pose a problem. Bars, such as the popular ***Oink***, take up much of the Centro Comercial Atlántico, on Avenida General Franco, as well as the custard yellow shopping centre further down the road, on the corner of Calle Anguila. For a relaxed cocktail just out of earshot of the main hurly-burly, ***Casablanca*** *(Calle Pérez Galdós)* is perfect. For a noisier one, sample from the range at shoreside ***Cafe Latino***, which has great canned jazz and, at weekends, a DJ.

For a late-night tipple (until about 3 am), the ***Blue Rock*** *(Calle de la Iglesia)* blues and rock bar at the northern end of the pedestrianised part of the street makes a refreshing alternative to the rowdier 'real British pubs'.

Getting There & Away

Bus Bus No 6 runs regularly from Corralejo's bus station to Puerto del Rosario (360 ptas, 40 minutes). You can also pick up the bus by the last Minitren stop south-east of town and at the Hotel Riu Palace Tres Islas.

Bus No 8 heads west to El Cotillo via La Oliva (325 ptas, 40 minutes, six daily).

Car & Motorbike There's a string of car rental companies, most of them acting as agents for the same supplier, near the Centro Comercial Atlántico on Avenida General Franco.

If you want only two motorised wheels, one option is Mal Fun Club (☎ 928 53 51 52) at Avenida Juan Carlos I, opposite the bus station.

Boat Fred Olsen ferries leave four to five times daily for Playa Blanca in Lanzarote. The trip takes 35 to 45 minutes and a one-way ticket costs 1850 ptas. Otherwise, hop onto one of Naviera Armas' five to six daily boats (1700 ptas).

At the Lanzarote end, Fred Olsen puts on

a free connecting bus as far as Puerto del Carmen for its 9 am and 5 pm services. The 9 am run continues to Lanzarote's airport. This free bus operates in the other direction too (see Getting There & Around under Puerto del Carmen in the Lanzarote chapter for details).

Getting Around

Minitren You know those irritating little trains which often transport sheepishly grinning tourists around resorts and theme parks? Well there's one in Corralejo and it actually comes in handy.

It runs every half hour, 9 am to 11.30 pm, from Avenida General Franco and takes in the port, bus station and most of the apartments at the northern end of the dunes in its circuit of the town. A ride costs 150 ptas.

Taxi Call ☎ 928 86 61 08 for a taxi. One from the town centre to the main beaches will cost about 500 ptas.

Bicycles & Blades Vulcano Biking (☎ 928 53 57 06), Calle Acorazado España 10, opens Monday to Saturday. You can rent bikes for 800/2000/4000 ptas per day/three days/week and roller blades for 500/1000/2000 ptas per hour/day/three days.

ISLA DE LOBOS

This bare 4.4 sq km islet takes its name from the seawolves *(lobos marinos)* that lived there. They were in fact monk seals *(focas monje)*, which have since disappeared.

You can go on an excursion to Isla de Lobos from Corralejo. Once you've disembarked there's little to do but go for a short walk, order lunch at the quayside *chiringuito* (kiosk) – you must reserve when you arrive if you intend to lunch there – and head for the pleasant little beach.

It's possible to camp here but you need a permit from the Oficina del Medio Ambiente (Environment Office; ☎ 928 85 20 38), Calle Professor Juan Tadeo Cabrera 10, in Puerto del Rosario.

The cheapest and fastest way to get there is on the *Isla de Lobos* ferry. Departing

Corralejo at 10.15 am, it leaves the island at 4.15 pm. A return ticket costs 800 ptas. See also Boating in the Corralejo section.

EL COTILLO

Once the seat of power of the tribal chiefs of Maxorata, the northern kingdom of Guanche Fuerteventura, El Cotillo has been largely ignored since the conquest. The exceptions to the rule were cut-throat pirates who occasionally sought to land here and the slowly growing invasion of less violent sun-seekers who prize the area's unaffected peacefulness. The developers have so far largely left this small fishing village on Fuerteventura's north-western coast alone, but for how long?

Apart from the delights of the sea (the better beaches stretch out south of town), the only object of note is the tubby little **Fortaleza del Tostón**. Built in 1797, the fort now seems oddly out of place, sitting isolated above the modest cliffs south of the port. The beaches between El Cotillo and Corralejo are generally small and pebbly. Experienced surfers should make for a spot known as Bubbles. Waves break over reef and rocks, you can pick out the casualties on the streets of El Cotillo and Corralejo.

It's a quiet spot; if you're after some frenzied nightlife, you should head over to Corralejo.

Places to Stay

El Cotillo is a rather nondescript, comparatively undeveloped haven with several groups of apartments.

Far from mundane is *La Gaviota (☎ 928 53 85 67)*, a laid-back, neo-hippy place which flies the Jolly Roger and charges 5000 ptas for a double.

Apartamentos Bar Playa (☎ 928 53 85 22, Calle San Pedro 12) is, in fact, some 200m from waterfront Bar Playa, where you can get directions. It has large rooms for up to four at 4000 ptas and ones for up to six for 6000 ptas.

Closer to the fort and the southern beaches are *Apartamentos Juan Benítez (☎/fax 928 53 85 03, Calle Caletón 10)*. They stand out like a sore thumb, but the apartments, starting at 6000/7500 ptas for single/double occupancy, are very clean.

More resorty is the comparatively large *Apartamentos Cotillo Lagos* (☎ *928 17 53 88, fax 928 85 20 99*) complex, a low-level development about 2km north of town in the satellite Urbanización Los Lagos. It's a characterless place but the apartments are comfortable and not a bad choice at 6500 ptas for a double.

Places to Eat
The most pleasant spot to eat and drink is *Restaurante La Vaca Azul*, presided over by a surreal, model cow (floodlit in lurid blue at night) right on the small pebble beach in the middle of town. They serve up decent food all day from noon to 10 pm.

There are a pair of good little places at the southern end of the village, above the tiny port. *Bar Cafetería Puerto Nuevo* has a rich selection of tapas while *Casa Chano* (*Calle Fuerteventura 1*) serves up standard fish and meat dishes for about 2000 ptas, including a side dish and wine.

Getting There & Away
Bus No 7 for Puerto del Rosario (450 ptas, 45 minutes) leaves at 6.45 am, noon and 5 pm. No 8 leaves for Corralejo (325 ptas, 40 minutes, six daily). The dirt road which follows the coast to Corralejo is normally passable for ordinary cars.

AROUND EL COTILLO
Zoo Safari, 1.5km north-west of the village of Lajares and 12 km from Corralejo, offers half-hour camel rides for 1000 ptas and a 1½-hour trip into the caldera of the long extinct Calderón Hondo volcano for 2500 ptas. Children are half price for each.

Península de Jandía

Most of the peninsula is protected by its status as the Parque Natural de Jandía, a designated nature park. The south-west is a canvas of craggy hills and bald plains leading to cliffs west of Morro Jable. Much of the rest is made up of dunes, scrub and beaches.

Somewhere along this peninsula, they say, German submarine crews used to hole up occasionally during WWII. You think these beaches are paradise now – just imagine them with not a single tourist, not one little apartment block, only you and your mates from the U-boat!

According to other stories, Nazi officials passed through here after the war to pick up false papers before heading on to South America. One version even has hordes of Nazi gold buried hereabouts – so bring your bucket and spade!

COSTA CALMA
Costa Calma, about 25km north-east of Morro Jable, is a 'Tidy Town' version of Caleta de Fuste. The beach is truly desirable and the developments are generally more tasteful. It's a superior resort but it lacks soul; its whole existence is due to tourism.

Places to Stay & Eat
Among the few cheaper options, *Bungalows Bahía Calma* (☎ *928 54 71 58, fax 928 54 70 31*, e *b_calma@lix.intercom.es*) at the southern end of the resort offers apartments (6000 ptas) and bungalows (8000 ptas).

A block north, cascading down the cliff and within a spit of the beach, the more upmarket *Apartamentos Maryvent* (☎/*fax 928 54 70 92*) has self-contained apartments for two to three people costing from 8500 ptas to 13,500 ptas. As with many places on the peninsula, both cater primarily to German package tourists.

Nearby, the unassuming *Restaurante Leo* (aka Restaurante Canario), in the Centro Comercial Costa Calma, does primarily Canarian specialities and has a daily special at 1000 ptas. *Restaurante Arena* is another decent eatery in the same complex, where you'll also find a couple of bars and a pair of pizzerias.

PLAYA DE SOTAVENTO DE JANDÍA
The name is a catch-all for the series of stunning beaches that stretch along the

south coast of the peninsula. For swimming, sun-bathing and windsurfing, this strand is the most beautiful in the Canaries (the dunes of Corralejo in the north of the island run a close second). It's a coastal paradise – miles and miles of fine white sand which creeps its way almost imperceptibly into the turquoise expanse of the Atlantic.

For 10 hyperactive days each summer, its drowsy calm is shattered by the daytime action and frantic nightlife as the beach hosts a leg of the Windsurf World Cup.

Various driveable trails lead down off the FV-2 highway to vantage points off the beach – its generous expanses mean you should have little trouble finding a tranquil plot for yourself.

MORRO JABLE
postcode 35625 • pop 6000
Competing with Corralejo for the title of Fuerteventura's premier tourist resort is Morro Jable, the island's southern-most town and altogether smarter than its brash northern rival.

Information
Tourist Offices The tourist office (☎ 928 54 07 76, fax 928 54 50 44, e turismo@ playasdejandia.com) is downstairs in the Centro Comercial de Jandía on Avenida Saladar. It opens 9 am to 2.30 pm (to 3.30 pm from October to May) on weekdays and 4 to 7 pm on Wednesday.

Post & Communications The post office is at the northern tip of Calle Gambuesas.

You can check your electronic correspondence over a beer at Pub Kuhstall in the Centro Comercial de Jandía.

Laundry You don't have to be a guest to use the laundrette facilities in major apartment blocks. At Apartamentos Alameda de Jandía, for example, pick up a 600 ptas token (good for one load) at reception.

FUERTEVENTURA

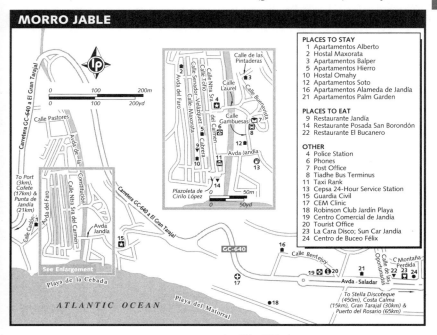

MORRO JABLE

PLACES TO STAY
1 Apartamentos Alberto
2 Hostal Maxorata
3 Apartamentos Balper
5 Apartamentos Hierro
10 Hostal Omahy
12 Apartamentos Soto
16 Apartamentos Alameda de Jandía
21 Apartamentos Palm Garden

PLACES TO EAT
9 Restaurante Jandía
14 Restaurante Posada San Borondón
22 Restaurante El Bucanero

OTHER
4 Police Station
6 Phones
7 Post Office
8 Tiadhe Bus Terminus
11 Taxi Rank
13 Cepsa 24-Hour Service Station
15 Guardia Civil
17 CEM Clinic
18 Robinson Club Jardín Playa
19 Centro Comercial de Jandía
20 Tourist Office
23 La Cara Disco; Sun Car Jandía
24 Centro de Buceo Félix

Medical Services Among several international clinics is CEM (☎ 928 54 03 33) in Edificio Don Carlos on Playa del Matorral.

Emergency The police station (☎ 928 54 10 22) is at Calle Laurel 1.

Things to See & Do
Beaches The magnificent Playa del Matorral, stretching eastwards for over 4km from Morro Jable, is great for indulging in a variety of watersports, churning a pedalo or just lazing on the hot sand. Such a stretch rarely gets crowded but for true solitude you need to be heading for seven further east. These are really only accessible with some kind of transport (from car via dune buggy to bicycle).

Diving If you're an experienced diver, you can explore the sea bottom with the Centro de Buceo Félix (☎/fax 928 54 14 18, @ info@tauchen-fuerteventura.de) at Avenida Saladar 27. One/three/ten dives cost 4000/11,700/33,200 ptas. Add on about 1000 ptas per dive if you use their gear. Beginners courses are only offered in German.

Windsurfing On an ideal stretch of coast for windsurfing, only one place, Robinson Club Jardín Playa (☎ 928 16 95 39), offers facilities – and then only if there's spare capacity (they give priority to members staying in their luxury activities complex). But they're friendly, accommodating folk who'll squeeze you in if possible. A 10- to 12-hour beginners course costs 35,500 ptas, including equipment. Hire of the gear costs 9000 ptas for five hours.

Sailing Robinson Club Jardín Playa (see the previous section) also has catamarans. The cost of an introductory course is as for windsurfing. Experienced sailors can hire the boats, which take two ideally (or up to five if you're just out for a bit of fun). They cost 20,000 ptas for five hours.

Boat Trips Magic (☎ 928 73 56 56) operates a couple of smart catamarans out of the port. Sailing at 10 or 10.30 am (also at 4 pm

from May to October), the cruises last five hours and cost 6900 ptas (children 3450 ptas). They include a barbecue lunch and allow plenty of time for offshore swimming and snorkelling.

Much the same is Maxi, which, in a previous existence (when she was called, prosaically, Fisher and Pykel) came second in the 1991 Whitbread Around the World sailing race.

If you have kids with you, you might consider Pedra-Sartaña which offers as an add-on – and perhaps a little direly if you're beyond puberty – 'fun and games with our pirate'. Sailings are Monday to Saturday. Tickets cost 6000 ptas (children 3000 ptas).

Cycling & Off-Road Driving Sun Car Jandía, beside La Cara disco, rents bicycles for 1200/3600/7000 ptas per day/three days/week.

It also hires out quads (basically four-wheel off-road motorbikes with fat tyres)

JANE SMITH

The waters off Fuerteventura offer excellent windsurfing opportunities.

for 4600/9100 ptas per hour/three hours. Fun they certainly are but, as they belt around the beaches and dunes of Playa de Barlovento de Jandía, they're not a very environmentally friendly form of locomotion.

Golf Just inland, 5km north of Morro Jable and up the Valle de Butihondo, an 18-hole golf course was being laid when we last passed by. Since every blade of grass has to be kept alive by desalinated water, you might think it kinder to the environment just to whack a ball up and down the sandy beaches if you're a golf addict. Brace your shoulders and take on the challenge of a 6km long bunker!

Markets There's a small Thursday market in a car park beside Avenida del Saladar, a little west of the tourist office, active in its way until 1.30 pm. With most stalls run by Moroccans, Africans and German dropouts, you'll be lucky to find anything that smacks particularly of the Canaries.

Places to Stay
A couple of cheap options in the centre of the town are *Hostal Omahy* (☎ 928 54 12 54, Calle Maxorata 47), where doubles with bathroom cost 4000 ptas, and *Hostal Maxorata* (☎/fax 928 54 10 87) at No 31, which has doubles with washbasin at 3000 ptas (4000 ptas with bathroom).

The welcoming *Apartamentos Hierro* (☎/fax 928 54 11 13, Calle Senador Velázquez Cabrera 16) has only two flats: a double at 6000 ptas and a quad at 8000 ptas.

Apartamentos Soto (☎ 928 54 14 19, fax 928 54 15 89, Calle Gambuesas) has fully equipped doubles/triples/quads which cost 6500/7500/12,500 ptas. Call by the adjacent Autos Soto if there's no response from reception.

A slight move up the ladder, *Apartamentos Alberto* (☎ 928 54 15 22, fax 928 54 13 10, Calle Cardon) offers apartments with a kitchenette, lounge room and phone. Doubles/triples/quads start at 6000/7500/ 10,600 ptas.

Climbing higher, huge *Apartamentos Palm Garden* (☎ 928 54 10 00, fax 928 54

10 40, Avenida Saladar), cascading like a ziggurat, has airy, attractive apartments starting at 8750 ptas while comparable ones at *Apartamentos Alameda de Jandi* (☎ 928 54 12 67, fax 928 54 15 29, Calle Bentejuy) cost pretty much the same.

Places to Eat
You can get the usual resort 'international cuisine' and fast food at innumerable places among the apartments, condos and shopping centres along Avenida Saladar.

Somewhere a little more interesting, and offering a variety of Spanish food, is *Restaurante Posada San Borondón (Plazoleta de Cirilo López)*. A full meal with wine will cost you about 2500 ptas. The main problem with this place – and one that can't escape you – is that it is trying to look like a steamship.

A quartet of *restaurants* on the waterfront behind San Borondón restaurant serve pleasant enough food in seaside surroundings. Stick to the fresh fish and you're bound to be satisfied.

For an earthier ambience and large servings of good Castilian cooking, try *Restaurante Jandía (Calle Senador Velázquez Cabrera 7)*.

Avenida Saladar may seem like one long eat-in. You can't go wrong but you can't go very right either. However, one exception is *El Bucanero*, a relative dwarf of a restaurant among the giant eateries. Their juicy *parrillada de pescado* (grilled fish) at 3500 ptas for two is several cuts above what is in too many places a few wizened offerings from the ocean.

Entertainment
The main nightlife action is along the beachfront part of the resort. A cluster of pubs is concentrated in the Centro Comercial de Jandía. Some, such as *Costa Sur* and *Pub Kuhstall*, cater to all types and age groups, but others, such as *Surf Inn,* aim at a younger and later-arriving crowd. When they start closing, you could head for *La Cara Disco (Avenida Saladar)*, a block or two east along from the Centro Comercial, or *Stella Discoteque (Avenida Saladar)*,

FUERTEVENTURA

450m farther on – look for the twin bronze lions and you're nearly there.

Getting There & Away

Bus The Tiadhe bus terminus is opposite the post office at the top of Calle Gambuesas in the town centre. The first No 1 bus for Puerto del Rosario (1055 ptas, two hours, nine daily) leaves at 6 am and the last leaves at 7 pm. The No 10 bus via the airport (1045 ptas, 1½ hours, three daily) is faster. Bus No 5 to Costa Calma (285 ptas, 40 minutes) runs frequently.

Boat Puerto de Morro Jable, the port, is 3km by road from the centre of town.

Trasmediterránea (☎ 902 45 46 45) has jetfoils leaving for Las Palmas de Gran Canaria (6265 ptas, 1½ hours) and Tenerife (8860 ptas) at 1.30 pm, Monday to Saturday, and at 3 pm on Sunday.

Naviera Armas ferries (☎ 928 54 21 13) head for Las Palmas (5000 ptas, about three hours, twice daily) at 3 pm on weekdays (3.30 pm at the weekend) and at 7 pm.

You can get tickets for both services at the port or at travel agents.

Getting Around

Taxi There is a rank in the town centre just off Avenida Jandía. To call a taxi, ring ☎ 928 54 12 57.

AROUND MORRO JABLE
Punta de Jandía

Twenty kilometres of graded but unsealed road winds out along the southern reaches of the peninsula to a lone lighthouse at Punta de Jandía.

Puerto de la Cruz, a couple of kilometres short (east) of the lighthouse, is a tiny, bedraggled fishing settlement and weekend retreat for locals. Two little restaurants, the *Tenderete* and *Punta de Jandía*, open only at lunchtime, serve up the local catch to tourists passing en route to the island's westernmost point. The latter serves the freshest of fish at 1300 ptas but particularly vile coffee.

Cofete

About 10km along the same road from Morro Jable, a turn-off leads north-east over a pass and plunges to Cofete (7km from the junction), a tiny peninsula hamlet at the southern extreme of the Playa de Barlovento de Jandía. Sandy tracks, negotiable on foot or by 4WD, snake off to this wind-whipped strand. *Restaurante Cofete*, open 11 am to 7 pm, does drinks and snacks and has a more sophisticated menu than you'd expect from a restaurant at the end of the road. They too do fresh fish – as well as *carne de cabra en salsa* (goat in sauce) – maybe a close relative of the semi-wild creatures you pass on the journey.

PLAYA DE BARLOVENTO DE JANDÍA

Much wilder than their leeward counterparts, the long stretch of beaches on the windward side of the peninsula are also harder to get to. You really need a 4WD to safely negotiate the various tracks leading into the area – but once you've found a spot you like, please don't chop up the dunes with your vehicle.

This stretch of coast can get very windy – though the flying sand doesn't seem to deter the nude bathers, who are as common as the partly clothed variety. Take care swimming here: the waves and currents can often be more formidable than the usually becalmed waters on the other side of the island.

Lanzarote

Covering 846 sq km and with a resident population of 85,000, Lanzarote is the fourth largest and most north-easterly of the Canary Islands. It measures only about 60km north to south and a mere 21km at its widest point east to west. It is known as the Isla de los Volcanes, with 300 cones peppered about it. The island's name is assumed to be a corruption of Lanzarotto (or Lancelotto) Malocello, the Genoese seafarer who landed on the island in the late 13th or early 14th century.

It hardly ever rains here, so all the water you use is desalinated sea water – not the tastiest stuff around, but better than cleaning your teeth with beer.

The immediate reaction of many who come to the island is that there is nothing here. True, it's a largely arid place but bizarrely so. UNESCO has declared the entire island a Biosphere Reserve. Its largely volcanic terrain is quite unique and those who take the time to move around the island, away from the three main resorts, will be pleasantly surprised by its stark, weird and very real beauty.

The island's approach to tourism has in no small measure been shaped by the inspiration of the artist César Manrique, who died in 1992. Not only has he left his personal stamp on many of the attractions around the island, but his ideas continue to inform policy on tourism development. The near absence of high rises – even in the three main resort areas – and careful adherence to traditional building styles in the interior is largely due to the vigilance of Manrique and his successors. Locals and visitors alike should be grateful such care has been maintained.

History

Lanzarote was the first of the Canary Islands to fall to Jean de Béthencourt in 1402, marking the beginning of the Spanish conquest. Along with Fuerteventura, Lanzarote was particularly exposed to frequent raids

Highlights

- Touring the lava landscape of Las Montañas del Fuego
- Enjoying a volcanic BBQ lunch at the Restaurante del Diablo
- Discovering the beaches and coves of Punta del Papagayo
- Wandering around the old town of Teguise, once the island's capital
- Visiting the bizarre and wonderful landmarks created by César Manrique
- Exploring the spectacular Cueva de los Verdes

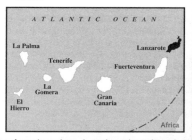

by Moroccan pirates operating from ports along the north-west African coast, barely 100km away. The then-capital Teguise was frequently sacked and many inhabitants hauled into captivity, later to be sold as slaves. The problem was especially grave during the 16th century and the Moroccans weren't the only source of grief. British buccaneers such as Sir Walter Raleigh, Sir John Hawkins and John Poole also visited the island, as did French bearers of the skull and crossbones such as Jean Florin and Pegleg le Clerc.

By the middle of the 17th century, misery, piracy and emigration had reduced the number of Conejeros (as the islanders are sometimes called) to just 300.

In the 1730s, massive and disastrous

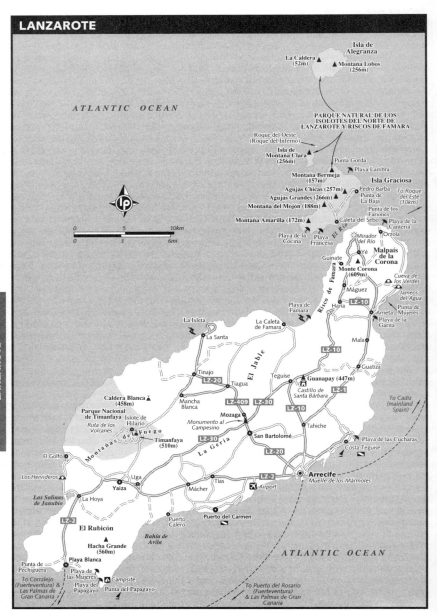

LANZAROTE

ATLANTIC OCEAN

Isla de
Alegranza

La Caldera
(52m)

▲ Montaña Lobos
(256m)

**PARQUE NATURAL DE LOS
ISOLOTES DEL NORTE DE
LANZAROTE Y RISCOS DE FAMARA**

Roque del Oeste
(Roque del Inferno)

Isla de
Montaña Clara
(256m)

Punta Gorda
Playa Lambra

Montaña Bermeja
(157m)

Isla Graciosa

Agujas Chicas (257m) ▲
Agujas Grandes (266m) ▲
Montaña del Mojón (188m) ▲
Montaña Amarilla (172m) ▲

Pedro Barba
Punta de
La Baja
To Roque
del Este
(10km)

Punta de los
Fariones

Caleta del Sebo
Playa de la
Cantería

Playa de la
Cocina

Playa
Francesa

Mirador
del Río

Orzola

El Río

Yé
Malpaís
de la
Corona

Guinate
Monte Corona
(609m)

Cueva de
los Verdes

Máguez

Jameos
del Agua

Playa de
Famara

Haría

Arrieta
Punta de
Mujeres

La Isleta

La Caleta
de Famara

Playa de la
Garita

La Santa

Mala

El Jable

Teguise

Guatiza

Tinajo

LZ-20
Tiagua

LZ-10

Guanapay (447m)

LZ-1

Caldera Blanca
(458m)

Mancha
Blanca

Castillo de
Santa Bárbara

**Parque Nacional
de Timanfaya**

LZ-409 **LZ-30**

Mozaga

To Cadiz
(mainland
Spain)

Islote de
Hilario

Monumento al
Campesino

LZ-10

Ruta de los
Volcanes

Timanfaya
(510m)

LZ-30

San Bartolomé

Tahiche

Playa de las Cucharas

El Golfo

Los Hervideros

La Gería

LZ-20

Costa Teguise

Uga

Arrecife
Muelle de los Mármoles

Las Salinas
de Janubio

Yaiza

La Hoya

Tías

Mácher

LZ-2

Airport

LZ-2

El Rubicón
▲
Hacha Grande
(560m)

Puerto
Calero

Puerto del Carmen

Bahía de
Ávila

ATLANTIC OCEAN

Punta de
Pechiguera

Playa Blanca

To Corralejo
(Fuerteventura) &
Las Palmas de
Gran Canaria

Playa de
las Mujeres

Campsite

Playa del
Papagayo

Punta del Papagayo

To Puerto del Rosario
(Fuerteventura)
& Las Palmas de Gran
Canaria

euro currency converter 1000 ptas = €6.01

Urban elegance in Tenerife's lovely La Orotava

San Andrés' beach is made of Saharan sand.

Colourful communications – Canary yellow?

Tenerife's most westerly point, Punta de Teno, offers fine views of La Gomera on a clear day.

Canarios don traditional dress for fiestas.

Streets ahead: discover La Orotava's old quarter.

The unique Roques de García offer spectacular views of Teide, Spain's highest peak, on Tenerife.

volcanic eruptions destroyed some of the island's most fertile land. Beyond the heartland of the great upheaval, though, islanders were to discover a rather ironic fact. The volcanic mix in the soil eventually proved a highly fertile bedrock for farming (particularly wine grapes), bringing relative prosperity to the descendants of those who had fled to Gran Canaria in terror of the lava flows.

Today, with tourism flourishing alongside the healthy if small agricultural sector, the island is home to 85,000 plus, of course, all the holiday blow-ins who at any given time can more than double the population. To give an idea of the scale: in just the first four months of the year 2000 alone, Lanzarote received nearly 600,000 visitors, of whom 40% were British and 25% were from Germany. About 1.7 million tourists visit the island annually.

Information

Books & Maps Noel Rochford's *Landscapes of Lanzarote*, published by Sunflower Books, gives some useful suggestions for drives and walks around the island of varying duration. More extensive in its coverage for walkers is the map pack, *Lanzarote*, produced by Discovery Walking Guides, which comes complete with walk descriptions written in their usual jaunty style.

See Maps in the Facts for the Visitor chapter for more details of the maps available.

Newspapers & Magazines The free monthly *Holiday Gazette & Tourist Guide*, although directed primarily at English-speaking expat residents, may give an idea or two about places to visit. The monthly *Gazette News* is of the same ilk – heavily reliant upon advertising and none too literate. Altogether more informative is the semi-official quarterly *Lancelot* (nominally 300 ptas but often available free), published in Spanish, English and German.

Activities

If lolling on the beach and dunking yourself in the ocean begins to bore, it may be time for something more active. The wilder, less visited and more rugged north coast has some of Europe's finest surfing breaks and a surf school based at Famara. By contrast, the beaches of the south coast are excellent for windsurfing and diving. The sea temperature rarely drops below 18°C while underwater visibility ranges between 6m and 20m, depending upon the season. Cycling, whether a gentle potter around your resort or a more strenuous outing along the lightly trafficked roads, is also possible. For details, see the Activities section within each of the three major resorts.

Diving Typical prices are 10,000 ptas to 18,000 ptas for a three-dive pack and about 28,000 ptas for 10 dives (allow 40,000 ptas if you hire all equipment). Otherwise, build in 2500 ptas per day for equipment hire. You're looking at around 35,000 ptas, all inclusive, for a two-day introductory course.

On Lanzarote, all divers must be registered; a one-year permit costs 2000 ptas.

Windsurfing Equipment hire is in the region of 2500 ptas for one hour, 5000 ptas for four hours, 6500 ptas per day and 27,000 ptas per week. A 10-hour beginners' course (two hours per day) costs around 25,000 ptas, including gear hire.

Cycling Rental prices vary but they average around 1500/4000/7000 ptas per day/three days/week.

Walking Feetbook Agencia (see Puerto del Carmen later in this chapter) and Canary Trekking (☎ 609 53 76 84, fax 928 59 08 61) both arrange half- and one-day guided walks, collecting you from and returning you to your hotel.

Accommodation

On all Lanzarote, there isn't a single youth hostel and only one camp site (see Punta del Papagayo later in this chapter).

Most accommodation is in the form of apartments and bungalows, the majority concentrated in the resorts of Puerto del Carmen, Playa Blanca and Costa Teguise.

As with neighbouring Fuerteventura, the main problem for independent travellers is that the bulk of these deal with tour operators, often exclusively, and are frequently full.

Arrecife is not the world's most fascinating capital but lone travellers without a booking might consider it as a temporary solution if nothing else turns up.

Otherwise, there is a spattering of alternatives at other points around the coast and a handful of inland options.

Getting There & Away

Air From Guasimeta airport (☎ 928 81 14 50), 6km south-west of Arrecife, Binter has up to six flights daily to Las Palmas de Gran Canaria (8860 ptas, 40 minutes) and four to Tenerife Norte (11,310 ptas, 50 minutes). Otherwise the traffic is made up of regular flights (Air Europa and Spanair) from the mainland and charters from all over Europe.

For a charter flight to the UK (around 20,000 ptas), contact or call by the airport booth of V.Travel 2000 (☎ 928 84 63 36, fax 928 84 63 35, **e** lanzarote@goflightline .com).

Boat See Getting There & Away under Arrecife for details on the ferry services to Fuerteventura and Gran Canaria.

Getting Around

Bus Arrecife Bus (☎ 928 81 14 56) provides the public transport. The service is frequent around Arrecife, especially to Puerto del Carmen and Costa Teguise. Fairly regular runs also connect with Playa Blanca in the south and such inland towns as Teguise. Otherwise services are minimal or nonexistent.

Car Rental places abound in all three major resorts.

Taxi As elsewhere, you have the option of moving around the island by taxi but it is an expensive way of doing things. The fare from Arrecife to Playa Blanca, for example, is 4500 ptas. For much the same amount you can hire a car for the whole day.

Arrecife & Around

ARRECIFE
postcode 35500 • pop 35,000

The island's capital is not its best advertisement. Aside from a couple of forts, one converted into a stylish art gallery and restaurant, and a fairly decent beach, it offers little of real interest. Its hotels and apartments can come in handy for those without reservations in the resorts – and it has a certain appeal simply because it's a living, breathing town which earns its living from doing much more than just catering to tourists.

History

The single biggest factor behind Arrecife's blandness is probably that it only became the island's capital in 1852. Until then Teguise ruled supreme – and the now-marginalised Teguise's architectural heritage shows what Arrecife missed out on by being a port for the erstwhile capital.

In 1574, the Castillo de San Gabriel first went up (it was subsequently attacked and rebuilt) to protect the port. Its sister further up the coast, the Castillo de San José, was raised in 1771. By the close of the 18th century, a semblance of a town had taken uncertain shape around the harbour. As its commerce grew and the threat of sea raids dropped off in the 19th century, Arrecife thrived. As the defensive imperatives for keeping the capital inland receded, the move of the island's administration to Arrecife became inevitable.

Orientation

Sun-blanched Arrecife presents no great navigational problems. With the notable exceptions of the Castillo de San José and port, everything of interest is located in a tight area around the centre. If you arrive by bus, drop off either in the heart of Playa del Reducto and walk eastwards or hang on until the bus station at the north-eastern flank of central Arrecife, from where you can easily zigzag into town.

The main streets for shops and res-

ARRECIFE

PLACES TO STAY
4 Pensión Guayermina
5 Hostal España
6 Pensión San Ginés
11 Hotel Miramar
18 Apartamentos Islamar
19 Apartamentos Arrecife
   Playa
20 Hostal Residencia
   Cardona
28 Hotel Lancelot

PLACES TO EAT
1 Covered Market
16 Tasca Tambo
25 Mesón Trasgu; Snack
   Bar Salida
27 Mesón La Tinaja

OTHER
2 Castillo de San José; Museo
   Internacional de Arte
   Contemporáneo
3 Bus Station
3 Bus Stop
8 Ayuntamiento (Town Hall)
9 Iglesia de San Ginés
10 Police Station
12 Post Office
13 Taxi Rank
14 Tourist Office
15 Castillo de San Gabriel;
   Museo Arqueológico
17 Viajes Insular
21 Redes Servicios Informática
22 La Antigua
23 La Polinesia
24 Trasmediterránea
   Ticket Office
26 Taxi Rank
29 Centro Medico Lansalud
30 Ciclo Mania

taurants are Avenida Generalísimo Franco and the pedestrianised Avenida León y Castillo.

Information

Tourist Offices The tourist office (☎ 928 81 18 60) is in a small pavilion opposite the post office. It opens 9 am to 1 pm and 4.30 to 7.30 pm (3 to 5 pm from July to September) on weekdays and 9 am to 1 pm on Saturday.

Money There are several banks with ATMs near the waterfront. American Express is represented by Viajes Insular (☎ 928 81 31 13) at Calle Doctor Rafael González Negrín 13.

Post & Communications The main post office, which has fax facilities, is at Avenida Generalísimo Franco 8.

To send or receive emails, pop into Redes Servicios Informática, Calle Coronel Bens 17, which charges 375/650 ptas per half hour/hour (250/350 ptas for students). It is wired 9 am to 2 pm and 5 to 8 pm, Monday to Friday, and 9 am to 2 pm on Saturday.

euro currency converter €1 = 166 ptas

The Life & Art of César Manrique

Some Lanzaroteños will tell you that César Manrique 'made Lanzarote'. Perhaps an overstatement, but the internationally renowned artist's love of his island home certainly left many traces across its length and breadth.

Born on 24 April 1919, he grew up in relative tranquillity by the sea. After a stint as a volunteer with Franco's forces during the 1936–9 Civil War, he eventually followed his heart's desire and enrolled in Madrid's Academia de Bellas Artes de San Fernando in 1945, after having already held his first exhibition five years earlier in his home town of Arrecife.

Influenced but not stylistically dominated by Picasso and Matisse, he held his first major exhibition of abstract works in 1954. In the following

JANE SMITH

years his opus toured most of Europe, and in 1964 he was invited by one of his admirers, Nelson Rockefeller, to the USA where he exhibited in New York's Guggenheim Museum.

But Manrique never forgot his birthplace and returned home in 1968 after his successful US tour brimming with ideas for enhancing what he already felt to be the incomparable beauty of Lanzarote.

He began with a campaign to preserve traditional building methods, especially in rural architecture, and another to ban the blight of advertising billboards on roadsides and across the countryside. A multifaceted artist, Manrique subsequently turned his flair and vision to a broad range of projects across the island. The whole of Lanzarote became his canvas. In all, he carried out seven major projects on the island, numerous others elsewhere in the archipelago and beyond, and at the time of his death had several more on the boil.

Medical Services The Hospital General (☎ 928 80 16 36) is north-west of the town centre on the highway to San Bartolomé. Near the beach is the Centro Medico Lansalud (☎ 928 81 58 54), Calle Coronel I Valls de la Torre 6.

Emergency The police (☎ 928 81 23 50) can be found at Avenida Coll 5.

Things to See

Castillo de San Gabriel The first building of any note in what was little more than a landing point for the odd caravel from Spain, this doughty fort was sorely tested on several occasions by Moroccan corsairs and European pirates in the years after its construction in 1574.

Today it is home to the **Museo Arqueológico**, a grandiloquent name for a very

modest, badly labelled collection of artefacts found on the island, including many from the Cueva de los Verdes (see Malpaís de la Corona later in this chapter). The 300 ptas admission fee might well be better spent on a couple of coffees. For the very keen, it opens 10 am to 1 pm and 4 to 7 pm daily.

Museo Internacional de Arte Contemporáneo Converted in 1994 by the Fundación César Manrique into an attractive home for modern art, the **Castillo de San José** was originally raised in the 18th century to deal with pirates and, at a time of famine on the island, to provide unemployed locals with a public-works job scheme.

It houses the most important collection of modern art in the Canaries. Aside from

The Life & Art of César Manrique

In Lanzarote's north-east, he directed the works to make the grotto of the Jameos del Agua accessible to visitors without ruining the natural beauty of the spot. Here too, he directed the construction of a music auditorium in a cavern of volcanic rock.

He chose to live not just in harmony with but directly amid the blue-black hardened lava flows that so characterise the island, building his house in a flow in Taro de Tahiche, about 6km north of Arrecife. Since his death in a car accident on 25 September 1992, this unusual house has served as home to the Fundación César Manrique (the César Manrique Foundation).

Farther north, the bizarre Jardín de Cactus, bristling with 10,000 cactuses of more than 1000 species, is another of his ideas. In the Montañas del Fuego, he installed the striking Restaurante del Diablo at the heart of the hostile, denuded volcanic terrain – and even thought to turn the still surging subterranean volcanic energy to good account so that the meat you eat there is grilled using its heat.

On the grand scale, it was primarily Manrique's persistent lobbying for maintaining traditional architecture and protecting the natural environment that prompted the Cabildo to pass laws restricting urban development.

The growing wave of tourist development since the early 1980s has, however, threatened to sweep all before it. But Manrique's ceaseless opposition to such unchecked urban sprawl touched a nerve with many Lanzaroteños and led to the creation of an environmental group known as El Guincho, which has had some success in revealing and at times even reversing abuses by developers. Manrique was posthumously made its honorary president.

As you pass through villages across the island, you'll see how traditional stylistic features remain the norm. The standard whitewashed houses are adorned with green painted doors, window shutters and strange onion-shaped chimney pots. Hotels beyond the resorts are sparse and the island seems to deal with the waves of tourism in a dignified and thoughtful way, weighing up the euros to be made against the quality of island life. In such ways, César Manrique's influence and spirit endure.

LANZAROTE

works by Manrique himself, artists such as Miró, Millares, Mompó, Oscar Domínguez, Gerardo Rueda, Sempere and Cárdena are on show. Manrique himself – that man's influence is everywhere on the island – designed the restaurant (see Places to Eat).

Both gallery and restaurant are well worth the 30-minute walk or 400 ptas taxi ride from the town centre. The gallery (admission free) opens 11 am to 9 pm daily and the bar, with its spectacular panorama, to 1 am (restaurant service until 11.30 pm).

Playa del Reducto Arrecife has quite a respectable beach of its own, a spit away from Calle Doctor Rafael González Negrín.

Special Events

Carnaval is celebrated here, as in the rest of the Canary Islands, with gusto – if not in quite the same style as in Las Palmas de Gran Canaria and Santa Cruz de Tenerife.

The other major fiesta is 25 August, Día de San Ginés, the day of the island's patron saint, which is celebrated in even the smallest pueblo.

Places to Stay – Budget

Pensión Guayermina (☎ *928 81 24 57 Avenida León y Castillo 98)* has simple singles/doubles/triples costing 2500/4000/6000 ptas.

The cheapest deal in town, if not the entire Canary Islands, is the basic but cheerful *Hostal España* (☎ *928 81 11 90, Calle Gran Canaria 4)*, where spartan singles/doubles cost just 1700/2500 ptas. Not surprisingly, it's often full so be sure to ring in advance.

Pensión San Ginés (☎ *928 81 18 63,*

El Molino 9), around the corner, is another cheap choice with little to distinguish it from the others. Rooms with bathroom come in at 2450/3100 ptas and it has a few basic singles at 1950 ptas.

More comfortable is **Hostal Residencia Cardona** (☎ *928 81 10 08, Calle 18 de Julio 11)*. Quite spacious rooms with bathroom cost 3300/4500 ptas. Don't take a front room though, they look straight across the narrow street to a noisy disco.

Places to Stay – Mid-Range

Soviet-style **Apartamentos Arrecife Playa** (☎ *928 81 03 00, Calle Doctor Rafael González Negrín 4)* has big but somewhat bleak apartments for 6000 ptas (6500 ptas for a triple).

Apartamentos Islamar (☎ *928 81 15 04, Calle Doctor Rafael González Negrín 15)* has spacious apartments with kitchen, TV and balcony for 6900 ptas.

Places to Stay – Top End

Waterfront **Hotel Miramar** (☎ *928 80 15 22, fax 928 80 33 66, Avenida Coll 2)* is slightly shabby. It's comfortable enough though and singles/doubles go for 6800/9200 ptas in summer.

Better value and top of the line is **Hotel Lancelot** (☎ *928 80 50 99, fax 928 80 50 39, Avenida Mancomunidad 9)*, which has singles/doubles/triples costing 8200/10,400/12,900 ptas.

Places to Eat

Mesón La Tinaja *(Calle Guenia 2)* is a pleasant little Castilian eating house with partly tiled walls and moderately priced food. **Tasca Tambo** *(Calle Luis Morote 28)*, does reasonable tapas and is another popular spot.

If you feel like a culinary excursion to northern Spain at a certain price, the Asturian and Basque dishes prepared by **Mesón Trasgu** *(Calle José Antonio 98)* could be for you. Count on about 4000 ptas per head.

If that seems steep, pig out next door – same kitchen, different cooks – at **Snack Bar Salida**, which does *bocadillos* (French-bread sandwiches), tapas, and main dishes for around 1500 ptas.

Calle Doctor Ruperto González Negrín is lined with pavement (sidewalk) cafes and makes a relaxing coffee stop or breakfast destination.

Last but very far from least, the **restaurant** (☎ *928 81 23 21)* at Castillo de San José – see Things to See earlier – is Arrecife's greatest gastronomic-cum-visual treat. From the museum, glide down the spiral staircase and spin into the lower level. Looking out over the port, it merits time for a relaxing tipple or, even better, a whole meal.

There's a small **covered market** *(Calle Liebre)* which opens until 1 pm, Monday to Saturday.

Entertainment

Bars For night-time entertainment, you're probably better off heading to Puerto del Carmen. Tamer but still worth investigating are the half dozen places on Calle José Antonio, including **La Antigua** at No 62 and **La Polinesia** on the corner of Calle 18 de Julio.

Getting There & Away

Air See the Getting There & Away section at the beginning of this chapter for details.

Bus Arrecife Bus crisscrosses the island from the bus station on Vía Medular. Many westbound buses also stop at Playa del Reducto. Bus No 2 (200 ptas, 40 minutes, about every 20 minutes) runs to Puerto del Carmen while No 1 serves Costa Teguise (145 ptas, 20 minutes, about every 20 minutes). Up to six daily go to Playa Blanca (415 ptas, 1½ hours) via Puerto del Carmen and up to seven to Teguise (110 ptas, 30 minutes) via Tahiche. Two buses head north for Orzola (415 ptas, 1½ hours), from where you can get a boat to the islet of Graciosa.

Car & Motorcycle There are plenty of rental companies – especially around Avenida Mancomunidad and Calle Doctor Rafael González.

Boat The weekly Trasmediterránea ferry to Cádiz (mainland Spain) stops here on the way from Las Palmas. It leaves at 10.30 pm on Saturday and arrives two days later.

Trasmediterránea also has ferries on Wednesday and Friday to Las Palmas de Gran Canaria (10 hours, 3900 ptas).

Naviera Armas (☎ 928 51 79 12) also puts four ferries per week on this run.

Puerto de los Mármoles is about 4km north-east of central Arrecife. You can get tickets at the Estación Marítima or at the Trasmediterránea office (☎ 928 81 10 19), Calle José Antonio 90.

Getting Around

To/From the Airport Arrecife Bus services run between the airport and Arrecife (110 ptas, 20 minutes, 17 daily). A taxi will set you back about 900 ptas.

To/From the Port The Arrecife–Costa Teguise bus calls in at the port. A taxi costs about 400 ptas.

Bus A couple of local buses *(guaguas municipales)* follow circuits around town, but you're unlikely to need them.

Taxi There's a taxi rank beside the tourist office on Avenida Generalísimo Franco and another on Calle José Antonio. Otherwise you can call ☎ 928 80 31 04 or ☎ 928 81 27 10.

Bicycle Ciclo Mania (☎ 928 81 75 35, e ciclomania@nexo.es), at Calle Almirante Boado Endeiza 9, rents mountain bikes for 1200/3600/6300 ptas per day/three days/week and city bikes for 1300/3900/7000 ptas. It opens 9.30 am to 1.30 pm and 5 to 8 pm on weekdays, and 9.30 am to 1.30 pm on Saturday.

COSTA TEGUISE

Only 9km north-east of Arrecife, Costa Teguise, except for a giant honeycomb near its northern limit, is a low-rise resort with a series of small but happy beaches. With a few exceptions, the holiday houses, apartments and bungalows are not in overly bad taste but the place is, like most resorts of its ilk, utterly devoid of character. There's not even a fishing village at its core to create the impression that it's anything other than a big holiday camp.

The main and most pleasant beach is Playa de las Cucharas. Those further south enjoy unfortunate views of the ports and industry near Arrecife. The Centro Comercial Las Cucharas shopping centre is the resort's focal point.

Information

There is a post office in the Centro Comercial Las Maretas. You can surf the net at Café Meral, Las Coronas, Avenida Mar 24. In the Lanzarote Gardens complex along Avenida Islas Canarias is a 24-hour medical service, Salus (☎ 900 10 01 44).

The fairly scrappily produced *El Listín* (free) gives details of what's on, in English. The Friday craft market in the Pueblo Marinero centre, 5 to 10.30 pm, merits a look. There's a laundrette beside Tommy's Bikes (see the next section).

Activities

You can sign up for **scuba diving** at long-established Calipso Diving (☎ 928 59 08 79, e calipso@arrakis.es), located in Centro Comercial Calipso; the Sealife Dive Centre (☎ 928 82 60 03, e sealifedive@teleline.es) in Centro Comercial Las Maretas; or Diving Lanzarote (☎ 928 59 04 07) on Playa de las Cucharas.

Lanzarote Surf Company (☎/fax 928 59 19 74, e ingo-f2@jet.es) on Playa de las Cucharas and with an office in Centro Comercial Peurto Tahiche gives **windsurfing** lessons and rents out gear. Alternatively, seek out Mick's Wind in Centro Comercial Las Maretas.

For **bicycle hire**, call by Hot Bike (☎ 928 59 03 04), a couple of shops from Calipso Diving. It also rents scooters (starting at 2900 ptas per day) and motorbikes (starting at 4900 ptas). Tommy's Bikes (☎ 928 59 23 27, e info@tommys-bikes.com), at Playa Galeón (the eastern continuation of Playa de las Cucharas), rents cycles and also arranges half- and one-day guided tours.

LANZAROTE

Olita Treks (☎ 928 59 21 48) does half-day **walks** for 4000 ptas, which includes collection from your accommodation and transport.

Acua Lanza **water park**, just beyond the town's western limit, opens 10 am to 5 pm (to 6 pm from June to September) daily and charges 1500 ptas (children 800 ptas).

Golf Costa Teguise (☎ 928 59 05 12) has the island's only 18-hole **golf course**.

Places to Stay
You may well not choose to stay at *Hotel Meliá Salinas (☎ 928 59 00 40, fax 928 59 03 90, Avenida Islas Canarias)*, where singles/doubles start at 27,000/32,350 ptas, including breakfast. But drift in for a drink and let your breath be taken away by the magnificent central atrium, all trees, flowers and pools, designed by César Manrique.

Places to Eat
There's no shortage of restaurants serving whatever sort of cuisine you may want – although Spanish seems to be hard to find! In the Centro Comercial Las Cucharas you'll find, for example, Tex-Mex at *Texas*, Greek at *Kovklaki* and *Shui Lun Kok* (which also does takeaways) ladling out the Chinese.

Entertainment
There are quite a few bars and discos in the shopping complexes. Two late-night favourites are *Bar Pis Pas* and *The Factory*.

Getting There & Away
Arrecife Bus No 1 connects with Arrecife (via Los Mármoles port) regularly from 7 am to midnight (145 ptas).

TEGUISE
Teguise, 12km north of Arrecife, is quite a surprise, an unexpected little treasure-trove amid the bare plains of central Lanzarote. The island's capital until Arrecife took the baton in 1852, it has preserved a fistful of monuments testifying to its leading role on the island over the centuries.

The son of Jean de Béthencourt, Maciot, moved in to what was a Guanche settle-ment, Acatife, and ended up living with Teguise, daughter of the one-time local chieftain. Various convents were founded and the town prospered. But with prosperity came other problems; pirates of various nationalities descended on the place several times – the only reminder of these attacks today is the ominously named Calle de la Sangre (Blood Street).

Teguise has a large Sunday morning market which, although rather touristy, is worth a browse.

Things to See
Sprawling **Palacio Spínola** on Plaza de la Constitución, was built between 1730 and 1780 and passed to the Spínolas, a prominent Lanzarote family, in 1895. Nowadays it serves as both museum and official residence of the Canary Islands government. The house deserves a leisurely inspection, although many of the furnishings are clearly not precious period pieces from some long-forgotten era. It opens 10 am to 5 pm daily (to 4 pm at weekends and in winter). Admission costs 300 ptas.

Across the square is the eclectic **Iglesia de la Virgen de Guadalupe**, which has suffered numerous remodellings (leaving it in a rather confused state) since it was first built in the 16th century.

Several monasteries dot the town and wandering Teguise's pedestrianised lanes is a pleasure in itself. Keep your eyes peeled for the Franciscan **Convento de Miraflores**, the **Convento de Santo Domingo** and the **Palacio de Herrera y Rojas**.

Castillo de Santa Bárbara is not only the oldest fort in the islands but about the only castle worthy of the name. Perched up on Guanapay peak, 1.5km east of Teguise, it was erected in the 16th century by Sancho de Herrera, expanded in later years and then allowed to fall into disuse. Since being restored, it houses the modest **Museo del Emigrante Canario**, a sparse collection relating to the long history of migration from the islands to Spain's American colonies. On its roof, note the battered, holed rowing boat bearing markings in Arabic. Washed up on the nearby coast, it's a poignant reminder of

LANZAROTE

a new wave of economic migration – from Africa to Spain.

The castle, which offers commanding views across the plains, is worth a visit for that reason alone. Admission prices and hours are as for the Palacio Spínola.

Places to Eat

Restaurante Acatifea (Plaza de la Constitución) is one of several enticing places to eat here. The interior is all deep, dark timber and whitewash, and meals start at around 1000 ptas.

Restaurante La Cantina, on the corner of Calle de León and Calle de José Betancourt, is in the same block as the Palacio de Herrera y Rojas. A full meal will cost about 2000 ptas per person.

Getting There & Away

Up to seven buses from Arrecife stop in Teguise en route to destinations such as Orzola and Haría.

SAN BARTOLOMÉ

Starting life as the Guanche settlement of Ajei, San Bartolomé ended up in the 18th century as the de facto private fiefdom of a militia leader, Francisco Guerra Clavijo y Perdomo, and his descendants.

A couple of kilometres north-west of town on the Tinajo road (just before the town of Mozaga), rises up the weird, white **Monumento al Campesino** (Peasants' Monument), erected in 1968 by (surprise, surprise) César Manrique to honour the unending and thankless labour that most of the islanders had endured for generations. Adjacent is what is called the **Museo del Campesino** (open 10 am to 6 pm, admission free) but it's hardly a museum; more a scattering of craft workshops which may or may not be functioning. Most people come here to eat – ironically, at a monument dedicated to those who so often endured hunger – at the architecturally exciting circular sunken *restaurant*. If you really want to understand the life of the *campesino* (peasant), you'll learn much more at the Museo Agrícola El Patio (see Tiagua in the North-West section).

El Grifo Museo del Vino is 3km south-west of the monument, along the road to Yaiza. Here, in the former *bodega* (old-style wine bar) and winery of the El Grifo company, you can see wine-making equipment, some dating back 200 years, and indulge in a little wine-tasting. The museum opens 10.30 am to 6 pm daily. Admission is free.

Around the Island

Many of Lanzarote's northern towns and villages are pretty enough in themselves. But the principal attractions are the combined work of nature and César Manrique: his house (now a gallery), a pair of breathtaking lava caves, cactus gardens and a stunning lookout point. Stash your pockets with cash since admission to the majority costs a hefty 1000 ptas (each). If you prefer to limit the financial damage, we recommend as a minimum Taro de Tahiche, where he lived, and the Jameos del Agua cave.

By contrast, at the island's barren heart, untamed nature takes your breath away and leaves you feeling decidedly puny. The aptly named Montañas del Fuego (Mountains of Fire), within the Parque Nacional de Timanfaya, were formed by a huge volcanic eruption that continued to growl for six whole years.

For scenery that's altogether gentler on the senses, brash Puerto del Carmen and its smaller, more discreet sister resorts along the south coast draws beach lovers and nightowls alike.

TAHICHE

A visit to the Fundación César Manrique, an art gallery and centre for the island's cultural life, is a must. Only 6km north of Arrecife, it was home to César Manrique who, on the island, enjoys a posthumous status akin to a mystical hero's. He built his house, **Taro de Tahiche**, into the lava fields just outside the town. The subterranean rooms are in fact huge air bubbles left behind by flowing lava.

Nowadays, there's a whole gallery devoted to Manrique across the decades, plus works by some of his contemporaries,

Seeing Red

Higgledy-piggledy cactuses, their leaves green, fleshy and the shape of giant rabbits' ears, are about all that grows around the small village of Guatiza. And grow they do, in profusion, hemming in the pueblo. They're a last reminder of what was once a thriving trade on Tenerife and the eastern islands.

Much more than a harsh desert plant, they're home and food to *la cochinilla*. To this day, these tiny insects are collected by the tens of thousands. Each one contributes a blood red droplet of the dye cochineal, used as a colouring in food and cosmetics.

Elsewhere, the once-thriving cochineal trade has long since withered, killed off by competition from synthetic dyes. But in Guatiza a centuries old cottage industry still just manages to persist.

including Picasso, Chillida, Miró, Sempere and Tàpies.

The Fundación opens 10 am to 6 pm Monday to Saturday (to 7 pm from July to October) and 10 am to 3 pm on Sunday. Admission costs 1000 ptas.

At least seven buses daily stop here on their way from Arrecife to Teguise and beyond. Get off at the Cruce Manrique (Manrique Intersection) and walk 200m down the San Bartolomé road.

GUATIZA

Just north of Guatiza, an uninspiring village 9km north of Tahiche, is the **Jardín de los Cactus**, signalled by an 8m spiky metal specimen, the work of – you've guessed it – César Manrique. Although it comes over as more a giant work of art than botanical garden, it has nearly 1500 different varieties of this prickly customer, every single one labelled. The garden opens 10 am to 5.45 pm, and admission costs 500 ptas.

ARRIETA & PLAYA DE LA GARITA

Next northwards is the fishing village of Arrieta, its only attraction the modest Playa

de la Garita. The village itself is a quiet, unassuming little redoubt, and you can stay in one of a few little pensiones and apartments.

Casitas del Mar (☎ 928 83 51 99), on the coast road between Arrieta and Punta Mujeres, is a discreet collection of bungalows that cost 6000 ptas for two.

Restaurante El Ancla (☎ 928 84 82 30), on the corner of Calle de la Garita and Calle de la Marina, will charge you 800 ptas to 1200 ptas for enticing main courses of fresh fish. It also has a few apartments at 4000 ptas per night but normally requires a minimum stay of four nights.

Bus No 9 from Arrecife to Orzola, which only runs twice daily, calls in here.

MALPAÍS DE LA CORONA

The 'bad lands of the crown' are the living (or dead) testimony to the volcanic upsurges that shook the north of the island thousands of years ago. Plant life is quietly, patiently, winning its way back, and it is here that you can visit two of the island's better known volcanic caverns.

Cueva de los Verdes & Jameos del Agua

More obviously than on any of the other islands, lava is the hallmark of Lanzarote. So it should come as little surprise that, after the lunar wonders of the Parque Nacional de Timanfaya (see that section later in this chapter), the flow of visitors should be strongest here, at the site of an ancient lava slide into the ocean. The cavernous **Cueva de los Verdes** and, farther 'downstream', the hollows of the **Jameos del Agua** (adapted by César Manrique into a kind of New Age retreat) are 1km distant from one another.

Cueva de los Verdes This yawning, 1km-long chasm is the most spectacular segment of an almost 8km lava tube left behind by an eruption that occurred 5000 years ago. As the lava ploughed down towards the sea (a little more than 6km of tunnel are above sea level today, and another 1.5km extend below the water's surface), the top layers cooled and formed a roof, beneath which the liquid magma continued to slither until the eruption exhausted itself.

You will be guided through two chambers, one below the other. The ceiling is largely covered with what look like ministalactites. But no water penetrates the cave. The odd pointy extrusions are where bubbles of air and lava were thrown up onto the ceiling by gases released while the boiling lava flowed; as they hit the ceiling and air, they 'froze' in the process of dripping back into the lava stream.

In spite of the name 'verde', there's nothing green about this cave. Some 200 years ago it was considered the property of a shepherd family, the Verdes! At other times, it served as a refuge for locals during pirate assaults on the island. All sorts of evidence of their presence – from bones to tools and ceramics – are displayed in Arrecife's under-endowed Museo Arqueológico.

Anyone with severe back problems might think twice about entering the cave – there are a few passages that require you to bend at 90° to get through. Similarly, it's no place for those who tend towards claustrophobia. Of less consequence, the New Age music is a rather gratuitous backdrop.

Guided Spanish/English tours last about 45 minutes. The Cueva opens 10 am to 5 pm daily, and admission costs 1000 ptas – worthwhile in itself for a great visual gag deep inside the cave. No, we're not telling – and urge you in your turn to keep it quiet from your friends.

Jameos del Agua The piped New Age music continues here, where it's rather more appropriate. The first of the caverns resembles the nave of a vast marine basilica. Molten lava seethed through here on its way to the sea, but in this case the ocean leaked in a bit, forming the azure lake at the heart of the Jameos. Manrique's idea of installing bars and a restaurant around the lake, adding a pool, a concert hall seating 600 (with wonderful acoustics) and the subtly didactic Casa de los Volcanes, was pure brainwave.

Have a closer look into the lake's waters. The tiny white flecks at the bottom are crabs. Small ones yes, and the only known examples, away from the deepest oceans, of *Munidopsis polymorpha* (blind crabs). Do take notice of the signs and resist the temptation to throw coins into the water – their corrosion could kill off this unique species.

The complex opens 9.30 am to 6.45 pm daily. Admission costs 1000 ptas. On Tuesday, Friday and Saturday, the bars' function becomes paramount and the place stays open until 3 am. Admission after 7 pm costs 1100 ptas.

Bus No 9 between Arrecife and Orzola, which only runs twice daily, stops at the turn-off for Jameos del Agua. The Cueva de los Verdes is a further 1km walk inland. The problem is, you'd have to get the 7.40 am bus from Arrecife and then wait until the bus heading back to the capital from Orzola passes (it leaves Orzola at 4.30 pm) or the bus from Arrecife on to Orzola (which leaves Arrecife at 3.30 pm).

Orzola

Most people just pass through this northern fishing town on their way to the Isla Graciosa. Some stop for a food break in one of several little restaurants flanking the port, but relatively few get wind of the beach a couple of kilometres west of the town – about the only one in this part of the island, which is otherwise dominated by steep uncompromising cliffs.

MINOR CANARIES

The string of tiny islets flung out north of Lanzarote are known as the Minor Canaries, and minor they certainly are. All except Isla Graciosa (aka La Graciosa) are part of a nature reserve, with access limited to researchers.

Isla Graciosa

Isla Graciosa makes an interesting half-day trip; anything longer is strictly for those who enjoy diverging from the beaten track for its own sake.

About 500 souls live on the island, virtually all in the village of Caleta del Sebo,

LANZAROTE

where the Orzola boat docks. Behind it stretches 27.5 sq km of largely barren scrub land, interrupted by five minor volcanic peaks ranged from north to south. About a 30-minute walk south-west of Caleta del Sebo is a pleasant little beach, and there's another at the northern end of the islet.

On a windy day, Caleta del Sebo can seem a cross between a bare Moroccan village and a sand-swept Wild West outpost (without anything particularly wild about it). This place is worlds away from the tourist mainstream – and perhaps the tourists are right.

There are three places to stay. Very near the church, *Apartamentos El Pescador* (☎ *928 84 20 36)* has apartments sleeping up to four at 4000 ptas. There's no sign, so you'll have to ask around.

Pensión Girasol (☎ 928 84 21 01), about 100m left along the waterfront from where the boat docks, has basic rooms at 2000 ptas (2500 ptas with balcony).

Pensión Enriqueta (☎ 928 84 20 51, Calle de la Mar del Barlovento 6) is a few blocks in from the port. It has simple but clean doubles for 2000 ptas (2500 ptas with bathroom). Both pensiones have restaurants.

Líneas Marítimas Romero (☎ 928 84 20 70) runs three (four between July and September) boats daily from Orzola in the north of Lanzarote across to the islet. Tickets cost 2000 ptas return (children 1000 ptas) and the trip takes 20 minutes. Unless you want to be Robinson Crusoed for the night, take the outbound 10 am or noon sailing. This allows time to explore before taking the last boat back at 4 pm (6 pm in summer).

THE NORTH-WEST
Mirador del Río

About 2km north of Yé, the Spanish armed forces set up gun batteries at the end of the 19th century at a strategic site overlooking El Río, the straits separating Lanzarote from Isla Graciosa. Spain had gone to war with the USA over control of Cuba, and you couldn't be too careful! In 1973, the ubiquitous César Manrique left his imprimatur, converting the gun emplacement into a spectacular lookout point.

It now has a bar and souvenir stand. Let your heart race at the nearly 500m sheer drop and the spectacular view of Isla Graciosa, stretched taut like a leopardskin far below – the best way, some would argue, to see this barren islet! The lookout opens 10 am to 5.45 pm, admission costs 400 ptas.

Guinate

The only thing that might draw you to the village of Guinate, about 5km south of Mirador del Río, is the **Tropical Park**, home to some 1300 exotic birds. Many of them are truly beautiful, but the bird show – parrots on scooters and so on – is a little silly. It opens 10 am to 5 pm daily. Admission costs 1300 ptas (children 500 ptas).

Beyond the park is another fine lookout overlooking El Río and the islets. Unlike Mirador del Río, here there's no bar, no souvenir stand – and no admission charge.

Haría

Shady Plaza León y Castillo, centre of this village, makes a delightful resting spot and, if the time is right, a lunch or mid-afternoon drink stop.

César Manrique moved into a farmhouse outside Haría after his house, Taro de Tahiche (see Tahiche earlier in this chapter), had become untenable because of all the visitors who liked to drop by to see how he was getting on.

Beside the plaza, ultra-friendly *Restaurante Papa Loca (☎ 626 60 62 66)* has *menús* at 750 ptas and 850 ptas or goat at 1850 ptas. Ask for Julio if you phone.

Up the hill, the vast *Restaurante Casa Kura* offers mains for around 1500 ptas.

Several daily buses connect Haría to Arrecife via Teguise and Tahiche.

Famara

As a young boy, before he hit the big time, Manrique whiled away many a childhood summer on the wild beach of Famara. The scrappy seaside hamlet of La Caleta de Famara doesn't seem to have changed much in many years and makes few concessions to the average tourist, apart from a couple of restaurants.

Discriminating surfers, however, feel the call of its waves, which offer some of Europe's finest breaks. Pedro Urrastarazu at Famara Surf Shop (☎ 928 52 86 76) rents boards and offers courses at all levels. Visit its Web site at www.famarasurf.com.

Famara Surf Shop can arrange accommodation in apartments, whether you're there to surf or sunbathe. Otherwise, Urbanización Famara, 2km north, is a relatively unobtrusive, step-terraced arrangement of holiday homes and little else. There you can stay at *Bungalows Famara (☎ 928 84 51 32)* starting at 7000 ptas (8900 ptas for up to four occupants) with a minimum stay of three nights.

One bus per day connects Arrecife with La Caleta, Monday to Friday only. It leaves La Caleta at 7 am and sets off back from the capital at 2 pm.

Tiagua

About 10km south of La Caleta and 8km north-west of San Bartolomé, the ecologically aware open-air **Museo Agricola El Patio** (☎/fax 928 52 91 34) in Tiagua recreates traditional agricultural life and has a small, incongruous display of West African sculpture. Signing – including some irritatingly edifying texts – is in English. The museum opens 10 am to 5.30 pm, Monday to Friday, and 10 am to 2.30 pm on Saturday. Admission costs 600 ptas.

Tiagua is on the bus route from Arrecife to Tinajo. The daily bus to La Caleta de Famara also calls in here.

PARQUE NACIONAL DE TIMANFAYA

The eruption that began on 1 September 1730 and convulsed the southern end of the island was among the greatest volcanic cataclysms in recorded history. A staggering 48 cubic million metres of lava spurted and flowed out daily, while fusillades of molten rock were angrily rocketed out over the countryside and into the ocean. When the eruption finally ceased to rage after six long years, over 200 sq km had been devastated.

The Montañas del Fuego (Mountains of

Goats

In the 1970s, some 14,000 goats grazed the arid hills and valleys of Lanzarote. By the early 1990s, numbers had plummeted to a mere 3000 and were continuing to fall. Now, at the beginning of a new century, they're on the increase again.

Until the 1960s and the advent of mass tourism, almost all the people of Lanzarote were engaged in agriculture or livestock rearing. Goats were their most versatile resource. Tougher than sheep, they're able to survive in a more desiccated environment and can chew on spiny, hostile plants that a sheep would look at with disdain.

Alive, they provided milk, which was either mixed with *gofio* (a roasted mixture of wheat, maize or barley), drunk fresh or transformed into cheese. Once slaughtered, they were a source of meat, both fresh and as *tocineta*, dried and long-lasting, like jerky. Their fat, where not used for food, would be rendered down into tallow for lighting and was the basic ingredient of a number of folk remedies. Their skins were used as rugs, for making clothing – and as a marketable currency when it came to bartering. Their yarn was (spun like sheep's wool) into blankets, jackets, socks and bags.

You're sure to see at least some of the estimated 15,000 which crop the sparse desert vegetation. They may look wild and free as they roam the hills but each and every last kid has its owner – and woe betide anyone who attempts a little goat-rustling on the side.

Fire), at the heart of this eerie 51-sq-km national park, are appropriately named. When you reach the Manrique-designed lookout and Restaurante del Diablo (note his lampshades in the form of giant frying pans) at a rise known as the Islote de Hilario, try scrabbling around in the pebbles and see just how long you can hold them in your hands. At a depth of a few centimetres, the temperature is already 100°C; by 10m, it's up to 600°C. The cause of this phenomenon is a broiling magma chamber some 4km below the surface.

Some feeble (or rather, given the harsh environment, decidedly robust) scraps of vegetation, including 200 species of lichen, are reclaiming the earth in a few stretches of an otherwise moribund landscape of fantastic forms and shades of black, grey, maroon and red. Fine, copper-hued soil slithers down volcano cones, arrested then by twisted, swirling and folded mounds of solidified lava – looking in parts like a liquorice-addict's idea of heaven.

The people running the show at Islote de Hilario have a series of endearing tricks. In one, they shove a clump of brushwood into a hole in the ground and within seconds it's converted by the subterranean furnace into a burning bush. A pot of water poured down another hole promptly gushes back up in explosive geyser fashion.

And the ***Restaurant del Diablo*** is, of course, a gag in itself – whatever meat you order you can watch sizzling on the all-natural, volcano-powered BBQ out the back. They do a *menú* at 1950 ptas and main dishes cost between 1400 ptas and 1800 ptas. The food's none too impressive but, hey, who's here for the cuisine?

Flesh-coloured buses with the Lanzarote tourist logo take you along the 14km Ruta de los Volcanes, an excursion through some of the most spectacular volcanic country you are ever likely to see. The trilingual taped commentary can be a bit painful at times, but it is informative. More frustrating, however, is the fact that you can't get out to simply experience the awesome silence and majesty of this stony waste. Buses leave every hour or so and the trip takes about 40 minutes.

A few kilometres south along the road that traverses the eastern edge of the park is a small geological museum, the **Museo de las Rocas** (about 5km north of Yaiza). It opens 9 am to 3 pm. From here you can also take a short camel ride.

North of the park on the same road is the much more informative **Mancha Blanca Visitor Centre**. It opens 9 am to 5 pm daily.

The main park installations open 9 am to 5.45 pm. The last bus trip along the Ruta de los Volcanes departs at 5 pm. Admission,

JANE SMITH

Once used for transport, camels are now popular with visitors.

which includes the bus excursion and the courtesy heat displays at the Islote de Hilario, costs 1000 ptas.

You can only get into the park under your own steam or on a tour bus – which you can organise through most travel agents and the larger hotels.

Walks

It is possible to walk within the park – but you'll need to plan in advance and you'll be part of a *very* select group. The 3km two-hour Tremesana guided walk leaves from the visitor centre (☎ 928 84 08 39) at 10 am on Monday, Wednesday and Friday. Reserve by phone or in person two days before. The more demanding Ruta del Litoral (9km, five hours) has no fixed days and you need to reserve in person. Each walk has a maximum of seven participants.

INLAND & WEST COAST
La Geria

From San Bartolomé (see that section earlier in the chapter), the LZ-30 highway proceeds south-west through what has to be one of the oddest-looking wine-growing regions around. The wine growers of Lanzarote have found the deep, black lava-soil, enriched by the island's shaky seismic history, perfect for the grape. The further south you go, the more common are these unique vineyards consisting of little dugouts nurtured behind crescent-shaped stone walls, known as *zocos*, implanted in the dark earth.

The *malvasía* (Malmsey wine) produced here is a good drop and along the road you pass a good half dozen *bodegas* (old-style wine bars) where you can buy the local produce at wholesale prices.

Uga Nothing much will keep you in this little hamlet, but it may be of interest to know that the camels used for tourist rides in the Parque Nacional de Timanfaya (see that section earlier) call Uga home.

Yaiza

Yaiza is something of a southern crossroads, so you'll probably pass through on your travels. There's no specific reason for hanging about but if you arrive at lunch time and are feeling peckish, you'll be able to find a few pleasant enough eateries. For Canaries cuisine in congenial surroundings try, for example, *La Era*, set in a 17th-century farmhouse surrounded by a courtyard and well-tended garden.

El Golfo & Around

The tour buses pile past this half-forgotten fishing village, which can make a pleasant alternative retreat for those uninterested in the hurly-burly of the international beach set.

Just south of the settlement begins a string of small and largely unvisited black-sand (or lava, if you prefer) beaches. The one near the Charco de los Clicos is particularly pleasant (although a little too pebbly) and protected. The Charco itself is a small emerald green pond, just in from the beach and overshadowed by a rocky cliff.

On the way along the coast road which eventually leads to La Hoya, stop by **Los Hervideros**, a pair of caves through which the sea glugs and froths. After about 6km you reach the long Playa de Janubio, behind which are **Las Salinas de Janubio**, salt pans from which sea salt is extracted.

There is just one place to stay in El Golfo and it's the charming *Hotelito del Golfo* (*☎/fax 928 17 32 72*), which has nine fully equipped doubles at 8500 ptas.

You'll find no shortage of eating options beyond the hotel, which is just at the entrance to the hamlet. On the waterfront, three eateries compete for your attention: the *Casa Torado*, *Lago Verde* and *Mar Azul*.

PUERTO DEL CARMEN

Lanzarote's premier resort straggles for 6km beside mostly golden sand. With sunshades four lanes deep, it's the island's best beach (those on Fuerteventura are, however, miles better), so it's hardly surprising that this is Lanzarote's biggest tourist development.

What else can you say? Walk the esplanade along Avenida de las Playas and you'll soon get a feel for the place from the signs: Ye Olde Spanish Inn, Pie In The Sky – For the Best in British Home Cooking, Tonight! Miss Sexy Bum Elections! Says it all really.

Information

Puerto del Carmen has two tourist offices within a kilometre of each other on Avenida de las Playas. The white one (☎ 928 81 17 62), halfway along Playa Grande, opens 9 am to 1 pm and 4.30 to 7.30 pm, Monday to Friday, and 9 am to 1 pm on Saturday. The other, a black kiosk overlooking the beach's northern end, was open weekdays only at the time of writing.

Check your emails at Networx Xpress (☎ 928 51 52 54) in the Centro Comercial Marítimo.

The post office is beside the roundabout at the junction of Avenida Juan Carlos I and Calle Guardilama in the western part of town. The police station (☎ 928 83 41 01) is directly behind it.

The Bookswop, Calle de Timanfaya 4, with a branch at Hotel San Antonio, is the best source of English-language reading on the island.

Activities

The main activity seems to be flaking out on the beach for its own sake or to recover from a heavy night, but there's no lack of opportunity for something less supine.

LANZAROTE

Bizarrely for a large resort with such reliable wind, no one in Puerto del Carmen hires windsurfing gear or offers lessons.

Cycling For bicycle hire, contact Sun Bike & Moto (☎/fax 928 51 34 40) in Centro Comercial Playa Blanca or Renner Bikes (☎ 629 99 07 55) in the Centro Comercial Marítimo.

Diving Among several enterprises, tried and trusted operators are Safari Diving (☎ 928 51 19 92) at the small, central Playa de la Barrilla; Centro de Buceo Atlántica (☎ 928 51 07 17), which operates from the first floor of Fariones Playa Suite Hotel on Calle Roque del Este; and Barakuda Club Lanzarote (☎ 928 51 27 65), based in Hotel Geria at the eastern end of Playa de los Pocillos.

Deep-Sea Fishing Contact MA (Motobarcas Arosa) Ana Segundo (☎ 928 51 37 36), Calle Teide 8, just west of the port, for half-day fishing trips.

Walking Feetbook Agencia (☎ 928 51 24 41), Calle Bentaguiare 4, organises half- and one-day walking expeditions.

Horse Riding Lanzarote a Caballo (☎ 928 83 03 14), at km17 on the road between Puerto del Carmen and Yaiza, does one- to three-hour horseback safaris.

Boating Two or three companies offer one-hour glass-bottomed boat cruises, departing from the Varadero (the port jetty). Tickets cost 1500 ptas (children 750 ptas).

Places to Stay
At last count there were more than 170 hotels, apartment blocks and bungalow complexes in Puerto del Carmen. Many deal only with tour operators but may oblige the independent blow-in if they have a room free.

Two bodies rent out apartments to all-comers. *Rodriguez y Ramos (☎ 928 51 22 49, fax 928 51 34 49, Calle Nuestra Señora del Carmen 5B)*, an exchange shop above

the port, just beside the parish church, normally insists upon a one-week minimum let. *Juan Ramón (☎ 928 51 40 35, 636 45 75 60)* has apartments at 6000 ptas (up to three occupants) and 7500 ptas (up to five).

There's just one standard pensión in Puerto del Carmen and it's a good one. The 14-room *Pensión Magec (☎ 928 51 38 74, Calle Hierro 11)* offers singles/doubles with washbasin for 2700/3200 ptas while doubles with bathroom cost 3700 ptas.

Apartamentos el Barranquillo (☎ 928 51 02 88, Calle del Ancla 7) is a short walk off Avenida de las Playas – far enough away to be insulated from the rowdiness but close enough to stumble home at the end of a long night. Apartments for two/three cost 5000/6500 ptas while ones accommodating up to five cost 8500 ptas. The complex has a bar and several swimming pools.

For a touch of luxury close to the old nucleus of town and the main happening scene along Avenida de las Playas yet with the beach at your feet, indulge yourself at *Hotel Los Fariones (☎ 928 51 01 75, fax 928 51 02 02, e fariones@infolanz.es, Calle del Roque del Este 1)*. Singles/doubles start at 13,275/18,700 ptas.

Places to Eat
Among all the sauerkraut, fish and chips and other delights on offer along the Avenida de las Playas pleasure zone, you'll occasionally stumble across a place offering some local cuisine. *Restaurante La Cañada (☎ 928 51 04 15, Calle de César Manrique 3)*, just off the Avenida, is one such rarity.

For a cluster of worthwhile restaurants serving essentially Spanish cuisine, take a walk to the port. There, *Casa Roja (☎ 928 51 66)* has an attractive terrace – most of the view, alas, being of the town's biggest car park. Next door is *Restaurante Varadero (☎ 928 51 31 62)*, its smaller terrace compensated for by the ample interior. Opposite, *La Lonja (☎ 928 51 13 77)* is both restaurant and fish shop. All, as you'd expect from their location, specialise mainly in fish dishes. The dark cube is *El Fondeadero (☎ 928 51 14 65)*, the restaurant of a hotel training school, which offers excellent value for money.

Outside town, **Restaurante La Finca** (☎ 928 51 35 50), on the road from Puerto del Carmen to Mácher, is only open for dinner and the chef often comes up with a few surprise dishes not listed on the excellent menu. Count on spending about 2500 ptas per head.

Entertainment

The bulk of the bars, discos and nightclubs are lined up along the waterfront Avenida de las Playas.

If you're not interested in the Miss Sexy Bum Elections, you could try **Waikiki**, **Paradise** or **Dreams** disco in the Centro Comercial Atlántico. Still on the Avenida and more or less opposite the white tourist office are the popular **César's** and – most in of the in places when we last passed through – **La Tropical**, a pub offering music and dancing.

If jazz is your scene, head for the altogether more sophisticated **Jazz Club** (☎/fax 928 51 41 70) just west of Hotel San Antonio. There's live Dixieland at lunchtime in summer and a couple of combos a night play through until 3 am, Tuesday to Sunday, year round.

Getting There & Around

Buses run the length of Avenida de las Playas with frequent stops, heading for Arrecife (200 ptas) about every 20 minutes from 7 am to midnight.

A free Fred Olsen bus leaves from the Varadero (the port jetty) in Puerto del Carmen at 9 am and 5 pm, linking with ferry runs from Playa Blanca to Corralejo (Fuerteventura). In the reverse direction, free buses for Puerto del Carmen meet the 9 am and 5 pm ferries from Corralejo on their arrival in Playa Blanca. The morning run continues to Lanzarote's airport.

To do the whole journey by sea, step aboard the catamaran Princess Ico, which sails four times per week for Corralejo (4000 ptas).

PUERTO CALERO

A few kilometres west of Puerto del Carmen and its complete antithesis, Puerto Calero is a pleasant, tranquil yacht harbour with a few cafes and restaurants.

The yellow submarine of Submarine Safaris (☎ 928 51 28 98) makes three one-hour dives daily, at 10 am, noon and 2 pm, reaching a depth of 27m. Tickets cost 6900 ptas (children 3900 ptas).

The large catamaran you see cruising the coast belongs to Catlanza (☎ 928 51 30 22 or ☎ 609 66 72 46). It sails westwards down the coast and anchors off Papagayo. The price of 8900 ptas (children 4900 ptas) includes lunch, drinks, loan of snorkelling equipment and a jet-ski ride. There are sailings at 9.30 am and 3 pm Monday to Saturday.

You can reserve these sea (or undersea) journeys through a travel agent or by calling direct.

For diving, contact Squatina Diving Center (☎ 928 51 18 80, fax 928 51 33 27).

PLAYA BLANCA

Not a bad little beach and a resort that's not yet out of control – but you're much better off crossing the ocean to Corralejo in Fuerteventura, where the beaches and dunes outclass Playa Blanca's. This said, the beaches at Punta del Papagayo to the east (see later in this chapter) are pretty and relatively isolated.

If it's thumping nightlife you're after, push on up the coast to Puerto del Carmen.

Information

The tourist office (☎ 928 51 77 94) is in the port at the rear of the ferry booking office. It opens 8.30 am to 12.30 pm and 2 to 5 pm on weekdays and 8.30 am to 12.30 pm on Saturday.

Activities

The main beach is about a 1km stroll along the waterfront, east from the port. Go beyond the tiny rock-and-sand beach you first encounter.

The large motor vessel César II (☎ 928 81 36 08) sails to the Isla de Lobos, off Fuerteventura (6500 ptas per head, Monday to Saturday) and has a Sunday special for the same price to one of the Papagayo

LANZAROTE

beaches. The Marea Errota (☎ 928 51 76 33), a handsome galleon, does twice-daily coastal cruises.

Places to Stay & Eat
One of the cheapest places to stay is **Apartamentos Gutiérrez** (☎ *928 51 70 89, Plaza Nuestra Señora del Carmen 8*). Just by the town church, prices for its six apartments range between 4000 ptas and 6000 ptas.

For something more stylish, **Apartamentos Bahía Blanca Rock** (☎ *928 51 70 37, fax 928 51 70 55*) has comfortable apartments in a complex just off Avenida del Papagayo and a 100m-stroll from the main beach. Prices vary hugely, according to season, from 6500 ptas to 11,400 ptas.

Modest **Restaurante Casa Jose** (*Plaza de Nuestra Señora del Carmen*), opposite the church, is superb for fish and serves a number of local dishes.

More stylish, **Restaurante El Almacen de la Sal** (*Paseo Marítimo 12*) is an excellent waterfront restaurant, open Wednesday to Monday. The fish dishes are the pick of the bunch and, although they can set you back up to 2000 ptas, are worth every peseta. It's about halfway between the port and the main beach.

Getting There & Away
Up to six buses daily (three on Sunday) run between Playa Blanca and Arrecife via Puerto del Carmen. The journey costs 415 ptas.

Fred Olsen ferries link Playa Blanca with Corralejo (Fuerteventura) four to five times daily. A one-way ticket costs 1850 ptas and the crossing takes 35 to 45 minutes. The competition comes from from Naviera Armas (1700 ptas), which has five to six sailings daily.

Free Fred Olsen buses leave Puerto del Carmen (9 am and 5 pm) to connect with the 10 am and 6 pm ferry departures. A free service also meets the 9 am and 5 pm ferries from Corralejo. The morning run continues to Lanzarote's airport.

PUNTA DEL PAPAGAYO
The south-east coast leading up to Punta del Papagayo is peppered with a series of pretty golden-sand coves. The promontory is a Reserva Natural Protegido (Protected Nature Reserve). The road beyond the rickety toll barrier (500 ptas per vehicle) is dirt but quite manageable in a saloon car. Or take the easy way and hop aboard the Ganges 6 motorboat (☎ 928 51 43 22), which sets out at least four times daily from Playa Blanca. The return trip costs 1400 ptas.

There's a seasonal **camp site** (☎ *928 17 34 52*), open May to September, where a plot costs 850 ptas. Since 2000 was its first, experimental year, play safe and ring in advance to check current arrangements.

Tenerife

Tenerife, all 2034 sq km of it, is the archipelago's largest island – and also its highest. From the heart of the island surges the Pico del Teide (3718m), Spain's tallest peak. The barren east coast contrasts starkly with the rich green north-west, and the vertigo-inducing cliffs of the north seem worlds away from the international holiday playgrounds of Playa de las Américas and the south-west.

There is something for everyone on the island – from whale-spotting to walking, from nightclubbing to bird-watching.

Most Tinerfeños, as the some 677,000 islanders are called, live in the north. A good half occupy the cities of Santa Cruz de Tenerife, the island and provincial capital, and the university city of La Laguna, a pearl of urban elegance 10km away.

Its main drawback is the sheer volume of tourists. However, most stick to the southern resorts and Puerto de la Cruz; elsewhere it is possible to feel you really are in Spanish territory and not a sunny version of Manchester or Munich. And if it does all get a bit much, you can easily escape westwards to La Gomera, La Palma or El Hierro, as yet not nearly as saturated.

History

Tenerife was the last island to fall to the Spanish, and the Guanches did not give up without a fight (see History in the Facts about the Islands chapter). The island's name appears to have been coined by the people of La Palma, who knew it as Tinerife – White Mountain (from *tiner*, mountain, and *ife*, white) – since all they could usually see was Teide's snow-capped peak.

Tenerife, like its neighbour and competitor Gran Canaria, soon attracted a big chunk of the settlers from Spain, Portugal, Italy, France and even Britain.

As elsewhere in the islands, sugar became the main export crop, later supplanted by wine as South American sugar undercut the market. Much of the wine was produced

Highlights

- Taking the cable car to La Rambleta, 200m below the volcanic peak of Teide, for breathtaking vistas
- Letting your hair down for Carnaval in Santa Cruz, second only to Rio de Janeiro's festivities
- Savouring the charming old mansions and late-night student bars of La Laguna
- Walking or driving through the Anaga mountains, winding up with the surf and a meal at Roque de las Bodegas
- Clambering down the Barranco de Masca and taking the afternoon boat back to Los Gigantes
- Roaming the streets of La Orotava's atmospheric old town

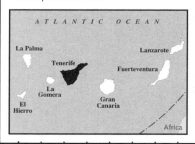

on Tenerife, giving it an enviable edge over the other islands. So much so that even when the importance of the wine trade diminished the island remained dominant until well into the 19th century. This prompted Madrid to declare Santa Cruz de Tenerife, by then the island's main port, the capital of the Canaries in 1821. The good and great of Las Palmas de Gran Canaria remained incensed about this until 1927 when Madrid finally decided to split the archipelago into two provinces, with Santa Cruz as the provincial capital of Tenerife, La Palma, La Gomera and El Hierro. Today, Santa

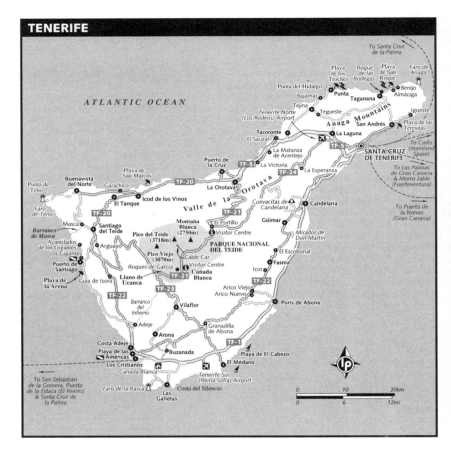

TENERIFE

Cruz shares the duties of regional capital of all seven islands with its rival, Las Palmas.

Information

Maps There's a shelf of competing small- and medium-scale maps of the island. Among the best is one by Editorial Everest at 1:150,000 (1997; 360 ptas). Buy the one with the green cover since, unlike the earlier (red) versions, this has street plans of Santa Cruz, Puerto de la Cruz, La Laguna, La Orotava and the south-western strip of Costa Adeje/Playa de las Américas/Los Cristianos.

Newspapers For an island with well under a million inhabitants, Tenerife has a disproportionately large number of newspapers. The most popular Spanish titles are *El Día*, *La Gaceta de Canarias*, *Diario de Avisos* and – a newcomer on the scene – *La Opinión de Tenerife*.

There's a profusion of English-language freebies. The most informative about the island are *Here & Now* and *Tenerife News*. Others, less literate, are only worth picking up if you want information about British bars, clubs, restaurants and more personal services.

Activities

The whole gamut of water sports, from diving to sailing, fishing to windsurfing, is available on the island. Most facilities are concentrated in and around the southwestern resort areas.

There's good scope for walking. You can follow 11 trails within the Parque Nacional del Teide, whose rangers lead guided walks daily. Other attractive areas are the Anaga mountains in the north-east and around the Valle de la Orotava. Ask at any tourist office for the *Footpaths* pack, a box of 22 looseleaf walks in English. Lonely Planet's *Walking in Spain* has detailed descriptions of a good week's worth of day hikes around the island while Discovery Walking Guides have three titles covering trails in the north, south and west of the island.

Accommodation

While finding a room is generally not a problem in Santa Cruz and the northern half of the island, the same cannot be said for the resort areas of the south, particularly around Costa Adeje, Los Cristianos and Playa de las Américas. Arriving here at night without a reservation can be a dodgy business, even if it's the low season and you are prepared to pay over the odds.

Cañada Blanca, near Las Galletas in the south, has Tenerife's only established camp site. However, there are 17 other sites around the island where camping is possible if you have official permission. Ask at the tourist office in Santa Cruz or call ☎ 922 27 81 00 or ☎ 922 63 04 88.

If you are interested in staying in farmhouses either on Tenerife or any of the other islands, you might like to contact AECAN (☎ 922 24 08 16, fax 922 24 40 03), who have a Web site at www.cip.es/aecan.

Getting There & Away

Air There are two airports on the island, with flights to all the other islands, the Spanish mainland and a host of European destinations, plus a few more exotic ones such as Venezuela and Havana.

Getting on for nine million passengers per year – often well in excess of 25,000

daily – pass through the modern **Tenerife Sur** (Reina Sofia) airport (☎ 922 75 95 10), about 20km east of Playa de las Américas. All international charter flights land here, as do nearly all scheduled international flights and others from a host of destinations in mainland Spain.

The airport has half-a-dozen car-rental offices, a post office, several banks, ATMs and exchange booths, and a modest tourist information office.

Practically all inter-island flights plus a few scheduled international and mainland services use the older and smaller **Tenerife Norte** (Los Rodeos) airport (☎ 922 63 56 35). There is an exchange booth, some car-rental reps, a bar and an information desk where you can get a map of Santa Cruz, but little else.

Boat For details of the weekly ship from Cádiz in mainland Spain, see Sea in the Getting There & Away chapter.

There are regular ferry, hydrofoil and jetfoil services from Tenerife to all the other islands. Details appear under Getting There & Away in the Santa Cruz and Los Cristianos sections.

Getting Around

To/From the Airports From Tenerife Sur, TITSA Bus No 487 departs more or less hourly for Los Cristianos (225 ptas) and Playa de las Américas (275 ptas) from 8.10 am to 10 pm. It's less than a half-hour ride to both destinations. No 341 departs at least hourly from 6.50 am for Santa Cruz (750 ptas, about 1½ hours). There are four buses (No 340) daily to Puerto de la Cruz (1175 ptas) via Tenerife Norte airport (750 ptas).

Call ☎ 922 39 21 19 for a taxi. Approximate fares are:

Los Cristianos	2100 ptas
Playa de las Américas	2400 ptas
Los Gigantes	5300 ptas
Santa Cruz	7400 ptas
Puerto de la Cruz	11,600 ptas

From Tenerife Norte, frequent TITSA buses go to Santa Cruz (150 ptas, 20 minutes).

euro currency converter €1 = 166 ptas

No 102 goes to Puerto de la Cruz (450 ptas) via La Laguna, only 3km away. Bus No 340 buses calls by the airport on its way between Puerto de la Cruz and Reina Sofia, the Tenerife Sur airport (four daily).

A taxi into Santa Cruz from Tenerife Norte costs around 1500 ptas. The fare to Puerto de la Cruz is around 3200 ptas.

Bus TITSA (Transportes Interurbanos de Tenerife SA) runs a spider's web of services all over the island, as well as providing the local bus service in the capital and other biggish towns. If you intend to use the bus a lot, get a Bonobus card. These cost 2000 ptas and are used instead of buying normal tickets. They represent a big saving – at least 30% and up to 50% on longer journeys. Insert the card in the machine on the bus, tell the driver where you are going and the amount is subtracted from the card. The card is good for any trip, intercity or local, throughout the island. It also gives you half-price admission into some of the island's museums.

Taxi You can take a taxi to anywhere you want on the island – but it is an expensive way to get around. You are much better off hiring a car. See Car & Motorcycle in the Getting Around chapter for details.

Santa Cruz de Tenerife

postcode 38003 • pop 203,800

Capital of both the island and the province of the same name (which embraces Tenerife and its smaller siblings, La Palma, La Gomera and El Hierro), Santa Cruz de Tenerife is a bustling port city – one of the busiest in all Spain. The long harbour gives protection to countless container ships, a cruise liner or two and a host of inter-island ferries and jetfoils. It's interesting enough for a day or so, although somewhat short on significant sights. With good bus transport, it makes a sensible base for exploring the north-east of the island – and here you feel you are truly in Canario territory, not the land of full English breakfasts and sauerkraut.

The townsfolk are known in the local slang as Chicharreros after the *chicharros* (horse mackerel) once favoured by the islands' fishermen.

HISTORY
Alonso Fernández de Lugo landed here in 1494 to embark on the conquest of the final and most-resistant island in the archipelago. But it was La Laguna, a few kilometres inland, that blossomed as the island's capital at first. Santa Cruz de Santiago, as it was then known, remained a backwater until its port began to flourish in the 18th and 19th centuries. Only in 1803 was Santa Cruz 'liberated' by royal decree from the municipal control of La Laguna, and in 1859 it was declared a city. From then on it has never looked back, its port giving it an advantage La Laguna could never match.

ORIENTATION
Taking Plaza de España as a hub, everything of interest lies within a kilometre or less. At the western edge is the bus station, while to the north-east is the terminal for jetfoils to/from Las Palmas de Gran Canaria.

With the exception of the Museo Militar de Almeyda (near the jetfoil terminal), most of the handful of sights and good shops lie within the central grid of streets leading inland from Plaza de España.

Maps
The small, in-your-palm town map handed out by the tourist office is refreshingly accurate.

INFORMATION
Tourist Offices
The tourist office (☎ 922 23 95 92) is in the Cabildo Insular de Tenerife building on Plaza de España. It opens 8 am to 6 pm, Monday to Friday, and 9 am to 1 pm, Saturday. Don't confuse it with the fairly uninformed tourist information kiosk in front of the adjacent post office.

Foreign Consulates

For a list of foreign consulates in Santa Cruz, see Embassies & Consulates in the Facts for the Visitor chapter.

Post & Communications

The main post office, from where you can send faxes, is on Plaza de España. Street phones abound. Otherwise, try the telephone office at Paseo de las Milícias de Garachico 3, which also has Internet access (700 ptas per hour). It opens 9 am to 10 pm, Monday to Friday, and 9.30 am to 2 pm and 5 to 9 pm at the weekend.

Email & Internet Access

If you're prepared for a short walk, the best choice in town, at a bargain 400 ptas an hour, are the friendly young folk at Yakiciber, Calle Ramón y Cajal 23 (☎ 922 27 52 08), open 10.30 am to 10 pm daily. An alternative is Bar Ciber El Navegante (☎ 922 24 15 00), Callejón del Combate 12, which charges 800 ptas per hour. It opens 10 am to 10.30 pm Monday to Saturday.

Bookshops

Titles in English carried by La Isla bookshop, Calle Robayna 2, include novels, a few Canaries guidebooks – and a larger selection of Lonely Planet guides.

Emergency

The main police station is at Avenida Tres de Mayo 32.

MUSEUMS

On the ground floor of the **Museo de la Naturaleza y El Hombre** is a multimedia, multiscreen display on volcanoes and the flora and fauna of the islands. Elsewhere are several Guanche mummies and skulls, a handful of artefacts including pottery, and a nicely arranged natural sciences section. The museum, which occupies a former hospital, opens 9 am to 8.30 pm daily except Monday. Admission costs 400 ptas (children 200 ptas). Admission is half price if you have a TITSA Bonobus card.

The **Museo de Bellas Artes**, on Plaza del Príncipe de Asturias, is home to an eclectic mix of paintings by Canarian and Flemish artists (including Bruegel), as well as sculpture, a weapons collection and old coins. It opens 10 am to 7.30 pm, Monday to Friday. Admission is free.

War buffs might want to check out the **Museo Militar de Almeyda**, on Calle San Isidro. The most famous item here is *El Tigre* (The Tiger), the cannon which reputedly blew off Admiral Nelson's arm when he attacked Santa Cruz in 1793 (much of the museum is devoted to the successful defence of the city and the capture of the invading force). It opens from 10 am to 2 pm daily except Monday, and admission is free.

AROUND THE CENTRE

Apart from the museums, there is really not an awful lot to see in Santa Cruz. It is a busy port city and simply meandering around is a pleasant way to while away the day. Starting a wander from the waterfront Plaza de España, whose centrepiece is a somewhat controversial memorial to the fallen of the 1936–9 Civil War, you could head inland along Plaza de la Candelaria and the pedestrianised shopping strip of Calle Castillo. A right turn along Calle José Murphy will, after a couple of blocks, bring you to the Museo de Bellas Artes and the **Iglesia de San Francisco**, a baroque church built in the 17th and 18th centuries.

Three small blocks south-west of Calle Castillo is the city's 19th-century **Teatro Guimerá**, whose austere facade belies a rather sumptuous interior (see Entertainment later for details). When we were last in town, the **Centro de Fotografía**, a photographic gallery on the other side of the small Plaza Isla de Madera, was about to be inaugurated; it might well be worth checking out.

Back towards the waterfront, on Plaza de la Iglesia, rises the striking bell tower of the city's oldest church, the **Iglesia de la Concepción**. The present church dates to about the same era as the Iglesia de San Francisco, but the original building went up in 1498 just after the island was conquered. At the heart of the shimmering silver altar is the Santa Cruz de la Conquista (Holy Cross

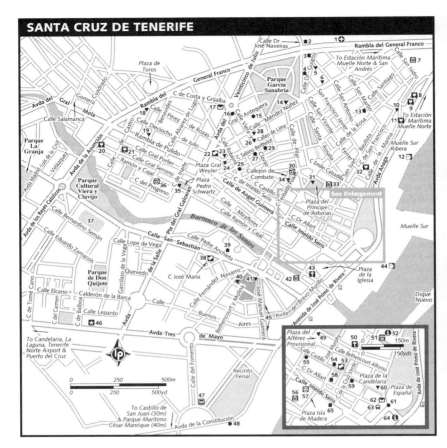

of the Conquest), which gives the city its name. Tradition has it that Alonso Fernández de Lugo, the Spanish commander, planted it in his camp to give thanks for his 1494 victory over the Guanches.

Check out too the anteroom to the sacristy (to the right of the altar). The altarpiece in the chapel beside it was carved from cedar on the orders of Don Matías Carta, a prominent personage who died before it was completed – he lies buried here and the pallid portrait on the wall was done *after* his death (hence the closed eyes and crossed arms). There's also a fine painting

of *La Adoración de los Pastores* (The Adoration of the Shepherds) by Juan de Miranda.

About another 10-minute walk southwest along the waterfront brings you to the 17th-century **Castillo de San Juan**. In the shadow of this protective fort there used to be a lively trade in African slaves. Nowadays, its squat, rectangular basalt form is overshadowed in its turn by the magnificent soaring concrete auditorium, the **Auditorio de Tenerife,** designed by the internationally renowned Spanish architect Santiago Calatrava.

SANTA CRUZ DE TENERIFE

PLACES TO STAY
2   Hotel Mencey
3   Hotel Contemporáneo
4   Hotel Taburiente
13   Pensión Mova
27   Pensión Casablanca
29   Pensión Valverde
39   Hotel Tanausú
54   Hotel Atlántico
58   Pensión Oviedo
59   Hotel El Dorado
65   Hotel Anaga

PLACES TO EAT
5   Mesón El Portón
6   Sidrería Mariano
10   Bar 3 de Mayo
14   Terrazas; Children's
     Playground
18   Terrazas
19   Don Pelayo; Rincón de la
     Piedra
23   Platillo Volante; Bar Zumería
     Doña Papaya
24   Mesón Castellano
26   Mesón Treinta y Ocho
28   Restaurante Vu-Do
31   Café del Príncipe

34   Mesón del Duque
35   Bar/Restaurant
40   Mercado de Nuestra Señora
     de África
41   Bar Mercado
49   Cafetería El Aguila
60   Terrazas

BARS & DISCOS
8   Charlie's Pub; The Camel
9   Nooctua; Yesterdays
11   Na-Na Disco Pub
20   Cervecería Rhín Barril
21   Bar Sucre
32   Bars

OTHER
1   Hospiten Rambla
7   Museo Militar de Almeyda
12   Estación Marítima Muelle
     Ribera (Fred Olsen Ferry
     Departures)
15   Ayuntamiento (Town Hall)
16   Gobierno de Canarias
17   Post Office
22   UK Consulate
25   La Isla Bookshop
30   Bar Ciber El Navegante

33   Museo de Bellas Artes
36   Yakiciber
37   Estadio Heliodoro Rodríguez
     López
38   French Consulate
42   Museo de la Naturaleza y El
     Hombre
43   Iglesia de la Concepción
44   Naviera Armas Ferry
     Departures
45   Rastro (Sunday Flea
     Market)
46   Police Station
47   Bus Station
48   Auditorio de Tenerife
50   Iglesia de San Francisco
51   Telephone Office
52   National Park Servicio de Uso
     Office Público Office
53   Irish Consulate
55   Manzana Megastore
56   Centro de Fotografía
57   Teatro Guimerá
61   Handicrafts Kiosk
62   Main Post Office
63   Bus No 015 for
     La Laguna
64   Tourist Office

Just beyond this contrasting pair is the **Parque Marítimo César Manrique** (for more on this remarkable local artist, see the boxed text 'The Life & Art of César Manrique' in the Lanzarote chapter). Here you can have a dip in one of the designer pools or just lie back on the loungers and drink in the pleasant view and something refreshing. It opens 10 am to 7 pm daily and admission costs 375 ptas (children 175 ptas).

ORGANISED TOURS
Several travel agents organise day tours of the island and to Tenerife's smaller cousin, La Gomera.

SPECIAL EVENTS
Carnaval – the Canarian fiesta par excellence – is *the* event in Santa Cruz, and throughout the island. Only Rio de Janeiro does it better, and even that famous party doesn't overshadow Santa Cruz's efforts by a great deal. The fun begins in early Febru-

ary and lasts about three weeks. Many of the gala performances and fancy dress competitions take place in the Recinto Ferial (fair grounds) but the streets, especially around Plaza de España, burst into a frenzy of outlandish activity as the whole island seems to participate in masked balls and an almost permanent state of good-natured frivolity.

Needless to say, finding a place to stay anywhere in Tenerife at this time – if you don't have an advance booking – is a rather tall order.

The founding of the city is celebrated on 3 May, but this is a sober affair in comparison to the Carnaval.

PLACES TO STAY – BUDGET
For a city this size, there are few budget places and most of the dirt cheap places are none too inviting.

Pensión Casablanca (☎ 922 27 85 99, Calle Viera y Clavijo 15) has had a facelift. The rooms are tiny but singles/doubles are

TENERIFE

good value at 2500/3500 ptas. The freshly tiled corridor bathrooms have had a nose job and are altogether sweeter than travellers once reported.

Only consider nearby **Pensión Valverde** (☎ 922 27 40 63, Calle Sabino Berthelot 46) as a fallback if Pensión Casablanca is full. Rooms with bathroom cost a reasonable 4000 ptas (3000 ptas without), or 5000 ptas if you want a triple, but you won't find the most cheerful of welcomes.

Altogether more friendly and a better budget option is **Pensión Mova** (☎ 922 28 32 61, Calle San Martín 33) where single/ double rooms cost 1900/3200 ptas (2400/ 3900 ptas with bathroom).

If all else fails, rock-bottom **Pensión Oviedo** (☎ 922 24 36 43, Calle Doctor Allart 24) has basic rooms with washbasin for 2000/3000 ptas.

PLACES TO STAY – MID-RANGE
Hotel Tanausú (☎ 922 21 70 00, fax 922 21 60 29, Calle Padre Ancieta 8), where rooms with bathroom cost 4500/7300 ptas, is a pleasant enough place.

Superior in both price and quality is **Hotel Taburiente** (☎ 922 27 60 00, fax 922 27 05 62, e hotel-taburiente@teleline.es, Calle Doctor José Naveiras 24A). Fully equipped singles/doubles/triples start at 7000/9600/12,900 ptas. With a swimming pool, sauna and dedicated garage, it has a lot going for it.

More central is **Hotel Atlántico** (☎ 922 24 63 75, fax 922 24 63 78, Calle Castillo 12), where singles/doubles cost 4750/ 8500 ptas, including breakfast.

Prices and service are similar at its sister, **Hotel El Dorado** (☎ 922 24 31 84, Calle de la Cruz Verde 24), which is under the same ownership. It is equally in the heart of things and charges 5000/8360 ptas for singles/doubles.

Lastly, **Hotel Anaga** (☎ 922 24 50 90, fax 922 24 56 44, Calle Imeldo Serís 19) is a good deal better than its gloomy lobby might suggest when you first arrive. Decent singles/doubles cost 3825/6265 ptas with shower (4850/7800 ptas with full bathroom), including breakfast.

PLACES TO STAY – TOP END
Stylish **Hotel Contemporáneo** (☎ 922 27 15 71, fax 922 27 12 23, e consultas.contem@ tenerife.net, Rambla del General Franco 116), has singles/doubles/triples at 9150/ 13,500/16,500 ptas.

If it's top class you want and the holiday budget's healthy, consider the huge, prestigious **Hotel Mencey** (☎ 922 27 67 00, fax 922 28 00 17, e mencey@ctv.es, Calle Doctor José Naveiras 38), where singles/ doubles begin at 24,000/29,000 ptas.

PLACES TO EAT
Breakfast & Juices
You probably wouldn't go out of your way for it, but minuscule **Bar 3 de Mayo** (Calle de la Marina 93) is not bad for breakfast, especially with all the great juices on offer (papaya, mango, strawberry and so on).

Superior for juices and fruit shakes is **Platillo Volante** (Calle Callao de Lima 3) and even one better for juices is its neighbour, **Bar Zumería Doña Papaya** ('Lady Papaya Juice Bar'), which has a wonderful selection of fresh fruits waiting to be pulped. Just lap up that vitamin C!

Restaurants
The **Mesón del Duque** (Calle Teobaldo Power 15) has wine barrels for tables and a fine old wooden bar – a perfect spot for a glass of red wine and a ración (a larger version of a tapa) of tortilla con chorizo – or head to the restaurant out the back for something more substantial. It closes on Monday.

Restaurante Vu-Do (☎ 922 27 98 32, Calle Viera y Clavijo 44) is a so-called Vietnamese spot, although much of the food looks like your average international Chinese fare. It's a pleasant enough place to eat though, and makes a change.

Down the road at No 38, **Mesón Treinta y Ocho** is an elegant place where fine Canarian food is served – don't expect to get away for less than 2500 ptas. It closes on Monday.

A little more down-to-earth is **Rincón de la Piedra** (Calle Benavides 32), an attractively decorated old Canarian house with lots of exposed wood beams. It closes Sunday and Monday lunchtime.

Its neighbour, **Don Pelayo** (☎ 922 24 19 66), specialises in Asturian cuisine from the north of Spain. Both hustling, bustling places are packed, particularly at lunchtime – rarely will you have seen barmen who can move at such speed and with such flair.

The small unnamed open-air **bar/restaurant** within Plaza Pedro Schwartz is popular. The food is average but the shady location is a big plus.

Sidrería Mariano (Calle Méndez Núñez 33) is the place to go if you're hankering for an Asturian-style cider to wash down your meal.

Mesón El Portón (Calle Doctor Guigou 18) is a swanky sort of eatery with fine food at fine prices – mains start at around 1500 ptas.

Also a little pricey but highly regarded is **Mesón Castellano** (Calle Callao de Lima 4).

Cafes & Terrazas

Cafes abound. Because of the pleasant climate, many have outside tables and make great places to sip and watch life pass.

Café del Príncipe, within the leafy Plaza del Príncipe de Asturias, is a lovely setting for a coffee or cocktail.

Cafetería El Aguila (Plaza del Alférez Provisional) is another choice spot.

Pleasant cafe terrazas to while away your time include those on Plaza de la Candelaria and Rambla del General Franco (near the Plaza de Toros) – and the shady number on the fringe of Parque García Sanabria, where you can let the kids romp in the adjacent playground.

On Sunday, **Bar Mercado**, right amid the flea market on Calle José Manuel Guimerá, is great for watching the action.

Self-Catering

The rather claustrophobic covered market, the **Mercado de Nuestra Señora de África**, is a little disappointing by Spanish standards. All the same, it's worth a visit if only to marvel at the variety of fish pulled from the ocean.

ENTERTAINMENT
Bars, Pubs & Discos

Bar Sucre (Calle Castro 15) couldn't be further from the tourist trail. Ordinary – nondescript even – it's a busy little hangout, usually packed with locals and serving up good *arepas* (an envelope of maize – corn – with a savoury filling) should you need food with your beer.

There are two or three concentrated areas of *marcha*. There's a bunch of bars on Plaza Isabel II and a few more at the western end of Calle Ramón y Cajal.

If you're gagging for Guinness, head for **Cervecería Rhín Barril** at No 74.

Nightlife takes off from about 2 am at the northern end of Avenida Anaga. Work your way from **Nooctua** at No 37 to its neighbour, **Yesterdays**. Next is **Charlie's Pub** and at No 41 **The Camel**, which calls itself 'The original friendly bar'. We can't vouch for the originality – after all, it hasn't been around all that long – but we're happy to endorse the friendly tag. Should you still have the energy to dance, drop in on **Na-Na Disco Pub** in the same block.

Theatre & Classical Music

The main venue for highbrow entertainment, whether music or theatre, is the **Teatro Guimerá** (☎ 922 29 08 38, Calle Imeldo Serís). The biggest event on the serious music calendar is the Festival de Música de Canarias, held annually in January and February.

Live Music

Big-name acts tend to perform at the **Plaza de Toros** or the **Recinto Ferial**. Ask at the tourist office if anything is on and for details of how to get tickets – often a bank such as La Caixa becomes the temporary box office for such events. Manzana Megastore, a music and book store at Calle Castillo 15, also often sells tickets to the big gigs.

SPECTATOR SPORTS
Football

Santa Cruz is home to CD Tenerife, who currently play in the second division. You can buy tickets at the *taquillas* (box office)

TENERIFE

of their stadium, Estadio Heliodoro Rodríguez López.

For information, call the club on ☎ 922 29 16 99 or ☎ 922 24 06 13.

SHOPPING

Many tourists – including those who briefly disembark from the cruise ships that moor in the harbour – come to Santa Cruz for the shopping, lured by the Canary Islands' status as a tax haven. The main shopping strip is the pedestrianised Calle Castillo and surrounding streets, especially Calle del Pilar (where there's a Corte Inglés department store) and Calle Bethencourt Alfonso. The most promising deals are on electronics, watches and so on, but even items such as jeans are worth considering.

If you're after something typical of the island, browse for ideas around the rectangular government-sponsored **handicrafts kiosk** opposite the main post office. All items are for sale. Then, perhaps, seek out some of the embroidery work in the shops along Calle Castillo, where you can even buy traditional Canarian costumes.

On Sundays there's a *rastro* (flea market) along Calle José Manuel Guimerá, leading up to the covered market (see Self-Catering under Places to Eat earlier).

GETTING THERE & AWAY
Air

Tenerife Norte is the nearest airport to Santa Cruz. It handles all flights between the islands, and very few others. See the Getting There & Away section at the beginning of this chapter for details.

Bus

TITSA buses radiate out from the bus station (☎ 922 21 93 99), beside Avenida de la Constitución, to pretty much every place of interest around the island. Major routes include:

No 102 Puerto de la Cruz via La Laguna and Tenerife Norte (525 ptas, 55 minutes, every 30 minutes)
No 103 Puerto de la Cruz direct (525 ptas, 40 minutes, over 15 daily)
No 106 and 108 Icod de los Vinos (750 ptas, 1¼ hours, over 15 daily)

No 110 Los Cristianos and Playa de las Américas direct (950 ptas, one hour, every 30 minutes)
No 111 Los Cristianos and Playa de las Américas via Guimar and Candelaria (950 ptas, one hour 20 minutes, every 30 minutes)
No 341 Tenerife Sur (750 ptas, 50 minutes, 20 daily)
No 014 and 015 La Laguna (150 ptas, 20 minutes, every 10 minutes or so)

Car & Motorcycle

Car-rental companies are scattered all over the city centre. Major operators also have booths at the Estación Marítima.

Boat

The Trasmediterránea (☎ 902 45 46 45) ferry to Cádiz via Las Palmas de Gran Canaria and Arrecife on Lanzarote (see Sea in the Getting There & Away chapter) leaves weekly at 9 am on Saturday.

Trasmediterránea runs three jetfoils per day (two on Sunday) to Las Palmas. The standard fare is 7350 ptas (4600 ptas off peak). The 9.30 am sailing continues on to Morro Jable in Fuerteventura (10,420 ptas). It also has a weekly boat to Santa Cruz de la Palma (from 3900 ptas, eight hours), which leaves at midnight on Thursday.

Naviera Armas (☎ 922 53 40 52) runs a fast ferry to Las Palmas twice daily and to Morro Jable (Fuerteventura) once daily. It also has a boat to La Palma (3600 ptas) on Friday and Saturday.

Líneas Fred Olsen (☎ 922 62 82 00) has six high-speed ferries daily to Agaete (from 3360 ptas, 1¼ hours), in the northwest of Gran Canaria, from where you can take their free bus onwards to Las Palma (35 minutes).

You can buy tickets for all three companies from travel agents or from the main Estación Marítima Muelle de Ribera building (which is where the Fred Olsen boats leave·from). Naviera Armas has its base farther to the south-west.

GETTING AROUND
To/From the Airport

See Getting Around at the beginning of the chapter for details of the regular buses serving both airports.

A taxi to Tenerife Norte will cost about 1800 ptas. For Tenerife Sur, the fare is around 7500 ptas.

Bus

TITSA buses provide the city service in Santa Cruz. No 914 runs from the bus station to the centre (Plaza del General Weyler and Plaza de España) about every 15 minutes (every half-hour at weekends).

Taxi

There are major taxi stands are on Plaza de España and at the bus station. Call ☎ 922 31 0000.

Around the Island

LA LAGUNA

postcode 38200 • pop 160,000
• elevation 542m
San Cristóbal de la Laguna (to give its full name) is one of the two urban jewels in Tenerife's crown (La Orotava is the other). The former island capital is a lively student town today and well deserves a visit. It is an easy day trip from Santa Cruz or Puerto de la Cruz and should not be missed.

History

Alonso Fernández de Lugo's troops ended up making a permanent camp in what is now known as La Laguna (the lagoon from which the name comes was only drained in 1837).

By the end of the 15th century, the old town as it is today was pretty much complete, and the Muy Noble, Ilustre, Leal y Fiel Ciudad de San Cristóbal de la Laguna (The Very Noble, Illustrious, Loyal & Faithful City of Saint Christopher of the Lagoon) – to give it its *fullest* name! – was a bustling city of merchants, soldiers, bureaucrats and the pious. In 1701 the university was established – it still flourishes today.

Although it's at barely more than 500m, it's appreciably cooler than the coast – another reason for making a pleasant day trip here.

Orientation

The bus station is about a 10-minute walk to the north-west of the old centre. The university, where you'll find the bulk of the bars and plenty of simple eateries, lies to the south of the old quarter. The little accommodation available is in the historic area, as are some nice restaurants, banks, the post office and the tourist offices.

Information

Tourist Offices It is only a tiny kiosk (☎ 922 63 11 94) but, staffed from 8 am to 8pm, Monday to Saturday, it wins the prize for the longest opening hours of any Canaries tourist information office. You'll find it on Plaza del Adelantado, just opposite Hotel-Apartamentos Nivaria. If you're interested in historical buildings, ask for a copy of the brochure in English, *Living History: San Cristóbal de La Laguna.*

Post & Communications The main post office is next to the Iglesia de Santo Domingo, on the street of the same name.

Emergency The police station is at Calle Nava y Grimón 66.

Canarian Mansions

Apart from the fine-balconied houses of La Orotava, La Laguna is where you will most fully appreciate the beauty and eccentricity of Canarian urban architecture – bright facades graced with ponderous wooden double-doors and pretty balconies. Broad, elegant, wood-shuttered windows conceal cool, shady patios, in the best cases surrounded by first-storey verandas propped up by slender timber columns. Wherever you see an open door, look inside – with luck the inner sanctum will also be open and you can see what lies behind the exterior walls.

The best place to start your wanderings is at Casa Lercaro, on Calle San Agustín. Built in 1593, long abandoned and now carefully restored, it houses the **Museo de la Historia de Tenerife.** The documents, maps, artefacts and descriptions are interesting enough in themselves (ask for the English

TENERIFE

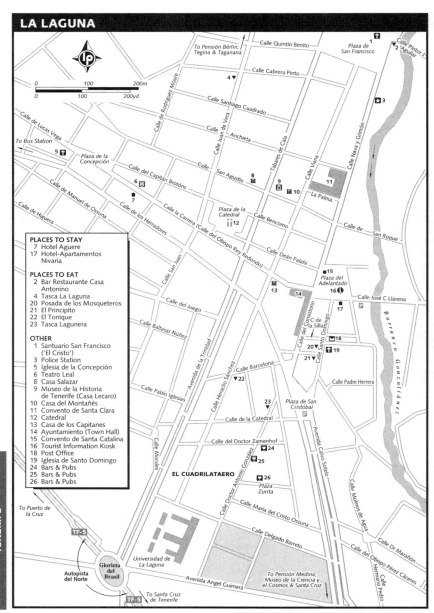

LA LAGUNA

PLACES TO STAY
7 Hotel Aguere
17 Hotel-Apartamentos Nivaria

PLACES TO EAT
2 Bar Restaurante Casa Antonino
4 Tasca La Laguna
20 Posada de los Mosqueteros
21 El Principito
22 El Tonique
23 Tasca Lagunera

OTHER
1 Santuario San Francisco ('El Cristo')
3 Police Station
5 Iglesia de la Concepción
6 Teatro Leal
8 Casa Salazar
9 Museo de la Historia de Tenerife (Casa Lecaro)
10 Casa del Montañés
11 Convento de Santa Clara
12 Catedral
13 Casa de los Capitanes
14 Ayuntamiento (Town Hall)
15 Convento de Santa Catalina
16 Tourist Information Kiosk
18 Post Office
19 Iglesia de Santo Domingo
24 Bars & Pubs
25 Bars & Pubs
26 Bars & Pubs

text), but the mansion alone is well worth looking over. It opens 10 am to 8 pm Tuesday to Sunday. Admission costs 400 ptas (with TITSA Bonobus 200 ptas, students 100 ptas).

Calle San Agustín and the surrounding streets are lined with fine old houses. Take a look inside **Casa del Montañés** at No 16. Peek too into the tranquil patio of No 28, the **Casa Salazar**, nowadays home to the bishop of La Laguna. The imposing **Casa de los Capitanes**, is beside the town hall on Calle La Carrera (aka Calle del Obispo Rey Redondo). You'll see others as you wander, so keep your eyes peeled.

Churches & Convents

Perhaps less enchanting (maybe because they are less original to the eyes of anyone who has seen the great cathedrals and monasteries of mainland Europe) are La Laguna's contributions to religious architecture.

The **Iglesia de la Concepción** was the island's first church and has undergone many changes. Elements of Gothic and plateresque styles can still be distinguished, and the finely wrought wooden mudéjar ceilings are a delight. The church opens 10 am to 12.15 pm and 5 to 7.15 pm Tuesday to Sunday.

A few minutes' walk east, the less interesting **catedral** was completely rebuilt in 1913. Inside is a fine baroque retable (reredos, altarpiece) in the chapel dedicated to the Virgen de los Remedios. It has also retained some fine paintings by Cristóbal Hernández de Quintana, one of the islands' premier 18th-century artists. The **Iglesia de Santo Domingo**, originally a hermitage and expanded in the 17th century, also contains some good examples of his work.

At the very northern end of the old quarter, the **Santuario San Francisco** (known as El Cristo by the locals), or the Santuario del Santísimo Cristo de La Laguna to give it its full name, contains a blackened wooden sculpture of Christ – the most venerated crucifix on the island. Core opening hours are 10.30 am to 1.00 pm and 4 to 9 pm daily. Admission is free.

Of the convents, the most interesting is the **Convento de Santa Clara**, which is closed for renovations until deep into 2002. You can, however, visit its fine 16th-century chapel, open 4.30 to 7 pm daily. Both it and the closed order in the **Convento de Santa Catalina** on Plaza del Adelantado are still active. You can visit the latter between 7 and 11.45 am, Monday to Saturday, and 6.30 to 8 pm on Sunday.

Museo de la Ciencia y el Cosmos

If you enjoy pushing buttons, watching balls and things jiggling around, and musing on the forces of nature, you can have fun here, even if you don't speak Spanish. It also has a planetarium. The museum (☎ 922 31 52 65) is on Vía Láctea, about 1.5km south of Plaza del Adelantado. It opens 10 am to 8 pm, Tuesday to Sunday, admission costs 400 ptas.

Special Events

The most important fiestas in La Laguna are the Romería de San Benito Abad on the first Sunday of July and the Fiesta del Santísimo Cristo from 7 to 15 September. Carnaval (February) and Corpus Christi (June) are also celebrated with gusto.

Places to Stay

Sleeping possibilities are extremely limited.

The only cheapies are a couple of pensiones in the suburbs. *Pensión Berlín* (☎ *922 25 50 43, Calle República de Venezuela 64)*, has single/double rooms for 3000/4000 ptas. *Pensión Medina (☎ 922 66 08 48, Calle Eduardo de Roo 68)* is in La Cuesta and charges 2100/3700 ptas.

Back in town, try the stylish *Hotel Aguere (☎ 922 25 94 90, fax 922 63 16 33,* @ *haguere@infonegocio.com, Calle La Carrera 55)*, opposite the Teatro Leal. Constructed in 1760, it has a delightful glass roofed patio. Rooms cost 6700/8250 ptas and are excellent value.

Hotel-Apartamentos Nivaria (☎ 922 26 42 98, fax 922 25 96 34, Plaza del Adelantado 11) also occupies a much-altered 18th-century building but has retained its

TENERIFE

Father of Gestalt

In 1913, at the age of 26, the German psychologist Wolfgang Köhler left the hot-house of the European academic world and migrated to the Canary Islands, where he took up a post at the Prussian Academy of Sciences on Tenerife.

Born in Tallinn, Estonia, and educated in Berlin and Frankfurt, Köhler launched the Gestalt theory of psychology, which attempts to understand learning, perception and other mental processes in terms of structured wholes.

When in 1913 he elected to leave behind his colleagues (including Kurt Koffka and Max Wertheimer) for sunnier climes, did he have an inkling of the madness that was about to befall the European continent or was he just plain lucky? In any event, he pursued his studies in Tenerife for the next seven years, investigating – among other things – chimpanzees' capacity for problem-solving and constructing simple tools.

His findings were eventually brought together in his ground-breaking *Intelligenzprüfungen an Menschenaffen (The Mentality of the Apes)*, published in 1917, as well as other books. In 1921 he returned to Berlin but, no great fan of a rather different and unpleasant kind of chimp – Adolf Hitler – he migrated to the USA in 1935.

own gracious patio. Studios for two cost 9600 ptas, apartments acommodating up to three cost 12,100 ptas.

Places to Eat

Bar Restaurante Casa Antonino (Plaza de San Francisco 6) has a cool bar inside and a small leafy courtyard in which to eat your filling meals. Count on spending 1500 ptas. You'll find plenty of other simple, economical eateries around the university.

Tasca La Laguna (☎ 992 63 33 30, Calle Juan de Vera 53) opens evenings only, Tuesday to Sunday. It's a great spot. The so-called tapas are actually sizeable portions of mouth-watering food. Try the *champiñones empanados* (breaded mushrooms).

Near-synonym *Tasca Lagunera (☎ 922 25 66 53, Calle Doctor Antonio Gonzalez 6)* is a more formal place which serves fine food. Mains cost between 1300 ptas and 1500 ptas. It closes Sunday lunchtime.

Slightly more expensive but worth those extra pesetas is the friendly *El Tonique (☎/fax 922 26 15 29, Calle Heraclio Sánchez 23)*, its walls lined with bottles of fine wine. They're but a sample of over 250 different varieties quietly maturing in its cellars. Mains cost around 1600 ptas.

For fine cuisine, take your pick between a pair of restaurants facing each other

across Calle Santo Domingo. Disregard the rather naff nouveau-rustic decor at *Posada de los Mosqueteros (☎ 922 25 49 65)* at No 24 and settle in to enjoy one of their main dishes at around 1400 ptas. Opposite at No 26, *El Principito (☎ 922 63 39 16)* is one of La Laguna's swishest restaurants. It's good value but you won't escape for much under 3500 ptas. It opens Tuesday to Saturday.

Entertainment

Bars & Pubs Students provide the nightlife and the bulk of the bars are concentrated in a tight rectangle north-east of the university, known as *El Cuadrilátero*. At its heart, pedestrianised Plaza Zurita is simply two parallel lines of bars and pubs. It would be invidious to single out a handful from so many – just set off bar-hopping and finding what suits your tastes – you won't have far to hop (or stagger).

Getting There & Around

Bus There is a stream of buses to Santa Cruz (No 015 is best as it takes you to Plaza de España) and a regular service to Puerto de la Cruz (Nos 101 and 102), La Orotava (No 062) and beyond.

Car Street parking is a minor hell. A big stretch of waste land just off Plaza del Ade-

View mighty Teide peak from La Gomera.

Stony silence on Hermigua's deserted beach

Picturesque Agulo makes the most of a break in La Gomera's rugged and forbidding coastline.

The islands' most important crop: banana terraces on La Gomera

Torre del Conde is still intact.

Playa de la Rajita, La Gomera

One bunch in a million

One *buenos dias* and you're everyone's friend in the Canaries.

lantado is used as a free car park and there's a paying underground one beneath Plaza de San Cristóbal.

THE NORTH-EAST
San Andrés & Around

The village of San Andrés, all narrow, shady streets, is 6km north-east of Santa Cruz. It is distinguished by the round tower, now crumbled, which once protected it and some good little fish restaurants, which themselves alone justify the short journey. Bustling *Marisquería Ramon*, just southwest of the tower, is packed to its fishy gills at midday. Pick your fish from the glass fronted fridge and go for the giant house salad at 625 ptas. Cheaper, if you can be squeezed in, is tiny *Bar Petón*, which is also a pebble's throw from the tower. The chalkboard menu lists the catch of the day.

It matters not one jot that the golden sands for the **Playa de las Teresitas**, just beyond the village, were imported from the Sahara. It's an extremely pleasant beach where the sunbathers are almost exclusively Spanish, whether local or from the mainland.

There are frequent buses (No 910) from Santa Cruz to San Andrés, continuing to Playa de las Teresitas. Bus No 245 goes north-east from San Andrés to the end of the road at Igueste, following another 6km of beautiful coastline.

If you have your own transport, you could head down to secluded Playa de las Gaviotas, a little before the road ends.

Taganana & the Anaga Mountains

A spectacular trip leads up the Barranco de las Huertas to cross the Anaga range (geologically the oldest part of the island) and plummets down on the other side to the little hamlet of Taganana. The views to the craggy coast from above it are breathtaking.

Taganana hosts an odd celebration in March/April (the date changes), in which an effigy of Judas Iscariot is burned in a kind of collective purging of the villagers' sins and guilty consciences!

Bus No 246 comes to Taganana six times daily from Santa Cruz.

There's little to the place, but it's only a few more kilometres to the coast and **Roque de las Bodegas**, which has four or five small restaurants and drink stands. *Casa Africa* is particularly popular. Local surfers and boogie boarders savour its beach – and, even more so, the rocky strand of **Almáciga**, 1.25km eastwards.

If you have your own wheels, backtracking up and into the Anaga mountain range and heading west at the intersection (follow signs for La Laguna) continues a spectacular excursion. It's a ridge ride with views of the ocean to both north and south and the islands of Gran Canaria and El Hierro rearing from the seas, if the air's clear. Take time to pause at the numerous *miradores* (lookout points) along the way.

Bajamar & Punta del Hidalgo

It's worth building in time to allow for a side trip to this part of the coast as you head towards La Laguna from Taganana. Once the mountain road has dropped to the plain, turn west for Tegueste. About 10 km beyond the junction, you reach the local seaside resort of Bajamar (via Tejina). The only swimming is in rock pools awash with Atlantic rollers but it is popular with Canarios and mainland Spaniards. As resorts go, it's pretty low key. Three kilometres north-east, Punta del Hidalgo is an extension of Bajamar. Locals try their luck on boogie boards in the surf of Playa de los Troches.

If you want to stay, you'll find a few sets of apartments in both locations. *Apartamentos Bellamar* (☎ 922 54 06 61, *Avenida Rafael González Vernetta*), has singles/doubles/triples at 5300/6100/6500 ptas. You could also try **Hotel Delfín** (☎ 922 54 02 00, *Avenida del Sol 59*). Singles/doubles cost up to 5000/7000 ptas.

Bus No 105 runs here every 30 minutes from Santa Cruz via La Laguna.

Tacoronte & El Sauzal

Tacoronte is one of the island's most important wine regions. Its fiesta of Cristo de

TENERIFE

Going Bananas

You're bound to see some of the islands' fields of bananas, grown close together in tight ranks, their large, light green leaves protruding in all directions like vegetable sunshades. Or maybe not: these days many are thriving under ugly, all-enveloping sheets of plastic which swathe a whole field, allowing only the tip of a mature plant or two to force its way up and out into natural sunlight.

JANE SMITH

Although bananas had been grown in the Canary Islands for centuries, they only really came into their own as *the* export cash crop around the 1870s. Today, they are still the single most important crop in the islands and the most important foreign currency earner after tourism.

Remaining even more dependent upon the yellow boomerang are the Latin American heirs of the Canary Islands' banana. It was the early Spanish conquistadors who took over the first samples from the archipelago and introduced the crop to the western hemisphere. The initial plantings took place after Columbus' first landfall at Hispaniola (the Dominican Republic and Haiti) and quickly spread to other islands and the mainland – for example, Fray Tomás de Berlanga, later Bishop of Panama, took some specimens to his new country in 1516.

To this day the banana remains a staple of the economies of countries such as Panama, the Dominican Republic, Guadeloupe, Jamaica, Costa Rica, Honduras, Guatemala, Brazil, Colombia and Ecuador.

So what's so great about bananas? Easily grown in tropical and sub-tropical environments, bananas brim with vitamins A and C, potassium and carbohydrates. People have been raving about them since ancient times – Alexander the Great encountered them during his conquests in India, three hundred years before Christ.

The banana plant is in fact an outlandishly large herb. After the first planting, it can take up to 15 months for fruit to appear. From its underground stem (or rhizome) springs a false trunk, all sappy and bendy (like rolled-up newspaper) that can grow up to 6m. The false trunk gives forth a huge spear-shaped mauve flower, from which will grow a bunch of anything up to 150 bananas, the whole divided into 'hands' of 10 to 20 'fingers' or pieces of fruit. As each plant only bears one bunch, the false trunk is pruned away to make way for new ones, sprouting from the same underground stem, to take its place.

There are hundreds of different types of banana scattered across plantations around the world, but one important distinction is between the sweet-tasting banana and the more starchy plantain (used primarily in cooking).

los Dolores is celebrated with harvest festivities on the first Sunday after 15 September – a good time to be here as much wine-tasting is done.

Downhill from the modern town centre is the **Iglesia de Santa Catalina** (signposted) – a bright, little, grey-stone, whitewashed church built in the Canaries colonial style.

TENERIFE

Around about a handful of traditional old houses. Otherwise, there really isn't a lot to the place.

Just beside the El Sauzal exit from the motorway is **Casa del Vino La Baranda**, a museum devoted to wine and its production. It opens 11 am to 8 pm, Tuesday to Saturday, and 11 am to 6 pm on Sunday. Admission is free.

Bus No 101 links these towns to Puerto de la Cruz and Santa Cruz every 30 minutes or hourly (according to the time of day).

La Matanza de Acentejo & La Victoria

La Matanza ('the slaughter') is where Bencomo's Guanches inflicted a nasty defeat on Alonso Fernández de Lugo's Spaniards in 1493. Two years later, however, de Lugo was back and this time he had better luck, winning a decisive victory over the Guanches just 3km south of the scene of his earlier defeat. Predictably, the village that eventually sprang up here was known as La Victoria.

Bus No 101 links these towns to Puerto de la Cruz and Santa Cruz.

PUERTO DE LA CRUZ
postcode 38400 ● pop 27,000

This is a coastal paradise, with palms swaying among the banana plantations, black sandy beaches and a limpid ocean. But it is also a forest of high-rise hotels, shopping malls, touts, 'traditional Sunday roasts' and street vendors flogging pirate Julio Iglesias tapes. However it's far from bad news: the western side and the older parts of the town centre, much of it pedestrianised, are pretty in places and not so obviously overrun.

Historically, Puerto de la Cruz was a secondary port much used by English traders. As maritime trade dropped off, it was the English who came to the rescue, erecting the monumental Grand Hotel Taoro as a kind of members' club. This marked the beginning of Puerto de la Cruz's vocation as a tourist recreation destination.

Orientation

The city spreads from east to west along the coast. Busy Plaza del Charco is a focal point

and most of the town's historic buildings lie in its immediate vicinity. To the east is the hideous jumble of high-rise hotels, discos, bars and international restaurants – plus the very pleasant Lago Martiánez, a watery playground designed by César Manrique.

Information

Tourist Offices The tourist office (☎ 922 38 60 00) is on Plaza de Europa. It opens 9 am to 8 pm (to 7 pm, July to September), Monday to Friday, and 9 am to 1 pm on Saturday.

Money American Express is represented by Viajes Insular (☎ 922 38 02 62), Avenida del Generalísimo 20A.

Post & Communications The main post office is on Calle del Pozo, opposite the bus station. There's a battery of telephones beside the little fishing port.

You can check your emails at Multicentro Sothís on Carretera del Botánico, opposite Hotel Botánico on the eastern side of town.

Bookshops The Book Shop, Calle Iriarte 42, has second-hand books in just about every major European language, with many titles in English. It's well worth a browse if you've exhausted your holiday reading.

Laundry Tip Top Lavandería, Calle Teobaldo Power 19, will wash a load of up to 5kg and return it, dried but not ironed, the same day for 950 ptas.

Emergency The main police station is on Avenida José del Campo Llarena.

Disabled Travellers Le Ro (☎ 922 37 33 01) is a specialist shop that rents wheelchairs and other appliances for the disabled, as well as offering a repair service. On Avenida del Generalísimo in the Apartamentos Martina building, it opens 9 am to noon on weekdays.

Things to See & Do

Created by César Manrique, the **Lago Martiánez**, with its fountains, whitewashed

TENERIFE

PUERTO DE LA CRUZ

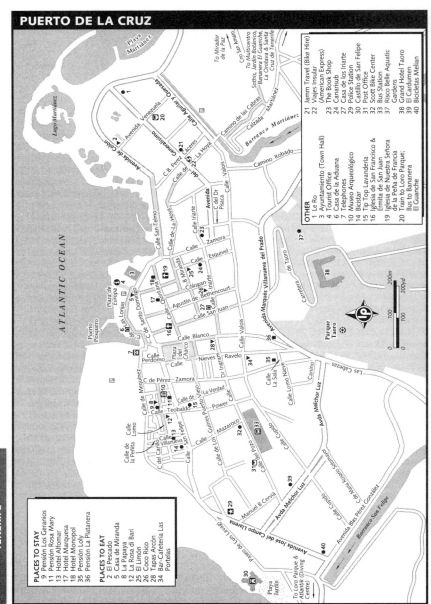

PLACES TO STAY
9 Pensión Los Geranios
11 Pensión Rosa Mary
13 Hotel Alfomar
17 Hotel Marquesa
18 Hotel Monopol
35 Pensión Loly
36 Pensión La Platanera

PLACES TO EAT
2 El Pescado
5 Casa de Miranda
8 La Papaya
12 La Rosa di Bari
25 El Limón
26 Coco Rico
28 Tapas Arcón
34 Bar-Cafetería Las Portelas

OTHER
1 Le Ro
3 Ayuntamiento (Town Hall)
4 Tourist Office
6 Casa de la Aduana
7 Telephones
10 Museo Arqueológico
14 Bicistar
15 Tip Top Lavandería
16 Iglesia de San Francisco & Ermita de San Juan
19 Iglesia de Nuestra Señora de la Peña de Francia
20 Train to Loro Parque; Bus to Bananera El Guanche
21 Jamm Travel (Bike Hire)
22 Viajes Insular (American Express)
23 The Book Shop
24 Canarisub
27 Casa de los Iriarte
29 Police Station
30 Castillo de San Felipe
31 Post Office
32 Scott Bike Center
33 Bus Station
37 Risco Belle Aquatic Gardens
38 Grand Hotel Taoro
39 El Cardumen
40 Bicicletas Melian

ATLANTIC OCEAN

TENERIFE

rocks and emerald green pools, makes a pleasant alternative to the town's black-sand beaches. It opens 10 am to 5 pm daily and admission costs 350 ptas. César Manrique also contributed to the design of the gardens that extend the length of **Playa Jardín**, the town's longest beach.

In the centre is the 17th-century **Iglesia de Nuestra Señora de la Peña de Francia**. The church has a fine mudéjar ceiling and some paintings by Luis de la Cruz in the retablo of the Capilla del Evangelio side-chapel.

On Plaza de Europa is the **Casa de Miranda**, dating from 1730 and now a restaurant (see Places to Eat later), while down narrow Calle de las Lonjas is the **Casa de la Aduana**, the customs house founded in 1620.

Another noteworthy old mansion is the **Casa de los Iriarte**, where this family of writers and artists had their family home. The laurels in the nearby **Plaza del Charco** were brought from Cuba in 1852. A block east brings you to the **Iglesia de San Francisco**, built onto the smaller **Ermita de San Juan**, constructed in 1599 and the town's oldest structure.

On Calle Lomo, just west of Plaza del Charco, the **Museo Arqueológico** has a modest collection of Guanche artefacts and mummies and some interesting early maps. It opens 10 am to 1 pm and 5 to 9 pm, Tuesday to Saturday, and 10 am to 1 pm on Sunday.

At the western edge of town, a little 17th-century fort known as the **Castillo de San Felipe** stands watch over Playa Jardín. It opens only for special exhibitions.

South of the city spreads the majesty of **Parque Taoro**, dominated by the grand old Grand Hotel Taoro – part of which now houses a casino. The Risco Bello Aquatic Gardens, an artificial tropical playground, which is situated in the heart of the park.

A good place for views of the town is the **Mirador de la Paz**, where you can enjoy a drink in one of the square's several bars. Along the road to La Orotava is the 200-year-old **Jardín Botánico**, open 9 am to 6 pm daily.

Loro Parque You can't fail to hear about saturation-marketed Loro Parque, 'Parrot Park' – or El 'Must' de las Canarias, as it calls itself – not least because every single litter bin in town bears its advertisement. Unless you object in principle to wild animals in captivity, including performing seals, dolphins and – oh yes – parrots on bicycles, it's really rather impressive. In addition to what is claimed to be the world's largest collection of parrots, there are sharks, manta rays and all sorts of other sealife in the aquarium, gorillas, crocodiles, chimps, tigers, flamingos, penguins – and even a bat cave.

It opens 8.30 am to 5 pm. Admission costs a hefty 2900 ptas. A free yellow train runs every 20 minutes from Avenida de Venezuela. Otherwise, it's about a five-minute drive west of town.

Bananera El Guanche At this functioning banana plantation, you can learn about the history of the banana trade plus everything you might want to know about bananas and their cultivation. The place is also bursting with all sorts of other exotic flora.

It's about 2km south-east of the centre on the road leading to the TF-5 motorway and La Orotava. A free bus runs every half-hour from Avenida de Venezuela. It opens 9 am to 6 pm and admission costs 1000 ptas.

Activities

Several places offer diving. Try Canarisub (☎ 922 38 30 07), Calle Esquivel 8, or Atlantik (☎ 922 36 28 01), based at the Hotel Maritim, about 2 km west of the centre.

El Cardumen (☎ 922 36 84 68), Avenida Melchor Luz 3, is a one-stop centre for a whole range of outdoor activities, including diving, climbing, canyon descending, parapente, walking and caving.

Scott Bike Center (☎ 922 37 60 81), which is located just north of the bus station on Calle Mazaroco, arranges one-day bicycle trips for 6800 ptas. The price includes transport to/from the start and finish of the ride, picnic and equipment hire.

TENERIFE

Organised Tours

Several travel agents organise day tours of the island and to nearby La Gomera.

Special Events

Puerto de la Cruz is big on fiestas. In February, the town pitches into Carnaval with a gusto approaching Santa Cruz's. On 3 May, crosses and chapels are decorated with flowers in a simultaneous celebration of the city's foundation and the Exaltation of the Cross. On the eve of the Saint's day of San Juan, grafted on to the pre-Christian celebration of midsummer's day, bonfires light the sky and, in a throwback to Guanche times, goats are driven for a dip in the sea off Playa Jardín. The town's main celebrations are in July, when there's a whole program of events, while the most rumbustious celebration, at least for the kids, is the Fiesta de Los Cacharros (see the boxed text 'Any Old Iron').

Places to Stay

Highly recommended *Pensión Rosa Mary* (☎ *922 38 32 53, Calle San Felipe 14)* is a congenial, immaculately kept little place. Its doubles (no singles) with bathroom cost 4000 ptas; it's often full.

Pensión La Platanera (☎ *922 38 41 57, Calle Blanco 29)* is a rather charmless, modern place but its rooms (4700 ptas) are clean, comfortable and have a bathroom.

Nearby, *Pensión Loly* (☎ *922 38 36 93, Calle de La Sala 4)* has simple doubles for 2500 ptas.

Around the Museo Arqueológico, in a quiet little barrio largely devoid of tourist trappings, is *Pensión Los Geranios* (☎ *922 38 28 10, Calle del Lomo 14)*. Doubles with shower cost 3800 ptas.

Not far up the road, *Hotel Alfomar* (☎/*fax 922 38 06 82, Calle Peñita 6)* has bargain singles/doubles with bathroom for 2200/3800 ptas (3500/5000 ptas in winter).

For a bit of tasteful elegance you can't go past two of the longest-established hotels in the town, both mid-range price and warmly recommended. *Hotel Monopol* (☎ *922 38 46 11, fax 922 37 03 10,* e *monopol@ interbook.net, Calle Quintana 15)* dates

Any Old Iron

If you happen to be in Puerto de la Cruz around sunset on 29 October, you'll think the tinkers have come to town.

All over the pueblo (and especially up and down Plaza del Charco) there's a clattering and a clanging as children rush through the streets, dragging behind them a string of old pots, kettles, pans, car spares, tin cans – just about anything metal that will make a racket.

It is the day of San Andrés (St Andrew) and the *Fiesta de Los Cacharros* (literally, the pots and pans feast) when, traditionally, the wine cellars were opened up and the new wine released.

Don't get the connection? Nor do we. It must have been hell if your hangover had already started to kick in. But nowadays, it's enormous fun if you're (feeling) young and frisky....

from 1742 and has been run as a hotel by the same family for three generations. The palm-fronded patio skirted by tiered wooden balconies is a tranquil haven. There's a pool and rooms, which start at between 5300 ptas and 7300 ptas according to the season, are excellent value.

There's mature woodwork everywhere at equally delightful *Hotel Marquesa* (☎ *922 38 31 51)*, near-neighbour at No 11, where rooms start at 5500/8000 ptas.

Places to Eat

There is an infinite number of uninspiring pizzerias and international food outlets at the eastern end of town around Avenida del Generalísimo. Somewhere different, though still very much in the tourist belt, is *El Pescado* at the corner of Avenida Venezuela and Calle Uruguay, where the fish and seafood are fresher than the service.

El Limón, at the junction of Calles Esquivel and B Miranda, is vegetarian, with great 'burgers', soups and fruit juices. Another tasty vegetarian place is *Coco Rico* run by a friendly German-Indian couple. They specialise in exotic pancakes and soulfood (the Indian *dhosas* bring tears to

TENERIFE

the eyes – of sheer pleasure, not because they're fiery). While one dish (around 600 ptas) doesn't constitute a meal, it makes a delightful snack. It closes at the weekend.

At **Bar-Cafeteria Las Portelas** *(Calle Cupido)* you can have a huge portion of *papas arrugadas y mojo picón* (wrinkly potatoes served with salsa) for 600 ptas and they do well-filled *bocadillos* (French-bread sandwiches) for between 175 ptas and 225 ptas. They advertise Canarian breakfasts, as if in defiance of the full-English-breakfast invasion.

Tapas Arcón *(Calle Blanco 8)* is another unassuming place which serves local grub in two sizes of traditional earthenware pot, so you know exactly how much you'll be getting.

There are a number of decent enough restaurants on pedestrianised Calle Lomo. Two where you can tuck into quality Canarian and Spanish cuisine are **La Rosa di Bari** at No 23 and excellent **La Papaya** *(☎ 922 38 28 11)* at No 10, go right through to their pretty rear patio.

More than two centuries old, **Casa de Miranda** *(Plaza de Europa)* enjoys low, wooden-beamed ceilings and tasteful period decor. For such an ambience, its mains, mostly between 1200 ptas and 1600 ptas, represent good value.

Entertainment
The bulk of the noisier bars and discos are clustered along and around Avenida del Generalísimo. Take your pick!

Getting There & Away
The bus station is on Calle del Pozo in the west of town. There are frequent departures for Santa Cruz (535 ptas, about 45 minutes). No 103 is direct while No 102 (signed, misleadingly, *directo* and *expreso*) calls by Tenerife Norte airport and La Laguna. Nos 325, 354 and 363 offer a regular service to Icod de los Vinos. No 340 passes by both island airports (1175 ptas to Tenerife Sur) four times daily and No 343 also has four daily services to Playa de las Américas. A number of routes pass through La Orotava.

A taxi to Tenerife Sur airport costs about 11,600 ptas – the equivalent, more or less, of three days' car hire! A taxi to Tenerife Norte costs around 3200 ptas.

Getting Around
There are taxi stands in Plaza del Charco and beside the bus station.

You can hire bicycles at Bicicletas Melian (☎ 922 38 29 17), Centro Comercial Ucanca, Avenida José del Campo Llarena. Also, at Jamm Travel (☎ 922 38 06 09), Avenida del Generalísimo 22, Bicistar (☎ 922 37 34 49) and Scott Bike Center (see Activities earlier).

AROUND PUERTO DE LA CRUZ
La Orotava
postcode 38300 • pop 38,000
• elevation 400m
La Orotava, 8km inland from Puerto de la Cruz, is perhaps the prettiest town on the island, outshining La Laguna, its only rival. It gives its name to the prosperous valley that spreads out to the west, and the noble mansions that grace the old centre of town seem a reflection of that wealth. The valley was settled soon after the Spanish conquest and by the 16th-century well-to-do families from La Laguna began building churches and convents, and later their own homes, in this town. The old quarter is about a five-minute walk uphill west from the bus station.

Information The tourist office (☎ 922 32 30 41) at Calle Carrera Escultor Estévez 2 opens 8.30 am to 6 pm (closed 9.30 to 10 am for breakfast – honest!) on weekdays. It sells a town map for 100 ptas. More useful if you're interested in exploring the historic buildings is *Villa de la Orotava: Street-Plan and Historic-Artistic Guide* (300 ptas), a map with multilingual descriptions which is also on sale here.

The post office is on Plaza Casañas, opposite Iglesia de la Concepción.

Things to See Congratulations to the town. Visited by only several thousand of the millions of tourists who flock to the island each year, its street and monument signing is exemplary.

TENERIFE

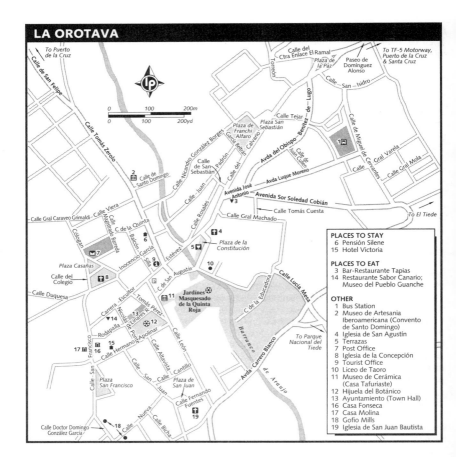

LA OROTAVA

PLACES TO STAY
6 Pensión Silene
15 Hotel Victoria

PLACES TO EAT
3 Bar-Restaurante Tapias
14 Restaurante Sabor Canario;
   Museo del Pueblo Guanche

OTHER
1 Bus Station
2 Museo de Artesanía
   Iberoamericana (Convento
   de Santo Domingo)
4 Iglesia de San Agustín
5 Terrazas
7 Post Office
8 Iglesia de la Concepción
9 Tourist Office
10 Liceo de Taoro
11 Museo de Cerámica
   (Casa Tafuriaste)
12 Hijuela del Botánico
13 Ayuntamiento (Town Hall)
16 Casa Molina
17 Casa Molina
18 Gofio Mills
19 Iglesia de San Juan Bautista

Wood is the most interesting architectural element, whether shaped into fine artesonado church ceilings or as an elegant balcony appended to a 17th- or 18th-century mansion.

The **Iglesia de la Concepción** is the Canaries' most notable contribution to baroque architecture. Behind it, Calle del Colegio climbs south to become Calle San Francisco, which is lined by impressive 17th- and 18th-century mansions.

Of the so-called Doce Casas (Twelve Houses), **Casa Fonseca** (aka Casa de los Balcones), built 1632, is perhaps the most outstanding. It boasts long and splendidly worked teak balconies and inside looks onto a leafy patio. It opens 8.30 am to 6.30 pm, Monday to Saturday, and 8.30 am to 1 pm on Sunday. Across the road is the **Casa Molina** (aka Casa del Turista), built 1590, open 9 am to 7 pm weekdays and 9 am to 2 pm on Saturday. In both places you can see (and buy) Canarian handicrafts.

Heading up and south, the street name changes to Calle Doctor Domingo González García. On the eastern side is a series of 17th- and 18th-century water-driven mills, once used to make *gofio* (a roasted mixture of wheat, maize or barley).

To the east, on Calle Fernando Fuentes, is the 18th-century **Iglesia de San Juan Bautista**, with an outstanding artesonado ceiling. Back towards the centre the **Iglesia de San Agustín**, beside Plaza de la Constitución, also boasts a fine carved wooden ceiling.

It's worth having a drink on the patio of the **Liceo de Taoro**, a private club, set back from this shady square. On top of the bill, you'll pay 200 ptas for day membership – a worthwhile investment for a squint at the sumptuous interior. Beside it, the lovely **Jardines Marquesado de la Quinta Roja**, open 8 am to 9 pm daily, cascade down the hillside. Admission costs 350 ptas. Garden lovers will also enjoy a stroll around the **Hijuela del Botánico**, open 9 am to 2 pm weekdays; admission is free.

Downhill on Calle Tomás Zerolo, are the **Iglesia** and former Convento de Santo Domingo. The latter now houses the **Museo de Artesanía Iberoamericana**, exhibiting handicrafts from Spain and Latin America. It opens 9.30 am to 6 pm Monday to Saturday. Admission costs 350 ptas.

If you have a passion for pots, visit the **Museo de Cerámica** in the restored 17th-century Casa Tafuriaste, Calle León 3. It opens 10 am to 6 pm, Monday to Saturday, and admission costs 300 ptas.

Special Events Corpus Cristi is celebrated with particular gusto in La Orotava. Tonnes of volcanic earth, flowers, branches and sand are hauled into the centre (especially around the 19th-century town hall) to create extraordinary 'carpets' in the streets and plazas.

Places to Stay & Eat Accommodation is thin on the ground.

You could try *Pensión Silene* (☎ 922 33 01 99, *Calle Tomás Zerolo 9*), which has singles/doubles with bathroom for 4500/7000 ptas.

At the top end, delightful *Hotel Victoria* (☎ 922 33 16 83, fax 922 32 05 19, e *hotel.victoria@teneriffa.com, Calle Hermano Apolinar 8*), is in an attractive refurbished 300-year-old Canarian mansion. Its 14 double rooms cost from 12,800/

16,000 ptas for single/double occupancy (including breakfast).

Restaurante Sabor Canario (Calle Carrera Escultor Estévez 17) is part of the Museo del Pueblo Guanche, (more a showcase for handicrafts than a museum). The restaurant is enticing enough though, especially if you get a seat in the patio. For quality, visit Hotel Victoria (see above) and its altogether more impressive patio. Mains cost between 1800 ptas and 2300 ptas. It closes Sunday evening and Monday.

For a cheap snack or meal, the more prosaic *Bar-Restaurante Tapias (Avenida José Antonio 6)* might be the go.

The *terrazas* that occupy most of Plaza de la Constitución are an agreeable spot to take the weight off your feet and enjoy a drink.

Getting There & Away Bus Nos 101, 345 and 352 come up from Puerto de la Cruz while Nos 101, 107 and 108 connect with Santa Cruz via La Laguna.

THE NORTH-WEST
Icod de los Vinos
postcode 38430 • pop 23,100

The main attraction in this wine-belt town is its weird tree, the **Drago Milenario**, reputedly a thousand years old. The oldest 'dragon tree' in the islands (see the boxed text 'The Tree with a Long, Shady Past' in the Facts about the Islands chapter) looks from a distance like a lopsided umbrella. Behind a high wall, it costs an extortionate 500 ptas to get up close, which you can do between 10 am and 7 pm (to 6 pm on Sunday) daily. In fact, for the best photos – and all for free – look across to it from the western side of the adjacent shady square.

On this square, **Iglesia de San Marcos** is worth a look. Its sober renaissance exterior hides a superb pine artesonado ceiling and silver high-altar. A few steps away, **Plaza de la Constitución** (aka Plaza de la Pila) is flanked by some fine old Canarian houses. The streets around here, forming the kernel of the old town, are worth a wander. From the plaza, head 200m up Calle San Antonio and get right up close – for free – to another venerable dragon tree, the **Drago Chico**.

TENERIFE

If you like butterflies, you might want to visit the **Mariposario del Drago**, a tropical garden aflutter with *mariposas* (butterflies). It opens 9 am to 6 pm daily. Admission costs 800 ptas (children 400 ptas). On the floor below, there's a continuous projection of the captivating, award-winning French film, *Microcosmos* (one hour 10 minutes long), showing, in giant close-up, life from an insect's perspective. The movie alone almost justifies the admission cost.

A few kilometres outside town, you can have a swim at the little beach tacked to the fishing village of **Playa de San Marcos** (bus No 362, hourly from Icod).

Places to Eat At Avenida de las Canarias 1, *Restaurante Carmen* is not a bad choice. Afterwards, try the *bodegas* (old-style wine bars) on Plaza de la Constitución, where you can sample Icod's wines, particularly the Malvasía, which flourishes in the local volcanic soil.

Getting There & Away Bus Nos 106, 107 and 108 go to Santa Cruz, Nos 354 and 363 head for Puerto de la Cruz and No 460 to Playa de las Américas.

Garachico
postcode 38450 • pop 5900
It is a real pleasure to simply wander the uneven streets and admire the traditional houses in this whitewashed fishing hamlet. They deserve special admiration, as Garachico has not been the luckiest town. Founded by Genoese merchants who had accompanied and to some extent bankrolled the conquistadors, Garachico soon developed into a centre of sugar production.

Its port was for a while the busiest on the island, but the 17th century brought a series of disasters which all but finished the place off. The long-suffering inhabitants were assailed by epidemics, freak storms that destroyed countless ships, fires, and finally, in 1706, a major volcanic eruption which buried the town in lava and destroyed the port. In 1905 another earthquake reminded the villagers of the ever-present dangers posed by nature.

Information There's a small tourist office (☎ 922 13 34 61), Calle Estéban de Ponte 5, open 10 am to 3 pm, Monday to Friday.

Things to See A stout little portside fort with curious whitewashed turrets, the **Fortaleza de San Miguel** was erected in the 16th century to protect Garachico from pirates. It was one of the few survivors of the 1706 eruption.

The central plaza is a pleasant place to hang around for late afternoon aperitifs and the **Iglesia de San Francisco** has a fine mudéjar ceiling.

The **Museo de Arte**, on Plaza Santo Domingo, is a modern art collection housed in what was a Dominican monastery. It opens 9 am to 1 pm and 4 to 7 pm daily. Admission costs 100 ptas.

For DIYers who need their holiday fix, there's also a small **Museo de Carpintería Antigua** (traditional carpentry museum) at Avenida República de Venezuela 17 on the seafront. It opens 9 am to 9 pm daily. Admission costs 200 ptas.

Activities The owners of El Jardín (see Places to Stay & Eat later) run diving courses.

Special Events The Romería de San Roque, held in August (the dates change), is the village's biggest yearly festival and worth being in town for.

Places to Stay & Eat Garachico has no truly budget accommodation.

An agreeably rambling building with huge rooms, *El Jardín* (☎/fax 922 83 02 45, e argonaut@arrakis.es, Calle Estéban de Ponte 8) is just behind the waterfront. It also has a pizzeria and diving school. They have five rooms with washbasin for 4000 ptas to 5000 ptas – and a very pleasant one with shower at 6000 ptas.

A stylish option is *Hotel San Roque* (☎ 922 13 34 35, fax 922 13 34 06) on the same street at No 32. The core of this elegant place dates from the 18th century. Singles/double occupancy costs from 18,000/ 26,000 ptas. This is something of a surprise

TENERIFE

packet: the beautiful rooms are equipped with TV, videos, CDs and minibar, and the use of the pool, sauna, tennis court, mountain bikes, fishing rods – and breakfast – is included in the price.

Pretty much the whole waterfront street, the Avenida Tomé Cano, is taken up with restaurants whose speciality, unsurprisingly, is fish. You can eat well for about 1500 ptas.

Getting There & Away Bus No 363 from Buenavista del Norte passes through en route to Puerto de la Cruz, as does the less frequent No 107 to Santa Cruz.

El Tanque
About 10 minutes west of Icod, the village of El Tanque is home to the Camello Center (☎ 922 13 61 91). For 1000 ptas (per half-hour ride), these people will dress you up as an 'Arab', lead you around for a few kilometres on a camel (with 50 other similarly attired tourists), stick you on a donkey as a follow-up and then pump 'traditional Arabian tea' down your throat in an 'authentic Arabian tent'. Hmm...

Buenavista del Norte & Punta de Teno
Buenavista, the most north-westerly village on the island, has little to recommend it. But 10km farther west is Punta de Teno, a startling spit of volcanic rock leaning out into the ocean. Behind it rise pale green, cactus-dotted mountains. You can see La Gomera from here and on a good day, sunset is a treat. If you're driving, note that in bad weather the road is prone to mud falls from the cliffs above, and therefore can be quite dangerous.

Bus No 107 goes to Santa Cruz from Buenavista. More frequent is No 363 to Puerto de la Cruz via Icod and Garachico. You need your own transport to get to Punta de Teno.

PARQUE NACIONAL DEL TEIDE
This national park attracts over 3.5 million visitors per year. Declared a national park in 1954, it was the third to be established in Spain. It covers the area once encompassed

by an enormous prehistoric volcano, measuring 45km in circumference and 17km in diameter, which collapsed in on itself. Spread over 18,990 hectares, Teide is Spain's fifth-largest national park.

In the north rises the great cone of the Pico del Teide, at 3718m the highest mountain in all Spain. To the south are the *cañadas*, a series of plains stretching away inside the old crater from the foot of Teide.

Most of the park lies above 2000m and presents a striking sight. Weird basalt, pumice and obsidian rock formations emerge from the sandy plains. A menacing black lava flow frozen in time reaches all the way down to the only road that crosses the park. The cable-car *(teleférico)* ride up to the top of the mountain is an experience in itself – an ascent of some 1200m in eight minutes!

Information
There are two park visitor centres. The main one at El Portillo opens 9 am to 4 pm daily. It has an excellent display on volcanoes and the park's animal and plant life. There's also an equally informative 14-minute video, 'The Sleeping Volcano', in a choice of five languages, including English. Outside, take time to browse around the Jardín Bótanico, where typical examples of park vegetation thrive.

The smaller centre at Cañada Blanca specialises in the history of the park and observes the same opening hours.

All telephone enquiries are via the national park's office in Santa Cruz (☎ 922 29 01 29).

Approaches to the Park
Four roads approach the park. Of these, the TF-24 on the northern side of the island ascends from La Laguna via La Esperanza and is by far the prettiest. It joins the TF-21 from Puerto de la Cruz and La Orotava at El Portillo, which has a couple of bar/restaurants. Continuing westwards for a further 14km of bizarre volcanic landscape, you reach the base of the cable-car.

A plan to control vehicle access will probably come into effect in mid-2001.

TENERIFE

While continuing to allow unimpeded through traffic, the idea is to establish a number of short-term car parks, from where a guide will lead groups of visitors. It will also be possible to leave your vehicle in designated sites outside the park limits and take a guided bus tour.

Pico del Teide

You have a couple of choices on how to get up close to the top of the mountain. Nearly everyone takes the cable-car, but it is also possible to hike up (see Walking later).

The cable-car (☎ 922 53 37 20) takes 8 minutes to whisk you up from 2356m to 3555m – about 200m short of the lip of the crater at the very summit. The return trip costs 3000 ptas and a one-way ticket costs 1700 ptas (if you plan to hike the other way). Get there early. The cabins, which hold around 35 passengers, start rolling at 9 am and you need to arrive before the tour buses pull in. At peak times you can be stuck in a queue for up to two hours. The last cabin down is at 5 pm.

Once at **La Rambleta**, the top, you can make two brief out-and-back walks or just sit and marvel. You could be on a stairway to heaven. If the atmosphere's clear below, the wrap-around views are soul stirring, with the islands of La Gomera, El Hierro, La Palma and Gran Canaria all peeking up from the Atlantic. If not, all you'll see beneath you is an airline porthole vista of cotton-wool cloud and more bloody cloud.

The height and rapid change of altitude can make you feel quite chilly on even the hottest day down below, so take a sweater.

Warning Oxygen is a little short up here, so anyone with cardiovascular or pulmonary problems should refrain from going up.

Roques de García

A few kilometres south of the peak, a bizarre set of rocks pokes up in an unlikely fashion from the plains around the parador hotel. Known as the Roques de García, they are the result of erosion on old volcanic dikes. The hard rock of the dikes has been bared while surrounding earth and rock has

been gradually swept away. The weirdest of the rocks, the Roque Cinchado, is wearing away faster at the base than above, and one of these days is destined to topple over (so maybe you shouldn't get up too close!). Spreading out to the west are the bald plains of the Llano de Ucanca. The road out to Los Cristianos is to the south-west and the road to Santiago del Teide is in the north-west.

Pico Viejo

The 'old peak' is the last of Tenerife's volcanoes to have erupted on the grand scale. In 1798, a 700m gash split open its south-western flank. Today, you can clearly see where fragments of magma shot over 1000m into the air and fell pell-mell. Torrents of lava gushed from a secondary, lower wound to congeal on the slopes. To this day, not a blade of grass or a stain of lichen has recolonised their arid course.

Walking

Only a small proportion of Teide's 3.5 million visitors venture far from the cable-car and the road that slices through the park. It's well-worth joining this select minority and it's quite possible even if you haven't got your own wheels.

Guided Walks Park rangers guide walks in both Spanish and English. The pace is gentle and there are frequent information pauses. Even though you'll huff and puff rather more than usual because of the high altitude, they're suitable for anyone of reasonable fitness (including children aged over 10).

Groups leave at 9.15 am and 1.30 pm daily from the El Portillo visitor centre and at 9.30 am and 1 pm from the Cañada Blanca centre.

Since each walk normally has a maximum of 10 participants, it's essential to ring and reserve a place the day before. Call ☎ 922 29 01 29.

Self-Guided Walks The general park brochure lists 12 walks, ranging in length from 600m to 15km, some of which are signed, and has a small and fairly useless map. Each walk is graded according to its level of difficulty (ranging from 'low' – the most frequent – to 'extreme'!). You're not allowed to stray from the marked trails, a sensible restriction in an environment where every tuft of plant life has to fight for survival.

Of these, among the most frequented is the 15km **Las Cañadas** day walk between the two visitors centres; longish, yes, but almost entirely on the flat. Pretty, it ain't. But the stark evidence of the activity of primeval volcanoes – nothing but the toughest grasses now grow – is deeply impressive. Set out along the broad track which begins just across the road from the El Portillo visitor centre. In a little over five minutes, cross a barrier which heralds the entrance to the park, and you're away. Within half an hour, you're amid whorls, hanks and twists of lava, looking like melted chocolate that might have congealed only yesterday. Allow four to five hours and remember to take plenty of water with you.

If you have a vehicle, drive it to the far end of the walk and take the morning bus (see Getting There & Away later) back to the start. This way, you're not dependent upon catching the afternoon bus back to your vehicle and can time the walk the way you want to.

You don't have to be a masochist to enjoy the challenge of walking from road level up to **La Rambleta** at the top of the cable-car, followed by a zoom down in the cabin lift. Get off the bus (ask the driver to stop for you) or leave your car at the small roadside parking area (signed 'Montaña Blanca' and 'Refugio de Altavista') 8km south of El Portillo visitor centre and set off along the jeep track that leads uphill. En route, you can make a short (half-hour maximum) almost level detour along a clear path to the rounded summit of Montaña Blanca (2750m), from where there are splendid views of Las Cañadas and the sierra beyond. Alternatively, make the Montaña Blanca your more modest goal for the day and head back down again (about 2½ hours, round trip).

For the full ascent to La Rambleta, allow

about four hours. And, of course, at the risk of stating the startlingly obvious, for an easier option, take the cable-car up and do the route in reverse!

Bagging the Summit Even though the steep there-and-back walk between the top of the cable-car and the summit takes only around 20 minutes, it isn't easy. The difficulty resides not in the climb but in the hoops you have to jump through before you set out.

There's a permit scheme in force that restricts the number of visitors who can pass above the barrier, and into the fragile, unique ecosystem fighting to survive in such inauspicious conditions for sustaining life, to 50 at any one time.

That's fair enough and understandable. But you can't just pick one up from the visitor centre. You need to pass by the national park's Servicio de Uso Público office (☎ 922 29 01 29) in Santa Cruz. On the 4th floor of Calle Emilio Calzadilla 5, it observes bureaucrats' hours: 9 am to 2 pm, Monday to Friday. Take along a photocopy of the personal details pages of your passport or ID. Permits, which are free, specify both the date and the two-hour window during which you're allowed beyond the *cordon sanitaire*. In addition to the permit, take your passport or ID with you on the walk since you'll probably be asked to produce it.

And enjoy the view – you'll have deserved it!

Places to Stay & Eat
Camping is not allowed in the park. The only place to stay is the *Parador de Cañadas del Teide (☎/fax 922 38 64 15)*, where singles/doubles cost from 12,400/15,500 ptas. There's also a huddle of restaurants a couple of kilometres north of the El Portillo visitor centre.

Getting There & Away
Scandalously, there's only one bus per day to the park from each side of the island. No 348 leaves Puerto de la Cruz at 9.15 am daily for the parador. No 342 simultaneously sets off for El Portillo from Playa de

TENERIFE

las Américas, calling by Los Cristianos 15 minutes later. Both call by the cable-car and will stop at intermediate points if you ask.

The return No 342 leaves El Portillo at 3.15 pm, calling by the cable-car at 3.40 pm. No 348 sets off from the parador at 4 pm.

And that, as far as public transport goes, is it. Of the park's 3.5 million visitors annually, the merest fraction arrive by bus; the remainder come in courtesy of their tour company's coach, by hired car or by taxi. Amid all the worthy lamenting of the deterioration of the park's environment, a few more buses and – we'd argue – a modest toll for private and hired vehicles would play their part in reducing the degradation.

THE WEST COAST
Santiago del Teide

There's not much to this little town but you will probably pass through it whether you use the buses or have your own transport. Five kilometres south on a branch road is the sleepy hamlet of **Arguayo**. It's home to the Centro Alfarero (pottery centre) and Museo Etnográfico 'Cha Domitila' – big words for what is essentially a roomful of traditional pots with modern reproductions, fired on the premises, for sale at inflated prices. Admission is free.

There are buses to Santiago from Puerto de la Cruz, Playa de las Américas, and Icod de los Vinos.

Masca

Six kilometres north-west of Santiago lies a true surprise. The narrow road rises steeply to a high ridge, only to then cascade down the other side into the Barranco de Masca in a series of tight switchbacks. The ride alone is a spectacle and the little farming village is charming. Old stone-houses look out across the palm-trees and the ravine walls to the Atlantic Ocean. A couple of restaurants and bars have opened up in strategic bits of the town so that the growing stream of tourists can admire the wonderful views in comfort.

Just outside town on the road to Santiago is a well-placed *terraza*. With views right down the gorge to the ocean, this must be one of the best seats for sunset on the island.

But Masca is no secret. Try to get there early in the morning before the tour buses disgorge their invading hordes.

For the Fiesta de la Consolación in the first week of December, many of the villagers wear traditional dress and bring out their timples (a string instrument resembling a ukelele) and other instruments for an evening of Canarian music.

A popular but demanding trek is down Barranco de Masca to the sea. Allow six hours hiking there and back or do it the smart way – ring the Nashira Uno office (see the next section) the day before and reserve a place on the 3.30 pm boat from the beach to Los Gigantes (1500 ptas).

There are two No 355 buses per day to/from Santiago del Teide.

Los Gigantes & Puerto de Santiago
postcode 38383 • pop 5600

The Acantilados de los Gigantes (Cliffs of the Giants) are sheer rock walls which plunge into the ocean. Across the small bight lies the little port and resort town of Los Gigantes and, next to it, Puerto de Santiago.

Both live on tourism, although on a much more modest scale than the Playa de las Américas phenomenon. Of the two settlements, Los Gigantes is easily the more pleasant (though Puerto de Santiago has a black-sand beach, Playa de la Arena, in its favour).

Information The tourist office for the two resorts (☎ 922 86 03 48), Avenida Marítima 36–37, is on the coast at Playa de la Arena, Puerto de Santiago.

Activities Of all the dive sites around the island, those off Los Gigantes, sheltered by the giant cliffs, lose fewest days each year through high winds. Take your pick from three diving centres beside the port. Los Gigantes Diving Centre (☎/fax 922 86 04 31, @ neville@intercom.es) has native English-speaking instructors and can arrange accommodation – for all-comers, not just visitors with webbed feet.

For boat trips, the launch Nashira Uno

How Tenerife Missed the Evolutionary Boat

The Galápagos islands, at the other end of the world, far off the Pacific coast of South America, are famous for having inspired Charles Darwin's theory of evolution.

Less well-known is that the first port of call for Darwin's ship, the Beagle, was to have been Tenerife. But, just as the crew were preparing to land, the island authorities told them they would have to spend a couple of weeks in quarantine. So the captain turned the nose of his boat and headed for the deep Atlantic.

Who knows? Had they landed, Tenerife's wealth of endemic plants, trees and animals, evolved over thousands of millennia in this island microcosm, might well have contributed to the development of Darwin's ideas. As he wrote regretfully in his journal, 'We have just left perhaps one of the most interesting places in the world, just at the moment when we were near enough for every object to create, without satisfying, our utmost curiosity'.

---

has daily whale- and dolphin-watching sailings (3000/4000 ptas for two/three hours). Call ☎ 922 86 19 18 or visit the office opposite Supermercado Los Gigantes. The sister boat, Feo, does half- and full-day deep-sea fishing trips (6000 ptas if you fish, 3000 ptas for spectators). For the really adventurous they organise parascending (4500 ptas for 12 exhilarating minutes being towed up high behind a motor boat).

Flipper Uno, a replica of an 18th-century galleon, does three-hour sailings twice daily (3000 ptas).

Places to Stay & Eat Accommodation possibilities here are largely limited to apartments. A particularly attractive option is *Aparthotel Poblado Marinero* (☎ 922 86 09 66, fax 922 86 06 79), which respects traditional building style and lies right on Los Gigantes port. Prices vary substantially according to season, beginning at 9000 ptas for twins and 13,000 ptas for apartments that can accommodate up to six.

Eating at one of the restaurants down by the port is also an enjoyable affair.

Getting There & Away Frequent buses No 473 go to Playa de las Américas and Los Cristianios. Up to six No 325 buses daily connect with Puerto de la Cruz.

Barranco del Infierno

From the village of Adeje, you can hike up one of the island's most spectacular ravines – the Barranco del Infierno (Hell's Gorge). A narrow path and steps make the 6km trek (there and back) possible for anyone of even average fitness – reckon on about a three-hour round trip. The deeper you get into the gorge, the higher its walls soar above you as they close in. On the way are a couple of pools in which you can dunk yourself and the end of the path is marked by a waterfall, which may be staunched to a mere trickle after a long dry period.

It's a popular trail so make an early start both to avoid the midday heat and to have the smug satisfaction of heading jauntily back down while the majority are still toiling up the valley.

Bus Nos 416 and 473 run regularly between Adeje and Playa de las Américas.

LOS CRISTIANOS, PLAYA DE LAS AMÉRICAS & COSTA ADEJE
postcode 38650 • pop around 200,000

What can you say about a place that lives entirely off its reputation as a year-round sun and fun scene? The beaches, although all artificial, are nice enough. Playa de las Américas is an uninterrupted stream of hotel-apartments, pubs, bars, discos, kitsch souvenir shops, and lots of bright lights and noise. Just what you'd expect and, taken in the right spirit, a good laugh – for a while anyway. Flanking it on either side, Los Cristianos and Costa Adeje are quieter. Los Cristianos manages to retain the merest hint

TENERIFE

The Luck of the Irish

On 12 January 1809, Leopoldo O'Donnell saw the light of day in Santa Cruz de Tenerife. Strange name for a Spaniard, let alone a Canario? Well, yes. Little Leopoldo was a descendant of the O'Donnell family, one of many Irish clans which fled the Emerald Isle after the disaster of the Battle of the Boyne back in 1690 (the street name José Murphy is a little hard to swallow, O'Shanahan is another good Canario name and the main street in La Palma's capital, Santa Cruz, is called Calle O'Daly).

Perhaps it was a bit of the Blarney and some fighting Irish spirit which set Leopoldo on the road of the soldier-politician. He, like just about anyone else hoping to make a mark in the Spanish world in those days, headed for the mainland just as soon as he could. A staunch conservative and partisan of Queen Isabel II, he played a distinguished role in the First Carlist War (1833–9), after which he ended up exiled in France. However, O'Donnell was destined to have more comebacks than Lazarus, and in 1843 he helped stage a coup to oust the government of General Baldomero Espartero. O'Donnell's prize was the captaincy-general of Cuba, which he held from 1844 to 1848.

He was soon back in Madrid, and in 1854 staged yet another revolt from which he emerged as minister for war. Heading the government again was Espartero, but O'Donnell eased him out two years later and became prime minister himself. During his two tenures, Spain remained uncharacteristically stable and O'Donnell made a name for himself in the war in Morocco, eventually receiving the title Duque de Tetuán.

After a break from leadership, he again returned to head the government in 1865–6 before being booted out by Queen Isabel, despite his longstanding support for her. She may well have regretted her decision to replace him, as he was one of her most faithful supporters; O'Donnell saw fit to leave the country, and died the following year in Biarritz in the French Basque Country. Isabel lost her throne a year later.

of an authentic local identity – but only just – while Costa Adeje, no less a concrete jungle than Playa de las Américas, seeks to create a separate identity that's more in the mind of local planners than anything on the ground.

Orientation
The desiccated Barranco del Rey river bed matters, if only in local political terms. It marks the 'frontier' between Costa Adeje, these days trying its hardest to distance itself from Playa de Las Américas' rock-bottom public image and especially, from the infamous Las Verónicas booze and butties complex with its seedy, violent reputation.

But Costa Adeje still has a good way to go. Playa de Torviscas, for example, on its northern side, boasts gems such as Mean Gene's Burgers and the Winking Frog pub, serving 'Frog Brekky' and 'Mighty Toad' lunches.

The tourist office map of Playa de las Américas indicates hotels and apartments, not streets, to help you navigate. It has to be this way; the place has developed so rapidly that most streets have no name – and those that do often have no plaque.

Information
Tourist Offices There are as many as seven tourist offices dotted around the place. The main ones are on the seafront just north of Barranco del Rey, on Avenida del Littoral and in the Los Cristianos Centro Cultural. For telephone queries, ring ☎ 922 79 76 68.

Post & Communications Of the several post offices, we've indicated on the town map a couple of more important ones.

Email & Internet Access There are several options. Internet Center run by a friendly young Spanish-English guy, is a congenial place. At Calle Juan XXIII 37, it

TENERIFE

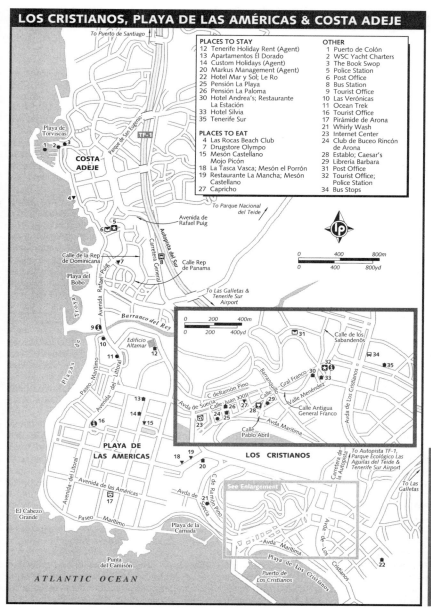

LOS CRISTIANOS, PLAYA DE LAS AMÉRICAS & COSTA ADEJE

PLACES TO STAY
12 Tenerife Holiday Rent (Agent)
13 Apartamentos El Dorado
14 Custom Holidays (Agent)
20 Markus Management (Agent)
22 Hotel Mar y Sol; Le Ro
25 Pensión La Playa
26 Pensión La Paloma
30 Hotel Andrea's; Restaurante
   La Estación
33 Hotel Silvia
35 Tenerife Sur

PLACES TO EAT
4 Las Rocas Beach Club
7 Drugstore Olympo
15 Mesón Castellano
   Mojo Picón
18 La Tasca Vasca; Mesón el Porrón
19 Restaurante La Mancha; Mesón
   Castellano
27 Capricho

OTHER
1 Puerto de Colón
2 WSC Yacht Charters
3 The Book Swop
5 Police Station
6 Post Office
8 Bus Station
9 Tourist Office
10 Las Verónicas
11 Ocean Trek
16 Tourist Office
17 Pirámide de Arona
21 Whirly Wash
23 Internet Center
24 Club de Buceo Rincón
   de Arona
28 Establo; Caesar's
29 Librería Barbara
31 Post Office
32 Tourist Office;
   Police Station
34 Bus Stops

To Puerto de Santiago

Playa de Torviscas

COSTA ADEJE

To Parque Nacional del Teide

Avenida de Rafael Puig

Calle de la Rep de Dominicana

Calle Rep de Panama

Playa del Bobo

To Las Galletas & Tenerife Sur Airport

Barranco del Rey

Edificio Altamar

Calle de los Sabandeños

Calle de Ramón Pino

Calle Juan XXIII

Valle Menéndez

Calle Antigua General Franco

Avda de Suecia

Avda Marítima

Calle Pablo Abril

PLAYA DE LAS AMERICAS

LOS CRISTIANOS

See Enlargement

Avenida de las Américas

Avda de Suecia

To Autopista TF-1, Parque Ecológico Las Águilas del Teide & Tenerife Sur Airport

El Cabezo Grande

Paseo Marítimo

Playa de la Carnada

Avda Marítima

To Las Galletas

Punta del Camisón

Playa de Los Cristianos

ATLANTIC OCEAN

Puerto de Los Cristianos

0   400   800m
0   400   800yd

0   200   400m
0   200   400yd

TENERIFE

has high-speed connections and charges 800 ptas per hour.

Bookshops Librería Barbara, Calle Pablo Abril 36, Los Cristianos, has a stock of German, French and English books. The Book Swop, on the first floor of the Puerto de Colón shopping complex in Costa Adeje, is a cheerful place which carries quite a wide range of second-hand books in English.

Laundry Whirly Wash (☎ 922 79 02 99) on Avenida de Suecia charges 800 ptas for up to five kilos (1200 ptas if they dry and fold for you). Give them a call and they'll even come round and collect your washing from your accommodation.

Medical Services If disabled visitors need specific help, contact Le Ro (☎ 922 75 02 89), in the same building as Hotel Mar y Sol, Los Cristianos (see Places to Stay later).

Emergency There are several police stations. Main ones include the branch just south of the bus station and another in the same premises as the tourist office, the Los Cristianos cultural centre.

Activities

For all of the following and any other activities available, you'll no doubt be deluged with possibilities and brochures and assailed by touts. Be firm.

Diving Two reputable outfits who don't need to tout are Ocean Trek (☎ 922 75 34 72), just beside Hotel Tenerife Sol, and Club de Buceo Rincón de Arona (☎/fax 922 79 35 50), down near the Los Cristianos port.

Fishing Deep-sea fishing trips can start at about 7500 ptas per person for a five-hour jaunt, or 10,000 ptas for a full day.

Sailing & Other Watery Activities You can hire luxury yachts or nippy catamarans, with or without skipper, for day trips or more extended excursions from WSC Yacht Charters (☎ 922 71 40 34) in Puerto

de Colón, Costa Adeje. Prices start at 60,000 ptas per day for a small yacht without crew taking up to eight people (you must be fully licensed). Crewed yachts start at 80,000 ptas per day.

WSC also offer parascending (3500 ptas for 10 minutes) and water-skiing (5000 ptas for 15 minutes, experienced practitioners only). Less intrusively and more affordably, they rent out kayaks for 1000/1500 ptas per half-hour/hour.

On a more modest budget, you can track down catamaran trips for around 3500 ptas per person for three hours, sometimes with food thrown in.

Whale Watching & Other Boat Trips
You will probably be hounded into taking a tour on one of the veritable fleet of competing boats and glass-bottomed catamarans which set out in pursuit of whales and dolphins (an estimated 700,000 visitors watch these magnificent creatures every year). Your average two-hour jaunt costs 2000 ptas, although some will charge up to double and throw in some food and drink of dubious value. See Whales & Dolphins under Ecology & Environment in the Facts about the Islands chapter for details of marine-friendly trips.

Organised Tours

Several travel agents organise day tours of Tenerife and over to the nearby island of La Gomera.

Places to Stay – Budget

The firm message must be that it's much safer and certainly cheaper to book a package outside Spain; the room rate some hotels and apartments quote to callers off the street can be as much as 100% more than what you can get through a tour operator. Travel agents in Britain, Ireland, Germany and the Netherlands brim with deals and special last minute offers.

Playa de las Américas & Costa Adeje
Since there are no pensiones hereabouts, it's either expensive hotels or apartments, which come in all shapes and sizes. The

entire area is often full to bursting so, if you do arrive without a reservation, head straight for one of the tourist offices, which can give you contact details for those agents which deal in apartments and studios.

Among these agents are: Tenerife Holiday Rent (☎ 922 79 58 18), Edificio Altamar, Local 2-bajo; Custom Holidays (☎ 922 79 60 00), Aparthotel California 6; and Markus Management (☎ 922 75 10 64), Apartamentos Portosin, Local 3.

Los Cristianos Here, while you may well end up doing the rounds of the apartment agents, the pensión scene is marginally more promising – though both options are often full.

Pensión La Paloma (☎ 922 79 01 98), in a lane off Calle General Franco in the heart of the town's pedestrian zone, has basic singles/doubles for 3000/4000 ptas.

Nearby, the altogether more welcoming *Pensión La Playa (☎ 922 79 22 64, Calle Paloma 9)*, charges 4000 ptas per day unless you stay for at least a week, in which case it comes down to 3200 ptas. Neither are anything special.

Places to Stay – Mid-Range & Top End

Playa de las Américas & Costa Adeje Again, the best thing to do if you arrive here without a reservation is try the tourist office and approach one of the above listed agents. There are at least 100 apartment blocks of all classes and plenty of big hotels – singling them out in the limited scope of this guide is virtually impossible.

To take an example at the less expensive end, *Apartamentos El Dorado (☎ 922 79 05 00, fax 922 78 75 30)*, a couple of blocks from the beach, has studios for two at 5250 ptas and apartments, accommodating up to three, for 6200 ptas.

Los Cristianos Although not on the scale of Playa de las Américas and Costa Adeje, there's no shortage of apartments and big hotels in Los Cristianos.

Hotel Andrea's (☎ 922 79 00 12, fax 922 79 42 70, Avenida Valle Menéndez) has singles/doubles starting at 4700/6800 ptas.

If that fails, you could try *Hotel Silvia (☎ 922 79 25 64, fax 922 79 79 20)* next door, where fully equipped apartments for up to two/three cost 6270/8360 ptas.

A much nicer version of the same thing is *Tenerife Sur (☎ 922 79 14 74, fax 922 79 27 74)*, a block east of Avenida de Los Cristianos. Prices start at 9500 ptas, rising to 15,000 ptas. The apartments are spacious and have balconies. There is also a pool.

Worth noting is *Hotel Mar y Sol (☎ 922 75 05 40, fax 922 79 05 73)*, at the eastern end of Calle General Franco. It is one of the few places on the island which caters properly for disabled guests.

Places to Eat

Playa de las Américas The place groans with restaurants. To name any seems almost churlish. Most fit into a general category of 'resort international' – you are unlikely to get any fine Canarian cuisine here but Yorkshire pudding and pizza are very popular.

One attractive but rather pricey spot is *Las Rocas Beach Club*, whose restaurant juts out over the water. It belongs to the Hotel Jardín Tropical, but accepts any diners.

Mesón Castellano Mojo Picón (☎ 922 75 02 73, Residencial Las Viñas) is a good restaurant serving quality mainland Spanish food – something hard to come by hereabouts. It closes on Sunday.

There's also a cluster of small places within the Residencia el Camisón building, in the no-man's land between Playa de las Américas and Los Cristianos. Each serves authentic Spanish cuisine to very much a Spanish clientele. Ones well worth the visit include *La Tasca Vasca*, offering mainly Basque food, *Restaurante La Mancha*, *Mesón Castellano* and *Mesón el Porrón*.

Drugstore Olympo is a handy 24-hour supermarket, which is on the corner of Avenida Rafael Puig and Calle República de Panama.

Los Cristianos Here, too, the bulk of the restaurants zero in on the lowest common denominator, churning out extremely

TENERIFE

uninspired stuff to shovel down the throats of unsuspecting foreign visitors.

Although nothing to write home about, *Restaurante La Estación (Calle Antigua General Franco 22)*, next door to Hotel Andrea's back entrance, at least has the distinction of being frequented by a largely Spanish clientele. The set menu is not bad at 1100 ptas. For a sandwich and fine fruit shake, try *Capricho* on Calle Juan XXIII.

Entertainment
Bars, Pubs & Discos Where do you start? Playa de las Américas is an ocean of bars and discos. At night its streets are awash with a tide of young northern Europeans, splayed out in various poses of catatonic splendour. This, apart from the sunshine, is what most of the younger set are here for. But older folk have plenty of pubs of a slightly less-hormonal character to choose from. And there's lots of German lager and fine British bitters (but do they travel well?) to be had.

The Los Cristianos end of the tourist zone is rather tranquil. In the town centre about the only bars thumping on into the night are *Establo* and *Caesar's*, next door to one another at Calle Pablo Abril 5.

Dance The Gran Ballet Clásico Español performs at the *Pirámide de Arona (☎ 922 79 63 60, Avenida de las Américas, Playa de las Américas)*. They present some reasonable interpretations of flamenco. The tip is that tickets are more cheaply secured through your hotel than by calling the above number.

Getting There & Away
Bus TITSA buses terminate at the bus station on the Carretera General in Playa de las Américas. Bus Nos 110 (direct) and 111 go to Santa Cruz (950 ptas, one hour), and No 487 goes to Tenerife Sur airport (275 ptas). Both pass through Los Cristianos (the stop is on Carretera de la Autopista). Plenty of other buses run between the two resorts, en route to destinations such as Los Gigantes, Las Galletas, El Médano, Arona and Puerto de la Cruz.

Boat Los Cristianos is the main jumping-off point for ferries to the three westernmost islands. There's healthy competition on the short run to San Sebastián de la Gomera. Fastest options (30 to 45 minutes) are Fred Olsen's Benchijigua Express (2570 ptas to 3110 ptas, five daily), and Trasarmas' Gomera Jet, (2050 ptas, three daily). If you want to enjoy a more leisurely sailing, Trasmediterránea has two ferries daily (2140 ptas, 1½ hours). At the time of writing, Trasarmas have withdrawn this run but claim that they will resume service.

Trasmediterránea has a daily ferry to Puerto de la Estaca on El Hierro (2615 ptas, 4 hours), sailing at 7.15 pm (8.30 am on Saturday, when it calls in to San Sebastián). Fred Olsen also has a daily run (2540 ptas), leaving at 8 am.

For Santa Cruz de la Palma, Fred Olsen's daily boat via La Gomera (3100 ptas) leaves at an inconvenient 7 pm, decanting you at your destination around midnight.

Getting Around
Bus Most TITSA buses running between Playa de las Américas and Los Cristianos and to other destinations beyond also act as local transport, making various stops along Avenida Litoral in Playa de las Américas. Tourist offices carry a map with bus stops and route numbers marked.

Taxi Watch the taxis here – some drivers feel tempted to dispense with the meter. The fare from Los Cristianos to Tenerife Sur airport is around 2700 ptas.

AROUND LOS CRISTIANOS
Parque Ecológico Las Aguilas del Teide
About 3km from Los Cristianos off the road to Arona, this much publicised (and evidently not 'ecological') attraction offers displays of trained eagles flying in low over the crowd as they zero in on morsels held out by their trainers. There's also an odd assortment of other beasties, including hippos and crocodiles. You can organise tickets through agents in the tourist areas, who will put you on a free bus to get out there.

It's just one of several such attractions in and around the resort. Others include Submarine Adventure in Puerto Colón, Atlantic Gardens banana grove, Aquario Atlántico (an aquarium), camel trekking and Aquapark (a water park with slides galore and a dolphinarium). The majority lay on free or subsidised buses to haul you in.

Las Galletas

Sun and sea apart, it's difficult to see what attracts people to this rather hodgepodge array of modern buildings and semi-high rises. Even the black sand and pebble beach are unremarkable. Still, it's a tranquil backwater compared to the rampant hedonism in Los Cristianos and its noisy neighbours.

Information There's a tourist office, open 9 am to 3.30 pm, Monday to Saturday, at the western end of Rambla Las Galletas, the promenade.

For dive courses and expeditions, try Tenesub Marine (☎/fax 922 73 16 05), Calle María del Carmen García 40, or Cita del Mar (☎ 649 19 46 19, fax 922 78 56 69), Avenida Fernando Salazar González 1.

Places to Stay & Eat Tenerife's only fully equipped camp site is *Camping Nauta* (☎ 922 78 51 18), at Cañada Blanca, a few kilometres north of Las Galletas, just off the road to Buzanada. Open year round, it charges 505 ptas per person/per tent/per car.

Pensión La Estrella (☎ 922 73 15 62, *Carretera General, Km 1*) is – as the address suggests – a bit of a walk from central Las Galletas. But the singles/doubles at 2000/3000 ptas, or 3800 ptas for doubles with bathroom, are OK.

Right in town, less-welcoming *Pensión Los Vinitos* (☎ 922 78 58 03, *Calle Venezuela 4*), provides simple rooms with own bath for 2500/3500 ptas.

Otherwise, try your luck at the various apartment blocks.

You'll find any number of waterfront restaurants. *Restaurante Varadero*, at the southern end of Avenida Fernando Salazar González, has a pleasant terrace overlooking the ocean.

THE EAST

Heading south from Santa Cruz, you have two choices: the TF-1 *autovía* (motorway) or the tortuous C-822, which once passed for the main highway along the east coast. The latter is infinitely slower and more scenic – if scenic is the right word to describe this bare, sinuous land cut up by *barrancos* (ravines) and carved farming terraces, buttressed by rough-hewn stone walls.

Candelaria

Candelaria, 18km south of Santa Cruz, is famous for its **Basílica de Nuestra Señora de Candelaria**, the Basilica of Our Lady of Candelaria, patron saint of the whole archipelago (see the boxed text, 'The Virgin of Candelaria'). Although the feast day is 2 February, official celebrations take place on 15 August (coinciding with the Feast of the Assumption). Pilgrims from all over the island converge on the town for festivities on both holidays. The basilica is open to visitors 7.30 am to 1 pm and 3 to 7.30 pm daily.

Flanking the large square where pilgrims assemble stand nine larger-than-life statues of Guanche leaders with their backs to the Atlantic, which laps the black sandy beach, one of several around Candelaria.

An original eating experience in the area requires your own transport. Head back to the autovía and take exit *(salida)* 9. Follow the TF-22 towards Güímar, then the signs for Cuevacitas de Candelaria.

Casa María (☎ 922 50 46 35) is outside the village (signposted) in a cave. The food is good and the locale a one-off!

Candelaria is an easy bus ride from Santa Cruz (Nos 122, 123, 124, 127 and 131).

Güímar

What brings most visitors here are the remarkable **Pirámides de Güímar** on the western outskirts of town. At first glance not so different from the agricultural terracing you see all over the island, these much restored remains are the raison d'être for a stimulating visitor centre. Its museum and a 15-minute documentary in a choice of six languages graphically illustrate Thor Heyerdahl's theory of pre-1492 cultural contact

TENERIFE

The Virgin of Candelaria

One morning near the end of the 14th century, a few years before the first European conquerors appeared on the scene, a statue of the Virgin Mary drifted in on the tide. A more prosaic interpretation is that it was the figurehead from a wrecked ship but, at a time when few ships ventured beyond the Straits of Gibraltar, such an explanation is equally – we choose the word deliberately – miraculous.

The Guanche fishermen who stumbled across it took it to their chief, the mencey of Güímar. The mencey kept it in his cave where, according to one version of the legend, it was venerated by his people, who gave it the name of Chaxiraxi, the Great Lady of All the World.

In 1526, Pedro Fernández de Lugo, commander of the conquering Spanish forces, gave orders for a sanctuary to be built to house the statue, which had been kept in safe custody by a Christianised Guanche.

First brought by the waters, the statue was also swept away by them during a violent storm in 1826. The one you see today was sculpted a year later by a local artist, Fernando Estévenez.

The basilica which the faithful visit today was completed in 1959.

---

between Europeans and American Indians. There's also a full-scale model of Ra II, the reed boat in which he crossed the Atlantic to demonstrate his theory. You can follow a 950m pyramids trail – though it must be said that one pile of stones looks very much like another. The complex opens 9.30 am to 6.00 pm daily and admission costs 1200 ptas (children 600 ptas).

Plenty of buses serve Güímar from Santa Cruz.

South From Güímar

The ride south on the TF-22 has its moments. Shortly after Güímar, the **Mirador de Don Martín** offers sweeping views of the coast and across to Gran Canaria. You then pass through farming villages such as El Escobonal and Fasnia, before hitting upon **Icor**, an even smaller, half-abandoned pueblo, notable because most of the houses are still built of brown stone rather than concrete.

Another 7km south lie **Arico Viejo** and **Arico Nuevo**. Surprisingly, it's the latter that is the most interesting, with pretty little white houses huddled around narrow lanes. From Arico to the end of the road in Los Cristianos/Playa de las Américas there is precious little of interest.

Those with wheels could make a 10km detour to the coast for **Porís de Abona**, a fishing village gradually metamorphosing into a minor tourist resort.

The turn-off north at Granadilla de Abona for the Teide peak makes for a scenic drive, passing through the hamlet of **Vilaflor**, known above all for its lacework, similar to that found in Venice.

Closer to Los Cristianos, the town of **Arona** is an agreeable little place. You might like to have a meal in the *Restaurante El Patio Canario (Calle Domínguez Alfonso 4)*, a charming French-run restaurant just up the road from the bus stop (No 480 for Los Cristianos).

On the coast **El Médano** is a rather dumpy sort of town, but the beach is pretty good. Windsurfers are virtually guaranteed good conditions and you can hire gear or take lessons at Hotel Playa Sur Tenerife (☎ 922 17 60 13). You'll find a few places to stay, among them *Hostal Carel (☎ 922 17 60 66, Avenida de los Príncipes 22)*, which was temporarily closed for mega renovations when we passed by.

Right on the beach is upmarket *Hotel Médano (☎ 922 17 70 00, fax 922 17 60 48, e reservas@medano.es)*, where singles/doubles come in at 7000/10,000 ptas. Bus No 116 runs to Santa Cruz while No 470 goes to Playa de las Américas via Las Galletas.

TENERIFE

La Gomera

Measuring 368 sq km and with a resident population of 17,000, La Gomera is, after El Hierro, the archipelago's least inhabited island. The Canarios call it the Isla Redonda (Round Island) and most visitors give it little more than a day trip from Tenerife. This is a shame, as more inquisitive travellers who hang around longer have found. In particular, the mountainous countryside and the ancient laurel forest of the Parque Nacional de Garajonay have considerable walking potential.

On the other hand, this relatively wild and sparsely populated island would be hard pressed to deal with too many more tourists – and some locals already feel that they have been overrun. The recent introduction of five fast ferries daily from Los Cristianos (Tenerife) and the inauguration of La Gomera's airport (even though it only receives three flights per day – so far) will inevitably increase the number of visitors. On the plus side, their impact is reduced since on arrival the majority are bundled into coaches which whisk them away to the island's inner reaches and decant them back at San Sebastián's small port at the end of the day.

Unlike its larger neighbours, Tenerife and Gran Canaria, La Gomera is used to receiving independent travellers. The bus service is good and accommodation, whether in a hotel, *casa rural* (house in the country), pensión or apartment, is relatively plentiful.

A kind of rocky fortress whose precipitous cliffs crash headlong into the ocean, La Gomera is the most 'dormant' of the islands. There has been no volcanic activity here for millions of years, which accounts for the virtual absence of cones, calderas and other geological signs. But evidence of the island's violent past does exist – *roques* (the odd rock formations that pile upward in various spots across La Gomera) are the most visible remains of lava fills, gradually exposed as the volcanic fissures eroded.

Agriculture still plays an important part

Highlights

- Walking through the misty forest of the Parque Nacional de Garajonay
- Taking a boat trip to the weird rock formations of Los Órganos and seeing dolphins on the way
- Staying in a *casa rural* in Benchijigua
- Having a drink at San Sebastian's parador, gazing over the water to where Teide peak spears the evening mists

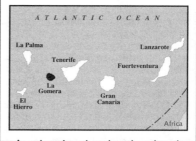

in the island's economy – 8.5 million kilograms of bananas were produced in 1999!

History

La Gomera's history has largely been one of isolation and is as tough as its terrain is difficult. Although the island is comparatively rich in spring water, agriculture has always been a challenge. The soil is poor and the sinuous, hilly country once made travel an arduous undertaking. Indeed, until the construction of modern roads the only access points inland from the coast were the deep *barrancos* (ravines) that radiate like spokes from the peak of Garajonay (1487m) and cut their way down to the small beaches and coves that long served as the only 'gates' to the island.

It was always tough eking out a living by farming the terraces that still spread over much of the island and Gomeros have a

LA GOMERA

long tradition of emigration; the island's population peaked at 29,000 in 1940. Although some of those who left in recent years merely opted for nearby Tenerife, only 28km away, most left for Venezuela and Uruguay. This is reflected in a variety of ways; for example, a lot of the music played on local radio will transport you to Latin America.

The whistling language of the Gomeros (see the boxed text 'Don't Mumble, Give a Whistle' under Language in the Facts about the Islands chapter) is still just about alive today. In an effort to preserve it from ex-

tinction, whistling is now a compulsory subject in primary schools and an optional one at secondary level. Three of the more touristy restaurants put on lunchtime performances, and those on a one-day guided tour from Tenerife can pretty much bank on having a display included in their itinerary.

Information

Books & Maps Tourist offices give out a free map, which is adequate for navigating the island's roads and has street plans of San Sebastián and Valle Gran Rey. *Caminos de la Gomera* at 1:50,000 (500 ptas), produced by the Cabildo (island government) for walkers, features main walking trails and times, the island's bus timetable and other useful information.

Far and away the most detailed for both walkers and motorists is *La Gomera Touring and Walking Map* (1:40,000) published by Discovery Walking Guides. They also produce the admirable *Walk! La Gomera* (2300 ptas) which has detailed descriptions and maps at 1:25,000 for 32 walks around the island. *Landscapes of Southern Tenerife and La Gomera* by Noel Rochford in the Sunflower series describes a number of walks and driving routes. Lonely Planet's *Walking in Spain* describes a couple of the choicest walks on the island.

Foto Junonia, at Avenida Colón 24 in San Sebastián de la Gomera, carries a few maps and guidebooks, mostly in Spanish and German.

Newspapers The island has one newspaper, *La Isla de Gomera*, which appears weekly.

Activities

One of the island's greatest pleasures is taking time out to trek around it. Recently, the Cabildo has invested considerably in preparing and signing (often little more than indicating the start of a route, it must be said) walking trails throughout the island. La Gomera, long a favourite with German hikers, is becoming increasingly popular among English-speaking walkers.

You can trek alone – good reference materials abound (see Books & Maps earlier) – or join an organised walk. Ring Caminos Reales (☎ 922 80 53 37) or Tamaragua Tours (☎ 922 14 10 56). See also the Valle Gran Rey section later in this chapter.

Similarly, cyclists can go it alone or hang in with a pack (again, see the Valle Gran Rey section). If you want to go off the land, the three major towns have diving schools and you can take a boat trip from Valle Gran Rey or Playa Santiago.

Beaches, accessible or otherwise, tend to be of the small, black, pebbly variety. The southern ones are more protected and suitable for swimming. One way to hang out on a beach of your own is to hire a boat and cruise the coast – some of the better ones are difficult to reach by land because no walking track leads to them.

Accommodation

With less than 30 hotels and *pensiones* across the island, the bulk of the accommodation is in private apartments and homes, the most tempting of them being the casas rurales sprinkled all over the countryside. Many of these are old farmhouses long abandoned by Gomero émigrés, now resurrected and refurbished. The easiest way to rent one is to call ahead to the central reservations number (☎/fax 922 14 41 01). They require a minimum stay of three nights (six nights from July to mid-September) and prices begin at 8800 ptas per casa.

During peak periods it can get a little squeezy, so when you arrive go to the tourist office in San Sebastián, ask for their island-wide accommodation list and phone ahead.

Free camping is prohibited on the island. There's only one private camp site, *Camping La Vista* (☎ 922 88 09 49) near El Cedro (see Around Hermigua in the Northern Gomera section later in this chapter).

Getting There & Away

Air La Gomera's spanking new airport (☎ 922 87 30 33), 4km from Playa Santiago, has precisely two flights daily to/from Tenerife Norte and one to/from Gran Canaria.

Boat The ferry terminal for the island is in San Sebastián. Nearly everyone who arrives by ferry comes from Los Cristianos (Tenerife) but there are also daily sailings to El Hierro and La Palma.

Fred Olsen (☎ 922 87 10 07) runs its Benchijigua Express (from 2420 ptas, 45 minutes, five daily) to/from Los Cristianos. For a more leisurely sailing, Trasmediterránea has two ferries daily (one on Saturday) which take 1½ hours (2140 ptas).

Trasmediterránea (☎ 902 45 46 45) runs a daily ferry to El Hierro at 5.15 pm

(2615 ptas, three hours) via Los Cristianos. On Saturday, it leaves at 10.30 am and goes direct.

Fred Olsen's daily boat for Santa Cruz de la Palma (3100 ptas) leaves at 8.30 pm and means a late arrival at your destination.

You can buy tickets for both lines at travel agents or the ferry terminal.

Getting Around

Bus The aqua coloured buses of the Servicio Regular de La Gomera (☎ 922 87 14 18) set out from the ferry terminal at San Sebastián and call by the bus station there. Three bus lines (with four departures per day) cover the island's main destinations.

All three services leave at 11.30 am, 6.30 and 9.30 pm. The time of the fourth departure varies according to the route.

Bus No 1 goes to Valle Gran Rey (700 ptas, 1¾ hours). It follows the TF-713 highway, then detours south of the Garajonay peak via Las Paredes and Chipude, rejoining the highway at Las Hayas. Its fourth departure is at 9.30 am,

Bus No 2 goes south to Playa Santiago (680 ptas), returning via Alajeró. Its fourth departure is at 6.45 am.

Bus No 3 runs north to Vallehermoso (575 ptas) via Hermigua. Its fourth departure is at 3.30 pm.

Car & Motorcycle There are plenty of car rental options in San Sebastián, Valle Gran Rey and Playa Santiago.

SAN SEBASTIÁN DE LA GOMERA

postcode 38800 • pop 4860
The capital and main port is the obligatory point of entry to the island. Aside from a few minor monuments, there's little to keep you here, although a stroll around the centre is pleasant enough if you have an eye for the remaining traditional houses squished between characterless concrete structures.

History

This settlement must have been the scene of much excitement back on 6 September 1492. After loading up with food, timber and water, Christopher Columbus led his three small caravels out of the bay and set sail westwards for the Indies, beyond the limit of the known world.

The town had barely been founded when Columbus arrived. Four years earlier, in 1488, there had been a terrible massacre in the wake of the failed uprising against Hernán Peraza, the island's governor. When it was all over, what had been the Villa de las Palmas (on a spot known to the Guanches as Hipalán) was rechristened San Sebastián.

The arrival of Columbus, and the consequent boom in transatlantic trade, helped boost the fortunes of the city, sited on a good sheltered harbour. Nevertheless, its population only passed the 1000 mark at the beginning of the 19th century. The good times also brought dangers as, like other islands, San Sebastián was regularly subjected to pirate attack from the English, French and Portuguese. In 1739, the English fleet actually landed an invasion force but the assault was repulsed.

The fate of the town was intimately linked with that of the rest of the island. Its fortunes rose with the cochineal boom in the 19th century, then collapsed with that industry which was unable to compete with synthetic dyes.

Orientation

You arrive by sea at the shipping terminal at the eastern end of town. Buses meet the morning and evening ferries and fan out across the island.

The main road, Calle Real (ex-Calle del Medio), leads north-west from the yacht harbour and small black-sand beach. Along it is the tourist office as well as the main sights. The bulk of the town's hotels and pensiones are here and on parallel Calle Ruíz de Padrón.

For good views of the town, its mountainous backdrop and the black-sand beach, walk up to the Mirador de la Hila.

Information

The tourist office (☎ 922 87 02 81), Calle Real 4, opens 9 am to 1.30 pm and 3.30 to

SAN SEBASTIÁN DE LA GOMERA

To TF-711 &
Hermigua

PLACES TO STAY
3 Pensión Colombina
6 Hotel & Apartamentos
   Villa Gomera
7 Pensión Colón
20 Pensión Gomera
23 Apartamentos San Sebastián
26 Pensión Residencia
   Hespérides
27 Pensión El Pajar
28 Hotel del Conde
29 Hotel Garajonay

36 Parador Nacional Conde
   de la Gomera

PLACES TO EAT
10 Club Junonia
15 Tasca los Frailes
17 Restaurante 4 Caminos
19 Restaurante La Tasca
22 Restaurante del Marqués de
   Oristano
24 Restaurante Cubino
33 Zumería Cuba Libre

OTHER
1 Oh Ribera
2 Laundry
4 Ermita de San
   Sebastián
5 Post Office
8 Casa de Colón
9 Le Pequeña Escuela
   de Buceo
11 Foto Junonia
12 Hospital
13 Bus Station
14 Cepsa Petrol Station
16 Cabildo Insular

18 Iglesia de la Virgen de la
   Asunción
21 Centro de Salud
25 Tourist Office; Pozo de la
   Aguada
30 Torre del Conde
31 Viajes Insular; Cicar
   Rentacar
32 Taxi Stand
34 Café Internet el Ambigú
35 Ayuntamiento (Town Hall);
   Police Station
37 Bus Terminal
38 Estación Marítima

ATLANTIC OCEAN

6.00 pm, Monday to Saturday, and 10 am to 1 pm on Sunday.

To check your emails, grab a coffee at Café Internet el Ambigú on Plaza de las Américas. It has a couple of machines and charges 850 ptas per hour. Open 8.30 am to 1.30 am daily, it booms out great jazz and folk, though the staff are a bit frosty.

For fresh farm produce and Germans selling clothing and natural potions, visit the small open air market, which is held every Wednesday and Saturday morning on Plaza de la Constitución.

There's a laundrette on Calle Real and the local police office is within the *ayuntamiento* (town hall).

Things to See & Do

The small town centre has a scattering of charming old mansions with leafy patios and wooden balconies, but is short on noteworthy monuments.

Set in a park just back from the beach, the **Torre del Conde** is where it all began. Beatriz de Bobadilla, wife of the ill-fated Hernán Peraza, had to barricade herself in this citadel in 1488 until help arrived. The fort had been raised in 1447, the first

Murder & Revenge in La Gomera

Love affairs can be a risky business, in or out of marriage. When, in 1488, Hernán Peraza, the son of the governor of La Gomera, Diego de Herrera, began to see Yballa, a young local beauty, his wife Beatriz de Bobadilla was none too impressed. Even less so was Yballa's Gomero suitor, Hautacuperche – who also saw in this a unique opportunity. He hatched a plan with other tribesmen to seize Peraza and compel him to confess his extramarital activities. In this way, Hautacuperche hoped not only to win back Yballa but also to extract from Peraza a promise of fairer treatment of the islanders by the colonial authorities, who had been particularly harsh with the local populace.

The chance to enact the plan was not long in coming. Tipped off that Peraza and Yballa were to meet clandestinely, Hautacuperche lay in wait. However, things didn't go according to plan and Hautacuperche ended up fatally spearing Peraza. There may well have been a touch of poetic justice in Peraza's death, since a few years earlier he had stood accused of murdering Juan Rejón, the unloved commander of the 1478 assault on Gran Canaria.

Were Peraza and Yballa really lovers? Another version of the story is that Peraza had five Guanche women seized for the benefit of his officers in a wild party. One of them, Yballa, resisted and was publicly mistreated by Peraza. Whichever way it went, Peraza's death unleashed a blood bath. Having killed the governor, the islanders laid siege to Beatriz de Bobadilla and the small Spanish contingent holed up in Villa de las Palmas, the precursor to modern San Sebastián.

Pedro de Vera in Gran Canaria got wind of the uprising and soon arrived to put a stop to it. His ruthlessness was bloodcurdling. According to one account, de Vera ordered the execution of all males above the age of 15. In an orgy of wanton violence, islanders were hanged, impaled, decapitated or drowned. Some had their hands and feet lopped off beforehand, just for good measure. The women were parcelled out to the militiamen, and many of the children were bundled off for sale as slaves. To complete the job, de Vera also ordered the execution of some 300 Gomeros living on Gran Canaria.

---

building of any note to be erected. It is about the only one to have been more or less preserved in its original state. It opens 10.30 am to 1.30 pm weekdays and admission is free, though there's not much to see inside unless reproductions of old maps give you a thrill.

Also worth a brief visit is the **Iglesia de la Virgen de la Asunción**. The central nave of the original hermitage was begun in 1450 but additions were made until well into the 18th century. On the wall of the northern aisle is a large mural depicting the islanders repelling an attack by the British fleet in 1743. In gratitude, the Gomeran commander had the adjacent side-chapel constructed with its fine painted artesonado roof.

The **Casa de Colón**, Calle Real 56, is where Columbus supposedly put up before heading off for the New World. Inside you'll find a few artefacts from Peru and maybe a temporary exhibition. It opens

4 to 6 pm on weekdays and admission is free.

On the subject of Columbus, nip out the back of the tourist office to have a look at the **Pozo de la Aguada**. They say that water drawn from this well was used to 'baptise America'.

The tiny **Ermita de San Sebastián** on Calle Real is reputedly the island's first chapel. History gave it a rough early ride. Sacked by passing Huguenots in 1571, plundered by Dutch freebooters 20 years later and trashed by Berber marauders in 1618, what remained was left as a ruin until it was comprehensively restored in 1650.

The main black sandy beach isn't bad. If you want something wilder and more secluded, a walking track heads south-west to the hamlet of **El Cabrito** from the TF-713 highway near the hospital. Ask around for it. The walk takes about two hours and the beach is quite pretty, with a huddle of houses set among palm trees and the mountainous terrain behind them serving as a colourful backdrop. Bring your own food and water.

Activities
For diving, contact La Pequeña Escuela de Buceo (☎ 639 989 089), a German operation at Calle Ruiz de Padrón 50. Catamaran Estela does four-hour cruises for 7000 ptas per person, including a snack and drinks. Ring ☎ 922 14 17 70 or inquire at the tourist office.

Special Events
The Fiesta de San Sebastián, the town's patron saint, is celebrated on 20 January and Columbus' first voyage is commemorated on 6 September.

Every five years on 5 October (the next time in 2003) the city celebrates the Bajada de la Virgen de Guadelupe, where a flotilla of fishing boats escorts the statue of the Virgin Mary from the chapel of Puntallana southwards to the capital.

Places to Stay – Budget
Pensión El Pajar (☎ 922 87 02 07, Calle Real 23) has basic, thin-walled rooms costing 3000 ptas. Beware, the hot water is only for the quick. They have a noisy bar and, at the rear, a small and undistinguished restaurant.

Quieter and with a much nicer internal garden is *Pensión Gomera (☎ 922 87 04 17)* at No 33. Simple rooms cost 4000 ptas for the first night and 3500 ptas thereafter.

If these are both full (which happens often enough), try the more modern *Pensión Colombina (☎ 922 87 12 57, Calle Ruíz de Padrón 83)*, which has singles/doubles for 3000/5000 ptas with bathroom. It's short on charm but clean and quiet. Otherwise, *Pensión Residencia Hespérides (☎ 922 87 13 05)* at No 42 has rooms for 4000 ptas with bathroom (3500 ptas without).

Spruce *Pensión Colón (☎ 922 87 02 35, Calle Real 59)* is a reasonable deal, offering comfortable singles/doubles with washbasin for 2500/3500 ptas. During termtime,

your morning slumbers may be disturbed by noise from the kindergarten below.

Places to Stay – Mid-Range
Hotels Of the handful of hotels, *Hotel Villa Gomera (☎ 922 87 00 20, fax 922 87 02 35, Calle Ruíz de Padrón 68)* is friendly and comfortable, and has singles/doubles for 4000/6000 ptas. Only slightly less trim is *Hotel Garajonay (☎ 922 87 05 50, fax 922 87 05 54)* at No 17. Here you'll be paying 4800/6200 ptas. The newest option is *Hotel del Conde (☎ 922 87 00 00, fax 922 87 13 14)*, next door at No 19, where rooms start at 5700/7700 ptas.

Apartments You may be met by touts with apartments to rent. They can be a good deal, starting at 4500 ptas a throw for two. Otherwise, keep an eye out for signs around town. At the quality end, *Apartamentos San Sebastián (☎ 922 87 13 54, Calle Real 20)* has large apartments for two costing 5500 ptas (6000 ptas sleeping up to three). If there's no one at reception, inquire at the exchange office next door. The apartments attached to Hotel Villa Gomera (see the previous section) also represent good value at 7000 ptas

Places to Stay – Top End
Parador Nacional Conde de la Gomera (☎ 922 87 11 00, fax 922 87 11 16) is a graceful four-star Canarian-style mansion. The views of Tenerife from the back garden are breathtaking. Single/double rooms cost 14,000/17,500 ptas.

Places to Eat
Airy, no-frills *Restaurante Cubino (Calle Trasera, aka Calle de la Virgen de Guadelupe)*, where most mains cost less than 1000 ptas, is excellent value.

Another good spot is *Club Junonia (Calle Real 51)* where you can eat well in their garden for equally modest prices.

Tasca los Frailes is primarily a bar and tapas place with a restaurant tagged on. Main courses cost between 1100 ptas and 1500 ptas.

High on atmosphere is *Restaurante La*

When Columbus Dropped By

When Christopher Columbus dropped anchor in the small harbour of San Sebastián de la Gomera in August 1492, he must have been filled with mixed emotions. The tiny Canary Island was to be his last stop in the known world; after so many years of grim determination and bitter disappointment, this was his chance to prove that there was a western sea route to the Orient – and that the world was round!

A Genoese sailor of modest means, Cristoforo Colombo (as he is known in his native Italy) was born in 1451. He went to sea early and was something of a dreamer. Fascinated by Marco Polo's travels in the Orient, he decided early on that it must be possible to reach the east by heading west into the sunset. Nice idea, but the rulers of Genoa, a considerable seafaring power, did not see such a dodgy enterprise as worthy

JANE SMITH

of investment. The young Columbus was undeterred and moved to Portugal in 1478, where he continued his career at sea and searched for backers for his idea. At every door he knocked the reaction was always the same, until finally the Catholic monarchs of Spain, Fernando and Isabel, gave him their patronage in 1492.

On 3 August, at the head of three small caravels – the *Santa María*, the *Pinta* and the *Niña* – Columbus weighed anchor in Palos de la Frontera, Andalucía, on the Spanish mainland.

Though single-minded when it came to westward exploration, Cristóbal Colón (as the Spanish call him) does not seem to have been above distraction. Legend has it that he took quite a shine to Beatriz de Bobadilla, the widow of the unlamented Hernán Peraza, during his stay on La Gomera. Still, he finally set sail on 6 September.

It was 12 October before Columbus' little flotilla again sighted land, just as his restless men were reaching the end of their patience with their commander's whims. The expedition 'discovered' several Caribbean islands on this trip, including Haiti and Cuba, and returned to Spain in March of the following year.

On his two subsequent voyages of discovery, Columbus chose again to land in San Sebastián, in October 1493 and May 1498. On this latter trip he found that Beatriz was married and some historians surmise that it is no coincidence that he didn't pass this way again on his final voyage in 1502.

Columbus founded Santo Domingo on Hispaniola and charted the coasts of Honduras and Venezuela; as an administrator, however, he ran into difficulties and was shipped back to Spain, clapped in irons, in 1500. His name was later cleared, allowing him to return to the new colonies.

In 1504 he died a forgotten and embittered man in Valladolid, Spain. To the last he remained convinced he had found a new route to the Orient and remained unaware that he had stumbled upon a continent unknown to the European world – America.

Tasca (Calle Ruíz de Padrón 34), which occupies a Canarian house with whitewashed walls. The *conejo en salmorejo* (marinated rabbit) is nicely washed down with a slightly sweet local house red. Next door at

No 36, small *Restaurante 4 Caminos* also serves up good food (about 1200 ptas for mains) – the upstairs dining area is particularly agreeable.

For a classier atmosphere and the option

of al fresco dining, try **Restaurante del Marqués de Oristano** *(Calle Real 24)*. Mains here average around 1700 ptas. It opens Monday to Saturday.

For a splurge, head up to the parador (see Places to Stay earlier), where a gourmet meal will cost you around 4000 ptas.

Zumería Cuba Libre *(Plaza de las Américas)* serves all the usual soft and hard stuff but particularly merits a stop for its fruit juices. Try, for example, their mango, banana or papaya at 400 ptas a pint pot.

Entertainment
One does not turn up in La Gomera for the rocking nightlife. A few of the restaurants have bars that stay open until about 2 am and there are two open-air terrazas with dancing: **Oh Ribera** up Barranco de la Villa and **La Planta**, open between June and September 3, at the southern end of Avenida de los Descubridores.

Getting There & Away
Bus See Getting Around at the beginning of the chapter for details.

Car & Motorcycle There is no shortage of car-rental offices. VipCar (☎ 922 87 04 61) and Rent a Car Piñero (☎ 922 87 01 48) both have booths in the ferry terminal and can have a vehicle waiting for you if you reserve in advance.

Taxi If money is no object, you can get a taxi (☎ 922 87 05 24) wherever you want, though it will almost certainly work out cheaper to hire a car.

Approximate fares from San Sebastián are 3000 ptas to Hermigua, 4000 ptas to Alajeró (4000 ptas) and 6000 ptas to Valle Gran Rey.

Boat See Getting There & Away at the beginning of the chapter for details.

PARQUE NACIONAL DE GARAJONAY
La Gomera's outstanding natural attraction is the ancient *laurisilva* (laurel forest) at the heart of the island's national park.

The 4000-hectare park is a haven for some of the planet's most ancient forest land. Although called laurisilva, there is much more to it than the several types of laurel that abound; as many as 400 species of flora, including Canary willows and Canary holly, flourish.

Up here on the roof of the island, cool Atlantic trade winds clash with warmer breezes, creating a constant ebb and flow of mist through the dense forest. Streams are few and as much precipitation comes from the mist as from rain. Indeed, conservation of the forest is essential to attract the mists and their moisture, which in turn feed the island's springs. Relatively little light penetrates the canopy, allowing moss and lichen to spread over everything. In the trees you may happen to spot rare laurel and long-toed pigeons.

What you see here was common across the Mediterranean millions of years ago until the frosty fingers of the last Ice age, which never made it as far as the Canaries, strangled it to death. Humans have done more damage in the islands than ice but in this case at least, they have acted to protect a good chunk of unique land before it was too late – the park was designated a UNESCO World Heritage site in 1981.

Information
Strangely, the main park visitor centre, in the north of the island, is well outside its limits and inconveniently distant from the nearest bus route. For details, see Northern La Gomera later in this chapter.

There are several trails in the southern part of the park and it's possible to walk from one side to the other in a day.

It is forbidden to light fires in the park except in a few designated areas. Free camping is also prohibited. It can get cold here, and the damp goes right through to the bones, even when it is not raining. Bring walking boots, warm garments and a rain-proof jacket.

Approaches to the Park
The TF-713 highway cuts east–west right through the park until it meets the TF-711

at the park's western extremity. The four daily buses between the capital and Valle Gran Rey make a detour south along a secondary road, branching off shortly before the Alto de Garajonay (the island's tallest peak) and continuing westwards along a decidedly tortuous route. They stop in such places as Igualero, Chipude and El Cercado before branching north again to rejoin the main road at Las Hayas.

Another less-travelled way to enter the park is from the north-east. From here a secondary road, signed Caserío el Cedro (get off bus No 3 at Cruce de El Rejo), twists and turns its spectacular way southwards through the laurisilva to meet the TF-713 (bus stop Cruce de la Zarcita) after 6km. Along the way are a couple of magnificent lookouts. Off it branches a driveable dirt road (signed Caserío de El Cedro) that meanders to El Cedro and the island's only camp site (see Around Hermigua later in this chapter), then along the northern boundary to Meriga.

A second minor sealed road connects the national park visitor centre in the north of the island to La Laguna Grande, about midway along the TF-713 between the park's eastern and western boundaries.

In & Around the Park

Many independent visitors make for the **Alto de Garajonay** (1487m), from where, clouds permitting, you have splendid views over the island. Another favourite stop is **La Laguna Grande**, just off the highway and ideal for picnics.

There's a popular and well-signposted walk up the Alto de Garajonay. Take bus No 1 from San Sebastián and get off at the Pajarito stop (where the bus turns south). From here it is about an hour's walk (signposted) to the peak. On a clear day you can see the islands of Tenerife, La Palma, El Hierro and sometimes even Gran Canaria. If you have your own transport or get a taxi, a much shorter trail (1.6km) leads up to the peak from El Contadero.

From El Contadero, another track, signposted Caserío de El Cedro, leads north. This is mostly descent and takes about two hours. It takes you through the heart of the park (it's a nature trail and the only one described in a free brochure handed out at the visitor centre).

On bus No 1's route, the detour along the south of the park is full of interest. **Chipude**, with its 16th-century Iglesia de la Virgen de la Candelaria, and **El Cercado**, known for its pottery production, are intriguing stops. Both villages lie amid rows of intensively farmed terraces. A dirt track and walking trail of about 3.5km climb from El Cercado to La Laguna Grande in the national park. In Chipude, *Pensión Sonya (☎ 922 80 41 58)* has singles/doubles with bathroom for 2500/4000 ptas.

SOUTHERN LA GOMERA

Those with transport or a will to walk and hitch could follow the steep, serpentine and narrow branch road south to **La Dama** from the Chipude bus stop, passing beneath the basalt, flat-topped 1243m peak of La Fortaleza (the Fortress). La Dama is little more than a smattering of houses and banana plantations high up above the Atlantic. You might dig up a room in one of a couple of apartments here, but don't bank on it. A few steep kilometres of track separate the town from a black pebbly beach, **Playa de la Rajita**, cheapened by the disused factory that sits glumly back from the shore. A rather punishing walk inland (unsignposted) and then back down the Barranco de la Negra gives better views.

A good but difficult hike runs from La Rajita north to Arguayoda (2km) and then about 6km eastwards to Alajeró, traversing two ravines in the process. Your orienteering skills need to be in good shape, though. At Alajeró you are on the No 2 bus route between San Sebastián and Playa Santiago.

Playa Santiago
postcode 38810 • pop 560

Until the 1960s Playa Santiago was about the busiest centre on the island, with food-processing factories (especially fish canning), a small shipyard and port facilities for the export of the familiar cash crops – bananas and tomatoes. But crisis hit the

It may go against the grain but Puerto Naos' black sand beach on La Palma is very inviting.

From people watching to...   ...space gazing at La Palma's observatory

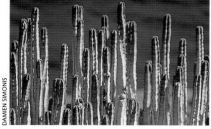

Known as the Pretty Island, La Palma receives the highest rainfall in the archipelago and boasts some of the most weird and wonderful vegetation in the Canaries as a result.

farming sector and by the 1970s the town had all but shut down, its populace having fled to Tenerife or South America.

Now tourism is coming to the rescue. Locals hope that their beaches (the playas de Santiago, Tapahuga, Chinguarime and En Medio), a huge tourist hotel belonging to the Fred Olsen shipping company and claims to the best year-round climate on the island will turn the place around. And should all these go belly up, the town remains La Gomera's most important fishing port, especially for tuna.

The three out-of-town beaches each lie at the end of a ravine. They can be reached on foot or by car along a dirt road which, once round the bounds of Hotel Jardín Tecina (see Places to Stay later) heads eastwards. As elsewhere on the island, the beaches – the usual narrow strip of black sand, pebble and stone – are underwhelming.

Information The tourist office, on waterfront Avenida Marítima, opens 10 am to 1 pm and 4 to 6 pm on weekdays and 10 am to 1 pm on Saturday.

Activities Two motor boats, Tina and Siron (see Activities under Valle Gran Rey for details), set out from the harbour on a coastal cruise every Tuesday and Sunday. A **diving school** has its base within Hotel Jardín Tecina.

Places to Stay The simplest apartments start at about 4000 ptas. Along Avenida Marítima are several perfectly decent pensiones and apartments, and prices get cheaper as you move inland and higher. On the waterfront, for example, *Apartamentos Casanova* (☎ 922 89 50 02) has apartments, accommodating up to three, for 4000 ptas. Also overlooking the beach, *Pensión La Gaviota* (☎ 922 89 51 35, fax 922 89 50 31) has double rooms with bathroom for the same price. Ask at *Restaurante el Bodegón* below, which is worth a visit in its own right for a simple snack.

Spread out on the cliffs overlooking the ocean and dominating the eastern side of town is grand *Hotel Jardín Tecina* (☎ 922

Not So Pretty Pussy

It happened in Australia (where a park ranger once told us he'd like all cats to have their tails docked from the neck downwards!) and it's happening in the Canaries.

Cats came with the Europeans. They may be sweet and cuddly around the house but they're also vicious killers. Seen from the perspective of a lizard, small rodent or bird, they lose their feline charm. And feral cats – born in the wild of domestic antecedents – are one of the islands' biggest environmental hazards.

The giant lizard (*Lagarto gigante*), for example, is becoming an endangered species, its falling numbers primarily attributed to slaughter by feral cats. The La Gomera sub-species, *Gallotia gomerano*, is all but wiped out and only five species survive in captivity. The Spanish Ornithological Association has condemned the role of feral cats in the decline in numbers of endemic bird species and, for the islands' regional ministry of the environment, the culling of these cats has become a priority.

---

14 58 65, fax 922 14 58 51) with its five pools, four restaurants and four bars. Prices vary a lot with the season, averaging around 15,500/24,000 ptas for singles/doubles with half board.

Places to Eat The waterfront is lined with modest little bars and eateries, and fish is the order of the day. *Restaurante El Paso*, on the corner of Avenida Marítima and Calle Santiago Apostol, is popular with locals and serves huge portions. Try their *ensalada mixta* (mixed salad) with avocado and asparagus – you'll have little room left for the main course. The food at *Restaurante la Cuevita*, beside the fishing port, is much the same as elsewhere on the seafront but, set inside a small cave, it makes a pleasant alternative to the usual beachside terraza.

The inventive *menú*, combined with heart-stopping ocean views from the terrace, of the main *restaurant* of Hotel Jardín Tecina is quite excellent value at 2500 ptas.

LA GOMERA

Just opposite, **Restaurante Tagoror** can't match either views or cuisine but in its more modest way, still represents good value for money.

Getting There & Away Four buses daily link Playa Santiago with San Sebastián, leaving from the little Plaza formed by the junction of Avenida Marítima and Calle de Santiago Apostol.

Alajeró
postcode 38812 • pop 325
• elevation 810m

The only sizeable village outside Playa Santiago in the south-east of the island, Alajeró is a pretty, palm-tree studded oasis on the road from the misty uplands down to the beach. The modest 16th-century **Iglesia del Salvador** is worth a quick look.

In September Gomeros from far and wide converge on Alajeró to celebrate the Fiesta del Paso, a chirpy procession that dances its way down from the mountains.

There are three casas rurales and several apartments in and around the village. You'll also find three modest bar/restaurants.

Bus No 2 passes by here (the bus stop is on the main highway) four times daily on its way back to San Sebastián from Playa Santiago.

To visit the island's only surviving *drago* or dragon tree (see the boxed text 'The Tree with a Long, Shady Past' in the Facts about the Island chapter for details) if you're driving, take an unsigned left turn 1.25km north of Alajeró as far as an old farm house, from where a trail drops steeply. If you're on the bus, get off at the Imada stop and turn left down a cobbled track to join this side road. Either way, allow a good 45 minutes for the round trip.

Benchijigua
One of the prettiest and most tranquil areas of inland southern Gomera is the wide terraced bowl of the upper reaches of the Barranco de Santiago. Along its northern reaches is Benchijigua, a smattering of half-abandoned hamlets.

A cluster of renovated cottages – yet another Fred Olsen initiative – make an excellent away-from-it-all base for a few days' walking. **Casas rurales** accommodating two/three/five people cost 8500/9600/10,700 ptas. It's essential to reserve in advance (☎/fax 922 14 41 01). From Las Toscas on the San Sebastián-Playa Santiago highway (bus No 2 runs past), take a dirt road northwards for 4km.

A couple of trails lead north into the park (going the other way, at least one is marked heading south into the area from the Roque de Agando by the TF-713 highway) and several others trace paths southwards along the ravines to the coast.

NORTHERN LA GOMERA
Hermigua
postcode 38820 • pop 475
• elevation 210m

Set in territory once known to the Guanches as Mulagua, Hermigua stretches south to north along the bottom of a pretty ravine, a long-established centre for banana cultivation fed by water falling from the Parque Nacional de Garajonay. Its small port, a few kilometres north, once made it an important export outlet and many of the island's notable families had their residence here. Although farming has lost much of its importance, the terraces scaling the steep slopes of the ravine are a pretty sight even today. Pretty, yes. But the peasants of the area long lived in misery, and revolts in 1690 and 1762 were mercilessly suppressed. At the heart of the original village, the Valle Alto, are the 16th-century **church** and **convent of Santo Domingo**.

On the opposite side of the highway from the convent is a handicrafts workshop, Los Telares, where you can buy handmade rugs and various other souvenirs. It has become something of an obligatory stop for busloads of day-trippers from Tenerife.

In September the town is transformed for a week by the crowds who gather from far and wide for the Fiestas de la Encarnación.

Bus No 3 linking San Sebastián and Vallehermoso passes through here four times daily.

Rough weather can make the nearby

stony – and none too enticing – beaches of Playa de Hermigua and Playa de Santa Catalina unsuitable for swimming and sunbathing. The nicest hereabouts, Playa de la Caleta, entails about an hour's walk (see Hermigua to Las Casetas later).

Places to Stay & Eat At the lower (northern) end of the village is the ***Centro de Iniciativas y Turismo Rural del Norte de la Gomera*** (☎ 922 14 41 01). Up at the top (southern) end, beside Hotel Villa de Hermigua, is ***Padimar*** (☎ 922 88 02 46). Both specialise in letting casas rurales, though the former's seem more genuinely rustic. Both are private rather than public-sector organisations. Padimar charges 5500 ptas for a studio, 6600 ptas for an apartment and 7700 ptas for a house, requiring a minimum stay of three nights.

Apartamentos Los Telares (☎ 922 88 07 81, fax 922 14 41 07), right by the convent, is excellent value, offering singles/doubles with bathroom and kitchenette for 2500/4000 ptas.

An altogether more luxurious option is cosy ***Hotel Rural Ibo Alfaro*** (☎ 922 88 01 68), 750m west of the main road. Here tasteful singles/doubles/quads cost 8500/10,000/16,000 ptas, including breakfast.

Hotel Villa de Hermigua (☎/fax 922 88 02 46) has singles/doubles costing 6500/9000 ptas, including breakfast. With a communal kitchen and terrace offering sweeping views of the valley, it too is no bad bet.

At the very southern end of the valley you can eat solidly for about 1700 ptas, including wine and a simple dessert, at ***Restaurante Las Chácaras***. For something more subtle at equally reasonable prices, pass by ***Casa Creativa***, a traditional house in the heart of the pueblo, which also does good juices. If you want views of the ocean, ***Restaurante El Faro*** (on the road leading to the Playa de Hermigua) can't be beaten.

Around Hermigua
El Cedro A walking track twists its way south from Hermigua via the Ermita de San Juan up towards the Parque Nacional de Garajonay. On the park borders, El Cedro is a rural hamlet amid farmed terraces and laurel thickets. The ravine and waterfall known as La Boca del Chorro are beautiful. In Hermigua, ask for the *sendero* (trail) to El Cedro and be prepared for a two- to three-hour hike. The simple Ermita de Nuestra Señora de Lourdes is a 1km wander out from the hamlet.

In El Cedro itself are four cottages for rent. Here too is ***Camping La Vista*** (☎ 922 88 09 49), the island's only camp site. It's a friendly place, open year round, with a bar and restaurant, and costs a bargain 300 ptas per person. It also runs a nearby ***refugio*** (mountain hut), complete with washing machine and TV, where a bed costs 1500 ptas.

For how to get there, see Approaches to the Park under Parque Nacional de Garajonay earlier in this chapter.

Hermigua to Las Casetas Clamped in between the craggy coast and the limits of the Garajonay park is a scenic dirt road, best attacked on foot or by mountain bike or 4WD. Initially heading north (to join it, follow the sign 'Playa de Hermigua') it eventually loops south to meet the TF-711 at Las Casetas (where there's a bus stop).

A signed branch track leads eastwards to **Playa de la Caleta**, to which there's also a footpath from Hermigua (allow about an hour, one way). It is one of the prettier black sand-and-pebble beaches in the north of the island, and there's also a little refreshment stand which is sometimes open.

Agulo & Lepe
postcode 38830 • pop 730
Five kilometres north of Hermigua, the village of Agulo was founded early in the 17th century. Along with the picturesque hamlet of Lepe, it squats on a low platform beneath the steep, rugged hinterland that stretches back towards the Garajonay park.

In Agulo, ***Hotel Rural Casa de los Pérez*** (☎ 922 14 61 22) has comfortable singles/doubles for 5000/7000 ptas.

Restaurante Zula, on the main road, does simple, economical food. Mains cost less than 1000 ptas.

Centro de Visitantes del Parque Nacional de Garajonay

The visitor centre (☎ 922 80 09 93) for the Garajonay national park, though inconveniently sited 2.5 km off the No 3 bus route, is well worth a visit.

The staff have piles of information on the park and the island in general while in the gardens and interior patio flourish a microcosm of La Gomera's floral riches. There are also handicraft displays and a tiny folk museum, and the centre runs a multilingual 20-minute video about the park. It opens 9.30 am to 4.30 pm daily. You can enjoy a drink or lunch at *Bar/Restaurante Tambur*, just outside the gardens.

If you have wheels, make the short detour to the **Mirador de Abrante** for a spectacular panorama of coast and ocean.

To linger over lunch with an equally soul-stirring view, take a turning left (southwest), signed Presa de las Rosas, about 2km before you rejoin the TF-711. After 0.75km, you will reach *Bar Terraza Amalaguigue*, where a filling three-course meal costs under 1500 ptas. For more subtle cuisine with plunging views down to Vallehermoso, continue for approximately a couple of kilometres, crossing over a small dam, to signed *Bodegón Roque Blanco*.

From the visitor centre, a minor sealed road leads south to La Laguna Grande, a picnic and play area within the park beside the TF-713. From it, a branch road takes you on a breathtaking drive along a ravine through the hamlets of **La Palmita** and **Meriga**. They are about as faithful a reflection of traditional rural Gomeran living as you will find on the island. It is said the older folk around here still use the Silbo Gomero (Gomero whistle) to communicate.

Vallehermoso

postcode 38840 ● pop 1540
● elevation 230m

The road winds a further 10km westwards from the visitor centre turnoff to the village of Vallehermoso, passing through traditional farming hamlets such as Tamargada along the way. Vallehermoso, with all

amenities, like Hermigua makes a good base for walking. This isn't the greatest beach territory, however. Three kilometres north of the village down a palm-studded valley, the rocky Playa de Vallehermoso is a bit of a disappointment. Just outside the town towers the volcanic monolith of the **Roque Cano**, whose rock walls rise up 250m.

Places to Stay & Eat If you go by the notices on walls, doors and windows, you'd think that just about every third house in the village has rooms to rent.

Bar/Restaurante Amaya (☎ 922 80 00 73, fax 922 80 11 38, Plaza de la Constitución 2) has basic singles/doubles starting at 1750/3500 ptas. For 2500/4000 ptas you can up the comfort level with your own bath, TV and fridge. The owners also rent out a couple of apartments. Their popular, bustling bar/restaurant is worth a stop.

Casa Bernardo (☎ 922 80 08 49, fax 922 80 00 81, Calle Triana 4) offers simple, clean singles/doubles/triples for 2000/3500/5000 ptas.

For more comfort, singles at *Hotel de Triana* (☎ 922 80 05 28, fax 922 80 01 28, Calle Triana s/n) cost 3500 ptas and doubles start at 5800 ptas. It's a pleasant place with a restaurant, where half board costs an extra 2000 ptas per person.

A good little place to eat with the locals is *Restaurante Triana*, just around the corner at No 19.

Around Vallehermoso

Los Órganos To contemplate this extraordinary cliffscape (something like a great sculpted church organ in basalt rising abruptly from the ocean depths), 4km north of Vallehermoso, you'll need to head out to sea. Boats making the trip actually set out from Valle Gran Rey and Playa Santiago in the south-west of the island (see those sections for details). The columned cliff face has been battered into its present shape by the ocean.

Alojera The main highway south of Vallehermoso snakes its way along the valley through farming villages (some abandoned) and up into the western extremity of the Parque Nacional de Garajonay. Shortly before the highway enters the park proper, a side road winds out, initially east then curling west, to Alojera, a sleepy settlement sprawled out above the black pebble Playa de Alojera. Tracks lead north to Tazo (about 5km) and Arguamul (8km). The best part of coming here is the spectacular drive down from the highway. If you want to stay, try *Apartamentos Ossorio (☎ 922 80 03 34)* at the entrance to the village. It has studios for 2500 ptas and an apartment for up to three at 3500 ptas.

Tazo & Arguamul In and around Tazo are some fine old traditional farm houses. The surrounding area also has the island's most extensive palm grove. The sap is used to make palm honey, a local speciality – the sap is boiled into a kind of thick dark syrup.

Arguamul, 3km beyond, is another tiny hamlet. Walking trails lead on a kilometre to Playa del Remo, and you could also walk south-east up to the ridge dominated by the Teselinde peak (876m) and then follow the Barranco de la Era Nueva down into Vallehermoso.

In dry weather you can get a car down this road: in wet weather it is often impassable.

VALLE GRAN REY
postcode 38870 • pop 3440

You'd better brush up on your German. The tourists, bar and waiting staff, even the signs, are German. The Canarios are in there somewhere but you have to look. This said, it's a place with some taste, a far cry from the horrors of lager-lout land in southern Tenerife!

As far as tourism on the island has taken off, Valle Gran Rey (Valley of the Great King, named after a Guanche leader called Orone) is where it's at. The majority of La Gomera's accommodation is here and it is not hard to see why. The valley itself is a deep gorge carved out from the ancient inland rock that fans out in a small fertile delta as it meets the ocean.

The area is one of the island's most pros-

perous, but farmers have stretched the possible to the limit, planting bananas and tomatoes deep into the steep valley.

Before you descend into the valley itself, you could stop in **Arure**. The views from the Mirador del Santo over the ravines and out to La Palma and El Hierro are splendid. A few kilometres farther south is another lookout, the Mirador César Manrique, with a restaurant (see Places to Eat).

Orientation & Information Valle Gran Rey is really a collection of little hamlets with a grand name. The high part is known as La Calera. From here the road forks to descend to La Playa (right) and Vueltas (left). Both have small beaches and plenty of accommodation, and Vueltas also serves as the area's harbour.

Street names and numbers are all but nonexistent, so pick a map from the tourist office (☎ 922 80 54 58) on Calle Lepanto in La Playa. It opens 9 am to 1.30 pm and 4 to 6.30 pm, Monday to Saturday, and 10 am to 1.30 pm on Sunday. An information office directed primarily at German visitors, La Paloma, is in the heart of Vueltas. Even more useful is Servicios Integrados La Gomera (☎ 922 80 58 66, fax 922 80 50 63) in La Calera, as you enter the resort. They seem to have fingers in every local pie and can arrange accommodation, walking tours, car hire, boat trips and more.

The post office is in Vueltas, while the banks (some with ATMs) and petrol station are in La Calera. To send an email or two, visit Gerardo's Internet bar in La Playa.

Activities The black sandy stretch of beach at La Playa is quite tiny, but inviting enough, and a few steps from several laid-back restaurants and bars. A dirt track leads north to the west-facing Playa del Inglés. The beach at Vueltas is not so pretty, but a dirt road leads east to Playa de Argaga and Playa de las Arenas.

For guided walks, contact long established Timah on ☎/fax 922 80 57 26 or via the Hotel Gran Rey (see the next section for details). OkoTours, on ☎ 922 80 59 40 or

LA GOMERA

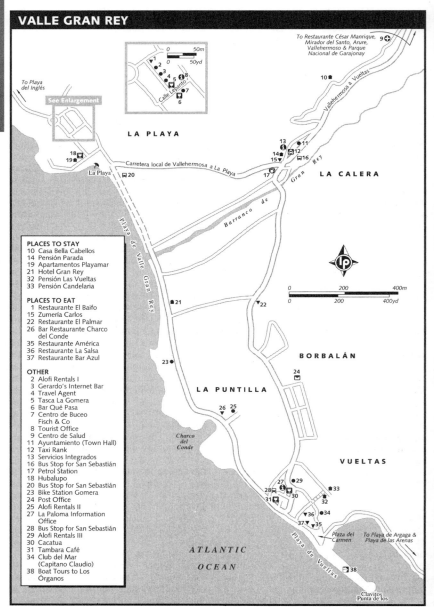

VALLE GRAN REY

LA PLAYA

LA CALERA

Barranco de Gran Rey

LA PUNTILLA

BORBALÁN

VUELTAS

ATLANTIC OCEAN

Charco del Conde

Plaza del Carmen

To Playa de Argaga & Playa de las Arenas

Clavijos Punta de los

To Restaurante César Manrique, Mirador del Santo, Arure, Vallehermoso & Parque Nacional de Garajonay

To Playa del Inglés

Carretera local de Vallehermosa a La Playa

Playa de Valle Gran Rey

Playa de Vueltas

PLACES TO STAY
10 Casa Bella Cabellos
14 Pensión Parada
19 Apartamentos Playamar
21 Hotel Gran Rey
32 Pensión Las Vueltas
33 Pensión Candelaria

PLACES TO EAT
1 Restaurante El Baifo
15 Zumería Carlos
22 Restaurante El Palmar
26 Bar Restaurante Charco del Conde
35 Restaurante América
36 Restaurante La Salsa
37 Restaurante Bar Azul

OTHER
2 Alofi Rentals I
3 Gerardo's Internet Bar
4 Travel Agent
5 Tasca La Gomera
6 Bar Qué Pasa
7 Centro de Buceo Fisch & Co
8 Tourist Office
9 Centro de Salud
11 Ayuntamiento (Town Hall)
12 Taxi Rank
13 Servicios Integrados
16 Bus Stop for San Sebastián
17 Petrol Station
18 Hubalupo
20 Bus Stop for San Sebastián
23 Bike Station Gomera
24 Post Office
25 Alofi Rentals II
27 La Paloma Information Office
28 Bus Stop for San Sebastián
29 Alofi Rentals III
30 Cacatua
31 Tambara Café
34 Club del Mar (Capitano Claudio)
38 Boat Tours to Los Órganos

via Alofi Rentals (see Getting Around later for details), also do small group day treks.

Two motor boats, Tina and Siron, cruise northwards to Los Órganos, a bizarre cliff formation (see Around Vallehermoso earlier), where you may also get to see dolphins and have a swim. Unfortunately, the success of these expeditions depends on prevailing winds and operators do not guarantee you will see either dolphins or Los Órganos. Departure is at 10.30 am from the Vueltas port. Tickets cost 5000 ptas (children 2500 ptas), including lunch.

To learn more about whales and dolphins rather than just taking a trip on the briny, contact Capitano Claudio at the Club del Mar (☎ 922 80 57 59) in Vueltas. The club, which also undertakes marine research, has four-hour sailings daily (3750 ptas).

See Whales & Dolphins under Ecology & Environment in the Facts about the Islands chapter for details of marine-friendly trips.

Bike Station Gomera (for details, see Getting Around later) has regular guided cycling expeditions while Fisch & Co (☎/fax 922 80 56 88), Calle Lepanto, organises diving and snorkelling expeditions.

Places to Stay About half-a-dozen pensiones are scattered evenly about Vueltas, La Calera and La Playa. Otherwise, the area swarms with apartments. You may want to get a list from the tourist office or reserve in advance through, for example, Servicios Integrados La Gomera (see Orientation & Information earlier), who have apartments ranging from 3500 ptas to 8000 ptas on their books.

The prettiest place to stay must be *Casa Bella Cabellos* (☎ 922 80 51 82), an enchanting old house with wooden balconies, high above La Calera. Turn right for the Centro de Salud as you approach La Calera from the north and continue beyond it. Simple rooms cost 3000 ptas and there's a studio for 4000 ptas. The owner also has four-bed apartments in the village, which costs 5000 ptas to 7000 ptas.

Vueltas seems to be nothing but apartments. Prices start around 3500 ptas and

head steadily upwards depending on quality, the number of beds and whim. If you just want a no-nonsense room, *Pensión Las Vueltas* (☎ 922 80 52 16), up the steps beside Supermercado El Puerto, has clean and comfortable doubles with bathroom for 3000 ptas. Just beyond, *Pensión Candelaria* (☎ 922 80 54 02) has doubles with bathroom starting at 4000 ptas.

Pensión Parada (☎ 922 80 50 52), near the bus stop in La Calera, has basic doubles for 3500 ptas. Ask at Zumería Carlos, just below.

In La Playa, *Apartamentos Playamar* (☎ 922 80 60 09), on the beach, has studios for as little as 3000 ptas (4000 ptas for the first night).

For something upmarket, *Hotel Gran Rey* (☎ 922 80 58 59, fax 922 80 56 51), on the waterfront about halfway between La Playa and Vueltas, has rooms for 8100/12,200 ptas, including breakfast.

Places to Eat Fresh fish, combined with a good local *mojo* (salsa/sauce), is generally great value. It's well-worth moving inland to try *Restaurante El Palmar*, set back from the road linking Vueltas with La Calera. It does a mean *atún* (tuna) *en mojo* for 975 ptas and most mains cost around 1200 ptas. On the coast in La Puntilla, *Bar Restaurante Charco del Conde*, beside the inlet of the same name, is also great for fish.

In Vueltas, *Restaurante La Salsa* serves up tasty vegetarian food from around the world. *Restaurante América* is mainly fishy and a full meal will cost around 2000 ptas. Next-door, kitsch *Restaurante Bar Azul* is garlanded with plastic flowers in a variety of ugly containers. But their mains, between 1100 ptas and 1700 ptas, are OK and they put on several vegetarian dishes at 1000 ptas.

In La Playa, *Restaurante El Baifo* offers an unusual mix of French and South-East Asian dishes, such as *gado-gado* (salad with peanut sauce).

In La Calera, *Zumería Carlos*, with a cornucopia of fresh fruit brimming from the fridge behind the bar, is great for juices.

Out of town on the road to Arure, try *Restaurante César Manrique* (☎ *922 80 58 68*) at the lookout point of the same name. Open 10 am to 10.30 pm, Wednesday to Sunday, it's a restaurant training school. Despite – or perhaps because of – this, the food, unlike the breathtaking views, fails to stun. However, it's well-worth dropping in for a drink – and a leak in what must be the toilets with the world's finest panorama.

Entertainment In Vueltas, a good place at sunset and on into the night is the balcony of *Tambara Café*, with views over the ocean. It opens 5 pm to 1 am. *Cacatua* has a lively patio but shuts shop at 11 pm and all day on Monday.

Then, it's time to move on to La Playa.

There, *Tasca La Gomera* is generally busy and does a nice line in exotic cocktails. At nearby *Bar Qué Pasa* salsa and merengue are the flavour while the music also thumps at *Hubalupo*.

Getting There & Away There are buses for San Sebastián (one hour 40 minutes, four daily) departing from at least three points (one stop each in Vueltas, La Playa and La Calera).

Getting Around Bike Station Gomera (☎/fax 922 80 50 82) in La Puntilla both rents bikes and organises cycle excursions. Around the resort, Alofi Rentals (☎/fax 922 80 55 54) has three branches which hire out bikes, scooters and motor cycles.

La Palma

Known in full as San Miguel de la Palma, the north-westernmost island of the archipelago lies 85km from Tenerife. It has also long been dubbed the Isla Bonita (Pretty Island) and it's easy enough to see why.

With rainfall and spring water more plentiful here than anywhere else in the Canaries (on average the sun doesn't come out at all 63 days per year!), La Palma's 708 sq km form the archipelago's greenest island. Its 86,110 inhabitants live fairly well from a combination of agriculture (it's hard to avoid banana plantations), fishing and the still modest tourist business. This comparative prosperity has not, however, been a constant and Venezuela has traditionally been the emigrant Palmeros' favourite place of escape. So much so that the Latin American country is often known around here as the 'eighth (Canary) island'.

The flourishing orchards, plantations and forests contrast strikingly with the hostile volcanic heights that form a kind of mountainous question mark down the middle of the island.

La Palma's most extraordinary feature is the huge horseshoe-shaped rock wall known as the Caldera de Taburiente. From it jut the island's highest peaks, including the Roque de los Muchachos (2426m), home to one of the world's most important astrophysical observatories. One statistic claims that, relative to its size, La Palma is the hilliest island in the world. What's sure is that it's the highest island in the archipelago after Tenerife.

Volcanic activity is far from over. The last eruption in the Canaries, a modest one, happened in the south of La Palma in 1971 while in late 2000 a less restrained polemic took place as seismologists blew their tops over whether the next big one would occur in 50 or more like 5000 years.

A more recurrent menace is forest fire. In 2000, one such fire raged for three full days and charred over 4,500 hectares, primarily of Canary pine, in the north-west of the

Highlights

- Enjoying a *barraquito* (coffee) on Placeta de Borrero, Santa Cruz de la Palma
- Relaxing on the black-sand beach of Puerto Naos
- Exploring the Parque Nacional de la Caldera de Taburiente
- Walking the ridgeback Ruta de los Volcanes
- Discovering the fine old balconies of Santa Cruz's old quarter

island. But Canary pines are a tough subspecies that start to sprout again no more than three months after the fire has left them as blackened stumps.

The southern end of the island is worlds away from its general lushness – a black wasteland interspersed with the reds and browns of other volcanic material and the pale green of what little flora attempts to reclaim the land.

The abrupt and often forbidding coastline does not offer the great sandy stretches that attract sun-seekers to La Palma's more easterly neighbours, yet the cliffs and rocky outcrops are occasionally interrupted by pleasant little black-sand beaches. For this reason alone the island may be spared the massive influx of tourists seen elsewhere in the Canaries, allowing those who do visit the luxury of exploring the ravines, hamlets

LA PALMA

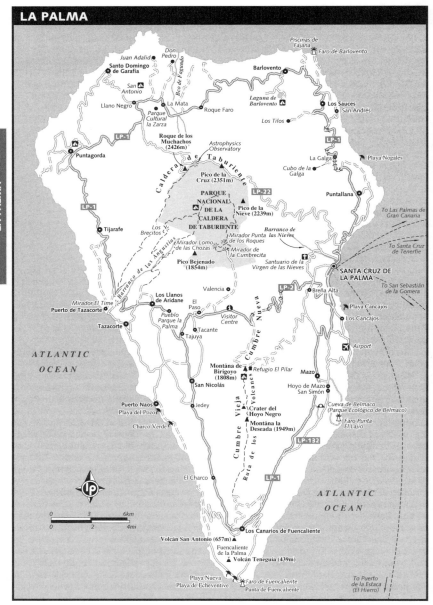

LA PALMA

and fertile countryside in comparative peace.

History

La Palma was not incorporated into the Crown of Castilla until 1493, the year after Alonso Fernández de Lugo had finished off the island's native opposition. This he had achieved only after a stroke of trickery. He invited the leader of the Benahoare (the Guanche tribe on La Palma), Mencey Tanausú, to abandon his impregnable stronghold in the Caldera de Taburiente for talks, only to ambush him and his men at the spot now known as El Riachuelo. Tanausú was shipped to Spain as a slave, but went on hunger strike and never saw the Spanish mainland.

By the following century, the few Benahoares who had not been enslaved or wiped out had been joined by a motley assortment of Spanish, Portuguese, Italian and Flemish migrants. The main exports became sugar, *malvasía* (Malmsey wine) and honey. In the meantime, the abundant Canary pine provided timber for burgeoning shipyards. By the late 16th century, as trans-Atlantic trade flourished, Santa Cruz de la Palma was considered the third most important port of the Spanish empire after Seville and Antwerp (in modern Belgium).

The fortunes of La Palma largely followed those of the other islands, as one cash crop succeeded another. Today, the banana remains a mainstay of the island's economy, although a wide range of crops are grown for local consumption. The cigars (half the menfolk seem to have one lodged permanently in a corner of the mouth) are of particular note and concede little to the product of Havana.

Information

Books & Maps The Firestone sheet covering all seven Canary islands has a reliable map of La Palma at 1:150,000. Michelin cover La Palma (at 1:125,000) on their No 222 map, *Tenerife, El Hierro, La Gomera & La Palma*.

For hiking, there are a pair of excellent maps and detailed accompanying walk de-

JANE SMITH

White-washed churches are common in the Canary Islands.

scriptions in *La Palma, East* and *La Palma, West* (Discovery Walking Guides). *Landscapes of La Palma and El Hierro* by Noel Rochford follows the usual Sunflower Books pattern, describing a number of possible walks and drives around the island, together with picnic suggestions.

Newspapers *La Isla de la Palma* appears weekly and its rival, *La Voz de la Palma*, hits the shelves every two weeks.

Pick up a copy of the free *Infomagazin*, which appears every three months in Spanish, English and German. It's informative, well written and several cuts above the usual free rags which live from advertising.

Activities

Walking is the main activity here, with a hike around part of the rim of the massive depression of the Caldera de Taburiente a must. Other possible treks take you south along the volcanic ridge of the Cumbre Vieja in the southern half of the island, while in the north the dense forest of Los Tilos is a green paradise. Several companies offer guided walks. Senderos Canarias (see Around Santa Cruz later in this chapter), for example, will pick you up from anywhere on the island.

LA PALMA

Ask at the tourist office in Santa Cruz for their three free hiking maps covering the northern, central and southern parts of the island. An island-wide walkers' map is also promised for late 2001 and a campaign is currently underway to sign all major walking trails.

Cycling, if you're not averse to a steep climb or two, is another agreeable way to experience the island.

Diving too is a possibility, and you'll find several dive centres around the coast. There are several black-sand beaches, a few of them quite pretty.

Accommodation

Camping Free camping is prohibited on the island. There are a few basic camp sites, but to use them you need to apply in advance by phone.

For the only camp site inside the Parque Nacional de la Caldera de Taburiente – a 6km hike from Los Brecitos, itself 10km of driveable dirt trail north from Los Llanos de Aridane – call the park visitor centre (☎ 922 49 72 77). The facilities are basic and it has room for 100 people. It's advisable to book well ahead (as much as one month in summer). You pick up the permit from the visitor centre, which is 3.5km east of El Paso. Bring a photocopy of your passport. The maximum stay is three days.

There are five camp sites outside the park. Phone the Consejería de Política Territorial y Medio Ambiente (Department of the Environment; ☎ 922 41 15 83) in Santa Cruz for those in Fuencaliente, by the Refugio El Pilar in the north of the Cumbre Vieja, and at San Antonio, south-east of Santo Domingo de Garafía, You need to apply at least a week in advance and collect your permit in person at least two days before you intend to camp. The office is just before the tunnel leading south to the airport.

The other two camp sites are outside Puntagorda (☎ 922 49 33 06) and beside the Laguna de Barlovento (☎ 922 69 60 23).

Hotels & Apartments There is a shortage of standard accommodation such as hotels and pensiones on the island. Resort apartments are spreading in a few areas, notably at Los Cancajos, just south of Santa Cruz, and Puerto Naos in the west, but these are aimed at pre-booked package tourists, mainly from Germany and Holland.

Casas Rurales Another pleasant, but by no means budget option, are *casas rurales*, renovated houses in the country. The Asociación de Turismo Rural has around 70 such places scattered across the island, mostly in the north (where alternatives are extremely thin on the ground). Try the central reservations office (☎ 922 43 06 25, ☎/fax 922 43 03 08), Casa Luján, Calle El Pósito 3, Puntallana. There's a Web site at www.infolapalma.com/islabonita in English, German and Spanish.

Getting There & Away

Air The inconvenient sea link schedules make wings an attractive alternative – for this reason flights are often booked solid. Binter connects La Palma airport (☎ 922 41 15 40) with Tenerife Norte (6860 ptas, up to 12 daily) and Gran Canaria (10,410 ptas, at least twice daily). Otherwise, traffic consists of one Iberia flight daily to Madrid and direct charter flights, mostly from Germany, with a few from Amsterdam and Zürich.

JMC, a relative newcomer to the skies, has a direct winter-only flight to La Palma from London Gatwick, on Fridays from November to March.

The airport, 7km south of Santa Cruz, has several car-rental agents, an exchange bureau (with a Western Union money transfer representative) and a small tourist office.

Boat Ferries from Tenerife (Santa Cruz and Los Cristianos) and La Gomera arrive in Santa Cruz de la Palma.

A Fred Olsen ferry departs daily from Los Cristianos at 7 pm, calls in at San Sebastián de la Gomera and then proceeds to Santa Cruz de la Palma, from where it heads back to Los Cristianos at 11.55 pm. The basic one-way fare is 3080 ptas.

Trasmediterránea has one boat per week to/from Santa Cruz de Tenerife – the big one that brings supplies from Cádiz on the mainland. It leaves Tenerife at midnight and arrives in La Palma at 8 am on Friday. Returning, it departs Santa Cruz de la Palma at 2pm on Friday. The basic fare is 3900 ptas.

Getting Around

Bus If you intend using the buses a lot to get around the island, you are better off buying a Bonobus card. Cards start at 2000 ptas and represent a discount of about 30% off the normal individual fares. They are on sale at bus stations and various shops such as newsagents.

There are 18 bus lines, covering most main destinations

Santa Cruz de la Palma

postcode 38700 • pop 18,705

The row of modern, gleaming-white buildings that greets the traveller who comes by sea to Santa Cruz might seem to promise little. Look inland and, as the waves of white walls give way to the farmers' green terraces and volcanic hills, you may be sorely tempted to strike immediately for the interior.

But hang on, because hidden from view as you get off the ferry is a quite enchanting old town centre, featuring some fine examples of Canarian architecture grouped in and around some charming little plazas.

HISTORY

The bay that is the town's window on the world was known to the Guanches as Timibucar, and the area around it as Tedote. The island's Spanish conqueror, Alonso Fernández de Lugo, had the first breakwater built, along with the settlement's first public buildings.

As Spain's imperial interests in the Americas grew in the 16th century, so did the fortunes of Santa Cruz, whose dockyards soon acquired a reputation as the best in all the Canary Islands. Such was the town's importance that King Felipe II had the first Juz-

gado de Indias (Court of the Indias) installed here in 1558, at which every single vessel trading with the Americas from mainland Spain was obliged to register.

Such prosperity did not go unnoticed; Santa Cruz was frequently besieged and occasionally sacked by a succession of pirates, including those under the command of Sir Francis Drake. The worst attack came in 1553, when Jean Paul de Billancourt (aka Jambe de Bois, or Pegleg) unleashed a merciless assault on the town.

ORIENTATION

Santa Cruz is a fairly small town, and most of interest lies within a few blocks of the waterfront Avenida Marítima, which runs north from the ferry port. It is about a 15-minute walk from the port to the Barranco de las Nieves which virtually marks off the northern confines of the town.

The heart of the old town and the prettiest part of Santa Cruz de la Palma lies around Plaza de España and Calle O'Daly, known to the Santacruceros as Calle Real.

INFORMATION
Tourist Offices

The well-informed tourist office (☎ 922 41 21 06) at Calle O'Daly 22 is housed in the impressive 17th-century Palacio de Salazar (see The Old Town section later). It opens 9 am to 1 pm and 5 to 7 pm, Monday to Friday, and 10.30 am to 1 pm on Saturday.

Post & Communications

The post office is on Plaza de la Constitución.

You can access the web at Copy.com, Calle A Cabrera Pinto 15. Open 9 am to 1.30 pm and 4 to 7.30 pm, Monday to Friday, and 9 am to 1.30 pm on Saturday, it charges 500 ptas per hour.

Newspapers

Odd, granted, but about the only place in town to find foreign newspapers is Buen Viaje Rent a Car, Avenida Marítima 25.

Laundry

There's a laundrette at Calle Díaz Pimienta 10, just behind the covered market.

LA PALMA

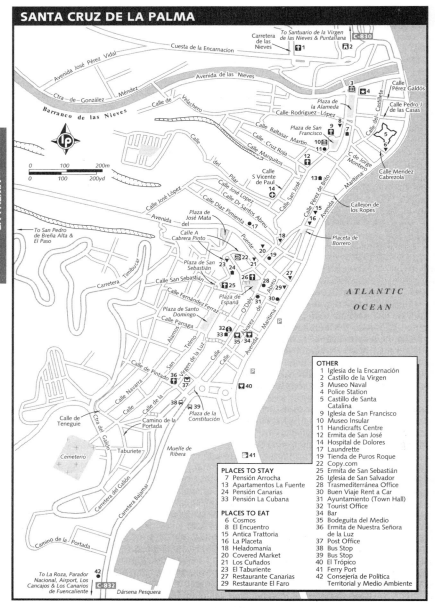

SANTA CRUZ DE LA PALMA

OTHER
1 Iglesia de la Encarnación
2 Castillo de la Virgen
3 Museo Naval
4 Police Station
5 Castillo de Santa Catalina
9 Iglesia de San Francisco
10 Museo Insular
11 Handicrafts Centre
12 Ermita de San José
14 Hospital de Dolores
17 Laundrette
19 Tienda de Puros Roque
22 Copy.com
25 Ermita de San Sebastián
26 Iglesia de San Salvador
28 Trasmediterránea Office
30 Buen Viaje Rent a Car
31 Ayuntamiento (Town Hall)
32 Tourist Office
34 Bar
35 Bodeguita del Medio
36 Ermita de Nuestra Señora de la Luz
37 Post Office
38 Bus Stop
39 Bus Stop
40 El Trópico
41 Ferry Port
42 Consejería de Política Territorial y Medio Ambiente

PLACES TO STAY
7 Pensión Arrocha
13 Apartamentos La Fuente
24 Pensión Canarias
33 Pensión La Cubana

PLACES TO EAT
6 Cosmos
8 El Encuentro
15 Antica Trattoria
16 La Placeta
18 Heladomanía
20 Covered Market
21 Los Cuñados
23 El Taburiente
27 Restaurante Canarias
29 Restaurante El Faro

LA PALMA

OLD TOWN

Buildings of historical importance all have information plaques in Spanish, English and German.

Calle O'Daly (Calle Real), named after an Irish trader who long ago made the town his home, is Santa Cruz's most venerable street. Its main feature is the 17th-century late-Renaissance **Palacio de Salazar**, now home to the tourist office. Along both sides of the cobbled, pedestrianised street is a mix of shops, bars and offices, most of which occupy centuries-old Canarian mansions.

From the rise behind Plaza de la Constitución (climb the steps about 100m south of the post office), the modest **Ermita de Nuestra Señora de la Luz** stands watch over the harbour – appropriately so since the chapel is also dedicated to San Telmo, patron saint of sailors and fishermen, whose guild paid for its construction in 1680. It opens 7 to 9 pm on Saturday and Sunday. Inside is a rich Baroque altarpiece, illuminated and visible through a window in the eastern door, even when the chapel is closed.

The ermita is one of several small 16th- and 17th-century chapels, most of them originally attached to monasteries, which the Dominicans and Franciscans established in the popular quarters of Santa Cruz, up above the choicer noble and bourgeois quarter nearer the coast.

Another chapel, dedicated to **San Sebastián**, is on the street of the same name behind the Iglesia de San Salvador. Yet another is the **Ermita de San José**, which has also given its name to the street on which it stands.

Just north of Restaurante Canarias (see Places to Eat later) on the waterfront is a series of wonderful, gaily painted **old houses**. Some date back to the 16th century and all sport balconies in a variety of styles. This penchant for balconies came with Andalucían migrants and was modified by Portuguese influences. The style was also exported, and similar balconies can be seen on noble houses in Venezuela, Cuba and Peru, where they came to be part of the so-called 'colonial style' of building.

It's lucky that the balconies are still there at all; King Felipe II apparently disapproved of balconies and sent orders to the islands that they be torn down. But the ship carrying the royal command never made it to La Palma, so the good citizens of Santa Cruz maintained their prized balconies, safe in their ignorance.

Plaza de España

Wander north along Calle O'Daly and you end up in the heart of old Santa Cruz. The main facade of the *ayuntamiento* (town hall) is a 16th-century Renaissance creation, and the imposing **Iglesia de San Salvador**, among the most opulent in all the islands, dates from the same period. Inside the town hall, there are magnificent tea-tree ceilings, or *artesonados*. The church, for its part, boasts a fine mudéjar ceiling, rich in traditional motifs such as the eight-point star whose roots lie in mainland Spain's Moorish period. Noteworthy among the artworks is a 16th-century Flemish carving of the crucifixion, *Cristo de los Mulatos*, in the Capilla de Ánimas side chapel.

The square itself – which boasts the archipelago's only surviving 16th-century fountain – is flanked by grand mansions. You'll see more such noble houses, most of them adorned with balconies in a variety of styles, as you head north along Calle Pérez de Brito.

Cigars

Even the most rabid antismoker might enjoy poking a nose into **Tienda de Puros Roque**, a wonderful small temple to nicotine in its finest form, and sniffing its rich aromas. Sr Roque, as the photos in his workshop attest, provided *puros* (cigars), the finest and the fattest, to Sir Winston Churchill, among other luminaries. His workshop is at Calle Pérez Volcán 10, just opposite the covered market.

AROUND THE BARRANCO DE LAS NIEVES

The **Iglesia de San Francisco**, another Renaissance church, is equally rich in works of art, the majority unmistakably baroque.

The plaque on the floor just inside the eastern portal commemorates one Baltasar Martín, killed while defending the church against assault by Pegleg and his French pirates in 1553.

The restored convent next door is architecturally interesting and worth a visit for its own sake. The small band of Franciscan monks who arrived with the conquering Spanish force began its construction in 1508, after having survived for 15 years in straw huts. Nowadays it houses the **Museo Insular**, the island's museum. Here, you'll find everything from Guanche skulls to cupboards of sad stuffed birds, animals, fish and pickled reptiles; shells and corals by the thousand; traditional household utensils; and a neat portrait of Franco with a feathery hat, upstairs among a dreary collection of anonymous and little-known Spanish artists. Convent and museum open 9.30 am to 1.50 pm and 4 to 6.20 pm, Monday to Friday. Admission costs 300 ptas.

Also on the square is the **Centro de Artesani**, which has a small exhibition of handicrafts for sale.

Gaze north across leafy Plaza de la Alameda (a good place to hover over a beer) and you'll think Columbus' Santa María got stranded here. But no, it's actually a rather weird idea for the town's **Museo Naval**, known as El Barco de la Virgen (the Virgin's Boat) to the locals. It opens 9.30 am to 2 pm and 4 to 7 pm, Monday to Thursday, and 9.30 am to 2 pm on Friday morning. Admission costs 150 ptas and it has some fascinating early maps of the coast and offshore islands on both sides of the Atlantic.

On the seafront, the **Castillo de Santa Catalina** was one of several built in the 17th century to fend off pirate raids. Across the ravine and higher is a smaller one, the **Castillo de la Virgen**. Tucked away up the same hill is the 16th-century **Iglesia de la Encarnación**, the first church to be built in Santa Cruz after the Spanish conquest.

SPECIAL EVENTS

Every five years (next time in 2005), Santa Cruz puts on its party clothes for the June–July celebration of the Bajada de la Virgen de las Nieves (Descent of Our Lady of the Snows). It's the island's principal fiesta – finding a place to stay at this time without having booked in advance is well-nigh impossible. The high point is the 'dance of the dwarves' which takes place along Calle O'Daly (the statue in Plaza de la Alameda of a perky little fellow under a huge tricorn hat gives an idea of what it's about).

Down this street also march the processions for Carnaval (February) and Easter Week, when members of lay brotherhoods parade in their blood-red robes and tall, pointy hoods, common in Spanish Easter parades but chillingly reminiscent of the Ku Klux Klan.

PLACES TO STAY – BUDGET

The choice is restricted but the quality's great.

Pensión Arrocha (☎ 922 41 11 17, Calle Pérez de Brito 77), in an old building rich in character, has basic singles/doubles for 2500/3500 ptas.

Pensión La Cubana (☎/fax 922 41 13 54, Calle O'Daly 24) is a travellers' and walkers' favourite. Clean, attractive rooms with external bathroom in this delightful old Santa Cruz house are excellent value at 3000/4000 ptas.

If you want your own bathroom, go for *Pensión Canarias* (☎ 922 41 31 82, Calle A. Cabrera Pinto 27) where pleasant, airy rooms cost from 3100/4300 ptas.

For all three, you'd be wise to reserve during winter months and if you're arriving from Tenerife by the late-night ferry.

PLACES TO STAY – MID-RANGE & TOP END

Apartamentos La Fuente (☎ 922 41 56 36, Calle Pérez de Brito 49) is a good bet. Studios start at 4700 ptas, while bigger apartments with balcony and sea views cost 7750 ptas.

About 8km south of town, the *Parador Nacional* (☎ 922 43 58 28, fax 922 43 59 99), inaugurated in 1999, is Spain's newest parador. Rooms cost 14,000/17,500 ptas.

PLACES TO EAT

A great little place for a beer and *arepa* (an envelope of maize – corn – with a savoury filling) is *Cosmos (Avenida Marítima 70)*.

For Canaries and Venezuelan specialities, take time out on the terraza of friendly *El Encuentro (Plaza de la Alameda)* where you can leave full and fulfilled with change from 1500 ptas. It also does great fresh juices.

El Taburiente, on the corner of Calles Poggio and A Cabrera Pinto, doesn't have a sign. But it doesn't need to, such is its reputation for unbeatable value food, prepared from prime-quality materials. Again, reckon on about 1500 ptas, including drinks.

Restaurante Canarias (Avenida Marítima 29) also offers hearty meals. The meat dishes are good and cost around 1300 ptas, the fish is fresh and they do a selection of original *platos combinados* (mixed dishes) at 800 ptas. Across the road, at No 27, intimate, low-ceilinged *Restaurante El Faro* is popular with Santacruceros. It closes on Sunday.

If you've a little extra money in your pockets, spill some of it at *La Placeta* (☎ 922 41 52 73, *Placeta de Borrero 1*) – count on 3500 ptas per head. The upstairs restaurant has an impressive Canarian/international menu. More modestly, call by for a breakfast *barraquito* (coffee Canaries style; see Drinks in the Facts for the Visitor chapter for details) on its terraza in the little square.

Just round the corner, *Antica Trattoria* (☎ 922 41 71 16) also operates as both restaurant and cafe with much the same prices. Stick to the house wines; the mark-up on others from their cellar is savage.

If you're self catering, take a trip around the small *covered market*, then cool off with a scoop or two of great ice-cream from *Heladomanía*, just behind. On the other side of the market, *Los Cuñados* makes most of the tantalising sweets and cakes on sale around the island and still finds time to make great bread. For your day sack, pick up a hunk of their *pan de jamón*, bread stuffed with ham, olives and raisins.

ENTERTAINMENT

Avenida Marítima is lined with cafes, *zumerías* (juice bars) and bars of a more nocturnal colouring. One block back, *Bodeguita del Medio (Calle Álvarez de Abreu 58)* is a bright little drinkery. Later in the evening, you could move across to the nameless *bar* at No 65.

La Roca, 2km south of the port in the Zona Industrial, dances until late and has live music at weekends. Best to take a taxi. Right beside the port entrance, *El Trópico* pulls in weekend revellers but can be a dull dump during the week – if you find it open. Both are active from July to mid-October but can't be guaranteed for the rest of the year.

GETTING THERE & AWAY
Air
See Getting There & Away at the beginning of the chapter for details.

Bus
Transportes Insular La Palma buses run to most destinations on the island. They depart from Carretera Bajamar, just off Plaza de la Constitución. Principal destinations are Los Llanos (No 1; 595 ptas) and Fuencaliente (No 3; 450 ptas).

Car & Motorcycle
There are plenty of car hire places in town, particularly along Avenida Marítima.

Taxi
You can use taxis to get around the island but, at 116 ptas per kilometre, they aren't cheap. The trip to Puerto Naos on the west coast, for example, will burn a hole over 4000 ptas wide in your pocket – more than the price of a day's car hire.

Boat
See Getting There & Away at the beginning of this chapter for details.

GETTING AROUND
To/From the Airport
Bus No 8 leaves every 30 minutes (hourly at weekends) on the quarter hour for/from the airport and take about 20 minutes,

LA PALMA

stopping at Los Cancajos. The fare is 160 ptas. A taxi costs about 1200 ptas.

Bus
Bus No 8 to the beach at Los Cancajos (140 ptas) are fairly frequent, stopping there en route to the airport. It takes about 45 minutes to walk there.

AROUND SANTA CRUZ DE LA PALMA
Santuario de la Virgen de las Nieves
A 2km hike or 4km drive from Santa Cruz leads to La Palma's main object of pilgrimage. To walk it (a 35- to 45-minute walk uphill, it's quicker coming down!): from the Museo Naval, follow the road, which becomes dirt track, westwards up the Barranco de las Nieves. By car, follow signs from the Avenida Marítima where it crosses the barranco.

This well-endowed 17th-century church and neighbouring *casa de romeros* (pilgrim hostel) are in typical Canarian colonial style, whitewashed, with tea-tree balconies. The church has a fine mudéjar ceiling. Above the altar, gleaming and plated with silver, gazes the image of the Virgin Mary that is brought down to Santa Cruz in grand procession every five years (see Special Events under Santa Cruz earlier). Note the naive ex voto canvases on the walls of the nave, painted in thanks to the Virgin for her intercession against the rages of the seas.

The spot is charming, surrounded by green slopes and palm trees, and those who walk up can give themselves a reward at the *restaurant bar*. Bus No 10 (140 ptas) comes up from Santa Cruz hourly.

Los Cancajos
A small strip of black-sand beach forms the nucleus of this small coastal resort with its scattering of restaurants, bars and discos. It's the base of Senderos Canarias, who organise hikes ranging between three and seven hours (from 3600 ptas). Ring to reserve on ☎ 922 43 30 01; they will collect you from anywhere on the island. La Palma Diving Center (☎ 922 18 13 93) is in Local

27 of the Centrocancajos shopping centre, a mournful cavern of a place with most of its lots unoccupied.

Restaurante Tiuna overlooks the beach. For more traditional dishes try *Mesón Canario*, in Centrocancajos, Local 314. For late night action, *H2O* is a disco which pulls in the young crowd from Santa Cruz while *Pub Guantanamera*, in Centrocancajos, often has live music at weekends.

Around the Island

PARQUE NACIONAL DE LA CALDERA DE TABURIENTE
Scan the enormous and ancient stone walls of this natural fortress from the south and you can appreciate how the terrain challenged the invading Spaniards back in the late 15th century. Here the last of the Benahoares, under Mencey Tanausú, took refuge and there was precious little Alonso Fernández de Lugo could do to dislodge them. Luckily for him, the chief had faith in the honour of his opponents and was induced to abandon his eyrie for 'talks' that proved to be none other than an old-fashioned ambush.

The Parque Nacional de la Caldera de Taburiente was declared a national park in 1954, the fourth in Spain. Its massive, broken wall of volcanic rock is about 10km in diameter and the only real opening, the aptly named Barranco de las Angustias (Gorge of Fear), lies to the south-west. The walls drop in some places as much as 2000m, and their crests are crenellated by shafts of rock, ancient volcanic plugs known as *roques*. The park, cloaked at its lower levels in dense thickets of Canary pine, covers 4690 hectares.

All may seem impressively still as you contemplate this extraordinary feat of accidental engineering, but the forces of erosion are hard at work. Landslides and collapsing roques are not infrequent, and some geologists give the caldera only another 5000 years before its last vestiges finally disappear – time enough for us to admire it at leisure.

In 1825 the German geologist Leopold von Buch applied the Spanish term 'caldera' (a large, deep pot or cauldron) to what he assumed to be a massive volcanic crater, the Caldera de Taburiente. The word stuck, to be used as a standard term for all such volcanic craters the world over. However, this caldera, although indeed largely made up of volcanic rock, was not in fact the result of a massive eruption, but has rather been slowly excavated by erosion over the millennia.

Water flows mainly along underground channels but occasionally crashes headlong in waterfalls down the caldera's many steep ravines. It flows to the south-west coast along the Barranco de las Angustias and is siphoned off to irrigate the lowlands beyond the park.

Approaches to the Park

The South No roads run right through the park. From the south you have two possible approaches. The most common is from the park's **visitor centre**, open 9 am to 2 pm and 4 to 6.30 pm daily. It runs a good 20-minute film on the park. The English version is on the half hour – or on request if things are quiet. The centre is also a good source of information and advice for walkers (see the next section). Bus No 1, which links Santa Cruz and Los Llanos, passes by the centre hourly.

Just across the road from the visitor centre is ***Pensión Nambroque*** (☎ 922 48 52 79), bleak but a good base for walkers with wheels. Good singles/doubles with bathroom cost 4000/5000 ptas.

Beside the centre is the turn-off north for **La Cumbrecita**, a 7km drive that takes you to a *mirador* (lookout) and information booth in the southern reaches of the park. That's as far as your motor will get you.

Alternatively, from Los Llanos (follow the signs for Los Barrios) a dirt trail leads 10km into the park, climbing steeply as far as Los Brecitos. From there it is a 6km hike to the park's only ***camp site*** (see Accommodation at the beginning of this chapter).

From both La Cumbrecita and the camp site, several walking trails lead off deep into the park.

The North The LP-22 (also signed VTF-8122) heads left 3km north of Santa Cruz and snakes across the centre of the island, skirting the caldera's northern peaks. You'll need your own wheels, no buses pass here.

If you simply want to sense what this massive eroded wall and its many gorges look like, the drive up, punctuated by a few strategic stops, is the best way to enjoy the island's star attraction. The most spectacular lookout is from the Roque de los Muchachos (the island's highest point at 2426m), which you can drive to. The turn-off for the Roque is the same as for the observatory buildings, which can't be visited. Go beyond the barrier, which is in force only from 8 pm to 9 am so that the stars have no terrestrial rival from car headlights.

Walking

Your best general walking reference is the free map, *Caldera de Taburiente*, handed out at the visitor centre, which has all the major trails marked up. The visitor centre also retails the excellent *Visitor's Guide* (1500 ptas), crammed with information about the park, including descriptions of its major trails.

The park trails are generally in good shape, but signposting, even at the beginning or end of a route, is scarce to nonexistent, so you'll need one of the above references. Come prepared for all weather extremes – when the sun is shining it's hot but it can easily turn damp and cold. Always take water and something to nibble.

Between July and September, the park rangers lead free guided walks, departing from the camp site at 10 am daily. Just turn up; there's no need to sign on in advance.

The South From the Mirador de la Cumbrecita you can undertake a couple of short, painless strolls. The first leads 1km westwards along a track to another lookout, the Mirador Lomo de las Chozas. Allow 30 to 40 minutes, out and back. A little more difficult is the descent to – and corresponding

LA PALMA

Starry Starry Night

When you gaze up into the crystal arch of sky above the Canary Islands, you cannot help but get some sense of what it is that excites astronomers the world over. The quality of the sky is such that the islands have been singled out as one of the best locations in the world for earthbound observation of the universe.

For more than 30 years astronomers have been peering into the night firmament from Tenerife and La Palma. Their efforts are coordinated by the Instituto de Astrofísica de Canarias (IAC), based at the university of La Laguna on Tenerife. The islands are also the base of the European Northern Observatory, shared by 12 Western European nations. Researchers from member countries apply for time on the telescopes, with a fifth of the allocations reserved for Spanish scientists.

The IAC has an observatory on the Teide mountain at Izaña (Tenerife) and another at Roque de los Muchachos on La Palma. The Teide observatory is used primarily for solar research and to study the Big Bang.

More famous is the cluster of domes, antennae and sensors which together make up the Observatorio Astrofísico de la Palma, on the very edge of the Parque Nacional de la Caldera de Taburiente. While astronomers at Teide are daylight creatures, their colleagues at the Roque de los Muchachos observatory are very much night owls. Even the locals support the scientists' efforts, with the island's lights being turned off once a year to allow certain experiments to take place. Making a virtue out of necessity, the occasion becomes one for impromptu partying – when stumbling in the dark presumably starts well before any inebriation.

Current research ranges from the study of the expansion of the universe through to star bursts, the observation of quasars and investigation of 'circumnuclear gas', eruptions of extragalactic supernovae, and studies on telescope making, optics and infrared instrumentation. The most important telescopes here are those of the Isaac Newton Group, whose big gun is the state-of-the-art William Herschel Telescope, an Anglo-Dutch instrument with a 4.2m diameter.

Neither observatory opens to the public.

steepish ascent from! – the Mirador Punta de los Roques. This too is about half an hour, down and up. You can combine the two by taking a linking track. Begin by dropping to the Mirador Punta de los Roques and allow 1¼ hours for the round trip.

An altogether more challenging hike strikes out north-north-east a little before the Mirador Punta de los Roques and continues to El Escuchadero, up inside the eastern wall of the caldera. Reckon on a good two hours each way.

Another possibility, if you have your own wheels (in fact doing anything in the park presupposes that you're independently mobile), is to follow the fork in the road to Valencia from the visitor centre rather than that to La Cumbrecita. Once you reach a flat section of road, a walking trail heads north (right) to the Pico Bejenado (1854m). Plan

on about 2½ hours, there and back, to enjoy the reward of one of the most inspiring – and least experienced – views out over the caldera.

From the camp site (itself a 6km trek from Los Brecitos), various walks can be done. They lead north part of the way up some of the ravines sliced into the walls of the caldera and circuit inside its heart below. Between July and September, park guides lead daily walks from the camp site. They're free and informal and you don't have to book a place in advance.

Near the camp site, the clear water from several barrancos runs together in the so-called Playa de Taburiente, where tired hikers can give themselves a refreshing rinse down.

The North You can walk around much of the length of the top of the rock walls that form the caldera. To home in on the most spectacular section, take the LP-22 (also called the VTF-8122) from just north of Santa Cruz and leave your vehicle at the turn-off for the Pico de la Nieve (2239m).

After 20 minutes walking, you can strike out along a narrow path in one of two directions: south-eastwards to the Ermita de la Virgen del Pino and on to the visitor centre beside the LP-2 highway or, even more spectacularly, with the caldera constantly on your left, north-west up to the Roque de los Muchachos (4½ to 5½ hours), where you'll need a friendly car to collect you. Less strenuously, press on to the summit of Pico de la Nieve, where, unless cloud obscures the valley, you'll have a panorama as splendid as any in the park, then return to your vehicle. The round-trip hike takes 1¾ to two hours.

If you don't want to do even this shorter walk, the drive west affords several opportunities to stop at lookouts and lean out over one of nature's most remarkable balconies before pushing on to the distinctive rock figures of the 'lads' *(muchachos)* that constitute the Roque de los Muchachos.

THE NORTH
Puntallana
postcode 38715 • pop 2025

San Juan de Puntallana still retains some relics of its centuries of inhabitation, among them the **Iglesia de San Juan Bautista**, but there is really not a lot to this small and largely neglected hamlet.

Nearby, however, is one of those delightful little finds still possible on an island relatively undamaged by mass tourism. **Playa Nogales** is a comparatively long stretch of black sandy beach backed by forbidding cliffs that by midday already cast their shadow across the sand. From Puntallana follow signs for Bajamar, then the turn-off signed 'Playa Nogales'. Park your vehicle at the top of the cliffs and pick your way down a steep dirt path.

La Galga
Somewhat larger than Puntallana, La Galga is in much the same vein and could be skipped without any great loss. A side road leads 4km west to the Cubo de la Galga, a small protected forest.

San Andrés & Los Sauces
postcode 38720 • pop 5436

Of all the island's villages, San Andrés, down on the east coast, is one of the best preserved. Walking its uneven cobbled streets, bordered by houses both trim and tumbledown, is a delight and the folk seem as pleasant as their homes. The large parish church, centrepiece of the village, has fine artesonado ceilings and a couple of lavish baroque altarpieces. The Fiesta de San Andrés is celebrated on 30 November.

Cheerful *Pensión Martín* (☎ 922 45 05 39, Calle San Sebastián 4) has simple singles/doubles for 2000/3000 ptas. Nearby at No 16, *Pensión Las Lonjas* (☎ 922 45 07 36), has rooms with bathroom for 3000/4000 ptas. *Restaurante San Andrés*, a friendly place on the plaza beside the church, does a good range of salads and has excellent fresh fish.

Los Sauces has nothing to detain you except possibly the **Molino El Regente**, a restored 19th-century watermill and minuscule folk museum. However, after a grand opening in which all the villagers received a free bag of freshly milled gofio, the grindstones haven't turned since. Unless and until they do, it's scarcely worth the detour up the steep hill beside the town hall. Admission, if you decide to go, costs 300 ptas.

Los Tilos
Much more stimulating is Los Tilos, 3km up the Barranco del Agua, entered from a turn-off about 1km before Los Sauces as you come from Santa Cruz. UNESCO declared this small subtropical forest a Biosphere Reserve in 1983, and it contains the biggest concentration of *laurisilva* (laurel forest) on the island (see the La Gomera chapter for more about laurisilva). Its visitor centre opens 8.30 am to 5 pm (to 6.30 pm in summer). There are several walking trails through the area. Just behind the visitor centre, one leads upwards (750 steps on the way) to a fine lookout – reckon

LA PALMA

on about 30 minutes up. A tougher hike (3½ to four hours one way) for those used to steep hill-walking leads south-west to the Corderos spring.

Los Sauces is on bus route No 11, connecting Barlovento and Santa Cruz. The fare to/from Santa Cruz is 445 ptas. For both San Andrés and Los Tilos, you'll need a vehicle or your own power.

Barlovento
postcode 38726 • pop 2766
• elevation 580m

Barlovento is a rather dull farming centre and local transport hub. A few kilometres south and 1.5km off the road is the **Laguna de Barlovento**, an artificial lake created in an extinct volcano. It's a disappointment, resembling some industrial holding tank, but at one corner is a small recreational area and camp site.

Hotel La Palma Romántica (☎ 922 18 62 21) is set back from the road 1km before the turnoff to the lake. The only three-star hotel in the north of the island, it's a charming place with a spacious conservatory, gym, swimming pool, sauna – and even a small observatory for stargazing. Singles/doubles cost 13,000/18,000 ptas, including breakfast.

At the **Piscinas de Fajana**, Atlantic waves keep a protected rock pool full of refreshing ocean water. Take the Santa Cruz road for a couple of kilometres, then the signposted left turn that leads you 1.5km down to the coast.

Eight buses (640 ptas) run daily (five at weekends) between Barlovento and Santa Cruz.

Parque Cultural La Zarza

The road between Barlovento and the hamlet of La Mata is spectacular, with one deeply incised gorge succeeding another.

The Parque Cultural La Zarza is just 1km west of the turn-off for La Mata. Cultural Park may be an overly grand term for a few Benahoare petroglyphs, or rock carvings (see also the Parque Ecológico de Belmaco in the section on The South later in this chapter), but it's well-worth stopping by to

visit them and take in the visitor centre display and 20-minute video about life before the Conquest. Both have an English version. Centre and site open 11 am to 5 pm daily (to 7 pm in summer) and admission costs 300 ptas.

Santo Domingo de Garafía
postcode 38787 • pop c. 400

This little town scarcely merits the 7km detour unless you are hungry for an excellent-value lunch. In that case, head for *Restaurante Berengal*, about 1km west of the small pueblo. Try their speciality, *terrina de pescado* (fish paté). Only the overcooked vegetables disappoint. Budget about 2500 ptas per head, it's only open at lunchtime. Try *Restaurante de Santo Domingo* in the village for more modest fare.

This is a soporific little place that won't detain you long. It started life as a busy community of Portuguese Jews, expelled from their home country at the end of the 15th century. The little of the old nucleus that remains is gathered around the 16th-century **Iglesia de la Virgen de la Luz** and the adjacent Plaza de Baltasar Martín, where there's a *bar* with tables outside.

A morning and afternoon bus (595 ptas, two hours) connects daily with Los Llanos.

Tijarafe
postcode 38780 • pop 2765

A brief wander around the cobbled streets of this farming village is a pleasant diversion. The area around is chopped up by high ridges and deep ravines. On the way south, if you have your own wheels, you could stop at the **Mirador El Time** and enjoy a drink as you contemplate the vistas across island and ocean.

A few buses pass by daily, running between Los Llanos and Puntagorda.

THE CENTRE
Breña Alta

Take the Los Llanos exit from the motorway, then a signed right turn in the village of Breña Alta. **Maroparque** (☎/fax 922 41 77 82) is a small, pleasant, well-managed zoo with attractive gardens which concentrate upon endemic flora. It opens 10 am to 6 pm daily and admission costs 1600 ptas.

From Breña Alta, the LP-2 highway climbs into the Cumbre Nueva ('new summit'), a heavily wooded mountain range that has its continuation in the Cumbre Vieja ('old summit') farther south.

The Parque Nacional de la Caldera de Taburiente visitor centre (see that section earlier in this chapter) is 3.5km east of El Paso.

At the end of the day, for a little-trafficked alternative scenic route back to Santa Cruz through lava fields, Canary pines and laurisilva, take the turning right (south) a couple of kilometres east of the visitor centre. This leads up to El Pilar recreational area, *refugio* (mountain hut) and camp site.

From El Pilar, a hiking trail leads south along the entire mountain ridge through the heart of the island's volcanic territory towards Fuencaliente. This is a demanding trek – you should reckon on six to seven hours to Los Canarios de Fuencaliente, from where you can get a bus to Santa Cruz. Known as the 'Ruta de los Volcanes', this classic route should only be attempted in good weather, which will also allow you to enjoy the ever-changing volcanic scenery and views to both east and west coasts of the island.

Driving on from El Pilar, the minor road rejoins the main Los Llanos–Santa Cruz highway, just near Breña Alta.

El Paso
postcode 38750 • pop 7192

A few local women of this small town still weave silk and the menfolk are mostly busy with farming in the surrounding countryside – bananas (of course), potatoes, tobacco, the vine and several vegetables are all grown in the area.

The restored 18th-century **Ermita de la Virgen de la Concepción de la Bonanza** (or 'La Bonanza' for short) is a curiously painted little chapel whose renovations mercifully left intact the splendid mudéjar roof above the altar. And that's about it for curiosity hereabouts....

About 1km east of town, you can eat well at *Restaurante La Cascada* for around 2000 ptas.

Around El Paso
A couple of kilometres along the LP-2 highway, heading towards Los Llanos, you'll see signs leading off the highway to **El Paraíso de las Aves** (☎ 922 48 61 60), with its wide selection of exotic birds and flora. A small, well-managed place, it opens 10 am to 6 pm daily, and admission costs 1000 ptas.

Los Llanos de Aridane
postcode 38760 • pop 20,230

Otherwise dull and modern, La Palma's second town has at its heart a charming little haven – Plaza de España. Shaded by mature laurel trees, its main feature is the gleaming white **Iglesia de Nuestra Señora de los Remedios**, built in the Canarian colonial style. The surrounding streets, particularly Calle Francis Fernández Taño, still preserve much of their traditional character.

About 500m east of town is the tourist-oriented **Pueblo Parque La Palma**, a mix of botanical garden and cultural centre. More than 6000 species of mostly subtropical plants thrive here. However, it's a German operation with German staff who are far from at home in Spanish and, plants apart, it has little to do with the island. It opens 10.30 am to 5 pm Monday to Saturday and admission costs 1500 ptas.

Cyclists should check out Bike 'n' Fun (☎ 922 40 19 27), Calle Calvo Sotelo. They rent mountain bikes (starting at 2100 ptas per day) and organise day rides around the island from 7500 ptas including transport to the start of the route and bike and equipment hire.

At the far, southern end of **Argual**, just west of Los Llanos and essentially a continuation of the town, a left turn brings you to a dusty, unkempt square, the Plaza de Sotomayor. It's surrounded by elegant buildings, the finest of which is the restored **Casa Massieu van Dalle**, which has a small Cabildo handicrafts exhibition and sales outlet. The house is considerably more interesting than the sparse display.

LA PALMA

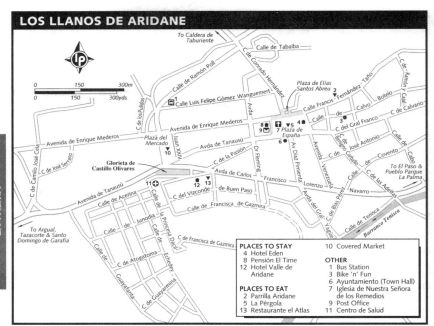

LOS LLANOS DE ARIDANE

PLACES TO STAY	10 Covered Market
4 Hotel Eden	
8 Pensión El Time	**OTHER**
12 Hotel Valle de	1 Bus Station
Aridane	3 Bike 'n' Fun
	6 Ayuntamiento (Town Hall)
PLACES TO EAT	7 Iglesia de Nuestra Señora
2 Parrilla Aridane	de los Remedios
5 La Pérgola	9 Post Office
13 Restaurante el Atlas	11 Centro de Salud

Places to Stay Unsigned *Pensión El Time* (☎ 922 46 09 07, Plaza de España) has basic singles/doubles/triples, attractively arranged around a central patio, for 3000/5000/7500 ptas.

Hotel Eden (☎ 922 46 01 04, fax 922 46 01 83), at the eastern end of the same square, is a better bet if it's comfort rather than aesthetics you're after. Here, singles/doubles with bathroom go for 3400/4800 ptas.

For even greater ease, check in at *Hotel Valle de Aridane* (☎ 922 46 26 00, fax 922 40 10 19, Glorieta Castillo Olivares 5), popular with walkers, where rooms cost 4800/5900 ptas.

Places to Eat Tucked away in a corner of Plaza de España, *La Pérgola* does decent pizzas and *bocadillos* (French-bread sandwiches) plus meat and fish mains for around 1500 ptas. For a filling meal with grilled meat specialities, consider *Parrilla Aridane*

(Calle Fernández Taño 17), open Tuesday to Sunday, which has a nice patio.

In Argual, *La Casona de Argual*, just opposite the Casa Massieu van Dalle, is in a beautiful early 18th-century house. Mains cost between 1500 ptas and 2000 ptas, it closes on Thursday.

Restaurante el Atlas, with mains costing around 1200 ptas, offers good value.

If you're catering for yourself, a browse around the small *covered market* can be rewarding.

Getting There & Away The bus station is on Calle Luis F Gómez Wanguemert. Buses to Puerto Naos (185 ptas) and Tazacorte (140 ptas) run frequently, as do those to Santa Cruz (595 ptas).

Puerto de Tazacorte
postcode 38770 • pop around 1500
Spare a brief thought for unremarkable Tazacorte as you pass through since it's the

spot where the conquistadors launched their campaign. Of more interest is **Puerto de Tazacorte**, 2km beyond. Go beyond the commercial port and some ugly housing blocks to the small marina and bijou development which marks the end of the road. With short streets of low-rise houses, each different from its neighbour, it's a brand new, model development and an example to other resorts, provided that it retains its model scale.

The motor boat Fancy II does a 2½-hour cruise (3000 ptas) daily except Thursday from the port.

Apartamentos Luz y Mar (☎ 922 40 81 63) has apartments which cost between 4500 ptas and 6500 ptas.

Restaurante La Gaviota specialises in seafood; it closes on Monday. Attractive *Taberna del Puerto*, about the only pre-development building still standing, enjoys a prime site overlooking the marina.

Puerto Naos

A side road south from Tazacorte tracks the coast from on high for about 5km before dropping down to the black-sand, palm-shaded beach of Puerto Naos, a growing population of apartments and a handful of restaurants and shops aimed at tourists – the great majority of them German.

If you have transport or don't mind walking about 20 or 30 minutes, you'll find a couple of other small beaches further south, the second of them, **Charco Verde** (Green Pond), comparatively protected from the Atlantic rollers.

Activities For such a small resort, there's no shortage of things to keep you active. Wanderzentrale (☎/fax 922 40 81 29), a Spanish-German outfit at Calle Jose' Guzman Pe'rez 9, organises day hikes starting at 3400 ptas. Bike Station (☎/fax 922 40 83 55), Avenida Cruz Roja, Local 3, rents beach tourers and mountain bikes. They also offer a range of challenging guided mountain-bike rides for between 4800 ptas and 6000 ptas for the day, including bike and equipment hire and transport. Tauchpartner (☎ 922 40 81 39), at the entrance to

town, does daily dives. The really adventurous can throw themselves off the escarpment behind the resort and parapente down, safely under the control of an instructor, who rides beside you. Parapente Biplaza (☎ 922 40 81 72, 610 69 55 70) operates from the promenade and charges 9000 ptas per descent.

Places to Stay & Eat The waterfront of Puerto Naos is lined with low-level apartment blocks. Among the cheaper ones is *Apartamentos Martín (☎ 922 40 80 46)*, which has doubles/triples/quads for 5000/6000/8000 ptas. Doubles/triples at *Apartamentos Playa Delphin (☎ 922 40 81 94)*, start at 6000/8500 ptas.

There are pleasant terrazas all along the waterfront. A couple of blocks back at Calle Maximilian Darias 5, *Ristorante Pizzería La Scala* does a fair version of Italian cuisine. A good spot for Canarian and mainland cooking is *Restaurante Mesón Don Quijote (Edificio La Palma Beach)*, one block from the foreshore.

Getting There & Away Weekday buses leave for Los Llanos (185 ptas) regularly, less so at weekends.

THE SOUTH
Mazo
postcode 38730 • pop 4749

A peaceful little spot, you'd barely know it was there as you trundle by on the bus from Santa Cruz, 13km away. The town, together with its neighbour, Breña Alta, is known for the production of handmade puros and various other handicrafts. Both are on sale at the **Escuela Insular de Artesanía**, signposted downhill off the highway. Here you can also see a range of products being fashioned. The trouble is, you can't do both at the same time since the shop opens 8 am to 3 pm while the workshops are in action 3 to 6 pm! Both open Monday to Friday.

A block further downhill, the 16th-century **Iglesia de San Blas** looks out over the Atlantic towards Tenerife. Inside, the altarpiece is baroque, as are many of the remaining artworks.

LA PALMA

Have a Cigar

Smokers who have been dying to try a Havana cigar, but have not yet had the chance, could do worse than puff on the local *puro*, made from La Palma tobacco which, to this day, is mostly hand rolled. The methods were brought back by reverse migrants from Cuba and, although not quite up to the standard of the real McCoy, are a respectably close substitute – they are also cheap and available across the islands.

LA PALMA

Corpus Christi is celebrated here in June with particular panache. Decorated wooden arches are raised in the streets. Beneath them, equally flamboyant tapestries of flower petals, moss, bark, seeds – everything natural – are spread. Visit the Casa Roja museum (300 ptas) for a sense of this fiesta. The ground floor presents the Corpus festival while upstairs is devoted to *bordado* (embroidery), another local craft. It opens 10.30 am to 2 pm and 3 to 6 pm, and 11am to 6 pm on Saturday.

Mazo has a bustling weekend market 3 to 7 pm on Saturday and 9 am to 1 pm on Sunday.

Getting There & Away Bus No 3 linking Santa Cruz (205 ptas) and Fuencaliente calls by six times daily on weekdays, less at weekends.

Parque Ecológico de Belmaco

Ecological Park is rather a grand name for a small but archaeologically important cave, once inhabited by Benahoare tribespeople who left behind petroglyphs, patterns of whorls and squiggles incised in the cave walls. The **Cueva de Belmaco** was the first such site to be discovered and recorded on the island, back in 1752. There are four sets of engravings and experts remain perplexed about their meaning. Legend has it that the cave was home to the local tribal chiefs, but there is no hard evidence for this.

A small museum and a series of interpretative panels in Spanish, English and Ger-

man give a detailed introduction to the life of the indigenous Benahoare people – and, indeed, to the life of many a peasant farmer on the island until quite recently. The complex opens 10 am to 6 pm (to 2 pm on Sunday) daily and admission costs 300 ptas.

The place is badly signposted from the LP-1 highway. The best bet is to take the first left after the Mazo exit heading south from Santa Cruz and then turn right (south) onto the LP-132. It's about 1km beyond San Simón. A few buses from Santa Cruz head down this way via Hoyo de Mazo. The nearest bus stop is about 400m south of the cave, just before the Bar Chaplin.

Los Canarios de Fuencaliente
postcode 38740 • pop 1728

The LP-132 Hoyo de Mazo road eventually rejoins the LP-1 road leading to Fuencaliente. The hot springs from which the area got its name have long since been buried by the anger of the volcanoes that as recently as 1971 were still erupting.

Things to See & Do In the village, you might want to pop into the **Taller de Artesanía**, Carretera General 104, which opens 10 am to 7 pm, Monday to Saturday. Here you can see traditional embroidery being done – and buy some.

The major attraction hereabouts is the volcanoes. From town, signs lead you to the first of them – **Volcán San Antonio**. You can follow a path half way around the yawning chasm of this great black cone, which last blew in 1949 and is now being repopulated by hardy Canary pines. At the time of writing, a visitor centre was nearing completion and there was talk of access to the crater rim being restricted.

From here you can walk south (signposted) or drive on to what was, in 1971, the scene of the Canary Islands' most recent eruption, **Volcán Teneguía.** You can scramble up its shattered rim if you want.

The less energetic and more sybaritic can take a short walk down the hill from the Volcán de San Antonio to enjoy a glass or two of organic wine at the family-owned *Bodegas Carballo*.

If you have wheels and feel like cooling off after so much exertion, **Playa de Echeventive**, down near the lighthouse at the southern tip of the island, is rarely busy. A kiosk sells cool drinks.

Places to Stay & Eat Offering basic singles/doubles for 2500/3500 ptas is *Pensión Los Volcanes (☎/fax 922 44 14 64, Carretera General 84)*. The owners have four apartments in the same building for up to three people at a bargain 3500 ptas.

Pensión Central (Calle Yaiza 4) and *Pensión Imperial (Calle San Antonio 1)*, under the same ownership, both have rooms with bathroom starting at 2500/3500 ptas. At the former, there are apartments for two at 4000 ptas and for five at 6000 ptas. For both, call ☎ 922 44 40 18).

Restaurante Llanovid (Calle de los Canarios s/n), with mains around 1200 ptas, is the best place in town. Its own local wines

are also for sale. You'll find a couple of more modest *parrillas* (grill places) on the main road in town.

Getting There & Away Six No 3 buses per day (two on Sunday) head north to Santa Cruz (450 ptas) and five (two on Sunday) to Los Llanos.

Fuencaliente to Los Llanos
The highway up the west coast of the island rides high above the seemingly limitless expanses of the Atlantic Ocean. The first settlement is **El Charco**, where you can call in at a mirador that has a small *bar*.

Another 10km north takes you through the village of **Jedey**, where some of the inhabitants still live in old stone houses. A little further north is a still smaller hamlet, **San Nicolás**. Just before you enter it there is a great place to eat, the sprawling *Bodegón Tamanca*, located in a cave.

LA PALMA

El Hierro

The smallest and westernmost member of the Canaries, El Hierro is known to locals as La Isla Chiquita (The Little Island). In the days when the earth was thought to be flat, the island was believed to mark the edge of the world.

Covering only 269 sq km, and with a population of just 8350 people, it is the least developed and most remote of the Canary Islands. The locals (often referred to as Herreños) often feel they are being ignored by the rest of the archipelago, and the reduction in air and sea links over the years has done nothing to alleviate the rancour.

El Hierro is also about as far as you can get from the stereotypical image of the Canary Islands. This is a rural island largely untouched by tourism. The high country, dripping with a wet swirling mist (which, by the way, can make driving hazardous) and divided up by rough stone walls into a green patchwork quilt of farm and grazing land, is more reminiscent of western Ireland than a sunny subtropical paradise. As on La Gomera, much of the coastline is rugged and forbidding, while the south is a mix of semi-arid, volcanic landscape and pine forest. The highest peak is Malpaso (1501m). Diving is possible in the protected marine park off La Restinga in the south, but there are few beaches to speak of.

History

El Hierro hasn't always been the tiny tot of the Canaries. About 50,000 years ago the area was hit by a quake so massive that a third of the island was ripped off the northern side – it slipped away beneath the waves, creating the crescent-shaped coast of El Golfo. It must have been a very dramatic event – the ensuing tidal wave may have been more than 100m high and probably crashed as far off as the American coast.

The last eruption was 200 years ago, but the island is still littered with about 500

Highlights

• Visiting the Ecomuseo de Guinea

• Taking the spectacular west-coast drive and seeing the amazing wind-blasted trees of El Sabinar

• Lunching at the Mirador de la Peña, overlooking El Golfo

• Hiking down to Las Playas from the magnificent Mirador de Isora

• Doing just the same down to Frontera from the Mirador de Jinama.

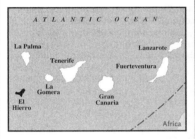

volcanic cones (and 300 more were covered up by lava flows).

How the island got its name is anyone's guess; there isn't a speck of iron *(hierro)* ore on the island. Perhaps the original inhabitants, the Bimbaches, called it *hero*, meaning milk.

Ptolemy identified the western edge of the island as the end of the known world in the 2nd century AD and it remained the 'zero meridian' until replaced by the Greenwich version in 1884.

After the Spanish conquest in the 15th century, a form of feudalism was introduced and Spanish farmers gradually assimilated with those locals who had not been sold into slavery or died of disease. In the subsequent quest for farmland much of El Hierro's forests were destroyed.

Today, the island's economy is based

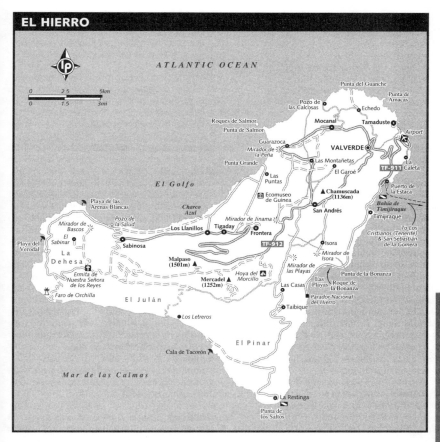

EL HIERRO

ATLANTIC OCEAN

Punta del Guanche
Punta de Amacas
Pozo de las Calcosas
Echedo
Roques de Salmor
Punta de Salmor
Mocanal
Tamaduste
Airport
Guarazoca
Mirador de la Peña
VALVERDE
Las Montañetas
TF-911
La Caleta
Punta Grande
El Garoé
Las Puntas
Puerto de la Estaca
Playa de las Arenas Blancas
Ecomuseo de Guinea
Chamuscada (1136m)
Bahía de Timijiraque
Pozo de la Salud
Charco Azul
Mirador de Jinama
San Andrés
Timijiraque
Mirador de Bascos
El Golfo
Los Llanillos
Tigaday
Frontera
To Los Cristianos (Tenerife) & San Sebastián de la Gomera
Playa del Verodal
El Sabinar
Sabinosa
TF-912
La Dehesa
Malpaso (1501m)
Isora
Mirador de Isora
Ermita de Nuestra Señora de los Reyes
Hoya del Morcillo
Mercadel (1252m)
Mirador de las Playas
Faro de Orchilla
El Julán
Las Casas
Las Playas
Roque de la Bonanza
Punta de la Bonanza
Parador Nacional del Hierro
Los Letreros
Taibique
El Pinar
Cala de Tacorón
Mar de las Calmas
La Restinga
Punta de los Saltos

EL HIERRO

on fishing, fruit-growing, livestock and tourism.

Information

Books & Maps The El Hierro map at 1:125,000 on the Michelin sheet No 122, *Islas Canarias*, covering the four western-most islands, is reliable enough for driving but far from perfect. The same applies to the El Hierro map (at 1:150,000) on the Fire-stone sheet covering all the islands. For walking, *Hierro* (sic), published by Freytag & Berndt at 1:30,000, is your best bet, though it weighs in at a hefty 1400 ptas.

Discovery Walking Guides' *El Hierro* covers a number of enticing trails in the north of the island. Beyond its remit, how-ever, are a number of equally enticing trails in the centre and south.

Landscapes of La Palma and El Hierro by Noel Rochford follows the usual Sun-flower Books pattern, describing a number of walking and driving routes around the island.

Newspapers Herreños read the Tenerife press. If they didn't, they'd be decidedly out of touch. On the island, *La Voz de El*

Hierro and *La Isla de El Hierro* both appear every two months.

Activities
Walking and diving are the two main activities that bring outdoor enthusiasts to the island. Other sports you can practice are cycling, canyon clambering, parapente, rock climbing and caving.

For details of two first-class companies that organise outdoor pursuits, see Activities within the Valverde section later in this chapter.

Special Events
The fiesta par excellence on El Hierro is the Bajada de la Virgen de los Reyes (Descent of the Virgin), held in early July every four years (2001, 2005). Most of the island's population gathers to witness or join in a procession bearing a statue of the Virgin, seated in a sedan chair, from the Ermita de Nuestra Señora de los Reyes in the west of the island all the way across to Valverde. Her descent is accompanied by musicians and dancers dressed in traditional red and white tunics and gaudy caps, and celebrations continue for most of the month in villages and hamlets across the island.

There are several other fiestas of note throughout the year:

25 April Fiesta de los Pastores (Shepherd's Feast) – La Dehesa
15 May Fiesta de San Isidro – Valverde
24 June Fiesta de San Juan – La Restinga & Las Puntas
June Fiesta de la Apañada (Festival of the Clever!) – San Andrés. Farmers gather for a livestock sale at which the smartest extract the best prices.
16 July Fiesta de la Virgen del Carmen – La Restinga
August Fiesta de la Virgen de la Candelaria – Frontera
8 December Fiesta de la Virgen de la Concepción – Valverde

Each year in May, La Restinga hosts Foto-sub, one of the world's major underwater photography competitions. For details and entry forms, contact the Valverde tourist office.

Watch Those Signs

In an effort to look rustic and rural, many of the island's signs for villages and side roads are in white longhand on wooden boards, some already faded and splitting. While a walker has time to assimilate their information, cyclists and motorists are often way beyond before they've managed to decipher the all-but-illegible message.

Accommodation
With about 800 beds available across the island, it's advisable to book ahead in busy periods such as summer and major fiestas. Winter, traditionally the peak season for the northern European invasion of other islands, is less of a squeeze here.

If you're in a group and planning to stay on the island for several nights, a *casa rural* (house in the country) is an attractive option. Meridiano Cero (☎ 922 55 18 24, fax 922 55 05 75) in Mocanal has a range of rural properties on its books. Prices vary from 7200 ptas to 8800 ptas per night and there's a minimum stay of three nights (six nights, July to September).

There is only one camp site – at Hoya del Morcillo (see Around the Island later in this chapter). Camping is prohibited elsewhere throughout the island.

Getting There & Away
Air The island's small airport (☎ 922 55 07 25) lies 10km east of town. Up to four flights daily connect with Tenerife Norte (7160 ptas), while there is a twice-weekly service to Gran Canaria (11,160 ptas, Friday and Sunday).

At the airport you'll find car rental offices, a bar and a shop selling local products such as cheese and wine as well as maps of the island.

Boat Trasmediterránea (☎ 922 55 01 29) runs a daily ferry service to Los Cristianos on Tenerife (2615 ptas, 7¼ hours), leaving at 11.45 pm, Sunday to Friday, and at 2 pm (via La Gomera) on Saturday. It has an office at Calle Doctor Dolkoski 3. Fred Olsen also sails daily to Los Cristianos (2540 ptas), leaving at 1.30 pm.

Boats depart from Puerto de la Estaca, 9km south of the capital.

Getting Around

Bus A very limited bus service covers the main destinations on the island from Monday to Saturday. Four buses fan out from Valverde at noon and leave their destinations early next morning to return to Valverde. For such a simple schedule, the printed timetable is truly inscrutable. To confirm schedules, ring ☎ 922 55 11 75. Destinations are Isora (125 ptas), Guarazoca (125 ptas) via Mocanal, Tigaday (400 ptas) via San Andrés and Frontera and La Restinga (325 ptas) via San Andrés and Taibique.

Car Rental firms such as Autos Bamir (☎ 922 55 01 83, fax 922 55 12 45) and Rosamar (☎/fax 922 55 13 32) will have a car ready and waiting for you at the port (Puerto de la Estaca) or the airport if you reserve in advance.

Bear in mind that there are only four petrol stations on the island: two are in Valverde, one is in El Pinar and another is in Tigaday. A full tank should be sufficient to get right around the island.

VALVERDE
postcode 38900 • pop 1630
• elevation 570

The only capital in the Canaries not located on the coast, the straggly white town of Valverde (or to give it its full title, La Villa de Santa María de Valverde) rises 570m above sea level, cradled by what remains of the walls of an ancient volcanic cone. Cloaked in a seemingly permanent mantle of low cloud and Atlantic mist, it is a rather dispiriting place and not a great introduction to the island. Once you've arrived on El Hierro, the transport options mean that it is not so easy to turn straight around and leave, so get out and see the rest of the island – it makes the melancholy capital well worth suffering.

History

When Jean de Béthencourt landed here with his motley crew in 1405, he wasted little time in defeating the Bimbaches of the area, then known as Armiche. When they surrendered, the invaders rounded most of the inhabitants up for sale into slavery, leaving some to escape into the hinterland.

Valverde only really came into being following a devastating hurricane in 1610. Much of the island's populace fled for shelter to this small hamlet, where a couple of churches had already been erected. In 1812 the town was made the seat of a *municipio* (town council) that covered the whole island, and in 1926 the island's first Cabildo Insular (local government) was established here.

Orientation

You'll find it a challenge to get lost here. Approaching from the airport or Puerto de la Estaca, the one-way main street (known for most of its length as Calle de la Constitución) winds its way up (and southwards) through town. On or near it you'll find the post office, banks, travel agencies, a couple of pensiones, car-rental firms and an assortment of shops.

Information

The well-informed tourist office (☎ 922 55 03 02, fax 922 55 10 52) is at Calle Doctor Quintero 4. It opens 8.30 am to 2.30 pm, Monday to Friday, and 9 am to 1.00 pm on Saturday.

The Instituto Tecnológico de Canarias intends to set up a few computers for general access within the tourist office building.

The hospital on Calle de la Constitucíon will be superseded by a new one, under construction when we last visited, on Calle de Santiago.

Things to See

Although it's pleasant enough to wander around for half an hour or so, the town is short on noteworthy sites. The 18th-century **Iglesia de la Concepción** is a relatively simple three-nave affair, crowned by a bell tower whose railed-off upper level serves as

EL HIERRO

VALVERDE

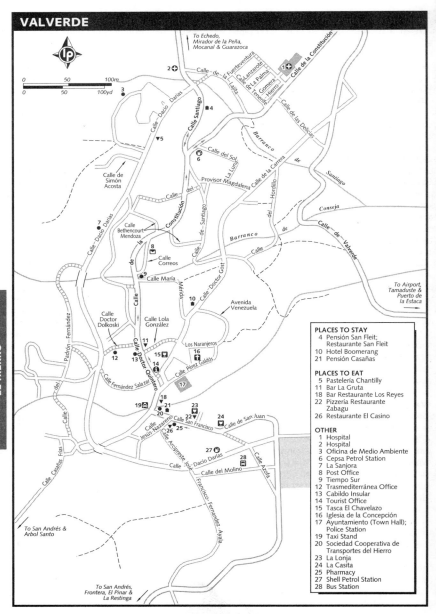

PLACES TO STAY
4 Pensión San Fleit;
   Restaurante San Fleit
10 Hotel Boomerang
21 Pensión Casañas

PLACES TO EAT
5 Pastelería Chantilly
11 Bar La Gruta
18 Bar Restaurante Los Reyes
22 Pizzería Restaurante
   Zabagu
26 Restaurante El Casino

OTHER
1 Hospital
2 Hospital
3 Oficina de Medio Ambiente
6 Cepsa Petrol Station
7 La Sanjora
8 Post Office
9 Tiempo Sur
12 Trasmediterránea Office
13 Cabildo Insular
14 Tourist Office
15 Tasca El Chavelazo
16 Iglesia de la Concepción
17 Ayuntamiento (Town Hall);
   Police Station
19 Taxi Stand
20 Sociedad Cooperativa de
   Transportes del Hierro
23 La Lonja
24 La Casita
25 Pharmacy
27 Shell Petrol Station
28 Bus Station

EL HIERRO

Inactive but still threatening, these cones are an ever-present reminder of El Hierro's volcanic past.

El Hierro's rocky coastline at Punta de Salmor

The Ermita de Nuestra Señora de los Reyes

Valverde's church keeps watch over the town.

It's not all sitting around in the Canaries.

The blue Atlantic laps the rust-red volcanic Playa del Verodal on El Hierro's west coast.

a lookout. Inside, the polychrome *Purísima Concepción* is the town's most prized piece of artwork. Up by the altar, an eagle lectern looks endearingly more like a rooster.

Activities

There are a couple of good outdoor activity outfits in town. Tiempo Sur (☎ 922 55 11 68, @ tiemposur@arrakis.es), Calle de La Constitución s/n, organises a one-day tour of the island with a little caving thrown in for 5000 ptas. La Sanjora (☎/fax 922 55 18 40, @ lasanjora@hotmail.com), at Calle Dacio Darias 65, offers rock climbing and parapente.

Both can set you up with horse riding and canyon clambering or organise guided bike rides and day hikes.

Places to Stay

Pensión San Fleit (☎ 922 55 08 57, Calle Santiago 24) provides singles/doubles at 3000/4000 ptas with a bathroom (2500/ 3000 ptas without).

A decidedly better choice is *Pensión Casañas (☎/fax 922 55 02 54, Calle San Francisco 9)*, which has spotless rooms with bathroom for 3500/4500 ptas. It also has three apartments, starting at 5500 ptas.

The only hotel in town is the *Hotel Boomerang (☎ 922 55 02 00, fax 922 55 02 53, Calle Doctor Gost 1)*, where singles/ doubles/triples cost 5700/7600/8600 ptas.

Places to Eat

To start the day, *Pastelería Chantilly (Calle Dacio Darias 62)* serves up quality coffee and rich croissants and pastries.

Breakfast over, it's slim pickings. For a quick snack or hamburger, you could do worse than *Bar La Gruta (Calle Lola González 10)*. *Restaurante San Fleit*, next door to the pensión of the same name, offers solid meals (basically meat and veg) for around 1500 ptas. *Pizzería Restaurante Zabagu (Calle San Francisco 9)* is decent enough – but stick to the *restaurante* dishes and steer clear of their pizzas.

Restaurante El Casino (Calle San Francisco) has a short but dependable menu with mains costing between 1000 ptas and 1550 ptas. It does a reasonable menu of the day at 1550 ptas but its veritable botanical garden of plastic plants are almost as hard to take as the old Tom Jones numbers that growl from the polythene shrubbery.

Best-value, though scarcely classy, is bustling *Bar Restaurante Los Reyes*. On the corner of Calle San Francisco, it's packed with locals from the first breakfast coffee to the last bedtime slug of brandy. Their *platos combinados* (mixed dishes) cost a bargain 750 ptas and they do a different Canarian special each day. The *restaurant* of Hotel Boomerang (see Places to Stay for details), though less enticing than you might expect from such a hotel, is another fair option, despite the lugubrious staff.

Entertainment

Well, we know you didn't come here for nocturnal entertainment. A capital can't get much quieter than this. *La Lonja (Calle San Francisco 11)*, open weekends only, is both a pub and disco. Nearby tiny *La Casita* (indeed a 'little house'), open daily, is *the* place for locals wanting to be seen. *Tasca el Chavelazo*, in pub mode until the early hours, rolls back the carpet and dances most of the rest of the night away. It opens – in principle – Wednesday to Saturday. Don't bank on any of them though; a weekend spent in tireless research of Valverde's nightlife revealed that all the options were tightly shut!

Getting There & Away

Air See Getting There & Away at the beginning of the chapter for details.

Bus The bus station is at the southern end of town on Calle del Molino. See the Getting Around section at the beginning of this chapter for details of the island's bus services. The latest timetable information can be had at the office of the Sociedad Cooperativa de Transportes del Hierro (☎ 922 55 11 75) on Calle San Francisco.

Car & Motorcycle You can go anywhere you want on the island in a taxi – call ☎ 922

EL HIERRO

55 07 29 between 7.30 am and 10 pm – but it is cheaper to hire a car instead. There are several car-rental firms up and down Calle de la Constitución and Calle San Francisco. A day tour in a taxi will cost about 10,000 ptas (so hire a car!).

Getting Around
A minibus (125 ptas) leaves at 8.15 am daily to meet the first flight from Tenerife and another (200 ptas) sets out half an hour before scheduled ferry arrival times. A taxi to the port or airport costs around 1300 ptas.

You can hire bikes from La Sanjora and Tiempo Sur (see Activities earlier).

AROUND VALVERDE
Echedo
Five kilometres north of Valverde, this tiny settlement is at the heart of wine-growing territory that benefits from the volcanic soil. A track leads west a few kilometres from the village to the **Charco Manso**, natural swimming pools scooped out of the volcanic rock.

Tamaduste & La Caleta
About 10km east of Valverde at the end of a side road leading north from the airport highway, **Tamaduste** is little more than a huddle of houses clustered around a relatively calm cove that is ideal for swimming, even though there's no beach. Out of the black volcanic soil grow low vines, thriving in the shadow of the rim of a former volcano.

There are several sets of apartments here. *Apartamentos Boomerang (Calle Tabaiba 6)* is right on the water's edge and has one/two-bedroom places on offer for 8300/9400 ptas. Reserve at Hotel Boomerang (☎ 922 55 02 00) in Valverde.

About 1km farther on from the turn-off to Tamaduste, is another turn-off south to **La Caleta**, where there are a few houses and a bar. You can splash around in the tiny bay or an ocean rock pool, or follow the steps and little bridge beyond to a basalt rock face bearing much weathered Bimbache petroglyphs (rock carvings).

Puerto de la Estaca
This is where you'll arrive and leave on the ferry. It's a frumpy, dishevelled little place devoid of interest. A secondary road, pushing on down the coast, is overshadowed by a tall and jagged volcanic ridge. After a couple of kilometres it passes through a tiny cluster of houses known collectively as **Timijiraque**. The beach isn't bad, but watch the undertow.

Divers should look out for Club de Buceo Hierro Sub (☎ 922 55 04 82), 5km south of the port. It offers courses and diving off the coast and/or from a boat year-round, and can provide accommodation.

As your eyes adjust after emerging from a 1km long road tunnel, notice the **Roque de la Bonanza**, a little rocky outcrop rising out of the sea just off the coast.

The road peters out in the grounds of the *Parador Nacional del Hierro (☎ 922 55 80 36, fax 922 55 80 86)*, in an area known as **Las Playas**. All singles/doubles cost 12,400/15,500 ptas per night (ask for one with a sea view), making it the island's premier establishment. From here, the only way out is by heading back to Valverde.

On the way back, to enjoy a splendid, breathtaking, windy stroll alongside the ocean, take the old road (now superseded by the tunnel and closed to traffic) that runs at the base of the cliff from the tunnel's southern end. If you're in a group, get the one who draws the short straw to meet you with the car where old and new roads merge, 800m beyond the tunnel's northern exit. There's only one slightly hairy 10m stretch where the sea has eroded a small cave, causing the road to collapse. Allow 30 to 40 minutes.

Around the Island

With your own transport you can rush around pretty much the whole island in a day, backtracking several times along fairly good roads. Unless you're really pushed for time, however, it's better to rent a car for, say, three days. This lets you explore the island in more leisurely mode, perhaps fitting in a walk or two. Using the infrequent buses and your own two feet you'll need several days. What follows is a series of routes which, if combined, present a roughly counter-clockwise tour around the island, starting from Valverde.

NORTHERN CIRCUIT

Following the TF-911 out of Valverde for 5km, you reach **Mocanal**, one of several farming villages that line the road. A 5km detour north leads down to the remains of the coastal hamlet of **Pozo de Las Calcosas**, with an ocean-side rock pool and a couple of restaurants.

Back on the highway, **Guarazoca**, 3km farther on, is another agricultural hamlet. The surrounding meadows are fertile ground and the whole area is frequently enveloped in sea mist.

If dumb animals make you dewy-eyed, you might like to visit Los Burros Felices ('Our happy donkeys are looking forward to seeing you'), a haven for ageing asses. It opens 11 am to 4 pm, Wednesday, Friday and Sunday. Admission is free but donations are welcome.

Just 500m beyond is the **Mirador de la Peña**. From the restaurant and bar, designed by César Manrique, you can enjoy magnificent views down the length of El Golfo. It opens 11 am to 10 pm, Monday to Saturday, and 11 am to 3.30 pm on Sunday. A steep walking trail leads down to Las Puntas (see El Golfo later in this chapter). Allow a good 2¼ hours. Another track trails off northwards towards Punta de Salmor and, offshore, the **Roques de Salmor**, an important nesting spot for various bird species and the last stand of the primeval *lagarto del Salmor* (lizard of Salmor), which now only survives in a few zoos.

The road doglegs back inland across highland fields. The largely abandoned houses of **Las Montañetas**, one of the island's oldest villages, are scattered around a bend in the road that leads to San Andrés. Although a few farmers continue to work the land and run small herds of sheep, goats and even some cattle up here, the thin soil

and unpleasantly damp climate has led most of them to move away.

As the road passes through a pine forest, much of it blackened by fire, take a signed left-turn opposite a spring to follow a dirt track north-east for 2.5km to the site of **El Garoé**, the ancient *arbol santo* (holy tree) of the Bimbaches. It was said to spout water, a myth perhaps explained by the mist-induced condensation on the tree's leaves. With patience, a drop or two of drinking water can indeed be collected. The original tree, a variety of laurel, was felled by a hurricane in 1610; the present one dates from 1949. Beneath it are several small cisterns, originally dug by the Bimbaches to hold the tree's off-flow.

Return to the sealed road, which then leads to **San Andrés,** 1100m above sea level, after less than a kilometre. Here, you can enjoy a hearty meal and local fare at no-frills *Restaurante Goyo* on the main street. Cereal and potato crops, cabbages, almonds, eucalyptus, figs and other fruits all flourish in the rich soil hereabouts. The plots are divided up by rough walls of volcanic stone, which recall some of the wilder countryside of western Ireland.

A couple of kilometres south-west of San Andrés and 0.5km west of the TF-912, the **Mirador de Jinama** affords magnificent views down over the fertile plains of El Golfo and towards the island of La Palma to the north – mist permitting. From here, you can take a glorious 3.5km trail (this, compared to 21km by road!) down an old donkey track to Frontera. Wear trainers (it's a little rough in places) and allow 1¼ to 1½ hours.

Another walking trail meanders its way south from San Andrés to the cheese-producing village of **Isora**. If you're driving, take the secondary road that branches off the TF-912 highway, just north-east of San Andrés. Beyond the village of Isora, perched high on El Risco de los Herreños ridge, is the **Mirador de Isora** with its magnificent panorama of Las Playas and the ocean. A steep track allows hikers to descend to the coast (reckon on at least an hour to get down). Otherwise, you can

EL HIERRO

follow another road south-west back to the highway and turn left (south) to follow signs for La Restinga. Yet another lookout, the **Mirador de Las Playas**, equally splendid, lies off to the left (east).

EL PINAR

A scenic sealed road snakes through **El Pinar**, the shady, protected pine forest that cuts an east to west stripe across the central highland.

Hoya del Morcillo and Around

The Hoya del Morcillo recreation area, 1.5km west of the highway, makes a pleasant picnic stop. It's also the island's only camp site (free at the time of writing), equipped with cooking facilities and showers. To camp here, you need a permit from the tourist office or Oficina de Medio Ambiente (Environment Office; ☎ 922 55 00 17, fax 922 55 02 71) in Valverde. If you send a request to the latter in advance, they'll fax back your permit before you even leave home.

Those with strong legs and an archaeological bent might like to visit the ancient site of **Los Letreros**, a scattering of petroglyphs (rock engravings) scratched into a lava flow by the Bimbaches and still undeciphered. A signed dirt track takes off a few kilometres beyond Hoya del Morcillo. After a little over 15 minutes' descent, you reach a visitor centre, under construction when we walked by. At the site itself, there's not a sign to help you – just a taciturn guardian, who'll want to see your passport. It's at least a four-hour round trip.

From the turning to Los Letreros, you can continue through the pines on the sealed road, (except for about 5km of firm dirt track), to link with the spectacular asphalt road coming round from Sabinosa (see El Golfo later in this chapter).

Las Casas & Taibique

Just south of the Hoya del Morcillo turn-off, the highway hits Las Casas and Taibique, a couple of hamlets that run into each other and seem to slide precariously downhill. You could have a quick look around the

quirky private **Museo de Panchillo** (signposted at the northern end of Taibique), Calle el Chamorro 57, a fascinating hotchpotch of everything that's ever come the way of the curator (and sole owner) and, just behind it, **Caracol**, a pottery studio. On the main street is *Hotel Pinar (☎ 922 55 80 08, fax 922 55 80 90)*, where excellentvalue singles/doubles with bathroom cost 4500/5500 ptas. Beneath it, *Bar Restaurante Luis el Taperio*, run by the same folk, is a popular spot serving good fare.

From Taibique it's another 15km south to La Restinga. A little over half way is a turnoff westwards for the **Cala de Tacorón**, a set of near-deserted coves facing the Mar de las Calmas, whose limpid waters are hard to resist. Have lunch or a cool drink at lone *Pizzeria Puesta del Sol*, a little *cabaña* (hut) perched on the lava flow which spews down to the shore – if it's still there, that is: its existence is under threat from developers who want to exploit this tranquil haven. It opens 1 to 8 pm, Monday to Saturday.

La Restinga

Home to the island's fishing fleet, La Restinga is also very much the place to be if you want to do some diving. The waters are relatively calm and the Reserva Marina Punta de la Restinga protects a range of ocean marine life, which is, in fact, a good deal more varied than the sparse flora and fauna that manages to cling on in the volcanic desert surrounding the pueblo.

You have a choice of four dive centres, all on or near the seashore and all offering much the same options. On Avenida Marítima are Centro de Buceo El Hierro (☎ 922 55 70 23) at No 16, El Submarino (☎ 922 55 70 68) at No 2 and Fan Diving Hierro (☎/fax 922 55 70 85) next door. Round the corner at Calle Gutiérrez Mont 40 is Centro de Buceo Meridiano Zero (☎ 922 55 70 76, fax 922 55 71 59). If it's closed, ask at Tasca La Laja – popular with the locals and worth a visit in its own right – down the road at No 45. You're looking at about 3800 ptas per dive (plus 1500 ptas for the gear) or around 33,000 ptas for 10 dives. A beginner's course costs about 45,000 ptas.

La Restinga's other claim to distinction is that it's home to the island's one and only laundrette. In a huge white elephant of a building at the western end of the harbour, its machines twirl 9 am to 1 pm, Monday to Saturday.

There are about a dozen holiday homes and apartment blocks in La Restinga, many on the waterfront. These apart, try *Pensión Casa Kai Marino* (☎ 922 55 70 34), right on the water's edge, which offers rooms with bathroom for 3500 ptas. *Pensión Matías I* (☎ 922 55 81 89, *Calle el Paral 2*) at the entrance to the village, has simple singles/doubles for 2000/2500 ptas.

The cure for hunger pangs hereabouts is fish. Several waterfront places will oblige. A little inland, a meal at *Restaurante Casa Juan* (*Calle Gutiérrez Mont 23*) will come in at around 2000 ptas. It closes on Wednesday.

The bus for Valverde leaves at 7 am and costs 325 ptas.

EL GOLFO

Beyond the junction with the La Restinga road, the TF-912 follows a sweeping crescent along the crown of the volcanic wall that overlooks El Golfo. To the south rears the peak of **Malpaso** (1501m), the island's highest point. An asphalt road, which becomes dirt (signed Ermita de Nuestra Señora de los Reyes) veers south off the highway and takes you to the foot of the mountain.

The TF-912 itself zigzags down to the coastal plain. The first village you encounter is **Frontera**, a name also used, confusingly, to cover all the settlements looking onto El Golfo. It's hard to miss the **Iglesia de Nuestra Señora de Candelaria**, built on the outskirts in 1818. Its bell tower is a striking, squat, three-storey edifice erected on a hill of volcanic ash so that it could be seen from all over the plains.

At **Tigaday**, one kilometre west, hang a right and follow the road north-east towards Las Puntas for the **Ecomuseo de Guinea**. This is really two centres in one. There are the restored and re-furnished Casas de Guinea, which were seasonal dwellings for the farmers who descended from the heights with their flocks or for the grape harvest. And there's the Lagartario, a centre for the study and reintroduction into the wild of the Lagarte Gigante del Hierro, the giant lizard endemic to the island. For both, you join a guided tour which, for the moment, is only in Spanish. The Casas open 10 am to 2 pm and 4 to 6 pm, Tuesday to Saturday, and 10 am to 2 pm on Sunday morning. The Lagartario opens 10 am to 2 pm and 4 to 6 pm on Tuesday, Thursday and Saturday. Admission to each costs 600 ptas or you can buy a combined ticket for 1000 ptas.

After another couple of kilometres, you reach **Las Puntas**. The star attraction is the old port building, now converted into what once held the Guinness Book of Records title of smallest hotel in the world: *Hotel Punta Grande* (☎ 922 55 90 81), whose impeccably kept four rooms cost 7000 ptas per night. There's a discount of 2000 ptas for single occupation.

A stone's throw away, *Apartamentos Noemí* (☎ 922 55 92 03), which belongs to the same owner, charges 6000 ptas for a double with kitchenette.

Pensiones and apartments are scattered all over the area. In Tigaday, *Pensión El Guanche* (☎ 922 55 90 65, *Calle de la Cruz Alta s/n*), has singles/doubles with bathroom for a bargain 2500/3500 ptas.

Sabinosa & Around

Six kilometres west of Los Llanillos, Sabinosa marks the western high point of El Golfo. Here, you can stay at *Pensión Sabinosa* (☎ 922 55 93 55, *Calle Valentina Hernández 7*), where singles/doubles with bathroom cost 3000/4000 ptas.

Follow the road as it winds down to the coast at **Pozo de la Salud** (the Well of Health). The little well is nothing to look at but its natural sulphurous spring water is used to treat various ailments and it's the raison d'etre for *Hotel Balneario Pozo de la Salud* (☎ 922 55 95 61, fax 922 55 98 01), where rooms cost 7600/9500 ptas and you can lie back and enjoy – at a price – a variety of water-based treatments.

Playa de las Arenas Blancas (White Sand Beach – just about the only white

euro currency converter €1 = 166 ptas

EL HIERRO

Contorted, wind-blasted junipers cover the hill of El Sabinar.   JANE SMITH

grains on the whole island) merits the 45-minute walk westwards from the hotel.

LA DEHESA
Faro de Orchilla
The spectacular sealed road from Sabinosa arches all the way round the west coast of what is known as La Dehesa (the pasture). You pass above a couple of beaches, including the rust-red volcanic **Playa del Verodal** (1km off the route) and negotiate a set of dramatic switchbacks before reaching the turn-off for the most south-westerly point of all Spanish territory: the **Faro de Orchilla**.

Although long ago robbed of its status as 'zero meridian' by Greenwich in the UK, the lighthouse still marks the first or last contact with land (depending on which way your bows are pointing) for mariners plying the rough Atlantic seas between Africa or Europe and the Americas. The 4.5km of dirt track down to the lighthouse make for a bumpy ride – you need to have a fervent love of lighthouses or a particular sense of place to bother.

Ermita de Nuestra Señora de los Reyes
Back on the asphalt road, head inland a few kilometres towards El Julán. An unassuming chapel contains the image of the Virgen de los Reyes (Madonna of the Kings), perched up high and gazing out like a china doll. Every four years, she goes walkabout (see Special Events earlier in this chapter).

El Sabinar
From the Ermita, follow the road – which soon becomes firm dirt-track – up this windswept height named after the *sabinas* (junipers), which grow here in such a malformed way. Bending before the ceaseless tradewinds that howl in from the east, they have become the island's symbol. Around 3km from the Ermita, take a signposted left fork.

Once back at the fork, you could curl north again for a further 2km to reach another spectacular lookout, the **Mirador de Bascos**. It's a matter of luck. The first time we came here, we had an uninterrupted view the length of El Golfo and all around to the islands of La Palma, La Gomera and Tenerife. The next time, we saw nothing but swirling cloud.

At the crossroads, 3.5km east of the Ermita, which mark the end of the sealed road, you have a choice: left along the firm dirt-track will take you to the TF-912 and back to Valverde. The right fork, which involves only about 5km of unpaved road, will lead you, via Hoya del Morcillo, to the road linking La Restinga and Valverde.

Language

Spanish, or Castilian, as it is often and more precisely called, is the most widely spoken of the Romance languages – the group of languages derived from Latin that includes French, Italian, Portuguese and Romanian.

Pronunciation

Pronunciation of Spanish is not difficult, given that many Spanish sounds are similar to their English counterparts, and there is a clear and consistent relationship between pronunciation and spelling.

Those steeped in the castellano of the central and northern mainland will be surprised by the Latin American lilt of the Canaries accent. It bears a closer resemblance to what you hear in Andalucía. The lisp (like 'th' in 'thin') you'd normally expect in 'z' and 'c' before vowels is pronounced more as a sibilant 's', and 's' is hardly pronounced at all – it's more like an aspirated 'h' – for example, Las Palmas sounds more like Lah Palmah! The swallowing of consonants like this is a marked feature of Canaries Spanish, and even solid speakers of the language may find themselves wondering just how much they really understood on hearing a lively *charla* (chat) among Canarios.

The Spanish of the Canaries has several other peculiarities. The standard second personal plural pronoun *vosotros* (you), is rarely heard. Instead, the more formal *ustedes* is used.

Where more than one option appears for vocabulary items below, the first cited is the most common usage in the islands. The -a/-o endings of some words indicate feminine and masculine forms, for example, an asthmatic woman is *asmática* while an asthmatic man is *asmático*.

Vowels

Unlike English, each of the vowels in Spanish has a uniform pronunciation which does not vary. For example, Spanish **a** has one pronunciation rather than the numerous versions we find in English, such as in 'cake', 'cat', 'cart', 'call' and 'care'. Many Spanish words have a written accent. This acute accent (as in *días*) indicates a stressed syllable; it doesn't change the sound of the vowel. Vowels are pronounced clearly even if they are in unstressed positions or at the end of a word.

a somewhere between the 'a' in 'cat' and the 'a' in 'cart'
e as in 'met'
i similar to the 'ea' in 'heat'
o similar to the 'o' in 'hot'
u as in 'put'

Consonants

Some Spanish consonants are the same as their English counterparts. The pronunciation of other consonants varies according to which vowel follows. The Spanish alphabet also contains the letter ñ, which is absent from the English alphabet. Until recently, the clusters **ch** and **ll** were also officially separate consonants (coming after **c** and **l** respectively), and you're likely to encounter many situations – for example, in lists and dictionaries – in which they're still treated that way.

b somewhere between 'b' and 'v'; also as the 'b' in 'book' when initial or preceded by a nasal such as **m** or **n**
c a hard 'c' as in 'cat' when followed by **a**, **o**, **u** or a consonant; as 's' before **e** or **i**
ch as in 'choose', although it often sounds more like a 'y' in the Canaries – Guanche is often pronounced as 'Guanye'
d as in 'dog' when initial or preceded by **l** or **n**; elsewhere as the 'th' in 'then'. Often not pronounced at all when at the end of a word.

g	hard, as in 'gate' when initial or before **a**, **o** or **u**; elsewhere it's much softer. Before **e** or **i** it's a harsh, breathy sound, similar to the 'ch' in Scottish *loch*.
h	always silent
j	a harsh, guttural sound similar to the 'ch' in Scottish *loch*
ll	similar to the 'y' in 'yellow'
ñ	a nasal sound like the 'ni' in 'onion'
qu	as the 'k' in 'kick'
r	a rolled 'r'; longer and stronger when initial or doubled
s	as in 'send'
v	same pronunciation as **b**
x	as the 'x' in 'taxi' when between two vowels; as the 's' in 'say' when preceding a consonant
z	as the 's' in 'sun' (not as the 'th' in 'thin' as in most of mainland Spain)

Greetings & Civilities

Hello.	*¡Hola!*
Goodbye.	*¡Adiós!*
Yes.	*Sí.*
No.	*No.*
Please.	*Por favor.*
Thank you.	*Gracias.*
That's fine/ You're welcome.	*De nada.*
Excuse me.	*Perdón/Perdone.*
I'm sorry. (forgive me)	*Lo siento/Discúlpeme.*
How are you?	*¿Cómo está?*
I'm fine, thanks.	*Estoy bien, gracias.*
What's your name	*¿Cómo se llama?*
My name is …	*Me llamo …*
Where are you from?	*¿De donde es?*
I'm from …	*Soy de …*

Language Difficulties

I understand.	*Entiendo.*
I don't understand.	*No entiendo.*
Do you speak English?	*¿Habla inglés?*
Could you write it down, please?	*¿Puede escribirlo, por favor?*

Getting Around

What time does the bus leave/arrive?	*¿A qué hora sale/llega la guagua/ el autobús/bus?*
Where is the bus stop?	*¿Dónde está la parada de la guagua/ del autobús?*
I'd like a … ticket. one-way	*Quisiera un billete … sencillo (or sólo de ida)*
return	*de ida y vuelta*

Directions

I want to go to …	*Quiero ir a …*
Can you show me (on the map)?	*¿Me puede indicar (en el mapa)?*
Go straight ahead.	*Siga/Vaya todo recto/ derecho.*
Turn left …	*Gire a la izquierda …*
Turn right …	*Gire a la derecha …*
at the traffic lights	*en el semáforo*
at the next corner	*en la próxima esquina*

Around Town

I'm looking for …	*Estoy buscando …*
a bank	*un banco*
the … embassy	*la embajada de …*
the post office	*Correos*
the public toilets	*los servicios/ aseos públicos*
the telephone centre	*el locutorio*
the tourist office	*la oficina de turismo*

Signs	
Entrada	Entrance
Salida	Exit
Abierto	Open
Cerrado	Closed
Información	Information
Prohibido	Prohibited
Comisaría	Police Station
Servicios/Aseos	Toilets
Hombres	Men
Mujeres	Women

Accommodation

youth hostel	*albergue juvenil* (or *albergue de la juventud*)
camp site	*camping*
hotel	*pensión/hostal/hotel*
Where is a cheap hotel?	*¿Dónde hay un hotel barato?*
Do you have any rooms available?	*¿Tiene habitaciones libres?*
How much is it ...?	*¿Cuánto cuesta ...?*
per night	*por noche*
per person	*por persona*
May I see it?	*¿Puedo verla?*
Is breakfast included?	*¿Está incluido el desayuno?*

Health

I'm ...	*Soy ...*
diabetic	*diabético/a* (m/f)
epileptic	*epiléptico/a* (m/f)
asthmatic	*asmático/a* (m/f)
antiseptic	*antiséptico*
aspirin	*aspirina*
condoms	*preservativos/condones*
diarrhoea	*diarrea*
medicine	*medicamento*
nausea	*náusea*
sunblock cream	*crema solar*
tampons	*tampones*

Time & Date

What time is it?	*¿Qué hora es?*
today	*hoy*
tonight	*esta tarde*
tomorrow	*mañana*
yesterday	*ayer*
Monday	*lunes*
Tuesday	*martes*
Wednesday	*miércoles*
Thursday	*jueves*
Friday	*viernes*
Saturday	*sábado*
Sunday	*domingo*

Emergencies

Help!	*¡Socorro!/¡Auxilio!*
Call a doctor!	*¡Llame a un médico!*
Call the police!	*¡Llame a la policía!*
Where are the toilets?	*¿Dónde están los servicios?*
I'm lost.	*Estoy perdido/ perdida.* (m/f)
Go away!	*¡Vete!/¡Fuera!*

Numbers

0	*cero*
1	*uno, una*
2	*dos*
3	*tres*
4	*cuatro*
5	*cinco*
6	*seis*
7	*siete*
8	*ocho*
9	*nueve*
10	*diez*
11	*once*
12	*doce*
13	*trece*
14	*catorce*
15	*quince*
16	*dieciséis*
17	*diecisiete*
18	*dieciocho*
19	*diecinueve*
20	*veinte*
21	*veintiuno*
22	*veintidós*
23	*veintitrés*
30	*treinta*
31	*treinta y uno*
40	*cuarenta*
50	*cincuenta*
60	*sesenta*
70	*setenta*
80	*ochenta*
90	*noventa*
100	*cien/ciento*
1000	*mil*
10,000	*diez mil*
one million	*un millón*

FOOD & DRINKS

Here are some basic words and phrases that can come in handy whatever kind of meal you're eating:

I'd like the set meal.	*Quisiera el menú del día.*
Is service included?	*¿El servicio está incluido?*
I'm a vegetarian.	*Soy vegetariano/ vegetariana.* (m/f)

bill (check)	*cuenta*
bread	*pan*
bread roll	*bollo*
breakfast	*desayuno*
butter	*mantequilla*
change	*cambio*
cold	*frío/a*
cup	*taza*
desserts	*postres*
dining-room	*comedor*
dinner	*cena*
food, meal	*comida*
fork	*tenedor*
glass	*vaso* or *copa*
hot (temperature)	*caliente*
ice	*hielo*
jam	*mermelada*
knife	*cuchillo*
lunch	*almuerzo* or *comida*
menu	*carta*
milk	*leche*
olive oil	*aceite de oliva*
plate	*plato*
pepper	*pimienta*
salt	*sal*
sauce	*salsa*
set menu	*menú del diá*
spoon	*cuchara*
sugar	*azúcar*
table	*mesa*
vinegar	*vinagre*
waiter/waitress	*camerero/a*

Food Glossary

Deciphering a menu in the Canaries is always tricky. However much you already know, there will always be dishes and expressions you are not familiar with. The following list should help you with the basics at least.

aceite	oil
aceituna	olive
agua	water
aguacate	avocado
ajo	garlic
almejas	clams
almendra	almond
almogrote	soft cheese blended with chile pepper
alubia	bean
anchoa	anchovy
arepas	envelope of maize with a savoury filling
arroz	rice
asado	roast
atún	tuna
bacalao	salted cod
bistek	beef steak
bocadillo	French-bread sandwich
bonito	tuna
boquerones	raw anchovy pickled in vinegar
(a la) brasa	char-grilled, barbecued
cabra	goat
cabrito	kid
cacahuete	peanut
calabacín	courgette (zucchini)
calabaza	pumpkin
calamares	squid
caldo	broth, stock,
cangrejo	crab
caza	hunt, game
cazuela	casserole
cebolla	onion
cerdo	pork
cereza	cherry
champiñones	mushrooms
charcutería	cured pork meats, or a shop selling them
chipirón	small squid
chorizo	red sausage
chuletas	chops
cilantro	coriander

cocido	cooked; also hotpot/stew
cocina	kitchen
conejo	rabbit
cordero	lamb
crudo	raw
dorada	sea bass
dulce	sweet
empanada	pie
ensaimada	sweet bread (of lard)
espárragos	asparagus
espinacas	spinach
faba	type of dried bean
fideo	vermicelli noodle
filete	steak
flan	crème caramel
frambuesa	raspberry
fresa	strawberry
frijol	dried bean
frito	fried
fruta	fruit
fuerte	strong
galleta	biscuit, cookie
gamba	prawn, shrimp
garbanzo (staple in Canaries diet)	chickpea
gofio	roasted mix of wheat, maize or barley
guindilla	hot chilli pepper
guisante	pea
haba	broad bean
hamburguesa	hamburger
harina	flour
helado	ice cream
hierba buena	mint
hígado	liver
higo	fig
horneado	baked
horno	oven
hortalizas	vegetables
huevos	eggs
infusión	herbal tea
jabalí	wild boar
jamón serrano	mountain-cured ham

jamón	ham
judías blancas	butter beans
judías verdes	green beans
langosta	spiny lobster
langostino	large prawn
lechuga	lettuce
legumbre	pulse
lengua	tongue
lenguado	sole
lentejas	lentils
lima	lime
limón	lemon
lomo	pork loin
maíz	sweet corn
mandarina	tangerine
manzana	apple
mayonesa	mayonnaise
mejillones	mussels
melocotón	peach
menta	mint
merluza	hake
miel	honey
mojo	salsa/sauce
morcilla	blood sausage (black pudding)
naranja	orange
nata	cream
nuez	nut (plural *nueces*), walnut
olla	pot
ostra	oyster
papas arrugadas	wrinkly potatoes, served with *mojo*
papas fritas	chips
pasa	raisin
pastel	pastry, cake
pato	duck
pavo	turkey
pechuga	breast, of poultry
perdiz	partridge
pescado	fish
pez espada	swordfish
picadillo	minced meat
picante	hot, spicy, piquant
pimiento	pepper, capsicum
piña	pineapple

pinchos morunos	kebabs
piñón	pine nut
plancha	grill, grilled, on the hot plate
plátano	banana
potaje	stew, potage
puerro	leek
pulpo	octopus
queso	cheese
rape	monkfish
rebozado/a	battered and fried
refrescos	soft drinks
relleno	stuffed
riñón	kidney
salado	salted, salty
salchicha	fresh pork sausage
salchichón	cured sausage
sandía	watermelon
sardina	sardine
seco	dry, dried
sepia	cuttlefish
sesos	brains
seta	wild mushroom
soja	soy
solomillo	fillet steak
sopas	soup
tarta	cake
ternera	beef
tomate	tomato
torta	round flat bun, cake
tortilla	omlette
tostado	toast
trucha	trout
turrón	almond nougat
uva	grape
vaca, carne de	beef
vegetal	vegetable
vegetariano/a (m/f)	vegetarian
verdura	vegetable
vieira	scallop
zanahoria	carrot
zarzuela	fish stew
zumo de naranja	orange juice

Drinks Glossary
Coffee

café con leche	with 50% hot milk
café grande/doble/ americano	in a large cup
café en vaso	in a small shot glass
café sombra	with lots of milk.
café solo	a short black
café con hielo	iced coffee
café cortado (or just *cortado*)	short black with a splash of milk (in the western islands, a *cortado* comes with sweetened condensed milk)
cortado natural	short black with fresh milk
cortado de condensado	short black with condensed milk
cortado de leche y leche	short black with both condensed and fresh milk
barraquito	*cortado* in a larger cup with added spices
con licor/alcohol	with a shot of liquor

Tea

té	tea
manzanilla	camomile
poleo	mint

Water, Soft Drink & Fruit Juice

agua (potable)	(drinkable) water
agua del grifo	tapwater
agua mineral	bottled water
con gas	fizzy
sin gas	still
refrescos	soft drinks
granizado	iced fruit crush
batido	flavoured milk drink/ milk shake
zumería	juice bar
zumo de ...	... juice
naranja	orange
aguacate	avocado
piña	pineapple

Alcoholic Drinks

cerveza	beer
cerveza de barril/ de presión	draught beer

clara	shandy (beer with a dash of lemonade)
botellín	small bottle
caña	small glass
jarra	pint-sized glass
vino	wine
blanco	white
tinto	red
rosado	rosé
de la casa	house
malvasía	malmsey wine, also produced in Madeira
dulce	sweet
seco	dry
sangría	a wine and fruit punch, usually with spirits

mistela (from La Gomera)	a mixture of wine, sugar, rum and sometimes honey
tinto de verano	a mix of wine and Casera (a brand of lemonade), or sweet, bubbly water
coñac	brandy
aguardiente	generic term for strong spirit (similar to schnapps or grappa)
licores	liqueurs
ron	rum
ron miel	honey rum
cobana	banana-based rum
güisqui	whisky
jerez	sherry

Glossary

abierto – open
aficionado – enthusiast
apartado de correos – post office box
artesonado – coffered ceiling
ayuntamiento – town hall

barranco – ravine or gorge. All but the two easternmost islands are rippled by ravines which cut paths from the mountainous centres to the coast; they often represent the only interruption to long coastlines of rocky bluffs and cliffs.
barrio – district, quarter (of a town or city)
biblioteca – library
buceo – scuba diving

Cabildo insular – island government
cajero automático – ATM (automatic teller machine)
cambio – exchange
Carnaval – festival celebrating the beginning of Lent, 40 days before Easter
carrete – film (camera)
casa rural – a village or country house or farmstead with rooms to let
casco – literally, helmet; often used as *casco antiguo* to refer to the old centre of town
caserío – traditional farmhouse or hamlet
catedral – cathedral
centro comercial – shopping centre, common in coastal resorts where they usually contain not only shops but also restaurants, bars and other facilities for tourists
cerrado – closed
comedor – dining room
comsaría – National Police station
Corpus Christi – festival in honour of the Eucharist, held eight weeks after Easter
correos – post office
cruz – cross

duro – common name for 5 ptas coin (literally 'hard')

este – east
entrada – entrance

ermita – chapel
estación – terminal, station
estación de guaguas – bus terminal/ station
estación marítima – ferry terminal

faro – lighthouse
fiesta – festival, public holiday or party
fin de semana – weekend

gofio – ground, roasted grain used in place of bread in Canarian cuisine
guagua – bus

hostal – commercial establishment providing accommodation in the one- to three-star range; not to be confused with youth hostels (of which there is only one in the islands)

IGIC – Impuesto General Indirecto Canario (local version of value added tax)
iglesia – church

lavandería – laundry
librería – bookshop
lista de correos – poste restante
llegada – arrival

madrugada – the 'early hours', from around 3 am to dawn; a pretty lively time in the cities and resorts!
marcha – action, nightlife, 'the scene'
mercado – market
meseta – high plateau
mirador – lookout point
muelle – wharf or pier
museo – museum, gallery

norte – north

oeste – west
oficina de turismo – tourist office

parador – chain of state-owned upmarket hotels
parque nacional – national park
pensión – guest house (one/two star)

piscina – swimming pool
playa – beach
pueblo – village
puerta – door
puerto – port

rastro – flea market
retablo – altarpiece
romería – festive pilgrimage or procession

salida – departure or exit
Semana Santa – Holy Week, the week leading up to Easter
Sida – AIDS

s/n – sin numero (without number); sometimes seen in street addresses
sur – south

tapas – bar snacks traditionally served on saucer or lid *(tapa)*
tarjeta de crédito – credit card
tarjeta telefónica – phonecard
tasca – pub, bar
terraza – terrace; outdoor cafe tables

valle – valley

zumería – juice bar

LONELY PLANET

You already know that Lonely Planet produces more than this one guidebook, but you might not be aware of the other products we have on this region. Here is a selection of titles that you may want to check out as well:

Spain
ISBN 1 86450 192 8
US$24.99 • UK£14.99

Spanish phrasebook
ISBN 0 86442 475 2
US$5.95 • UK£3.99

Walking in Spain
ISBN 0 86442 543 0
US$17.95 • UK£11.99

Barcelona
ISBN 1 86450 143 X
US$14.95 • UK£8.99

World Food Spain
ISBN 1 86450 025 5
US$12.95 • UK£7.99

Andalucia
ISBN 1 86450 191 X
US$17.99 • UK£10.99

Morocco
ISBN 0 86442 762 X
US$19.99 • UK£12.99

Madrid
ISBN 1 86450 123 5
US$14.99 • UK£8.99

Europe on a shoestring
ISBN 1 86450 150 2
US$24.99 • UK£14.99

Catalunya & the Costa Brava
ISBN 1 86450 315 7
US$17.99 • UK£11.99

Portugal
ISBN 1 86450 193 6
US$19.99 • UK£12.99

Available wherever books are sold

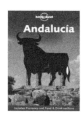
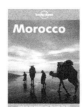

LONELY PLANET

Guides by Region

Lonely Planet is known worldwide for publishing practical, reliable and no-nonsense travel information in our guides and on our Web site. The Lonely Planet list covers just about every accessible part of the world. Currently there are 16 series: Travel guides, Shoestring guides, Condensed guides, Phrasebooks, Read This First, Healthy Travel, Walking guides, Cycling guides, Watching Wildlife guides, Pisces Diving & Snorkeling guides, City Maps, Road Atlases, Out to Eat, World Food, Journeys travel literature and Pictorials.

AFRICA Africa on a shoestring • Cairo • Cape Town • Cape Town City Map • East Africa • Egypt • Egyptian Arabic phrasebook • Ethiopia, Eritrea & Djibouti • Ethiopian (Amharic) phrasebook • The Gambia & Senegal • Healthy Travel Africa • Kenya • Malawi • Morocco • Moroccan Arabic phrasebook • Mozambique • Read This First: Africa • South Africa, Lesotho & Swaziland • Southern Africa • Southern Africa Road Atlas • Swahili phrasebook • Tanzania, Zanzibar & Pemba • Trekking in East Africa • Tunisia • Watching Wildlife East Africa • Watching Wildlife Southern Africa • West Africa • World Food Morocco • Zimbabwe, Botswana & Namibia **Travel Literature:** Mali Blues: Traveling to an African Beat • The Rainbird: A Central African Journey • Songs to an African Sunset: A Zimbabwean Story

AUSTRALIA & THE PACIFIC Auckland • Australia • Australian phrasebook • Australia Road Atlas • Bushwalking in Australia •Cycling New Zealand • Fiji • Fijian phrasebook • Healthy Travel Australia, NZ and the Pacific • Islands of Australia's Great Barrier Reef • Melbourne • Melbourne City Map • Micronesia • New Caledonia • New South Wales & the ACT • New Zealand • Northern Territory • Outback Australia • Out to Eat – Melbourne • Out to Eat – Sydney • Papua New Guinea • Pidgin phrasebook • Queensland • Rarotonga & the Cook Islands • Samoa • Solomon Islands • South Australia • South Pacific • South Pacific phrasebook • Sydney • Sydney City Map • Sydney Condensed • Tahiti & French Polynesia • Tasmania • Tonga • Tramping in New Zealand • Vanuatu • Victoria • Watching Wildlife Australia • Western Australia **Travel Literature:** Islands in the Clouds: Travels in the Highlands of New Guinea • Kiwi Tracks: A New Zealand Journey • Sean & David's Long Drive

CENTRAL AMERICA & THE CARIBBEAN Bahamas, Turks & Caicos • Baja California • Bermuda • Central America on a shoestring • Costa Rica • Costa Rica Spanish phrasebook • Cuba • Dominican Republic & Haiti • Eastern Caribbean • Guatemala • Guatemala, Belize & Yucatán: La Ruta Maya • Healthy Travel Central & South America • Jamaica • Mexico • Mexico City • Panama • Puerto Rico • Read This First: Central & South America • World Food Mexico • Yucatán **Travel Literature:** Green Dreams: Travels in Central America

EUROPE Amsterdam • Amsterdam City Map • Amsterdam Condensed • Andalucía • Austria • Baltic States phrasebook • Barcelona • Barcelona City Map • Berlin • Berlin City Map • Britain • British phrasebook • Brussels, Bruges & Antwerp • Budapest • Budapest City Map • Canary Islands • Central Europe • Central Europe phrasebook • Corfu & the Ionians • Corsica • Crete • Crete Condensed • Croatia • Cycling Britain • Cycling France • Cyprus • Czech & Slovak Republics • Denmark • Dublin • Dublin City Map • Eastern Europe • Eastern Europe phrasebook • Edinburgh • Estonia, Latvia & Lithuania • Europe on a shoestring • Finland • Florence • France • Frankfurt Condensed • French phrasebook • Georgia, Armenia & Azerbaijan • Germany • German phrasebook • Greece • Greek Islands • Greek phrasebook • Hungary • Iceland, Greenland & the Faroe Islands • Ireland • Istanbul • Italian phrasebook • Italy • Krakow • Lisbon • The Loire • London • London City Map • London Condensed • Madrid • Malta • Mediterranean Europe • Mediterranean Europe phrasebook • Moscow • Munich • Norway • Out to Eat – London • Paris • Paris City Map • Paris Condensed • Poland • Portugal • Portuguese phrasebook • Prague • Prague City Map • Provence & the Côte d'Azur • Read This First: Europe • Romania & Moldova • Rome • Russia, Ukraine & Belarus • Russian phrasebook • Scandinavian & Baltic Europe • Scandinavian Europe phrasebook • Scotland • Sicily • Slovenia • South-West France • Spain • Spanish phrasebook • St Petersburg • St Petersburg City Map • Sweden • Switzerland • Trekking in Spain • Ukrainian phrasebook • Venice • Vienna • Walking in Britain • Walking in France • Walking in Ireland • Walking in Italy • Walking in Spain • Walking in Switzerland • Western Europe • Western Europe phrasebook • World Food France • World Food Ireland • World Food Italy • World Food Spain **Travel Literature:** Love and War in the Apennines • The Olive Grove: Travels in Greece • On the Shores of the Mediterranean • Round Ireland in Low Gear • A Small Place in Italy

INDIAN SUBCONTINENT Bangladesh • Bengali phrasebook • Bhutan • Delhi • Goa • Healthy Travel Asia & India • Hindi & Urdu phrasebook • India • Indian Himalaya • Karakoram Highway • Kerala • Mumbai

LONELY PLANET

Mail Order

Lonely Planet products are distributed worldwide. They are also available by mail order from Lonely Planet, so if you have difficulty finding a title please write to us. North and South American residents should write to 150 Linden St, Oakland, CA 94607, USA; European and African residents should write to 10a Spring Place, London NW5 3BH, UK; and residents of other countries to Locked Bag 1, Footscray, Victoria 3011, Australia.

(Bombay) • Nepal • Nepali phrasebook • Pakistan • Rajasthan • Read This First: Asia & India • South India • Sri Lanka • Sri Lanka phrasebook • Tibet • Tibetan phrasebook • Trekking in the Indian Himalaya • Trekking in the Karakoram & Hindukush • Trekking in the Nepal Himalaya
Travel Literature: The Age of Kali: Indian Travels and Encounters • Hello Goodnight: A Life of Goa • In Rajasthan • A Season in Heaven: True Tales from the Road to Kathmandu • Shopping for Buddhas • A Short Walk in the Hindu Kush • Slowly Down the Ganges

ISLANDS OF THE INDIAN OCEAN Madagascar & Comoros • Maldives • Mauritius, Réunion & Seychelles

MIDDLE EAST & CENTRAL ASIA Bahrain, Kuwait & Qatar • Central Asia • Central Asia phrasebook • Dubai • Hebrew phrasebook • Iran • Israel & the Palestinian Territories • Istanbul • Istanbul City Map • Istanbul to Cairo on a shoestring • Jerusalem • Jerusalem City Map • Jordan • Lebanon • Middle East • Oman & the United Arab Emirates • Syria • Turkey • Turkish phrasebook • World Food Turkey • Yemen
Travel Literature: Black on Black: Iran Revisited • The Gates of Damascus • Kingdom of the Film Stars: Journey into Jordan

NORTH AMERICA Alaska • Boston • Boston City Map • California & Nevada • California Condensed • Canada • Chicago • Chicago City Map • Deep South • Florida • Hawaii • Hiking in Alaska • Hiking in the USA • Honolulu • Las Vegas • Los Angeles • Miami • Miami City Map • New England • New Orleans • New York City • New York City City Map • New York City Condensed • New York, New Jersey & Pennsylvania • Oahu • Out to Eat – San Francisco • Pacific Northwest • Puerto Rico • Rocky Mountains • San Francisco • San Francisco City Map • Seattle • Southwest • Texas • USA • USA phrasebook • Vancouver • Virginia & the Capital Region • Washington, DC City Map • World Food Deep South, USA
Travel Literature: Caught Inside: A Surfer's Year on the California Coast • Drive Thru America

NORTH-EAST ASIA Beijing • Cantonese phrasebook • China • Hiking in Japan • Hong Kong • Hong Kong City Map • Hong Kong Condensed • Hong Kong, Macau & Guangzhou • Japan • Japanese phrasebook • Korea • Korean phrasebook • Kyoto • Mandarin phrasebook • Mongolia • Mongolian phrasebook • Seoul • South-West China • Taiwan • Tokyo
Travel Literature: In Xanadu: A Quest • Lost Japan

SOUTH AMERICA Argentina, Uruguay & Paraguay • Bolivia • Brazil • Brazilian phrasebook • Buenos Aires • Chile & Easter Island • Colombia • Ecuador & the Galapagos Islands • Healthy Travel Central & South America • Latin American Spanish phrasebook • Peru • Quechua phrasebook • Read This First: Central & South America • Rio de Janeiro • Rio de Janeiro City Map • Santiago • South America on a shoestring • Trekking in the Patagonian Andes • Venezuela
Travel Literature: Full Circle: A South American Journey

SOUTH-EAST ASIA Bali & Lombok • Bangkok • Bangkok City Map • Burmese phrasebook • Cambodia • Hanoi • Healthy Travel Asia & India • Hill Tribes phrasebook • Ho Chi Minh City • Indonesia • Indonesian phrasebook • Indonesia's Eastern Islands • Jakarta • Java • Lao phrasebook • Laos • Malay phrasebook • Malaysia, Singapore & Brunei • Myanmar (Burma) • Philippines • Pilipino (Tagalog) phrasebook • Read This First: Asia & India • Singapore • Singapore City Map • South-East Asia on a shoestring • South-East Asia phrasebook • Thailand • Thailand's Islands & Beaches • Thailand, Vietnam, Laos & Cambodia Road Atlas • Thai phrasebook • Vietnam • Vietnamese phrasebook • World Food Thailand • World Food Vietnam

ALSO AVAILABLE: Antarctica • The Arctic • The Blue Man: Tales of Travel, Love and Coffee • Brief Encounters: Stories of Love, Sex & Travel • Chasing Rickshaws • The Last Grain Race • Lonely Planet Unpacked • Not the Only Planet: Science Fiction Travel Stories • On the Edge: Extreme Travel • Sacred India • Travel with Children • Travel Photography: A Guide to Taking Better Pictures

ON THE ROAD

Travel Guides explore cities, regions and countries, and supply information on transport, restaurants and accommodation, covering all budgets. They come with reliable, easy-to-use maps, practical advice, cultural and historical facts and a rundown on attractions both on and off the beaten track. There are over 200 titles in this classic series, covering nearly every country in the world.

 Lonely Planet Upgrades extend the shelf life of existing travel guides by detailing any changes that may affect travel in a region since a book has been published. Upgrades can be downloaded for free from **www.lonelyplanet.com/upgrades**

For travellers with more time than money, **Shoestring** guides offer dependable, first-hand information with hundreds of detailed maps, plus insider tips for stretching money as far as possible. Covering entire continents in most cases, the six-volume shoestring guides are known around the world as 'backpackers bibles'.

For the discerning short-term visitor, **Condensed** guides highlight the best a destination has to offer in a full-colour, pocket-sized format designed for quick access. They include everything from top sights and walking tours to opinionated reviews of where to eat, stay, shop and have fun.

CitySync lets travellers use their Palm™ or Visor™ hand-held computers to guide them through a city with handy tips on transport, history, cultural life, major sights, and shopping and entertainment options. It can also quickly search and sort hundreds of reviews of hotels, restaurants and attractions, and pinpoint their location on scrollable street maps. CitySync can be downloaded from **www.citysync.com**

MAPS & ATLASES

Lonely Planet's **City Maps** feature downtown and metropolitan maps, as well as transit routes and walking tours. The maps come complete with an index of streets, a listing of sights and a plastic coat for extra durability.

Road Atlases are an essential navigation tool for serious travellers. Cross-referenced with the guidebooks, they also feature distance and climate charts and a complete site index.

LONELY PLANET

ESSENTIALS

Read This First books help new travellers to hit the road with confidence. These invaluable predeparture guides give step-by-step advice on preparing for a trip, budgeting, arranging a visa, planning an itinerary and staying safe while still getting off the beaten track.

Healthy Travel pocket guides offer a regional rundown on disease hot spots and practical advice on predeparture health measures, staying well on the road and what to do in emergencies. The guides come with a user-friendly design and helpful diagrams and tables.

Lonely Planet's **Phrasebooks** cover the essential words and phrases travellers need when they're strangers in a strange land. They come in a pocket-sized format with colour tabs for quick reference, extensive vocabulary lists, easy-to-follow pronunciation keys and two-way dictionaries.

Miffed by blurry photos of the Taj Mahal? Tired of the classic 'top of the head cut off' shot? **Travel Photography: A Guide to Taking Better Pictures** will help you turn ordinary holiday snaps into striking images and give you the know-how to capture every scene, from frenetic festivals to peaceful beach sunrises.

Lonely Planet's **Travel Journal** is a lightweight but sturdy travel diary for jotting down all those on-the-road observations and significant travel moments. It comes with a handy time-zone wheel, world maps and useful travel information.

Lonely Planet's eKno is an all-in-one communication service developed especially for travellers. It offers low-cost international calls and free email and voicemail so that you can keep in touch while on the road. Check it out on **www.ekno.lonelyplanet.com**

FOOD & RESTAURANT GUIDES

Lonely Planet's **Out to Eat** guides recommend the brightest and best places to eat and drink in top international cities. These gourmet companions are arranged by neighbourhood, packed with dependable maps, garnished with scene-setting photos and served with quirky features.

For people who live to eat, drink and travel, **World Food** guides explore the culinary culture of each country. Entertaining and adventurous, each guide is packed with detail on staples and specialities, regional cuisine and local markets, as well as sumptuous recipes, comprehensive culinary dictionaries and lavish photos good enough to eat.

OUTDOOR GUIDES

For those who believe the best way to see the world is on foot, Lonely Planet's **Walking Guides** detail everything from family strolls to difficult treks, with 'when to go and how to do it' advice supplemented by reliable maps and essential travel information.

Cycling Guides map a destination's best bike tours, long and short, in day-by-day detail. They contain all the information a cyclist needs, including advice on bike maintenance, places to eat and stay, innovative maps with detailed cues to the rides, and elevation charts.

The **Watching Wildlife** series is perfect for travellers who want authoritative information but don't want to tote a heavy field guide. Packed with advice on where, when and how to view a region's wildlife, each title features photos of over 300 species and contains engaging comments on the local flora and fauna.

With underwater colour photos throughout, **Pisces Books** explore the world's best diving and snorkelling areas. Each book contains listings of diving services and dive resorts, detailed information on depth, visibility and difficulty of dives, and a roundup of the marine life you're likely to see through your mask.

OFF THE ROAD

Journeys, the travel literature series written by renowned travel authors, capture the spirit of a place or illuminate a culture with a journalist's attention to detail and a novelist's flair for words. These are tales to soak up while you're actually on the road or dip into as an at-home armchair indulgence.

The new range of lavishly illustrated **Pictorial** books is just the ticket for both travellers and dreamers. Off-beat tales and vivid photographs bring the adventure of travel to your doorstep long before the journey begins and long after it is over.

Lonely Planet **Videos** encourage the same independent, tough-minded approach as the guidebooks. Currently airing throughout the world, this award-winning series features innovative footage and an original soundtrack.

Yes, we know, work is tough, so do a little bit of deskside dreaming with the spiral-bound Lonely Planet **Diary**, the tearaway page-a-day **Day-to-Day Calendar** or a Lonely Planet **Wall Calendar**, filled with great photos from around the world.

TRAVELLERS NETWORK

Lonely Planet Online. Lonely Planet's award-winning Web site has insider information on hundreds of destinations, from Amsterdam to Zimbabwe, complete with interactive maps and relevant links. The site also offers the latest travel news, recent reports from travellers on the road, guidebook upgrades, a travel links site, an online book-buying option and a lively traveller's bulletin board. It can be viewed at **www.lonelyplanet.com** or AOL keyword: lp.

Planet Talk is a quarterly print newsletter, full of gossip, advice, anecdotes and author articles. It provides an antidote to the being-at-home blues and lets you plan and dream for the next trip. Contact the nearest Lonely Planet office for your free copy.

Comet, the free Lonely Planet newsletter, comes via email once a month. It's loaded with travel news, advice, dispatches from authors, travel competitions and letters from readers. To subscribe, click on the Comet subscription link on the front page of the Web site.

Index

Text

Bold indicates maps.

Bold indicates maps.

Boxed Text

MAP LEGEND

BOUNDARIES

.... International
.... Regional

HYDROGRAPHY

.... Coastline
.... River, Creek
.... Lake
.... Canal
⊙ ⟿ .... Spring, Rapids
⤛ ≋ .... Waterfalls
.... Swamp
+ × .... Cemetery

◉ .... Island Capital
Las Palmas de Gran Canaria
● Maspalomas .... Town
○ Tapira .... Village

■ .... Place to Stay
▲ .... Camping Ground
⛺ .... Caravan Park
⌂ .... Chalet or Hut
▼ .... Place to Eat
▢ .... Pub or Bar
✕ .... Airport
↗ .... Ancient or City Wall
▣ .... Archaeological Site
§ .... Bank
↗ .... Beach

ROUTES & TRANSPORT

.... Freeway
.... Highway
.... Major Road
.... Minor Road
=========== Unsealed Road
.... City Freeway
.... City Highway
.... City Road
.... City Street, Lane

AREA FEATURES

.... Building
.... Park, Gardens

MAP SYMBOLS

🚏 🚉 .... Bus Stop, Station
🏰 .... Castle or Fort
⛪ ⛪ .... Cathedral or Church
⌒ .... Cave
⌒⌒⌒ .... Cliff or Escarpment
◥ .... Dive Site
▣ .... Embassy
⛴ .... Ferry or Boat Terminal
✛ .... Hospital
@ .... Internet Cafe
⚱ .... Monument
▲ .... Mountain or Hill
🏛 .... Museum
☗ .... National Park
← .... One Way Street

Note: not all symbols displayed above appear in this book

.... Pedestrian Mall
⇀ ═ ═ ═ .... Tunnel
├─┼─●┼─ .... Train Route & Station
─ ─ Ⓜ ─ .... Metro & Station
──◫── .... Tramway
⊩─⊪─⊩ .... Cable Car or Chairlift
─ ─ ─ ─ ─ .... Walking Track
· · · · · · · .... Walking Tour
─ ─ ─ ─ ─ .... Ferry Route

.... Market
.... Beach, Desert

🅿 .... Parking
)(.............. Pass
✚ .... Police Station
✉ .... Post Office
🛍 .... Shopping Centre
⛷ .... Ski Field
🏛 .... Stately Home or Palace
🏄 .... Surf Beach
🏊 .... Swimming Pool
☎ .... Telephone
▲ .... Temple
🚽 .... Toilet
❶ .... Tourist Information
▣ .... Transport
▲ .... Volcano
◢ .... Windsurfing
🔖 .... Zoo

LONELY PLANET OFFICES

Australia
Locked Bag 1, Footscray, Victoria 3011
☎ 03 8379 8000 fax 03 8379 8111
email: talk2us@lonelyplanet.com.au

USA
150 Linden St, Oakland, CA 94607
☎ 510 893 8555 TOLL FREE: 800 275 8555
fax 510 893 8572
email: info@lonelyplanet.com

UK
10a Spring Place, London NW5 3BH
☎ 020 7428 4800 fax 020 7428 4828
email: go@lonelyplanet.co.uk

France
1 rue du Dahomey, 75011 Paris
☎ 01 55 25 33 00 fax 01 55 25 33 01
email: bip@lonelyplanet.fr
www.lonelyplanet.fr

World Wide Web: www.lonelyplanet.com *or* AOL keyword: lp
Lonely Planet Images: lpi@lonelyplanet.com.au